Channelling Mobilities

M000237210

The history of globalisation is usually told as a history of shortening distances and acceleration of the flows of people, goods and ideas. *Channelling Mobilities* refines this picture by looking at a wide variety of mobile people passing through the region of the Suez Canal, a global short cut opened in 1869. As an empirical contribution to global history, the book asks how the passage between Europe and Asia and Africa was perceived, staged and controlled from the opening of the Canal to the First World War, arguing that this period was neither an era of un-hampered acceleration, nor one of hardening borders and increasing controls. Instead, it was characterised by the channelling of mobilities through the differentiation, regulation and bureaucratisation of move-ment. Telling the stories of tourists, troops, workers, pilgrims, stow-aways, caravans, dhow skippers and others, the book reveals the complicated entanglements of empires, internationalist initiatives and private companies.

VALESKA HUBER is a Research Fellow at the German Historical Institute London.

Channelling Mobilities

*Migration and Globalisation in the Suez
Canal Region and Beyond, 1869–1914*

Valeska Huber

CAMBRIDGE
UNIVERSITY PRESS

CAMBRIDGE
UNIVERSITY PRESS

University Printing House, Cambridge CB2 8BS, United Kingdom

Cambridge University Press is part of the University of Cambridge.

It furthers the University's mission by disseminating knowledge in the pursuit of education, learning and research at the highest international levels of excellence.

www.cambridge.org
Information on this title: www.cambridge.org/9781107595385

© Valeska Huber 2013

First published 2013
First paperback edition 2015

A catalogue record for this publication is available from the British Library

Library of Congress Cataloguing in Publication data
Huber, Valeska, 1980–
Channelling mobilities: migration and globalisation in the Suez Canal Region and beyond, 1869-1914 / Valeska Huber.
   p.   cm.
Includes bibliographical references.
ISBN 978-1-107-03060-2
1. Migration – Egypt – Suez Canal Region – History.   2. Trade routes – Egypt – Suez Canal Region – History.   3. Muslim pilgrims and pilgrimages – Egypt – Suez Canal Region – History.   4. Suez Canal Region (Egypt) – History.   I. Title.
HB2121.7.S9H83   2013
304.80962´15–dc23

2012038173

ISBN 978-1-107-03060-2 Hardback
ISBN 978-1-107-59538-5 Paperback

Contents

Figures and maps

Acknowledgements

This book not only deals with mobilities of various sorts, but has itself moved between a number of institutions and countries over the last few years, accumulating many debts on the way. It originated as a doctoral dissertation, examined at the University of Konstanz on 25 May 2009. My first and deepest words of thanks belong to my supervisor, Jürgen Osterhammel, who has guided this research from its very beginnings until completion. I am grateful for his constant support and unceasing encouragement as a supervisor, and for his prodigious example as a global historian.

I am also grateful to the examination committee of the University of Konstanz consisting of Aleida Assmann, Bernhard Kleeberg (both acting as oral examiners) and Clemens Wischermann (third referee). My colleagues at the Arbeitsgemeinschaft für Globale und Internationale Geschichte provided a most stimulating and friendly academic home where to discuss research, academic travels and teaching.

I profited immensely from a year as a Visiting Fellow at the History Department of Harvard University. The comments of the second referee of the dissertation, Roger Owen, have greatly improved this study. To participate and discuss parts of this work in graduate seminars of Sven Beckert, Sugata Bose, Engseng Ho and Roger Owen and with various graduate students opened up many new avenues of thought. Sven Beckert has also given valuable advice for the transformation from dissertation to book.

My return to London in many senses brought the project full circle, with the very first ideas concerning this book and its final completion many years later both taking place in the UK. Some first steps towards the present study were already taken in my MPhil dissertation, supervised by Richard Evans (University of Cambridge). The manuscript was completed after leaving Konstanz for the German Historical Institute London. I would particularly like to thank the director of the institute, Andreas Gestrich, for granting me the time to finish the manuscript.

It is the nature of long and longwinded projects that one accrues many debts towards readers and audiences that cannot be named individually. I have been fortunate to present parts of this work at conferences and colloquia in different countries and continents. I have been even more fortunate that many people have read and commented on parts of this book at various stages, among them On Barak, Felix Brahm, Johann Büssow, Fred Cooper, Angela Davies, Ben Fergusson, Will Hanley, Jan C. Jansen, Bernhard Malkmus, Emran Mian, Niels P. Petersson, Tom Poole, Penny Sinanoglou, Suzanne Smith and two anonymous reviewers. All remaining shortcomings are of course to be blamed entirely on the author.

In archives and libraries in five countries, I have been assisted by many people, again too numerous to list here, who have gone beyond their duty to locate relevant material. Particular thanks are due to the staff of The National Archives of Egypt, Dār al-Wathāʾiq, in Cairo and to Riham Salem who helped me with the sources there. The Association du Souvenir de Ferdinand de Lesseps has courteously granted access to its collections. Every effort has been made to trace copyright holders and to obtain their permission for the use of copyright material. The author apologises for any errors or omissions and would be grateful if notified of any corrections that should be incorporated in future reprints or editions of this book.

The research and writing of the dissertation could not have materialised without help from a number of bodies: the Studienstiftung des Deutschen Volkes, the Exzellenzcluster 'Kulturelle Grundlagen von Integration' in Konstanz and the German Historical Institutes in London and Paris. I am very happy that the book that emerged out of the dissertation has found its home at Cambridge University Press and would like to thank Michael Watson and his team, especially Chloe Dawson, Sarah Payne and Cheryl Prophett, for their guidance and meticulous help with production.

Finally, I could not have completed this book without the continuous support of friends and family who provided a stable base despite the various translocations of the author. My parents have read the manuscript in different incarnations and have always accompanied me with their advice and encouragement. My partner has shared the lowest and highest points of this effort and has persistently and patiently put things into perspective convincing me when it was time to move on. Our two daughters joined us in the interval between the completion of the dissertation and the appearance of the book and begin their own journeys as this project comes to an end.

Transliteration and Translation

The transliterations are based on the system used by the *International Journal of Middle Eastern Studies*. Where there is a standard English spelling, names and terms appear without diacritics (Port Said instead of Būr Saʿīd etc.). Less commonly used place names and names of people are rendered with the ʿayn and hamza but without further diacritical signs. Names of people, places, ships and companies appearing in the sources have been spelt according to their appearance in these documents rather than according to the transcription currently in use. All foreign language quotations are translated by the author.

Abbreviations

AFL	Association French Lines, Le Havre
ANMT	Archives Nationales du Monde du Travail, Roubaix
ANOM	Archives Nationales d'Outre-Mer, Aix-en-Provence
CADN	Centre des Archives Diplomatiques de Nantes
CCIMP	Chambre de Commerce et d'Industrie Marseille-Provence
DWQ	Dār al-Wathā'iq al-Qawmiyya, Cairo
FAL	Fine Arts Library, Harvard University, Cambridge/MA
GehStA PK	Geheimes Staatsarchiv Preußischer Kulturbesitz
OIOC	Oriental and India Office Collections, British Library, London
Quai d'Orsay	Archives du Ministère des Affaires Etrangères, Paris
SHD	Service Historique de la Défense, Château de Vincennes, Paris
TNA	The National Archives, London

Introduction: mobility and its limits

At a time of global connections, localities matter. On several occasions in 2008 and 2010, when deep-sea cables running through the Suez Canal were damaged, the internet connections of about 75 million people were disrupted: these cables carry most of the data traffic between Europe and the Middle and Far East. Even in an age of digital information transfers, physical spaces of transmission play a decisive part. In an interconnected and interdependent world, hubs and chokepoints are also crucial to understanding the ebbs and flows of natural resources. One might look at the example of those large shipping companies, for instance, who have decided to redirect their oil tankers from the Suez Canal to the much longer Cape of Good Hope route because of the fear of pirate attacks near the Horn of Africa or at commentators calling attention to the Suez Canal as a weak point in the West's oil supply, which was under threat during the upheavals of early 2011 in Egypt.

The aim of this book is to study the Suez Canal as a nodal point and lynchpin of various forms of mobility during an earlier wave of global interconnection, showing that the history of globalisation can best be understood by analysing one specific – and specifically global – locality. After its opening in 1869, the Canal developed into a thoroughfare carrying not only information and goods but also individuals and their ideas. Rapidly, the desert strip of the Isthmus became an important crossroads between Europe, Asia and Africa, where the growing passenger traffic shuttling between, for example, Great Britain and India intersected with caravan routes and the circuits of dhows in the Red Sea.

Tensions between different forms of mobility became particularly tangible where the caravan route connecting Cairo and Damascus crossed the Suez Canal: at a location where camels had for centuries been the only mode of conveyance, they now had to wait for steamers to pass before they could be shuttled across the new Canal with the help of a float – a powerful symbol of the simultaneous acceleration and deceleration that was characteristic of this global junction. Travellers admired the image of gigantic steamships crossing the desert while associating the caravans with a

Figure 1 'The Suez Canal – Passage through the Highest Cut', postcard published by the Oriental Commercial Bureau Port Said (Egypt), no date.

bygone age. The supposed 'backwardness' of caravans and other traditional forms of desert mobility, however, could not be judged so easily when it came to the emerging international control regimes: during epidemics, for instance, camel guards patrolling the Canal were essential in securing the strict prohibition of contact between the Canal and the surrounding desert. In countering the dangers connected with an acceleration that was otherwise so desirable, recourse to practices deemed traditional or 'backward' was thus inevitable.

The simultaneity of steamship and camel in a single location encapsulates the gap in the scholarship that the present study sets out to fill. Mobility and acceleration are conventionally seen as central processes in shaping the history of globalisation. The Suez Canal appears in the literature on global history and the history of globalisation as soon as the 'time-space compression' starting in the second half of the nineteenth century is mentioned.[1] In works on imperial expansion, the Suez Canal is equally present.[2] Yet the increasingly rapid mobility which the Suez Canal came to symbolise had two sides: on the one hand a modernising force in the eyes of western observers, on the other a force that was difficult to control

---

[1] Harvey, *The Condition of Postmodernity*, p. 240; Rosenberg (ed.), *A World Connecting*, esp. pp. 352–7.
[2] Headrick, *The Tools of Empire*, pp. 150–6.

and which was connected with problems such as the worldwide propagation of disease or the movement of unruly individuals or groups. The period around 1900 was neither – as often implied – an era of unhampered acceleration, nor one of hardening borders and increasing controls. Rather it was characterised by the *channelling* of mobility, or to be more precise, the differentiation, regulation and bureaucratisation of different kinds of movement.

The maritime shortcut of the Suez Canal is perfectly suited to this revision of global history. It has become a symbol of the 'shortening' of distances around 1900 and of the triumphant version of acceleration that stressed the transformation of a desert by means of modern technology. Yet it also highlighted the dangers and anxieties connected with this same acceleration. At this very location colonial traffic and troop transportation crossed the circuits of tourists, the journeys of pilgrims to Mecca, the trajectories of nomads and caravans, the work-related movements of seamen and coal heavers and the illicit passages of stowaways, smugglers and microbes. This kaleidoscope of movement shows how, in the context of the technological innovations of the second half of the nineteenth century, mobility became a marker of Western modernity. But it also makes clear how certain forms of mobility were increasingly regulated and stigmatised. While acceleration is often taken for granted, multiple processes of exclusion and deceleration were in fact in play.

With the aim of developing this thesis, the book asks a number of questions. Although the Canal is frequently mentioned in passing in narratives of globalisation and empire, and there are a number of surveys depicting the engineering achievement and its diplomatic and economic context, it has not so far received attention as a global locality worth being studied in detail. Yet in order to understand the tension between acceleration and deceleration as crucial to the process of globalisation, it is useful to ask what happened on the ground in one particular location. Who travelled through the Canal and why? How was the passage between Europe, Asia and Africa perceived, described, staged and controlled from the opening of the Canal to the First World War? For whom was the Canal experience pleasurable and for whom hard work? Where and how was political, military and police control present in a waterway that was by no means a no-man's-land, yet did not belong to one single political entity? Who had the power to move at full speed or to hamper the movement of others? For whom did travelling become an increasingly standardised routine and for whom did it mean resistance and the breaking of (globally drafted) rules and regulations?

Three main themes will help to systematise these questions. First, the distinction between different *categories of mobility* is at the core of the

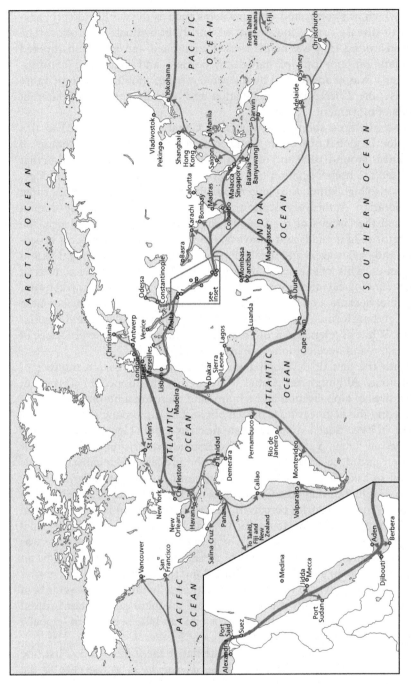

World map with principal steamship routes. Inset: Suez Canal and Red Sea.

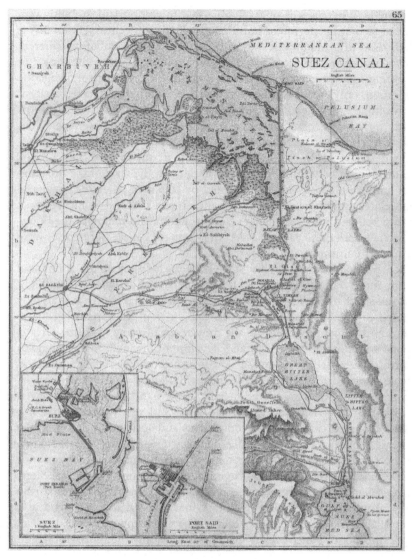

Figure 2 Map of the Suez Canal: *The World-wide Atlas of Modern Geography*
(Edinburgh: W. & A. K. Johnston, 1897), p. 65.

argument. Whereas it is undisputable that migration and mobility were crucial to the transformation of the late nineteenth century,[3] mobility is often used in a monolithic way with authors either conflating different forms of mobility in the sense of a global population 'on the move' or shedding light on a single form of mobility, for instance transatlantic migration, only. Yet it is crucial to develop a more multifaceted analysis of 'multiple mobilities'.[4] Mobilities were discriminated according to the mode and purpose of movement associating them with different velocities and different historical moments, calling some forms of movement modern and others 'backward' relegating them to a bygone age.[5] Increasingly, the distinction between different mobilities – at the level of the imagination and of politics – was also effected by classifying them according to race, class, gender, religion or nationality. It was a central political project of imperial and internationalist actors to define and maintain the boundaries between these categories. At the same time these boundaries were frequently contested and transgressed.

Secondly, and connected with the above, by focusing on the differential treatment of various mobilities, the chapters of this book will highlight various facets of the tension between *acceleration and deceleration* already alluded to. The distinction between categories of movement became a central instrument to speed up the movement of some of them, such as troops and colonial travellers, and develop a bureaucratic apparatus to control and if necessary detain or repatriate others. Acceleration and deceleration were partly related to the technological developments creating expectations of unhampered speed.[6] Western travellers often perceived the shortcut to Asia and Africa as slow and easily corruptible, for instance when it came to strike movements and accidents, but also to the increase of bureaucracy and logistics connected to the Canal passage. Such controls were particularly burdensome at specific instances, for instance when epidemic disease outbreaks loomed, or concerning specific travellers, such as pilgrims on their way to Mecca. These implementations point to the political imperatives relating to fast connections on the one hand and controllable movement on the other. The interruption of the caravan route in order to construct the Canal was thus only the most visible and

---

[3] See, for example, Conrad, *Globalisierung und Nation*, p. 13; Osterhammel, *Die Verwandlung der Welt*, pp. 183–252: 'Sesshafte und Mobile'.

[4] Huber, 'Multiple Mobilities'; Roche, *Humeurs vagabondes*; Urry, *Mobilities*; Clancy-Smith, *Mediterraneans*. See also the growing field of 'mobility studies' represented by journals such as *Mobilities* (since 2006) or *Transfers* (since 2011).

[5] Fischer-Tiné and Gehrmann (eds.), *Empires and Boundaries*, pp. 1–7; Fischer-Tiné, *Low and Licentious Europeans*.

[6] On perceptions of speed and slowdown in Egypt, see also Barak, *On Time*.

extreme contrast between acceleration and deceleration that shall be explored in the chapters to come.

Third, the book contributes to the investigation of the emerging *rules of globalisation* including the arsenal of forced mobility (in the guise of expulsion or repatriation) or forced immobility (such as the refusal to grant travel permits), for instance when dealing with pilgrims, unwanted workers or illicit travellers without funds.[7] It does so by combining a focus on mobile agents of globalisation with the close examination of a specific space, which was never regulated by a single system such as an empire. Rather the global and the local as well as many levels in between were especially tightly enmeshed.[8] The book uncovers the different levels of rulemaking and standardisation, ranging from the local and regional to the level of empire, defined as 'an interconnected zone constituted by multiple points of contact and complex circuits of exchange',[9] the often neglected level of inter-imperial contact and competition and the level of international conferences and meetings. By unearthing this interaction, it offers a more precise meaning of 'the global' as precisely the interplay and competition between these different levels. Additionally, the book points to the limits of such rule making and to incidences of 'rule breaking', not only because of the often contradictory interests of these different levels, but also due to the multiple evasions of mobile individuals who undermined the bureaucratic control measures.

The book thus adds to recent debates regarding globalisation and its history. Ten years after the publication of A. G. Hopkins' *Globalization in World History*, several authors have convincingly argued for the need to historicise this concept of the social sciences and buzzword of our times.[10] Others have contributed to our understanding of the 'global' more generally by providing broader synthetic works on worldwide interconnectedness and its limits.[11] Yet some have also questioned the concept and called for caution. Frederick Cooper contended that globalisation is too broad (and too fashionable) a term to carry much analytic value and criticised the Eurocentric, generalising tendencies brushing over the various levels between the local and the

---

[7] For different sets of such 'rules of globalisation' or 'world orders', see Conrad and Sachsenmaier (eds.), *Competing Visions of World Order*.

[8] See Hopkins, 'Introduction: Interactions Between the Universal and the Local', in Hopkins (ed.), *Globalization in World History*, pp. 1–38, at pp. 7–11.

[9] Magee and Thompson, *Empire and Globalisation*, p. 16.

[10] Hopkins (ed.), *Globalization in World History*; Osterhammel and Petersson, *Geschichte der Globalisierung*.

[11] Bayly, *The Birth of the Modern World*; Osterhammel, *Die Verwandlung der Welt*.

global.[12] Jürgen Osterhammel has also recently warned historians to use the concept of globalisation in a naive and imprecise way.[13]

Other authors have taken a different road, using the concept of globalisation in a more differentiated and flexible way meaning more than mere interconnectedness. Adam McKeown has convincingly shown how borders, sometimes seen as antagonists of globalising forces, in fact were part and parcel of the same process.[14] In imperial Germany, nationalism and globalisation, also often seen as opponent forces, were intricately linked and in fact drew on each other, as Sebastian Conrad demonstrated.[15] Gary B. Magee and Andrew S. Thompson have compellingly connected 'empire' and 'globalisation' in terms of the 'cultural economy' of the British world.[16]

The present study contributes to these more cautious and multifaceted approaches, analysing the Canal both as hub and as chokepoint and teasing out the contrast between free flows and controls. 'Global' is not used indiscriminately in this book, but carries several distinct yet overlapping meanings, which are developed in successive chapters, such as new perceptions of time and space, economic interconnection and worldwide labour migration. What is more, visions of the global were often competing, ranging from conceptualisations of the global as universal, the global as imperial or the global as juxtaposition of heterogeneous elements. Hence this study uses globalisation neither as a mere cliché of unlimited interconnectedness nor as a precisely defined analytical tool, but rather as an overarching and flexible concept that binds the different levels and actors together instead of referring to one set of institutions or one centre of power. In this manner it highlights the layering or *jeux d'échelles* and the multitude of actors belonging to different entities, such as empires, private companies or international conferences, as well as the friction between them.[17] The study of mobility in the Suez Canal and its regulation can thus show that globalisation 'was made' rather than simply happened.

In order to develop these themes of hub and chokepoint, free flows and control, *Channelling Mobilities: Migration and Globalisation in the Suez Canal Region and Beyond, 1869–1914* follows different agents of globalisation who are not usually in the spotlight and whose trajectories met at this global crossroads. In the manner of a historical ethnography interested in a multitude of actors, it tries to catch a glimpse of the different mobile people it encounters.[18] It takes snapshots with the tourists

[12] Cooper, *Colonialism in Question*, pp. 91–112.   [13] Osterhammel, 'Globalizations'.
[14] McKeown, *Melancholy Order*.
[15] Conrad, *Globalisierung und Nation*, esp. pp. 316–24.
[16] Magee and Thompson, *Empire and Globalisation*.
[17] See Revel (ed.), *Jeux d'échelles*, esp. pp. 15–36.
[18] See also Clancy-Smith, *Mediterraneans*, p. 9.

enchanted or bored by what they are seeing and spends time during the passage with routinely travelling troops and colonial officials, as they complain about the latest health restrictions. It follows workers in their attempt to find employment in global labour markets and accompanies pilgrims trying to get to their holy destination in Mecca, with or without travel permits. It shares the (often unsuccessful) adventures of 14-year-old stowaways from Liverpool, encounters destitute travellers from different colonial territories and meets seamen from Europe and Asia looking for hire in the Canal area or complaining of their rough treatment on board. It joins caravans and boards dhows facing new restrictions on income opportunities and freedom of movement.

To follow these individuals on the move, a wide variety of sources will be used. Clearly, the material available on the different forms of mobility is highly unequal. Ego-documents and literary sources describing the Canal passage are mainly available for privileged travellers, while the voices of other mobile people make themselves heard through consular and police records. This reliance on official sources with their obvious emphasis on those 'problematic cases' coming into contact with official authorities and the information that the officials found useful to preserve obviously shapes the findings of this study. Also, with an emphasis on global mobility and imperial circuits, the perspective of the local population, of Egyptian newspapers or Ottoman travellers for example, is largely omitted. Yet, these official documents are used to tease out individual stories as well as broader patterns of bureaucracy and control. Colonial and consular archives are furthermore complemented by the documentation of international conferences as well as company archives.

In the remainder of this introduction, the main themes of the book will be explored in four sections, setting the scene for the following chapters. Beginning with a global perspective that highlights the new modes of transportation and communication and their implications for the mobility of people around the world, the introduction then turns to a consideration of the political uses of and attitudes toward this mobility in imperial contexts. The discussion will then gradually narrow the focus, via the maritime spaces of the Indian Ocean, the Mediterranean and the Red Sea, and finally settle on the central arena explored in this book – the Suez Canal – before outlining the arguments presented and providing a map of the individual chapters.

Global connections

That the influence of the Suez Canal radiated far beyond its Egyptian locale became evident in 1871 at a famous meeting a long way from the

Nile. Henry Morton Stanley's first greeting to the missionary and explorer David Livingstone, on the occasion of their encounter near Lake Tanganyika in Central Africa – the famous explorer had by then been missing for four years – has been called 'one of the best-known remarks' of the nineteenth century and 'a classic example of Victorian banality'.[19] In the exchange that followed, Livingstone apparently said: 'tell me the general news: How is the world getting along?' To this wide-ranging question, Stanley answered by reporting the opening of the Suez Canal as the one decisive event that Livingstone had missed while out of touch with the 'civilised world'.[20]

The Suez Canal did not stand alone in the nineteenth-century revolution of technology and transportation, yet for Stanley and Livingstone, both travellers by profession, it was its most impressive element. In the three years before the Canal's opening, the interested public witnessed two other spectacular and mediatised moments of global unification. First, on 27 July 1866, the American continent was connected to Europe, after many years of effort, by the transatlantic telegraphic cable.[21] Messages could now overcome the distance between the continents within a couple of hours. Another connective moment of global resonance occurred some months before the opening of the Canal. On 10 May 1869 the Union and Central Pacific Railroads, linking the United States from coast to coast, joined up at Promontory Summit in Utah, just north of the Great Salt Lake with the president of the Central Pacific Railroad, Leland Stanford, fastening the last rail with a golden spike and a silver hammer. The telegraphic message 'it is done' was dispatched to destinations across the country and – via the newly laid cable – to Europe, and the event was celebrated worldwide.[22]

The telegraph connecting Europe and America, the new railway between America's east and west coasts, and finally the opening of the Suez Canal on 17 November 1869, represented high points in the development of global connections. This moment found forceful expression in Jules Verne's novel, *Around the World in Eighty Days*, published in 1872. When Verne's hero, Phileas Fogg, accepted his wager, travelling around the globe in 80 days had become feasible for the first time in history. The technological successes led to a novel perception of global unity – at least among Europeans and North Americans – and expressions such as the

---

[19] Anstruther, *Dr. Livingstone I Presume?*, p. vii; see also Driver, *Geography Militant*, pp. 121–2.

[20] Stanley, *How I Found Livingstone*, pp. 414–15.

[21] Gordon, *A Thread Across the Ocean*, p. 207.   [22] Orsi, *Sunset Limited*, p. 17.

annihilation of time and space or the shrinking of the globe became commonplace.[23]

Steam engines in trains and ships were the essential motors of the nineteenth-century transport revolution.[24] The railway was the technology that changed the perception of space and distance most drastically.[25] In the British context, the bulk of this transformation took place between 1830 and 1852: in 1830, less than 100 miles of rails linked the major cities; by 1852 the number had grown to 6,600 miles.[26] In the United States the railway was crucial in creating a unified national space.[27] In Russia the new technology served to make the vast Siberian landmasses more manageable and exploitable.[28] Colonial territories such as India were soon equipped with a railway system to facilitate the extraction of raw materials and the movements of troops.[29]

In parallel to faster overland transportation, mobility across oceans and seas was transformed by the construction of larger ships, owing to the increased use of iron and the introduction of steam engines. Not least because of the opening of the Suez Canal, the steamship would gradually displace the sailing ship, although for some time steam and sail were competing technologies.[30] In the British context, as in many others, the experience of travelling on the new ships was made more uniform by the regulation of passenger densities fostered by agencies such as the Colonial Land and Emigration Commission, founded in 1840, and by legislation such as the British Passenger Act of 1855.[31] At the same time, steamships and railways made transportation cheaper and thus more accessible. The new means of transportation were not only faster, but also ran according to timetables, which in turn led to an increasing demand for the standardisation of world time.[32]

---

[23] See Osterhammel, 'Raumerfassung und Universalgeschichte im 20. Jahrhundert'; Darwin, *After Tamerlane*, p. 300; Kern, *The Culture of Time and Space 1880–1918*; Borscheid, *Das Tempo-Virus*; Kaschuba, *Die Überwindung der Distanz*.

[24] For an overview, see Bagwell, *The Transport Revolution from 1770*.

[25] See, for example, Schivelbusch, *Geschichte der Eisenbahnreise*; Schivelbusch, 'Railroad Space and Railroad Time'; Harrington, 'The Railway Journey and the Neuroses of Modernity'.

[26] Freeman, *Railways and the Victorian Imagination*, p. 1.

[27] Cronon, *Nature's Metropolis*, pp. 74–81.

[28] Marks, *Road to Power*; Cvetkovski, *Modernisierung durch Beschleunigung*.

[29] Kerr, *Building the Railways of the Raj, 1850–1900*; Headrick, *The Tools of Empire*, pp. 180–191; Headrick, *The Tentacles of Progress*, pp. 49–96; Adas, *Machines as the Measure of Men*.

[30] Gardiner (ed.), *The Advent of Steam*, p. 7; Graham, 'The Ascendancy of the Sailing Ship, 1850–85'; Foulke, 'Life in the Dying World of Sail, 1870–1910'.

[31] Magee and Thompson, *Empire and Globalisation*, pp. 72–3; Northrup, *Indentured Labour in the Age of Imperialism*, pp. 83–4.

[32] See Blaise, *Time Lord*.

The same decades that witnessed the rapid transformation of landscapes by the introduction of the railway, enabling goods and people to move at hitherto unknown speeds, also experienced a previously unseen velocity in the transfer of news and information. In 1837 the first electric telegraphs were patented almost simultaneously in Britain and the United States. The first submarine cables were laid some years later, including the cable that connected Calais and Dover from 1851 on. This was followed, as indicated, by the European-North American cable in 1866. Telegraphy transformed diplomacy, centralised colonial decision-making and changed the consumption of news.[33] The new medium even found its way into poetry. In his poem 'The Deep-Sea Cables' Rudyard Kipling alluded to the frequently used trope of the annihilation of space and time in an era of global interconnectedness when he described the telegraph as uniting the world while its cables had simultaneously 'killed their father Time'.[34]

Space was not only criss-crossed by rails and cables but it was also measured and depicted. The middle third of the nineteenth century marked a shift in the history of exploration and cartography. Expeditions into 'unknown' regions, often with a clear imperial agenda, and the increasing sophistication of mapmaking and surveying methods, led to the gradual disappearance of the white spots that in the eighteenth century had covered large parts of Africa in the geographical imaginations of educated Europeans.[35] The new cartographical depictions claiming scientific exactitude began to restructure perceptions of distance and space.[36] Not only the maps but also the journeys of exploration themselves became more standardised; they were now funded and publicised by institutions such as the Royal Geographical Society in London, founded in 1830.[37] More instantaneous press coverage resulting from the novel telegraphic immediacy of news generated excitement in a growing reading public, which closely followed the fate of explorers such as David Livingstone and Henry Morton Stanley. Distance and mobility were now experienced, as it were, from one's own armchair.[38] By 1900,

---

[33] Wenzlhuemer, *Connecting the Nineteenth-Century World*, pp. 77–84, 88–92; Nickles, *Under the Wire*; Hugill, *Global Communications since 1844*; Headrick, *The Invisible Weapon*; Wenzlhuemer (ed.), *Global Communication*.

[34] Kipling, *Rudyard Kipling's Verse*, p. 199.

[35] See Conrad, 'Geography and Some Explorers'.

[36] Black, *Maps and Politics*; Schneider, *Die Macht der Karten*, esp. pp. 45–9; Dipper and Schneider (eds.), *Kartenwelten*, esp. Zoe Laidlaw, 'Das Empire in Rot: Karten als Ausdruck des britischen Imperialismus', pp. 146–59.

[37] Collier and Inkpen, 'The Royal Geographical Society and the Development of Surveying 1870–1914'.

[38] For 'armchair geographers', some of whom were decidedly critical of Stanley's methods, see Driver, *Geography Militant*, pp. 14, 48, 127–8.

authors such as Halford Mackinder could claim that the 'Columbian epoch' of exploration had come to an end,[39] while the historian Gaston Dodu declared at the same time that 'one has never spoken as much of explorers and explorations as in these recent times'.[40]

Although the expanding networks of transportation resulted in the more rapid movement of larger numbers of people over greater distances than ever before, this is not to argue, as nineteenth-century believers in progress and some proponents of mid-twentieth-century modernisation theory have done, that the early modern period was static and immobile.[41] On the contrary, early modern Europe displayed a wealth of mobile practices, ranging from emerging colonial enterprises and the travels of the *Lumières* and other members of the Republic of Letters, to the movement of troops, missionaries, pilgrims, workers, journeymen, religious fugitives (such as the Sephardic Jews expelled from Spain and the Huguenots who fled France after the revocation of the Edict of Nantes), among many others.[42]

This 'culture of mobility', as Daniel Roche has termed it, could also be detected in parts of the world other than Europe. Innumerable mobile practices and communicative networks characterised precolonial India – the idea of a 'timeless and unchanging India' disseminated by colonial thinkers and officials was thus a mere myth. Roads and canals constructed in *ancien-régime* Orissa, for instance, continued to have an impact in the colonial period, even if colonial rulers often denied this.[43] The existence of mobile groups, such as circulating labourers, merchant networks, itinerant rulers and travelling storytellers, equally deflates the notion of a static pre-colonial India.[44] Most obviously, seas and oceans such as the Mediterranean, the Indian Ocean and the Atlantic were all marked by specific and often extensive 'mobilities'.[45]

It is the case, however, that the theme of mobility acquired a new intensity in the nineteenth century with regards to both the number of people on the move and – perhaps most importantly – their speed and the distances they covered. Since the 1820s, migration across the Atlantic had been steadily increasing.[46] An estimated 52 million Europeans departed

---

[39] Mackinder, 'The Geographical Pivot of History', 421.
[40] Dodu, *Vers les terres nouvelles (explorateurs – explorations)*, p. vii.
[41] See, for instance, Lerner, *The Passing of Traditional Society*.
[42] Roche, *Humeurs vagabondes*.   [43] Ahuja, 'Opening up the Country', 128.
[44] Markovits, Pouchepadass and Subrahmanyam (eds.), *Society and Circulation*, esp. pp. 5–6.
[45] For an overview, see Hoerder, *Cultures in Contact*.
[46] See, for instance, McKeown, 'Global Migration, 1846–1940', 155–89, at 164.

for North and Latin America between 1860 and 1914 alone.[47] Australia became another popular destination. And yet not only emigration abroad but also migration between different European countries shaped modern Europe.[48] These mass movements were paralleled by other currents such as the large numbers of Russians settling in Siberia or Asian contract labourers employed in Africa or the Caribbean.[49]

As well as forced and free migrations, the nineteenth century also witnessed the emergence of organised tourism, which became associated above all with the name of Thomas Cook.[50] Egypt in particular was popular among European upper middle classes in these new circuits of tourism.[51] Package tours made the 'exotic' available at minimum risk if not at minimum cost. In the 1870s a tour from London to the first Nile cataract and back still amounted to between £81 and £117 first class and between £76 and £104 second class (depending on the period and the steam line); a trip further upstream to the second cataract was about £30 more. The fare included coupons for the hotels, landing expenses at Alexandria, the hiring of donkeys and guides during the stops on the Nile, 'backsheesh' for officers and crews and 'all provisions on the Steamers, except wine and other drinks'.[52]

Alongside the comfort of travel and the exoticism associated with the 'Orient', Egypt's historical heritage was the main reason for its particular attractiveness to bourgeois travellers of the second half of the nineteenth century. Heinrich Stephan, head postmaster of the North German Confederation and later of the German Reich, noted in 1872 that few non-European countries exerted a similar, almost magical attraction on mind and soul: 'If history ennobles the soil, the valley of the Nile belongs to the most ancient nobility of the countries of this world.'[53]

Yet by the time Stephan was writing, the Nile was complemented by a new waterway in Egypt – the Suez Canal. If the river stood for age-old civilisations, the Canal represented novelty and progress. And if tourist mobility was not entirely unpolitical, imperial politics of mobility developing in the second half of the nineteenth century strongly differentiated between various mobilities, as the following section will show.

---

[47] Moch, 'Dividing Time', pp. 51–2. There are different numbers in circulation ranging from 52 million to 63 million, see Reinecke, *Grenzen der Freizügigkeit*, pp. 27–8, n. 3.

[48] See Sassen, *Guests and Aliens*; Bade, *Europa in Bewegung*.

[49] Hoerder, *Cultures in Contact*, chs. 13 and 15. See also Cohen (ed.), *The Cambridge Survey of World Migration*; Christopher, Pybus and Rediker (eds.), *Many Middle Passages*.

[50] Withey, *Grand Tours and Cook's Tours*; Brendon, *Thomas Cook*.

[51] Simoën, *Le voyage en Egypte*, p. 16. See also Gregory, 'Scripting Egypt'.

[52] Cook, *Programmes and Itineraries of Cook's Palestine Tours*, pp. 60–1.

[53] Stephan, *Das heutige Aegypten*, p. v.

Empire and mobility

The opening of the Suez Canal coincided with the period of what is often termed 'new imperialism'.[54] Many elements of this form of imperialism, such as great power competition, the unequal concessions preceding construction, faith in progress through technology and global interconnection, to name but a few, were concentrated in the Canal Zone. Many of the projects leading to the increased interconnection traced above were linked to the imperial permeation of space. It is well known that the nineteenth century was the century of colonial expansion par excellence: while in 1800 roughly 35 per cent of the earth's surface had been under West European domination, just before the First World War this number had grown to 85 per cent.[55] Often the new transport and information infrastructures were financed not directly by the colonial state apparatus, but through private companies. But in addition to the frequently indirect financial involvement of the colonial powers, government contracts – for example, for postal services – were essential to the success of the engineering projects.[56] Not only the building of infrastructure but also many mobile practices themselves – such as the voyages of exploration organised under the umbrella of the Royal Geographical Society – were directly or indirectly linked to imperial enterprises. Yet, as the following section will highlight, such projects also illustrate the ambivalent relations between empire and mobility and point to inter-imperial relationships that were not always without friction.

Enterprises of expansion, along with the colonial structures themselves, relied to a critical degree on the mobility of objects and information, such as the reliable transportation of mail, but they also depended on the faster and more standardised mobility of the colonising agents. Families circulated between Britain and India, sending their children to school in Britain, marrying their daughters to colonial officers and finally retiring in Britain after long years of colonial service.[57] These circulatory patterns not only tied together families separated by large distances but also created a tighter-knit structure of colonial rule. Yet empires depended on other mobilities as well, for example South Asian and

---

[54] Kubicek, 'The Proliferation and Diffusion of Steamship Technology'. See also Burbank and Cooper, *Empires in World History*; Darwin, *The Empire Project*.
[55] Conrad, *Globalisierung und Nation*, p. 37.
[56] Marsden and Smith, *Engineering Empires*; Kubicek, 'British Expansion, Empire, and Technological Change'; Headrick, *The Tools of Empire*; Headrick, *The Tentacles of Progress*.
[57] See Buettner, *Empire Families*, esp. pp. 146–251.

Arab lascars on the steamships or indentured labourers staffing the different sites of empire.[58] The increasingly fast and efficient connections between colonies and their 'motherlands' also reverberated in the political thinking of the time, for instance in the concept of a 'Greater Britain'.[59] There were numerous writers and pamphleteers who proposed an organic view of the British Empire according to which Britain was now closely (and apparently indivisibly) connected with its parts and peripheries. In one of his lectures, John Robert Seeley, Regius Professor of Modern History at Cambridge University and one of the most famous proponents of such a view, underlined the shift between the eighteenth and nineteenth centuries:

In the last century there could be no Greater Britain in the true sense of the word because of the distance between the mother-country and its colonies and between the colonies themselves. This impediment exists no longer. Science has given to the political organism a new circulation, which is steam, and a new nervous system, which is electricity. These new conditions make it necessary to reconsider the whole colonial problem. They make it in the first place possible to realise the old utopia of a Greater Britain, and at the same time, they make it almost necessary to do so.[60]

Seeley thus associated the new infrastructures with the new possibilities that the European states had to maintain closer political control over vast distances. He argued that in an age when 'distance is abolished by science' a European nation not only *could* have dependencies that were far away yet closely connected, but was *obliged* to grow in order to compete with Russia and the United States.[61]

As a counterpart to the idea that the new global arteries of transport and mobility were rendering new political entities possible, the task of bringing mobility to backward and immobile countries also formed an important element in the self-understanding of colonisers. In this view, mobility was part of the package of civilisation and progress and thus part of the civilising mission of western imperial enterprises.[62] The building of roads and railways was essential for territorial control – for example through the display of the colonial presence via touring officials[63]– as

---

[58] Northrup, *Indentured Labour in the Age of Imperialism*; Hoerder, *Cultures in Contact*, pp. 45–76.
[59] See Bell, 'Dissolving Distance' and *The Idea of Greater Britain*.
[60] Seeley, *The Expansion of England*, pp. 73–4.   [61] Ibid., p. 75.
[62] For civilising missions of different kinds see Barth and Osterhammel (eds.), *Zivilisierungsmissionen*; Fischer-Tiné and Mann, *Colonialism as Civilizing Mission*; for a more explicit connection with mobility see Ahuja, 'Opening up the Country'.
[63] Pouchepadass, 'Itinerant Kings and Touring Officials'.

well as for the rapid extraction of raw materials and revenues. However, mobility was also fashioned as a marker of modernity, in contrast to the apparently immobile qualities of pre-colonial India, for instance, even at the price of negating existing forms of mobility, with the association of modernity and mobility mentioned above continuing well into the twentieth century. The contrast between the mobility of Western modernity and the static and immobile features of the 'East' was even internalised by anti-colonial thinkers, such as Mohandas Karamchand Gandhi. To mobilise the stagnant and static village dwellers was to make them modern.[64]

Sometimes, this connection between Western civilisation and mobility was believed to be so direct that foregrounding the travelling practices of one's culture was considered a key to its cultural valorisation. The director of the Cairo-based newspaper *Arafate*, for example, stated, in reference to the important tradition of Muslim travel and travelogues:

One might be astonished to hear us speak of *Muslim travellers*. The Muslims also had *travellers?* one has to ask oneself. In effect our state is so dilapidated! We do not have routes, means of communication, nor postal services and securities ... Well, in the ancient times, when Muslims followed the Qur'an, they had order and security everywhere. They had excellent routes, rapid means of communication, and an admirable postal service.[65]

The mobility connected with roads and postal services thus figured strongly in the progress-preaching ideas of nineteenth-century colonisers (and sometimes of the colonised, as the above quotation illustrates), and colonialism as a practice depended to a large extent on the mobility of its agents. Yet there was an increasingly stark difference between mobilities with positive connotations and those with very different implications. Being mobile could make you modern, but it could also mean the contrary.

The stigmatisation of certain wandering groups, for instance, took place inside Europe as well as outside of it. Discrimination against the Sinti and Roma and other mobile populations had already begun in the fifteenth century with their migrations being more strictly regulated.[66] The distinction between 'good' and 'bad' mobility was thus already clearly drawn in earlier periods, with 'vagabonding' becoming an increasingly criminalised activity since the early modern period. However, from the eighteenth

---

[64] Markovits, Pouchepadass and Subrahmanyam (eds.), *Society and Circulation*, pp. 1–2.
[65] Salem Bey, 'Les voyageurs musulmans', pp. 419–20. For Muslim travel practices see Eickelmann and Piscatori, *Muslim Travellers*; see also Euben, *Journeys to the Other Shore*.
[66] Lucassen, 'Eternal Vagrants'. For other forms of early modern mobility control, see Roche, *Humeurs vagabondes*, p. 381; Siegert, *Passagiere und Papiere*; Moatti and Kaiser (eds.), *Gens de passage en Méditerranée de l'Antiquité à l'époque moderne*.

century onwards, the authorities' concern regarding wandering people of all kinds intensified with the last decades of the eighteenth and the first of the nineteenth witnessing a real onslaught of the settled 'civilised' life against its mobile counterparts.[67]

In the European context this trend was particularly visible in the large cities, which had to digest an influx of poor migrants from the countryside. Some contemporaries perceived these migrants as pathological nomads. In his work *London Labour and the London Poor* of 1851, Henry Mayhew divided the whole of humanity into two groups: the sedentary (and respectable) and the mobile. He declared that '[o]f the thousand millions of human beings that are said to constitute the population of the entire globe, there are – socially, morally, and perhaps even physically considered – but two distinct and broadly marked races, viz., the wanderers and the settlers – the vagabond and the citizen – the nomadic and the civilized tribes'.[68]

Likewise in British India, the stigmatisation and regulation of wandering people increased as the nineteenth century progressed. During this period, the ideal of a settled society became paramount.[69] 'Wandering tribes' came to be seen as inherently criminal and dangerous. This concern regarding mobile populations that could not be identified through censuses and taxed was expressed in a growing state apparatus. Accordingly, certain mobile groups fell prey to measures of forced settlement and persecution and were discussed in sensational literature of all kinds. The Pindaris who had fought against the British in the late eighteenth and early nineteenth centuries were now dispersed. In the 1830s, the colonial government also took steps against the 'thagis', a well-organised fraternity that had travelled throughout India for several hundred years and was known for the ritual murder of other wayfarers. A special police force captured over 3,000 of them; most were executed, imprisoned for life or settled by force.[70]

Sedentarisation policies became more widespread in the aftermath of the Indian Uprising of 1857–58. Now the measures became a 'matter of special urgency, as only a settled village society, wholly under the supervision of a conservative landed elite, could guarantee the British the security they required'.[71] As Metcalf and others argue, through such

---

[67] Osterhammel, *Die Entzauberung Asiens*, p. 267.
[68] Mayhew, *London Labour and the London Poor*, p. 1.
[69] See Ludden, 'Presidential Address', p. 1063.
[70] See, for instance, Thornton, *Illustrations of the History and Practices of the Thugs*; Sleeman, *The Thuggs or Phansingars of India*; Hutton, *A Popular Account of the Thugs and Dacoits*; Tuker, *The Yellow Scarf*; Ghosh, *British Policy towards the Pathans and the Pindaris*.
[71] Metcalf, *Ideologies of the Raj*, p. 123; Satya, 'Colonial Sedentarisation and Subjugation', 314–36.

measures the British contributed to a more rigidified and essentialised caste system. Similar developments can be observed in other colonial contexts, for example in the French dominions in North Africa where Bedouin were more and more closely surveyed.[72] Africa's increasing colonisation resulted in border demarcations that frequently cut through traditional trajectories. In the case of internal colonisation, for instance in the large land-based empires, settlement policies also played an important part.[73] These examples illustrate that sedentarisation policies were the answer to a wide range of issues relating to imperial consolidation and control.

The colonial preoccupation with mobile populations gave rise to new administrative practices aimed at gaining trustworthy information about them. The introduction of censuses and new passport practices in India were part of such an effort, ultimately aiming to create a controllable 'immobile' population.[74] Measures like the census were occasionally accompanied by more traditional identification measures such as tattooing on the forehead and branding.[75] In any event, as the nineteenth century progressed, the techniques were increasingly 'modernised' with skull measurements, photographs and fingerprinting becoming more and more widely disseminated.[76] In relation to identification practices, colonies often served as 'laboratories of modernity'.[77]

Yet in Europe similar techniques and practices were also introduced over the course of the nineteenth century. The professionalisation of the police, the codification of citizenship, a sense of growing responsibility of states towards their citizens and a clearer definition of territories and their boundaries, all added to the stigmatisation of mobile people and rendered the control practices already in place more efficient.[78] The emphasis on mobility should not hide the fact that large population groups were sedentary by the nineteenth century. Steve Hochstadt has argued that it 'is clear that human societies have become more geographically stable over the span of recorded history' and that the focus on mobility has been a result of the 'myopic historical vision of modernization' concentrating on a short span of time rather than the *longue durée*.[79] Still, the 'mobilisation' accompanying the European 'modernisation' process went hand

---

[72] Trautmann, 'The Nomads of Algeria under French Rule'.
[73] See, for instance, Köksal, 'Coercion and Mediation'.
[74] Cohn, 'The Census, Social Structure and Objectification in South Asia'.
[75] Singha, 'Settle, Mobilize, Verify', 165.   [76] Sengoopta, *Imprint of the Raj*.
[77] Prakash, *Another Reason*, p. 13.
[78] See, for example, Raphael, *Recht und Ordnung*; Caplan and Torpey (eds.), *Documenting Individual Identity*; Torpey, *The Invention of the Passport*; Fahrmeir, *Citizens and Aliens*.
[79] Hochstadt, *Mobility and Modernity*, pp. 280–1.

in hand with efforts by various states to stabilise or immobilise parts of their populations.

The period before the First World War is often seen as marked by an openness that was followed by stricter controls after 1914, but the picture that emerges from these examples is in fact more complex. It involves a developing internationalism and increasing interconnections on the one hand, with imperial ambitions creating new constraints and attempting to monopolise certain trajectories on the other. The nineteenth century, and particularly its second half, saw a pronounced acceleration and the development of new kinds of technologised mobilities defined in the language of civilisation and progress.[80] The new technologies created a need for international standardisation and often crystallised in nodal points where different empires overlapped. At the same time the territories that were opened up, mapped and made accessible to European influence most often came under the power of one single empire. In the context of growing state apparatuses, the need for efficient taxation and clearly defined territories demarcated by defendable borders was foregrounded – as was the distinction between positively connoted and stigmatised mobilities. It will emerge in the following chapters that the balancing act between the freedom of movement and the control of population flows as well as the limits of colonial control and inter-imperial competition crystallised in places such as the Suez Canal where openness had to be guaranteed, while at the same time certain mobilities were to be tracked and controlled.

Approaching the Suez Canal

The technological developments outlined above led to closer integration and political permeation of seas and oceans such as the Mediterranean and the Indian Ocean.[81] They had obviously been shaped for centuries by a variety of maritime mobilities, but the introduction of the steamship and the increase in colonial traffic had a heavy impact on them, creating entirely new professions and impeding more traditional ways of crossing the seas.[82] In what follows, the transformation of the seas, particularly the

---

[80] Bayly, *The Birth of the Modern World*, p. 451.

[81] Studies of the Mediterranean and of the Indian Ocean are legion – see for the Mediterranean: Braudel, *The Mediterranean and the Mediterranean World*; Horden and Purcell, *The Corrupting Sea*; Abulafia, 'Mediterranean History as Global History'. For the Indian Ocean: Chaudhuri, *Trade and Civilisation in the Indian Ocean* and *Asia before Europe*; Pearson, *The Indian Ocean*; Bose, *A Hundred Horizons*; Metcalf, *Imperial Connections*. For an example of the wide-ranging literature on seas and oceans more generally, see Lambert *et al.*, 'Currents, Visions and Voyages'.

[82] See Ewald, 'Crossers of the Sea'; Ho, *The Graves of Tarim*, esp. pp. 244–9; Tagliacozzo, *Secret Trades, Porous Borders*.

Red Sea, as a precondition for the Canal's construction, will first be reviewed. Then the construction of the Canal itself, especially the ideological and political preconditions, and the building process determined by the use of forced labour and growing mechanisation will receive some attention.

The maritime space that was perhaps most drastically transformed by the introduction of the steamship and the eventual opening of the Suez Canal was the Red Sea. Because of its dry and barren shores – flanked by steep mountains and lacking fresh water – its coral reefs and adverse winds, the Red Sea was notoriously difficult to navigate. In the early modern period, many merchants preferred the terrestrial caravan route from the Indian Ocean to the Mediterranean. Often, merchandise was brought by ship from India or East Africa to the entrance of the Red Sea in southern Arabia. From there, caravans crossed the Arabian Peninsula from south to north transporting spices, perfumes, ivory and other goods, thus avoiding the Red Sea altogether.

Yet despite its complicated conditions, the Red Sea soon came to be a site of competition between the interests of different trading and shipping companies and between the Ottoman Empire and European influence. Following the Ottoman conquest of Egypt in the early sixteenth century, transhipment nodes developed into trade emporiums such as Mokha, whose early successes continue to make it a worldwide synonym with the coffee trade to this day. John Ovington, an East India Company chaplain, observed around 1693 that 'of late', Mokha had become the principal port in the Red Sea.[83] In addition to its importance as a trade route, the Red Sea also served pilgrims (who nevertheless often preferred the less dangerous terrestrial route) as a means of accessing Mecca.[84] After 1650, the Red Sea was divided into a northern part, restricted to Egyptian navigation, and a southern part, dominated by Yemeni, Indian and European ships. This separation was confirmed by an Ottoman decree in 1774. Napoleon Bonaparte's expedition into the region in 1798 and the ascent to power of Muhammad 'Ali as viceroy of Egypt contributed to the Red Sea's opening, but there was still very limited European influence in the region.[85]

Regardless of this legacy of limited European involvement, the Red Sea was already being explored as a shortcut to India before the Suez Canal's opening transformed it into one of the busiest sea routes in the world. In

[83] Ovington, 'Ovington's Notes on the Red Sea Ports', p. 173.
[84] Eschelbacher Lapidoth, *The Red Sea and the Gulf of Aden*, pp. 15–16; Tuchscherer, 'Trade and Port Cities in the Red Sea', esp. p. 36.
[85] Raymond, 'A Divided Sea', esp. pp. 53–6.

1785 James Capper recommended the land route across the desert to Suez and then on to India by ship. He tried to allay the worries of his contemporaries regarding this journey with a simple calculation. If the expenses were shared among two or three travellers, the desert route would turn out cheaper than travelling around the Cape of Good Hope. Furthermore 'the navigation of the Red Sea being now tolerably well known', all other problems possibly encountered, Capper insisted, could be fixed 'by means of a little money properly applied'.[86] Nevertheless, the overland route remained something for the adventurous and usually required some prior desert experience. Its standardised use depended on two preconditions linking the locality of the isthmus with the general developments mentioned in the first part of this introduction.

One of these preconditions was a thorough exploration of the Red Sea, the other was the introduction of steam navigation.[87] Before steamships emerged to cut their way straight through the waves, the strong northerly winds made the navigation of Suez-bound sailing vessels extremely difficult for three-quarters of the year. The Red Sea thus became a testing ground for steam navigation. In 1822 the naval officer James Henry Johnston began to campaign for a steamer service between Calcutta and Suez.[88] Eight years later the *Hugh Lindsay* was the first steamship to navigate the Red Sea's complete length.[89] In the following years, the practicability of steam navigation during the northeast monsoon (October to January) was established more firmly, although the southwest monsoon of the summer months remained an obstacle to the still fairly weak engines.[90]

Even if the Red Sea became increasingly navigable, the desert strip between the Red Sea and the Mediterranean still had to be crossed. In 1829 the Royal Navy lieutenant Thomas Waghorn started to provide organised overland transportation between Suez and Alexandria, despite many critical voices.[91] The *Asiatic Journal and Monthly Register for British and Foreign India, China and Australasia* promoted the route in 1834 anticipating that the British government would endorse it; the journal's emphasis on the picturesque desert trip on the back of 'dromedaries,

---

[86] Capper, *Observations on the Passage to India*, p. 2.
[87] Searight, 'The Charting of the Red Sea'.   [88] Headrick, *The Tools of Empire*, p. 133.
[89] Ewald and Clarence-Smith, 'The Economic Role of the Hadhrami Diaspora', p. 281. See also Blyth, 'Aden, British India, and the Development of Steam Power in the Red Sea'.
[90] Farnie, *East and West of Suez*, p. 8.
[91] Howarth and Howarth, *The Story of the P&O*, pp. 37–46; Lamb Kenney, *The Gates of the East*, pp. 7–13.

mules or donkies [sic]' brought the contrast between steam navigation and 'desert mobility' into sharp relief. Readers were informed that one had to allow ten to twelve days for the transit between Alexandria and Suez – a necessary precondition for the success of the overland route, however, was that Egypt's viceroy Muhammad 'Ali abstained from imposing heavy duties on transit goods.[92]

While a parliamentary commission had still rejected the route in 1834, in 1835 the Peninsular Steam Navigation Company, later Peninsular and Oriental (P&O), was founded, venturing first into the Mediterranean and then 'east of Suez'.[93] In the same year, the monthly India mails, mercantile correspondence and bills were diverted from the Cape to the Red Sea route, with passengers starting to use the new trajectory in 1836.[94] In 1839 the British Navy shifted from sail to steam, thereby underlining the success of the new technology. Waghorn now began to organise camel caravans across the desert to transport coal (which had to be imported from Europe) to Suez thus making the fuel's price considerably cheaper compared with its shipment via the Cape route. This of course marked the removal of a further impediment to the use of the new route.

By now the overland route had lost its adventurous flair and had been transformed into a reasonably short transfer during which passengers barely came into contact with the desert they traversed.[95] The passage became increasingly standardised. In the summer of 1834, an anonymous British officer had reported, in a letter to the editor of *The Times*, that Muhammad 'Ali had given orders to build a railway between Cairo and Suez.[96] The project was realised by British engineers with the construction of the section between Alexandria and Cairo between 1852 and 1856 and its extension to Suez in 1858.[97] After its realisation, the Peninsular Steam Navigation Company reached an agreement with Khedive Isma'il that the price of the passage would be fixed and that passengers would be conveyed between Alexandria and Suez in less than 30 hours. Furthermore the agreement demanded that sufficient numbers 'of European water closets, indicating by a notice in French or English those destined for ladies and those for gentlemen' had to be provided and 'kept in a state of efficient repairs and in a thoroughly clean and

---

[92] 'Egypt', *Asiatic Journal and Monthly Register for British and Foreign India, China and Australasia*.

[93] Harcourt, 'The High Road to India'. For the early history of the company, see Harcourt, *Flagships of Imperialism*.

[94] Karabell, *Parting the Desert*, p. 56.   [95] Farnie, *East and West of Suez*, p. 57.

[96] 'Steam-Navigation to India', *The Times*, 13 August 1834.

[97] Peters, *Building the Nineteenth Century*, p. 180.

healthy condition'.[98] As this example illustrates, the creation of shipping lines such as P&O was essential for the standardisation of intercontinental travel. In the British Empire P&O's role was certainly dominant, yet it still had to face competitors on a global scale. In the mid-1840s, for instance, Austrian Lloyd established a bimonthly service between Trieste and Alexandria.[99] The French shipping line *Messageries Maritimes* was another important rival.

Importantly, the rivalry at work here was not only economic but political as well. The establishment of P&O and the overland route were closely linked to the Eastern or Oriental Question, which had been on the political agenda since Napoleon's occupation of Egypt.[100] It gained increasing virulence during the course of the nineteenth century against the background of the weakening Ottoman Empire, which despite its attempts at reform could not maintain an equal position with the other powers. The emerging power vacuum coupled with the new traffic in the Red Sea region led to increased competition between western companies and more importantly European states for dominance in areas formerly controlled by the Ottoman Empire. This could take the shape of new types of control, such as the supervision of foreign warships.[101]

Before the opening of the Canal, Egypt and more specifically the Suez Canal Region had thus already developed into a strategic location at the crossroads of political rivalries and – as the result of the diversion of troop transportation from the Cape of Good Hope to the overland route – as a passageway between Britain and India. Even before its realisation, the Suez Canal region was charged with multiple meanings: a strip of barren desert between two seas that had to be mapped and calculated, but also a project deeply charged with mystical power; drawing on the most up-to-date technology of the time, yet simultaneously infused with the legends of ancient Egypt and the land of the Bible.

The construction of the Suez Canal captures much of late nineteenth-century attitudes towards progress and ties together many of the phenomena mentioned in earlier parts of this introduction, particularly the impact of new communicative channels on perceptions of time and

---

[98] SHD, BB4 1492, *Sous-Dossier chemin de fer Egyptien*: Agreement made and ratified on the day and date underwritten, between the undersigned acting respectively on behalf of his Highness Ismaïl Pacha, Kedeve [*sic*] of Egypt on the one part and the Peninsular and Oriental Steam Navigation Company of London on the other, 2 January 1869.

[99] Farnie, *East and West of Suez*, p. 23.

[100] For an overview, see Macfie, *The Eastern Question*; see also Anderson, *The Eastern Question*.

[101] SHD, BB4 1017 and 1036; more generally on French–British rivalry Marlowe, *Perfidious Albion*.

space and as focal points of imperial competition. The story of the Canal's creation has attracted a great deal of attention, in both academic and popular writing; the project has often been described as one of the epic success stories of the nineteenth century, much in line with the completion of the Pacific Railroad and the laying of the transatlantic cable. The idea of cutting a canal through the Isthmus of Suez was not new to the nineteenth century but had in fact been repeatedly voiced over the centuries as both a utopian dream and a technological challenge. The Pharaoh Sesostris III had built a canal from the Nile to the Bitter Lakes; this was re-excavated by the Persian ruler Darius I and then restored during the Roman occupation of Egypt in 98 BC.[102] A little less than 1,800 years later, the famous Ottoman traveller, Evliya Çelebi, returning from Mecca in 1670–71 with the Cairo caravan passing in proximity to the Red Sea, proposed the construction of a Suez Canal, suggesting that it would make the journey cheaper and safer.[103]

In the late eighteenth and early nineteenth centuries, the project of building such a canal gained new urgency. During the Napoleonic expedition to Egypt, the engineer Jacques-Marie Le Père was commissioned to assess the project's feasibility. In 1803 he published his *Mémoire sur la communication de la mer des Indes à la Méditerranée par la mer Rouge et l'isthme de Suez*, in which he concluded that a 10 metre difference between the levels of the two seas rendered a canal impossible.[104] But several decades later, followers of the French utopian thinker Henri de Saint-Simon again took up the project, with writers such as Gustave d'Eichthal developing the theme of Orient and Occident as two distinct and opposing worlds that had to be brought together.[105] For the group surrounding Saint-Simon's successor, Barthélemy Prosper Enfantin, the Suez Canal became a central remedy for resolving this opposition. Their ideas combined the vision of a united world with a reverence for technology and engineering understood as keys to saving the world from conflict and war. For Michel Chevalier the dispute between east and west could be solved through the development of a tightly knit system of travel and transportation of which the Suez Canal would be a crucial segment allowing an expansion of European civilisation. In this manner, as he saw it, Europe would soon carry its progress and culture throughout the world, rendering it peaceful and united.[106]

---

[102] According to Herodotus, the Canal had first been built by Necos (610–595 BC) and then re-excavated by Darius I. Herodotus, *Histories* vol. ii, ch. 158, sect. 1.
[103] Faroqhi, 'Red Sea Trade and Communications as observed by Evliya Çelebi', 93.
[104] Spillmann, 'Le percement de l'isthme de Suez', 6–10.
[105] d'Eichthal, *Les deux mondes*, for example pp. 17–22; Picon, *Les saint-simoniens*.
[106] Chevalier, 'Exposition du système de la Méditerranée'.

Enfantin was the most eccentric of Saint-Simon's disciples. Born in 1796, he formed a new church in 1829, calling himself the 'father' and his followers 'apostles'. His idea of unifying the world by digging across the isthmus involved an orientalist vision of the marriage between a female Orient and a male Occident. In an epistolary poem he stated that it was his and his disciples' task first to create a new European route between ancient Egypt and Judea, directed towards India and China, and later to construct a similar connection at Panama. He continued:

> We will thus place one foot on the Nile,
> The other on Jerusalem,
> Our left hand will cover Rome
> And still rest on Paris.
> Suez
> Is the centre of our working life,
> There we will commit the act
> That the world is waiting for
> To confess that we are
> Male.[107]

Even if no one else used equally graphic expressions, Enfantin was not the only one interested in the construction of a global crossroads at Suez. From the 1830s onwards he attempted to turn his ideas into reality. In 1833 he left for Egypt with some of his disciples to negotiate a deal with the viceroy allowing them to research local conditions and eventually build the Canal.[108] While manoeuvring in Cairo's diplomatic arena and investigating the geographical conditions of the isthmus, he met Ferdinand de Lesseps who would become his more successful rival.[109] In 1846 a separate canal building project got underway with the establishment of the *Société d'études pour le canal de Suez*; the chief figure tied to this project was the Austrian engineer Alois Negrelli who established that the Red Sea and the Mediterranean were actually at the same level.[110] In any event, many accounts of the Canal's construction centre on de Lesseps who, because of his personal friendship with the Egyptian viceroy Sa'id, obtained the concessions to build the Canal in 1854 and 1856.[111]

---

[107] Enfantin, 'Lettre d'Enfantin à Barrault, 8 août 1833', pp. 55–60, at pp. 56–7; see also d'Allemagne, *Prosper Enfantin et les grandes entreprises du XIXe siècle*; Lajard de Puyjalon, *L'influence des Saint-Simoniens*.

[108] Carré, *Voyageurs et écrivains français en Egypte*, pp. 261–77.

[109] Karabell, *Parting the Desert*, p. 35.

[110] See, for instance, Moghira, *L'isthme de Suez*, pp. 62–3.

[111] These accounts either tend to be hagiographical depictions of Ferdinand de Lesseps (from Ritt, *Histoire de l'isthme de Suez* to Karabell, *Parting the Desert*, ch. 4: 'A man, a plan, a canal', pp. 38–49) or, as part of the Egyptian national historiography, they describe how Sa'id was tricked into the concessions that led to the sacrifice of thousands of peasants

The concessions can be understood in the framework of an emerging informal empire, with European firms taking advantage of the weakness of local states. These concessions, which the Ottoman government only approved in 1866, allowed the *Compagnie universelle du canal maritime de Suez*, an international shareholders' company incorporated under Egyptian law yet controlled by foreigners, the exclusive right to operate the Canal for 99 years; the company was also granted land and supplied with workers.[112] This represented a method of domination grounded in highly unequal economic relations – most of the profit generated went to the European investors with little advantage for the local economy.[113]

At the beginning, the enterprise was far from either profitable or uncontested. Despite publicity campaigns and 200,000 shares being sold in France, the Suez Canal Company could not raise sufficient funds and thus depended on financial help from the Egyptian government.[114] In addition to the viceroy's backing, de Lesseps also had to gain the support of other political representatives. Napoleon III was easily convinced – de Lesseps happened to be the godfather of his wife Eugénie. However, the Ottoman sultan, Abdülmecid I, was not willing to ratify the concessions, as the British, and above all their prime minister, Viscount Palmerston, were ardently opposed to the very idea of the Suez Canal. Palmerston saw the entire undertaking as an instrument of the French, aimed at gaining the upper hand in the 'Eastern Question'. True, the Indian Uprising rebellion of 1857 had shown how relevant faster communication between India and Great Britain could be, as the news of the uprising had only slowly reached Britain and the soldiers sent as reinforcements had arrived in India after a long delay.[115] Richard Burton, who had gained fame for his journey in disguise to the holy sites in Mecca and Medina, summarised the conflict: 'The English want a rail road, which would confine the use of Egypt to themselves. The French desire a canal that would admit the hardy cruisers of the Mediterranean into the Red Sea. The cosmopolite will hope that both projects may be carried out.'[116]

Despite this political struggle, construction work began in 1859. First estimates suggested that work on one of the globe's biggest building

who died on the building sites and eventually to Egypt's dependency from the West (Jalāl and Mashhūr, *al-Sīrāʿ al-dawlī ḥawla istighlāl qanāt al-Suways*; Barakāt, *Taṭawwur al-milkiyya al-zirāʿiyya fī miṣr wa athāruha ʿala al-ḥaraka al-siyāsiyya*).

112 Boutros-Ghali and Chlala, *Le Canal de Suez*, pp. 1–3 and 4–9.
113 Piquet, 'The Suez Canal Company's Concession in Egypt', 109; also Piquet, *Histoire du Canal de Suez*. See also Hansen and Tourk, 'The Profitability of the Suez Canal'.
114 Karabell, *Parting the Desert*, p. 140.
115 Farnie, *East and West of Suez*, p. 45. On the Indian Uprising as global event, see Carter and Bates, 'Empire and Locality'.
116 Burton, *Sir Richard Burton's Travels in Arabia and Africa*, p. 23 n. 10.

sites would last only six years.[117] The intrinsic relationship between expanding mobility and the Canal had already begun before its opening: most of the required engineers moved to Egypt from France. As Nathalie Montel has shown, many of them had been trained at the *École polytechnique* in Paris and had started their careers at the French railway companies, on which the structure of the Suez Canal Company was actually modelled.[118] In addition to these engineers, the construction work depended on large numbers of forced labourers, a practice known as *corvée*.[119] In the concessions, Sa'id had agreed to furnish the company with *fellahin* who mainly came from Upper Egypt. During its building process the Canal had thus already added a new form of mobility to the region by causing significant local migrations.[120]

De Lesseps was wary of the use of forced labour. After all, the anti-slavery movement in the United States and elsewhere was at its height. Still he was forced to rely on the *corvée* system to gather the number of workers needed for his undertaking (a peak of 23,318 workers was reached in April 1862). Working conditions on the building sites were very harsh, with the Egyptian historiography referring to thousands of deaths.[121] In 1862 the British Parliament, in line with its generally critical stance regarding the Canal project, voiced official protests against the *corvée*, which had been used just some years earlier by the British themselves during construction of the railway across the isthmus.[122] Palmerston was particularly critical, stating that it had to be regretted that at a time when England and France were in need of cotton cultivation, 30,000 to 40,000 workers were instead building a canal and harbours impractical for navigation.[123] In this manner, the fight against forced labour could be used as a political weapon in the interimperial power game between Britain and France.

Sa'id died in 1863, resulting in a transformed political situation in Egypt. His nephew Isma'il ascended to power; intent on ruling in an explicitly modern fashion he began to call for an end to the *corvée*.[124]

---

[117] Farnie, *East and West of Suez*, p. 55.

[118] Montel, *Le chantier du canal de Suez*, esp. p. 30.

[119] See Brown, 'Who Abolished Corvée Labour in Egypt and Why?'

[120] McKeown, 'Global Migration, 1846–1940', 115.

[121] Karabell paints an overly romanticised picture of the *corvée* stating that the forced labourers earned decent money and were treated well (Karabell, *Parting the Desert*, pp. 169–80). Montel gives a more detailed and balanced account (Montel, *Le chantier du canal de Suez*, pp. 38–42; p. 52 for the rations that workers received; pp. 62–4 for (British) protests against the *corvée*).

[122] Peters, *Building the Nineteenth Century*, p. 186.

[123] Karabell, *Parting the Desert*, p. 200.

[124] An example of Isma'il's belief in 'progress' (and his anglophile attitudes) can be found in the fact that he decorated the walls of his palaces with Arabic quotations from Samuel Smiles' *Self-Help* (Farnie, *East and West of Suez*, p. 66).

Isma'il also worked to bring the Canal more clearly under Egyptian control and to check the company's dominance by transforming the Canal Region into an Egyptian province in 1864.[125] While he was generally sympathetic to the Canal project, viewing it as an important step in Egypt's modernisation, he was also suspicious of dependence on foreign powers and resented the fact that 'even if your company is essentially Egyptian and you have given it since the beginning the title of universal, it is indisputable that it is most particularly French'.[126]

The discontinuation of the *corvée* in May 1864 forced the Suez Canal Company to rely more heavily on semi-skilled European and Levantine workers and foremen, to increase wage rates, and to mechanise the building process as fast and as far as possible, for example by the deployment of various dredgers.[127] The new general director of the company, François Philippe Voisin, reorganised the working routine and created a hierarchical and centralised logistical structure. Western visitors were impressed with the degree of mechanisation. Observing the proceedings in 1866, the explorer Thomas Kerr Lynch was particularly amazed by a machine that, moving along a rail, cut the banks perpendicularly. The European machines that finally dug the global shortcut of the Suez Canal through Egyptian sands were operated by a Mediterranean workforce, as Lynch also noted that at that point there were not many Arab workers but rather Maltese, Greeks and Ionians. He was amazed at how the construction was turned into 'simply a work for the dredging-machine, and one happily exempted from that awful sacrifice of human life and labour which formerly attended similar Egyptian enterprises, in one of which 120,000 Egyptians perished'.[128]

Accompanying such developments was a change in political attitudes towards the Suez Canal project. The imperial and economic expansion of the 1860s fostered the demand for accelerated communication between Europe and Asia. As a result, once the creation of the Canal seemed unstoppable, the British opposition weakened. In May 1862 a French navy captain investigating the political situation on the Red Sea reported to the French Minister of the Navy and the colonies that the British had begun to occupy strategic points in the sea to gain access to coaling stations, telegraphs and so forth. He noted new constructions pointing to the fortification of Perim, an island Britain had occupied as early as

---

[125] Farnie, *East and West of Suez*, p. 69.
[126] DWQ, 'Abdīn 243, 0069–004754: Isma'il to Ferdinand de Lesseps, 23 April 1869.
[127] Montel, *Le chantier du canal de Suez*, pp. 255 ff.
[128] Lynch, *A Visit to the Suez Canal*, pp. 44–5.

1857, and wondered how France could counterbalance this British rein-forcement.[129] In conjunction with the changing British attitude, the Ottoman sultan issued a *firmān* approving the project in 1866.

The major influx of people into a former desert region slowly trans-formed it into an inhabited territory, creating the need for secondary infrastructures to supply food, water and shelter and for bureaucracy and policing. The influx of European employees and Egyptian service providers meant that the Canal towns were marked from the outset by a particularly international character – as one visitor of the building site noted: 'Port Said is quite a city: we count 1,023 Europeans and 1,578 Arabs, we have restaurants, cafés, tailors and canteens'.[130] In 1862 the foundations of Port Said, the emerging town at the Mediterranean entrance of the Suez Canal, were laid in concrete – until then there had been only wooden shacks to accommodate the workers.[131] A newly con-structed canal brought fresh water from the Nile to Ismailia and Suez rendering this resource easily available at Suez for the first time. This offered Suez a profound advantage over Port Said, to which water was first conveyed by pipeline from Ismailia in April 1864. By the mid-1860s, the three towns in the Canal area – Suez, Ismailia and Port Said – were prospering with a population either directly connected to the Canal build-ing or else supplying services to the workers. By now the opening of the Canal which would take place after ten years of construction work, was eagerly awaited.

Outline of the book

While the history of the Canal's imagination and construction form an important backdrop, *Channelling Mobilities* goes far beyond this well-known history, with the Canal serving both as a specific case study and as an example for developments occurring in different regions of the globe. Studying a newly constructed and strategically important 'global locality' makes it possible to write global history in a novel and especially fruitful way, avoiding the limitations of concentrating on a single commodity, a single mobile group or a single idea by which historians in recent years have attempted to turn global history into a manageable undertaking. The con-centration on a clearly bounded space of research also makes it possible to develop a more precise argument than those works covering a whole maritime space. Hence a micro-exploration of the Canal and its everyday

---

[129] SHD, BB4 1036: Capitaine de frégate (name not readable) Ministre de la Marine et des Colonies, Aden, 4 May 1862.
[130] Berchère, *Le désert de Suez*, p. 20.   [131] Perkins, *Port Sudan*, p. 12.

processes forms the centre of the present work. Yet an investigation interested in the workings of a global locality cannot emphasise the global and local levels alone but has to show how one and the same space is integrated into different geographies, sometimes changing the focus, the angle and the zoom from the bird's eye view to that of the magnifying glass and to all scales in between. In this manner, the intertwining of the different functions necessary to guarantee successful transportation – imperial competition, internationalist endeavours, political movements in Egypt, local controls and the mobilisation of workers – will be followed in various contexts. What is more, different chapters venture 'east of Suez', for instance when it comes to the mobility of Mecca pilgrims or alleged slave traders.

The small-scale investigation adds to the understanding of imperial geographies that crystallise around specific nodal points, contributing to debates on the character of imperial space and modifying older approaches of a centripetal or a centrifugal vision of empire, where integration either comes in from the edges or spreads out from the metropole. It does so by shedding light on a place in-between that is crucial as a meeting place and as a location that structures and interconnects this imperial space. Furthermore it provides a link with the interest in networks voiced by many proponents of the 'new imperial history', who have emphasised the movements of different agents of empire by tying these networks and movements back into a specific location and shedding light on the power struggles over global mobility concentrated in this location.[132] Finally it helps to illuminate the everyday practices of colonialism that have been neglected for too long.[133]

Three organising principles – the different phases of the global management of mobility between 1869 and 1914, the different forms or categories of mobility and the different spatial configurations connected with the Canal – structure our journey through this book. While the three parts, 'Imperial relay station', 'Frontier of the civilising mission' and 'Checkpoint' investigate different forms of organising and perceiving space as well as provide a rough chronology of the experiments with the regulation of movement, most of the individual chapters focus on different mobilities intersecting at the Canal. With every chapter thus adding a specific perspective and often moving from the level of perception to the level of regulation, an increasingly complex picture of the Suez Canal route will emerge, assembling a mosaic of the different angles from which one and the same space can be analysed.

---

[132] For a good summary of the different approaches on 'imperial space', see Lambert and Lester, 'Imperial Spaces, Imperial Subjects', in Lambert and Lester (eds.), *Colonial Lives*, pp. 1–31, esp. pp. 3–13.

[133] See, among others, Clancy-Smith and Gouda (eds.), *Domesticating the Empire*; Buettner, *Empire Families*.

If the Canal possessed various facets as a connector – maritime, imperial, infrastructural – it was also a boundary in different senses. For one it functioned as a *boundary between imagined spaces*. As a transition between Europe and Asia, the Canal rapidly became a space that structured the journey of numerous colonial officers and troops. Travellers to their colonial stations in India, for example, often sent their first postcards from here and associated the place not only with increasingly standardised rituals, such as the purchase of tropical equipment in Port Said's department store, or fancy-dress parties during the passage through the Canal, but also with the shift from European hierarchies to colonial ones and vice versa.

Furthermore, the Canal became a 'frontier of the civilising mission' where the distinction between those forms of mobility that were deemed civilised and those that were perceived as backward and in need of a civilising mission was drawn most sharply. While the mobility of the Canal was often perceived as being progressive and 'modern', it was contrasted with the mobility of Bedouin and caravans on both sides of the Canal and of dhow boats on the Red Sea. The new Canal route also interacted with these mobilities in several ways. Not only did it interrupt the old caravan route between Egypt and Syria, which could only be upheld by the installation of a ferry service, it also transformed the Red Sea into a main global shipping artery, which in turn led to the increasing control and identification of ships traditionally navigating this sea.

Finally the Suez Canal was turned into a checkpoint where states and empires had to face up to their responsibilities for their mobile subjects and had to select who had to undergo certain controls and who did not. It thus became a space where the boundaries between different travellers were negotiated and hardened as a strategy for coping with increasing and increasingly rapid mobility. Growing capacities led to more and more situations in which such controls and measures of identification became necessary – for example in connection with people who fell sick on the journey, who were destitute or who stowed away from their country of origin.

In addition to moving successively from the biographies of privileged travellers to those of workers and on to stowaways and other marginal people on the move, the three parts also follow a rough chronology illustrating the dynamisation of regulation and standardisation at global level, as well as the emerging patterns of resistance to these increasingly rigid rules, and adding to the argument that the Canal facilitated movement but at the same time helped introduce new forms of control which in turn often slowed down traffic. The first part traces the emergence of the new transportation system created by the Canal during the first two decades of its existence as well as its dependence on workers and other personnel. The second part looks at alternative mobilities in the Canal Zone and beyond, after the firm establishment of the Canal system and at the partial reliance of some of the control mechanisms on these 'traditional' forms of mobility, which were at the same time targets of controls and slowdowns. The last part goes on to scrutinise the control and identification measures that were tightened up in the years between 1900 and the First World War. During this period, the attempts to contain, control and channel mobility were accompanied by new ways of evading these controls.

The three chapters following this introduction deal with what I call 'imperial infrastructure'. This is first approached in Chapter 1, 'Rites de passage and perceptions of global space', through the perceptions of passengers travelling on the big steamers, looking at the part that Port Said and the Canal came to occupy in their records. It makes the point that these perceptions became increasingly standardised by the wide dissemination of media such as travel guides, travelogues and postcards. At the same time it is necessary to differentiate between perceptions of the global in the late nineteenth century as they shifted between the global as universal, the global as imperial and the global as cosmopolitan and multiethnic. In Chapter 2, 'Regimes of passage and troops in the Canal Zone', the political preconditions and implications of this 'imperial infrastructure' move to centre stage. The chapter reveals the complicated governance of a global locality by disentangling the different scales of rulemaking, from the treatment of troops on the ground to the level of international law and its limits. By concentrating on the global relocation of imperial troops, the chapter can furthermore demonstrate how, in the Canal Zone, empires observed each other's military strategy closely and how the Canal became a barometer of inter-imperial relations. In Chapter 3, companies and workers, crucial for the functioning of such a new system of transportation, play the leading role; specific attention will be paid to working conditions and strike movements of Canal workers, coal heavers and seamen.

Chapters 4, 5 and 6 look more closely at those groups perceived by western travellers as representing 'traditional' mobility in the region, such as the Bedouin, caravans, dhow ships and Muslim pilgrims. It will be argued that various western agents perceived these mobilities through the lens of the civilising mission, which was very often connected with a particular occupation of empires with religion. Yet in fact these mobilities deemed 'traditional' were not transformed along the lines envisaged by many observers, but rather entered into an intricate interaction with western agents who very often relied on seemingly 'traditional' knowledge and skills in their attempt to exert closer control in the region. Chapter 4 deals with the Bedouin and caravans, both in close proximity to the Canal and further 'east of Suez'. Chapter 5 shows that dhows in the Red Sea were increasingly suspected of participating in slave-trading networks between the African and Arab coasts of the Red Sea, which served as a pretext for tighter controls. Chapter 6 returns to the domain of steamships, analysing the growing regulation of the pilgrim traffic journeying through the Canal.

From the regulation of specific groups, Chapters 7 and 8 move to more wide-ranging moments of control. In Chapter 7, 'Contagious mobility and the filtering of disease', we turn to the attempt to transform the Suez Canal into a semi-permeable membrane, designed to keep out microbes that cause epidemic disease. Chapter 8, 'Rights of passage and the identification of individuals', deals with the identification of individuals in the Canal Zone, be they destitute, stowaways, prostitutes or criminals.

The conclusion returns to the three main themes of the book and particularly to the tension between the freedom of movement and its limits, specifying the process of 'channelling mobilities' and clarifying the understanding of globalisation and mobility as they emerge throughout this book.

Part I

Imperial relay station: global space, new thresholds 1870s–1890s

1 *Rites de passage* and perceptions of global space

It was a cold evening after heavy rain and the half-flooded streets reeked. But we undefeated tourists ran about in droves and saw all that could be seen before train-time. We missed, most of us, the Canal Company's garden, which happens to mark a certain dreadful and exact division between East and West. Up to that point – it is a fringe of palms, stiff against the sky – the impetus of home memories and the echo of home interests carry the young man along very comfortably on his first journey. But at Suez one must face things. People, generally the most sympathetic, leave the boat there; the older men who are going on have discovered each other and begun to talk shop; no newspapers come aboard, only clipped Reuter telegrams; the world seems cruelly large and self-absorbed. One goes for a walk and finds this little bit of kept ground, with comfortable garden-gated houses on either side of the path. Then one begins to wonder – in the twilight, for choice – when one will see those palms again from the other side. Then the black hour of homesickness, vain regrets, foolish promises, and weak despair shuts down with the smell of strange earth and the cadence of strange tongues. Cross-roads and halting-places in the desert are always favoured by djinns and afrits. The young man will find them waiting for him in the Canal Company's garden at Port Said.[1]

The Canal Zone was not only a focal point of Saint-Simonian utopias, technological achievements and political rivalries – it also had a specific location in the spatial imaginations of ordinary passengers. The Canal and the towns on its shores were erected from scratch; they were literally put on the map. As they were places without a past, it was not yet clear, in 1869, what position they would come to occupy in the minds of contemporaries, or, in line with the cartographic metaphor, on their personal maps of the world. In the first decades after the opening of the Canal, the region became emblematic as a point of transition between Europe and Asia. As implied in the quotation from Rudyard Kipling, passage through the Canal became a veritable *rite de passage* associated with standard

---

[1] Kipling, 'A Return to the East', p. 244.

behaviours, such as a changing dress code and specific celebrations. It gained this position via the establishment of defined images and perceptions, which were then put into motion with the help of official publications, newspapers, travel descriptions, guidebooks and visual images, such as photographs and postcards.[2]

Despite the emphasis on passengers occupying the upper decks of the big steam liners, which ploughed the seas between the continents, the aim of this chapter is not to trace individual trajectories and cast the characters in full detail. Drawing on a wide range of travelogues, of which only few feature explicitly in this chapter, it will centre on how the patterns used to describe the Canal and its cities were established, put into motion, and reproduced by a large amount of travellers, both western and non-western. Often these patterns were articulated in oppositions, such as home and away, exotic and familiar, backward and modern, acceleration and deceleration and, of course, east and west. Travellers' observations shifted between different visions of the region: as a bridge unifying the globe, as a border zone between two worlds and as an outpost of competing empires. Linking the globality of the Suez Canal to the individual perceptions of travellers using it, the following discussion will focus on these rival visions of a global space in the first two decades after the opening of the Canal, veering between expressions of universality and imperial connotations which form the basis for the chapters to come, before the last section turns to the way in which media disseminated and solidified these images and ideas.

As implied in the title of this chapter, in the following the concept of the *rite de passage* will be connected to conceptualisations of global space. Since the anthropologist Arnold van Gennep elaborated the concept, it has been linked to the passage between different stages, be they temporal, spatial, or social. These passages always carried the germ of social upheaval and had to be tempered by certain rites.[3] Van Gennep already used spatial metaphors to describe the passage from one stage to another. In the following, such *rites de passage* will be linked to spatial configurations even more explicitly than in his work. They carried both personal and global connotations of different kinds, helping us to understand the emergence of certain competing images of the global solidifying with an astonishing rapidity between 1870 and 1890, most notably the

---

[2] For analyses of descriptions of the Canal opening: Haddad, 'Digging to India'; Murray, *Imperial Ways*; Simons, 'Dichter am Kanal' and 'Heinrich von Stephan und die Idee der Weltpost'. More generally on travelogues of Egypt: Barrell, 'Death on the Nile'.
[3] See van Gennep, *Les rites de passage*.

global as universal, the global as juxtaposition of heterogeneous elements and the global as imperial.

Global unification

In line with the Saint-Simonian ideas mentioned in the introduction, the Canal Company disseminated the idea that the role of the Canal was to represent the unification of the globe. Yet this unification could mean at least two things: either the Europeanisation of the world or the fusion of east and west at this particular locality. In the following we will trace these different meanings by a visit to the opening ceremony and a perusal of the Canal Company's journal. To a certain extent these meanings referred back to a pre-existing set of images. The theme of Egypt as the world's crossroads had a long tradition. Even before the Canal's opening, Khedive Isma'il made reference to it, when, explaining that he was looking forward to the opening of this new path of commerce and civilisation, he voiced his pride as ruler of Egypt, which was to become, as it had once been, the 'hyphen' between Europe and the Far East.[4]

The opening of the Canal

On 17 November 1869, the Suez Canal was finally inaugurated with great pomp. The festivities for the new waterway stretched the budget of Khedive Isma'il, whose financial situation had already been strained, not least due to the Canal's construction.[5] The opening of the Canal changed the Khedive's map of the world and shifted his sense of Egypt's location. 'My country is no longer part of Africa', he was reported as saying on the eve of the opening, 'I have made it part of Europe.'[6]

To underline the European character of the opening ceremonies, western etiquette was observed and the list of invitees featured many notable European guests. Empress Eugénie of France took up the prime position in this hierarchy. On her yacht, *L'Aigle*, she was the first to pass through the Canal, followed by a procession of 55 ships. Other royal representatives included Emperor Franz Joseph I of Austria, Prince Henry of the Netherlands and the German heir to the throne, Friedrich Wilhelm (later to be Friedrich III of Prussia and Germany). Some royal guests, for example the Ottoman sultan himself,

---

[4] DWQ, 'Abdīn 243, 0069–004754: Isma'il to Ferdinand de Lesseps, 23 April 1869.
[5] See Owen, *The Middle East in the World Economy*, pp. 122–30.
[6] Busch, *Verdi's Aida*, p. 6, quoted in Carter and Harlow (eds.), *Archives of Empire*, p. 555.

had turned down the invitation. The British had sent their ambassador in Constantinople, Henry Elliot, together with Admiral Sir Alexander Milne. Their ship *Psyche* occupied the eighth position, just after the royal guests of honour.[7] Following the considerable international turmoil caused by the building of the Canal, questions such as the order of the ships proceeding through it were of crucial importance.

Although the opening ceremonies and the party in Ismailia unfolded without major incident, the first passage did not proceed entirely smoothly: even if a boat that had got stuck in the Canal the night before the opening was able to be removed just in time, during the procession, some Austrian ships that had pushed in before the Prussian ship (thus ignoring the politically delicate line-up), ran aground three times – much to Prince Friedrich Wilhelm's dismay, as he noted in his diary.[8] The captain of Eugénie's ship reported back to his officials that the transit had been extremely challenging, a genuine 'tour de force'. As the Canal was still very narrow, they had passed dredgers at a distance of only 25 centimetres, demanding outright 'mathematical precision'. The empress herself had been so moved by the transit that she was taken by a brief fit of nerves and had come to the bridge in tears to congratulate the captain.[9]

Besides emphasising western habits, for example in the fashionable menu that was offered, other elements of the opening ceremonies did not follow European etiquette. In order to illustrate the meeting of east and west, a Bedouin camp was erected next to the Khedive's palace in Ismailia. The 'exotic' was thus deliberately put on display to exhilarate European participants. In his diary, Friedrich Wilhelm contrasted the splendid European-style ball in Ismailia (commenting on the dresses of the most famous guests) with his incognito visit to the Bedouin camp – for him, the highlight of the event – where he met, to their mutual delight, Empress Eugénie. Yet they pretended not to know each other as they secretly watched the 'howling, fire-eating dervishs biting into snakes'.[10]

There were also attempts to herald not simply the juxtaposition but the actual fusion between east and west. The ceremony included a religious service during which representatives of different religions blessed the

---

[7] Stanley, *My Early Travels and Adventures in America and Asia*, pp. 51–2; Karabell, *Parting the Desert*, p. 249 and pp. 253 ff.; Montel, *Le chantier du canal de Suez*, pp. 341 ff.; Farnie, *East and West of Suez*, pp. 84–7; Carter and Harlow, *Archives of Empire*, ch. 10: 'The Suez Canal: The Gala Opening', pp. 555–71.

[8] Friedrich Wilhelm, *Tagebuch*, pp. 66–7.

[9] SHD, BB4/1048, Sous-dossier voyage à Suez de S. M. l'impératrice 1869: Commandant l'Aigle à l'amiral de la Marine et des Colonies, Ismailia, 18 November 1869.

[10] Friedrich Wilhelm, *Tagebuch*, p. 69.

Canal. Sheikh Ibrahim al-Saqqa of al-Azhar University offered a Muslim benediction. The Greek Orthodox archbishop of Jerusalem and the Catholic priest Marie-Bernard Bauer – Eugénie's confessor, who in his eulogy compared Ferdinand de Lesseps to Christopher Columbus – served as Christian representatives. Lord Houghton, one of the trustees of the Royal Geographical Society, was not convinced by Bauer's comparison, however, remaining instead true to British scepticism regarding the Canal project:

Now, what is this Canal through the Isthmus of Suez? . . . I have seen it compared to the discovery of America, in fact I have seen it placed above the discovery of America, because it has been said to unite two worlds was a finer thing than to discover one. I cannot agree with this sentiment, nor do I think that its consequences can ever be compared to those of the circumnavigation of the Cape by the great Portuguese navigator.[11]

The Canal's perception as part of either Europe, or Asia, or Africa and the extent to which it would change global spatial configurations were thus already up for debate at the time of its opening. While the Khedive saw the Canal as a European work that had Europeanised his entire country, others, such as Friedrich Wilhelm, were amazed by all those things 'oriental' and 'exotic' connected to it. In a third conception, and in line with the trans-religious ceremony, the Canal was neither European nor 'oriental', but represented the whole world in a single place. Watching the first procession passing through the Canal, the proud building site manager, François Philippe Voisin, captured this idea of simultaneity describing the crowd who admired this first Canal passage: 'A multitude of all languages, all races, all colours, all dresses gathered in the wide streets of the nascent city.'[12] In the decades following the bombastic opening event, the three different visions of the Canal, stressing either its European features, its 'oriental' character, or the hybridity of the budding Canal towns, all re-emerged in different versions.

A road of civilisation and progress

Most visitors at the opening ceremonies agreed that the Canal epitomised European civilisation and progress as well as human perseverance.[13] The travel agent Thomas Cook took part in the opening ceremonies and, perhaps not unexpectedly, with the future of his business in mind, called

---

[11] 'Session 1869–70. Fourth Meeting 10th January 1870', *Proceedings of the Royal Geographical Society* XIV/1, p. 89.
[12] Voisin-Bey, *Le canal de Suez*, p. 303.
[13] See, for instance, Friedrich Wilhelm, *Tagebuch*, p. 66.

the Canal 'the greatest engineering feat of the present century'.[14] Newspaper articles propagated such images of the triumph of progress and technology together with descriptions of the pomp of the celebrations.[15] The Prussian director of postal services, Heinrich Stephan, equally praised the engineers' masterly achievements – although, true to the growing national antagonisms of the period, he expressed his disappointment that the Canal had not been built by Prussians.[16]

Even if during the first years of service, the extent of the Canal's usage left much to be desired – in December 1869 the coal merchant Worms called the 'dead quiet' Canal a failure – many observers continued to view it positively on the grounds of its unifying virtue as a global junction.[17] Author M. F. Proeschel even attributed revolutionary powers to the Canal: 'The Suez Canal, which has put the Orient at two steps of the Occident and vice versa, is an event that will cause a revolution among civilised and uncivilised peoples.'[18] The celebratory image of the Canal as connector between Europe and Asia was naturally also upheld in the Canal Company's official rhetoric and publicised via its main print publication, the weekly *Le Canal de Suez: Journal maritime et commercial* (from 1872 onwards the *Bulletin décadaire de la Compagnie universelle du canal maritime de Suez*, appearing every ten days). The newspaper's main goal was to convince shareholders of the wisdom of their investment, even at a time when the value of the shares kept falling. The journal reported on all shipping lines starting to use the Canal and offered descriptions of the novel connections forged by it. For the most part, the idea of a shrinking globe was conveyed in terms of economic connections and transported goods with an emphasis on commodities, such as tea, rice and cotton.[19]

In these positive assessments, cartographical re-scaling and a vanishing of distances were perceived as important elements in the civilising mission of the Canal.[20] The increasing involvement of the United States in the Indian Ocean theatre, the economic inclusion of Japan, the growing commerce in the Persian Gulf and in Cochinchina and the colonial activity of the Netherlands in East Asia were all assessed in terms of

---

[14] *Excursionist and Tourist Advertiser*, 1 July 1869, quoted in Said, *Orientalism*, p. 88.
[15] See, for instance, *The Illustrated London News*, 55/1567, 20 November 1869; 55/1570, 11 December 1869; 55/1571, 18 December 1869; Haddad, 'Digging to India'.
[16] Simons, 'Dichter am Kanal', p. 244.   [17] Quoted in Bonin, *Suez*, p. 32.
[18] ANMT, 1995060/1026 'Le canal de Suez et l'avenir commercial de la France': *Moniteur industriel*, 20 January 1870.
[19] See 'Le trafic du thé par le canal' and 'Commerce de la Cochinchine – riz de Saïgon', *Le canal de Suez: Journal décadaire de la Compagnie universelle du canal maritime de Suez*, 24–26 August 1871; 'Les cotons de l'Inde et le canal de Suez', ibid., 31 August 1871.
[20] See, for instance, 'La communication électrique entre l'Inde et l'Europe', *Le canal de Suez: Journal maritime et commercial*, 15 April 1870.

advancement and progress.[21] Of course Ferdinand de Lesseps himself played a vital part in singing the praises of his project, inserting it into a larger context that illustrated his universal vision of a unified and thus peaceful world: 'It will be the honour of the second part of our century to have opened to the world the great channels of communication, which, in establishing continuous relations between the peoples, will slowly bring about a universal pacification and will end the barbarities of war.'[22]

The Canal Company's self-presentation became even more confident as – after the difficulties and disappointments of the first years – the traffic through the Canal began to increase. While in 1879 only 1,477 ships passed through the Canal, the figure was 2,026 a year later. The number climbed to 2,727 in 1881, then to 3,198 in 1882, levelling out (with the exception of a slight slump in 1897, when 2,986 ships were counted) at around 3,500 by 1899.[23] At the same time, the number of passengers using the Canal was continuously rising: from 26,758 in 1870 to 101,551 in 1880 and 282,511 in 1900.[24] In 1899 de Lesseps' triumph took visible form with erection of his statue at the Canal's Port Said entrance carrying the slogan *Aperire Terram Gentibus* ('To open the earth to the nations') capturing the universal aspirations of the Canal project.[25] Soon a wealth of metaphors such as the key to the Orient or the hyphen between east and west came to be used to describe the Canal. Yet such metaphors could point not only to Europeanisation or fusion between east and west but also to the more or less awkward coexistence of European and Asian features in a space that rapidly came to be associated with personal *rites de passage* in a world of empires.

In-between space

The opening of the Canal, in connection with other developments outlined in the introduction, led to the growth of passenger traffic that served the purposes of colonial careers, migration and tourism. Whereas previously, only a negligible number of travellers had ventured on (or could

---

[21] See, among many others, 'Les États-Unis d'Amérique et le canal de Suez', *Le canal de Suez: Journal maritime et commercial*, 10 March 1871; 'Le progrès dans les Indes', ibid., 21 September 1871; 'La civilisation au Japon', ibid., 26 September 1871; 'Le golfe Persique', ibid., 26 October 1871.

[22] 'Séance du 2 février 1877', *Bulletin trimestriel de la société khédiviale de géographie du Caire, fascicule 4: Compte rendu des séances de la société de la géographie*, p. 406.

[23] Compagnie universelle du canal maritime de Suez, *Assemblée générale des actionnaires, 46e réunion 7 juin 1900*, p. 22.

[24] *Le canal maritime de Suez Note, tableaux et planches* (Ismailia, no year), tableau 4.

[25] On Bartholdi's statue and the connections with New York's Statue of Liberty: Kreiser, 'Public Monuments in Turkey and Egypt', 106.

afford) a world tour, this changed after 1869.[26] Just over a month after the opening, on 25 December 1869, *The Times* noted, with great astonishment, the arrival in Calcutta of seven American tourists who were on their way around the world.[27] Just some years later, astonishment of this sort had waned – now the astonishing aspect could only be the speed of passage, as in the case of Jules Verne's fictional hero Phileas Fogg, touring the world in 80 days. Not only were more people travelling to faraway places, but they were also writing about their experiences more frequently, bringing the world to European readers' doorsteps.

The increasing propensity for travel led to a large output of travel narratives, with the passage through the Canal emerging as a standard incident. Clearly in the last third of the nineteenth century, travel narratives were by no means a new genre. Even before the Canal had opened, the journey to Egypt particularly had become a bourgeois pastime engendering an extensive literature creating the impressions in visitors such as William Makepeace Thackeray, that they had already seen the sights some time before.[28] Nevertheless, Joseph Conrad attributed the great number of writing world tourists to the Suez Canal:

Nowadays many people encompass the globe. That kind of victory became to a certain extent fashionable for some years after the piercing of the Isthmus of Suez. Multitudes rushed through that short cut with blank minds, and alas, also blank note-books where the megalomania from which we all more or less suffer, got recorded in the shape of 'Impressions'. The inanity of the mass of travel-books the Suez Canal is responsible for took the proportions of an enormous and melancholy joke.[29]

Yet the Suez Canal was not only partly to blame for the increase in travel writing, it also figured prominently in these depictions themselves. In the following we review the increasingly standardised perceptions of a cast of characters comfortably peopling the upper decks of the slow-moving steamers and trying to make sense of the new waterway and the artificial-looking towns on its shores.

Port Said

The Suez Canal Company upheld the straightforward image of the Canal as a connection between east and west and as a road to progress and

[26] For the limited number of world tours before 1869, see *Nouvel abrégé de tous les voyages autour du monde, depuis Magellan jusqu'à d'Urville et Laplace.*
[27] Alliance française Port Said, 'Port Said après l'inauguration du canal', 27.
[28] Thackeray, 'Notes of a Journey from Cornhill to Grand Cairo', pp. 228, 250.
[29] Conrad, 'Preface', p. xii.

civilisation expressed in the articles of the *Bulletin décadaire*. Yet the numerous travelogues referred to by Conrad increasingly tended to associate the Canal passage and Port Said with more ambivalent images, as did officials employed in the town. These ambivalent images came to be defining features of Port Said and, perhaps, of the emerging imagination of the global more generally. Two depictions, framing the period under observation in this chapter, capture the extreme poles of these images. On arriving at his new post in 1870 the French Consul at Port Said, Pélissier de Raynaud, congratulated himself on serving in this location and predicted that the city's development would be a success story.[30] However, such enthusiasm soon became reversed; in April 1891 the British Consul, W. Burrell, offered evidence in his resignation letter to the degree to which Port Said had become a hardship post of the British Empire over the preceding two decades. After describing the disagreeable climate – it had according to Burrell destroyed both his and his wife's health – he concluded with remarkable frankness that he regretted giving up his position in the consular service, but that 'after years of dreary work in such a place as Port Saïd, there is but little prospect of obtaining a change from the incessant drudgery of this post, which with its other great disadvantages, becomes unbearable after a stay of several years'.[31]

The disappointment voiced by Consul Burrell was echoed in many statements of passers-by who had gone ashore while waiting for their steamer's allotted time for passage through the Canal. For most travellers to Asia, Port Said was the first port of call outside of Europe; a stay in Port Said, often extending overnight before the opening of the Canal for night traffic in 1887, thus came to be an experience shared by almost all travellers between Europe and Asia. Some passengers even decided to take a hotel room – most of them named after fashionable Parisian counterparts, yet naturally much less grand – for the sake of a night on firm ground. Many went shopping at the Simon Arzt department store to augment their tropical apparel and had a look around town before recording their impressions once back on board.[32] In line with the period's guidebooks, they predominantly concluded that there was not much to see besides a particularly diverse population that many termed 'cosmopolitan'.[33]

[30] 'Le consulat français à Port-Said', *Le canal de Suez: Journal maritime et commercial*, 6 June 1870.
[31] TNA, FO 78/4394: Consul Burrell to Marquis of Salisbury, Port Said, 9 April 1891.
[32] MacMillan, *Women of the Raj*, p. 22; Marshall, *Passage East*, p. 64.
[33] See Murray, *A Handbook for Travellers in Lower and Upper Egypt* (7th revised edn.), p. 287.

If, from its first days onwards, the port's international character was what had made it notable, for authors such as Louis Aubert-Roche, François Philippe Voisin and other representatives of the Canal Company this had been a very positive feature, carrying in it a germ of global solidarity.[34] In the following decades, this internationality would remain striking for those travelling through the Canal – albeit not always in a positive way. In any event, some found the sight of the diverse population quite fascinating. Lala Baijnath, an Indian judge and reformer on his way to Europe, referred to the diversity encountered in Port Said by alluding to the new science of ethnology:

We got to Port Said in the morning and found ourselves in quite an ethnological museum of races and people, though not generally of the best sort. Port Said is always full of vessels discharging or taking cargo, or waiting to pass through the Canal. Men-of-War of all nations, emigrant ships and troopers all meet here, and the sight is extremely interesting.[35]

Travellers in the opposite direction, from Europe to Asia, had often hoped for a more 'oriental' and less 'cosmopolitan' experience. A few travellers were, to be sure, less dissatisfied, for example the painter George Rodier, who concluded that despite the 'cosmopolitan' sailors frequenting the numerous cafes and bars, his eyes were dazzled by the 'grand oriental extravaganza'.[36]

This range of descriptions is not all that different from depictions of port scenes in other places. However, together with its specific geographic location, it was the artificial and newly built character of Port Said, erected on soil excavated during the Canal's building process with a long man-made breakwater instead of a natural harbour, that distinguished it from, for example, its older and bigger sister Alexandria. Many travelogues hinted at the artificial character of the newly built Canal towns by using a large number of descriptive analogies and comparisons. Besides images such as the key to the Orient or the hyphen between Orient and Occident, mentioned above, a variety of other places were invoked to try and capture the characteristics of the new locality. During the building period, many names had already been coined for the towns such as 'the Marseilles of the Red Sea', 'the Venice of the desert', or 'an Egyptian Calcutta'.[37]

As the waterway's construction progressed, the environment of its towns became increasingly multi-ethnic and multilingual. With the

---

[34] See, for instance, Aubert-Roche, *Rapport sur l'état sanitaire des travailleurs et des établissements du canal maritime de l'isthme de Suez.*

[35] Baijnath, *England and India*, p. 4.   [36] Rodier, *L'Orient*, p. 9.

[37] Leconte, *Promenade dans l'isthme de Suez*, p. 113; Karabell, *Parting the Desert*, p. 241; Farnie, *East and West of Suez*, pp. 43, 69.

construction work nearing completion, Port Said had established itself as the most important of the towns, a place where, according to one observer, 'you speak bad Italian to the Arabs, even worse Greek to the French, and an impossible Arabic to the Dalmatians'.[38] Once it was finally completed, a Calcutta-based reporter covering the opening ceremonies, and very impressed by what he saw, called Port Said the 'silver gate between the Orient and the Occident', which was to become within 50 years another Venice and rival to Alexandria.[39] Another visitor wandering about during the inauguration festivities, came to a very different conclusion (albeit perhaps with more foresight), employing yet another city analogy to capture its improvised nature and dedication to 'money-grubbing and crude amusements' featuring storehouses, factories and shops on the one hand and brothels, nightclubs and casinos on the other, namely 'San Francisco in miniature'.[40]

Soon, these and similar comparative analogies to characterise this in-between space became legion. Félix Charmetant, a French missionary on his way to Zanzibar, used a Middle Eastern analogy, describing Port Said as a Mediterranean caravanserai.[41] Yet he also compared Port Said, with its rectangular streets traced on the drawing board, to the cities that were springing up during the same period on the American continent.[42] With its rectangular layout and peculiar wooden houses, most visitors agreed that Port Said seemed somewhat artificial and inauthentic. Even its stones had to be imported, the *Egyptian Gazette* indicated in 1900: apparently they had been taken from, among other places, the ruins of Famagusta and Rhodes – thus to build the modern town, historic heritage elsewhere had been destroyed.[43]

Some travellers found the amorphous character of Port Said and its lack of authenticity and 'oriental features' outright disappointing. A French doctor, Henri Couvidou, travelling in 1875, described his disenchantment at arriving at Port Said after the spectacular coastlines of the Provence, Italy, Malta and Greece.[44] For Couvidou, Port Said was not 'oriental' enough; missing the exoticism he had been hoping for, he complained that European tourists did not want to see factories, similar

↳ *for cultural capital*

---

[38] Quoted in Karabell, *Parting the Desert*, p. 235.
[39] Dall, *From Calcutta to London by the Suez Canal*, p. 61.
[40] Quoted in Duff, *100 Years of the Suez Canal*, p. 103.
[41] Charmetant, *D'Alger à Zanzibar*, p. 7.   [42] Ibid., p. 8.
[43] 'Where Port Said's Stones Come From: The Ruin of Famagusta', *Egyptian Gazette*, 10 January 1900.
[44] Couvidou, *Voyage à travers l'isthme*, p. 13. For the category of the 'picturesque' see Buzard, *The Beaten Track*, p. 15; Mazower, *Salonica, City of Ghosts*, pp. 185–9.

to those in Europe, when they were travelling.[45] Nevertheless, the multi-
coloured and multilingual shopping advertisements that lined the streets
of Port Said were impressive signs of a global presence: 'The necessary
and the superfluous are displayed in Arabic, Greek, French, English,
Turkish, Dutch, and soon, God willing, in Chinese.'[46]

Alongside these depictions of Port Said as 'neither east nor west', were
efforts by other authors to pin down what exactly was 'western' and what
'oriental' about the place. Many visitors noted a clear separation between
the European and Arab quarters. A European traveller in 1869 admired
the splendour of Port Said, viewing its blue basins, straight avenues and
long jetties as 'monuments to an industrious civilisation', while dismissing
the irregular contours of the Egyptian district as 'a rough example of the
easy-going life-style of the Orient'.[47] Later visitors reiterated this contrast
between the European city and the Arab neighbourhoods, including the
American explorer Mary French Sheldon who found Port Said's jetty very
'picturesque', but the Arabic quarters, where one would not want to walk
alone after closing time, 'most villainous'.[48]

But even those travellers who did not perceive the boundary between
the European and the Arab parts of the city as so clear-cut, but were rather
bemused by the mixture they encountered in this global meeting point,
tried to define specific elements of this mixture as eastern or as western.
When it came to crime and vice (one of the few trademarks of Port Said
acknowledged at the time), most authors attempted to draw such a
boundary. For Paul Bourde, a correspondent for the Paris newspaper *Le
Temps* who was on his way to Tonkin, it was not the shopping opportunities but above all the extent of prostitution that was notable. He
described Austrian women whose beauty had diminished as the distance
from home had increased and obese Levantines in tight clothes with their
hands full of false jewels. For Bourde Port Said, a rough place where
European girls and gamblers waited for those who had made their luck in
India or elsewhere, thus represented the embodiment of a corrupted
Europe rather than the beginning of the Orient.[49]

As was the case with many of his co-passengers, the Indian traveller
N. L. Doss, whose travel account was published in Calcutta in 1893, went
on shore to avoid the nuisance of coaling. He also struggled to place Port
Said geographically, concluding that it was rather a European than an
African town, with mainly Europeans frequenting the cafes and drinking
places of which there were too many for such a small city. Doss seemed to

[45] Couvidou, *Voyage à travers l'isthme*, p. 64.   [46] Ibid., p. 55.
[47] Quoted in Modelski, *Port Said Revisited*, p. 56.
[48] French Sheldon, *Sultan to Sultan*, p. 24.   [49] Bourde, *De Paris au Tonkin*, pp. 14–15.

agree with Bourde that the consumers of the unsavoury goods and services on offer were mainly European, but that the immorality itself contained elements from both the East and the West. In conclusion, Doss repeated the image of Port Said as 'the place where at the present day the vice of the east and the vice of the west find a common refuge'.[50] This theme of Port Said as, in the words of Behramji Malabari, a Parsi newspaper editor and social reformer, 'a mixture of European and Asiatic vices', became a standard feature in the travelogues.[51] Nevertheless, other travellers had no difficulty in associating the town with either eastern or western depravity in a clear-cut manner. T. N. Mukharji esteemed the Suez Canal in Thomas Cook's manner, as 'one of the greatest feats of modern engineering' and as an example of what an individual endowed with the 'power of organisation, enterprise and perseverance' could achieve, yet Port Said represented the dark side of Europe where the 'dregs of all European countries' gathered.[52] In sharp contrast Rachel Humphreys, travelling during the First World War, asserted that Port Said was 'the refuse heap for all the nations of the East'.[53]

Whether the characteristics of Port Said were seen as clearly attributable to either east or west, or whether they were perceived as a global mixture, the increasingly uniform descriptions of westward as well as eastward travellers shared the unease of placing it on the map as part of Asia, Africa or Europe. The travelogues also highlight the extent to which Port Said had become not primarily a location representing global unification, but rather a border zone *between* different worlds. What the travellers termed 'cosmopolitanism' was thus not a universal ideal, but rather denoted an uneasy mingling of distinct groups of people. The difficulty of placing Port Said and its society in flux was part of the perception of the town as a space of disorder par excellence. More than once, this global space of unruliness was explicitly contrasted with another global space: the steamer with its ordered and hierarchical social life on which the passengers passing through the Canal were noting in their observations.

Rites de passage in the Canal and the Red Sea

Accompanying such perceptions of Port Said as a global locality was a more personal response to the passage through the Canal and – depending on the direction of the journey – to the arrival in the Red Sea and the

[50] Doss, *Reminiscences, English and Australian*, p. 25.
[51] Malabari, *The Indian Eye on English Life*, p. 18; Burton, *At the Heart of the Empire*, pp. 154–87.
[52] Mukharji, *A Visit to Europe*, pp. 15–16.   [53] Humphreys, *Travels East of Suez*, p. 7.

Mediterranean respectively: its experience as an individual *rite de passage* marking the transition between home and away. In this regard, it is useful to recall the discussion of the *rite de passage* offered by the anthropologist Arnold van Gennep in 1909, who described it as a three-phase process of departure, liminal state and assimilation.[54] As van Gennep conveys the process by using spatial metaphors (for example by equalling the passage between different life stages to the passage between different rooms in a house), the analogy of the journey through the bottleneck of the Suez Canal is evident. What is more, in the case of the Canal, the spatial crossing was often also connected with a more personal transformation in van Gennep's sense.

Whereas, as indicated, the Canal's opening was widely celebrated for its unification of the globe, prompting wonder at the new ease and speed of European-Asian travel, getting between the two continents remained a considerable undertaking and brought the tension between acceleration and deceleration that the Canal came to represent to the fore. Contrary to all expectations, the passage through the Canal – a symbol for the speeding up of global traffic – was often resented as being terribly slow. Prince Friedrich Wilhelm had already found it rather boring and the painter Rodier, who had written so favourably about Port Said, considered it 'not very picturesque'.[55] Most travellers, in fact, experienced disillusion and weariness during the monotonous passage, despite the striking image they were offered of ships traversing the desert. Journalist Paul Bourde placed such feelings in a direct relationship with the experience of modernity, again denying any sense of the picturesque or colossal in relation to the Suez Canal. He felt that this grandeur became apparent when reading the statistics but not when physically experiencing the Canal journey, which was contrary to all expectation mediocre and disappointing. Bourde concluded that such deception was frequent with 'large modern enterprises'.[56]

Travelling in the other direction, Bhagvat Sinh Jee, the 18-year-old ruler of Gondal, one of the princely states of the Bombay Presidency, was happy to arrive at Aden and the Red Sea after a long Indian Ocean crossing during which – despite all comforts and luxuries – he and his company had felt like 'prisoners confined within the wooden walls of the steamer'.[57] In line with Bourde's observation, he was himself disappointed with the Canal: although, he admitted, it was 'one of the greatest

[54] van Gennep, *Les rites de passage*.
[55] Friedrich Wilhelm, *Tagebuch*, p. 67; Rodier, *L'Orient*, p. 10.
[56] Bourde, *De Paris au Tonkin*, pp. 16–17.
[57] Sinh Jee, *Journal of a Visit to England in 1883*, p. 17.

monuments of modern engineering skill' he wished he had followed some of his co-passengers and taken the overland route from Suez for some sightseeing in Cairo and Giza and then the steamer from Alexandria to Brindisi to avoid the Canal, which 'awfully disgusted' him.[58] Despite this assessment, Sinh Jee did purchase some photographs for his album while in Port Said, which, he duly noted, as many had before him, 'seems to be a sort of meeting place for all nations'.[59]

Maintaining their admiration for the Canal as a technological achievement, Indian travellers however were frequently disappointed with it as a symbol of Western civilisation. The newspaper editor and social reformer, Behramji Malabari, expressed his ambivalence in an especially vivid manner:

The Suez Canal is a splendid piece of work; but the passage through it is dreadfully slow. It becomes too monotonous as we drag our way painfully along. The wild and weird-looking country beyond, on both sides, interests me more than the immense feat of engineering before me. Whilst the steamer is crawling, you more than once realize the force of the expression – 'Dull as ditch water.' It is seldom, indeed, one finds that phrase so vividly illustrated as in the Suez Canal.[60]

Implicitly, Malabari underscored the Canal's function as not only a connection between Asia and *Europe* but also a new boundary between Asia and *Africa* – a function that many Europeans neglected. He also stressed the slowness of the passage through what was one of the major accelerators of world traffic. In his preference for the Asian and African coasts of the European Canal, Malabari furthermore appeared to view not only its technological achievement but also its uniformity as somehow symbolic of Europe and European modes of controlling both nature and large parts of the world's population.

If the portrayals of the opening ceremony often revealed an eagerness to distinguish the 'modern' Canal from 'oriental' or orientalised Egypt, in the travel literature of the following decades, the Canal was not so clearly separable from images associated with Egypt. The trip from Europe to Asia, and more specifically to India, evoked adventures reaching back to Columbus and Vasco da Gama. Often, however, both the Canal, symbol of progress, and the 'encounter with the Orient' were disappointing to eastward travellers.

For those who undertook the journey more than once, the Suez Canal passage quickly became a routine associated with certain standard behaviours. The Canal represented the place where people and crews changed clothing to prepare for the Red Sea's heat: in the language of British

---

[58] Ibid., p. 20.   [59] Ibid., p. 21.   [60] Malabari, *The Indian Eye on English Life*, p. 18.

colonials, the tweed of the *homi-cide* gave way to the light linen of the *Suez-cide* and the hot broth served at 11 o'clock was replaced by ice and lemons.[61] To relieve the boredom of the Canal passage, travellers often organised fancy dress parties with accessories purchased at Port Said's Simon Arzt department store, mentioned above.[62]

Eventually the steamer would of course reach either the Mediterranean or the Red Sea. Only very few assessed the Canal as positively as the missionary Pyjanmohana Chaudhuri, who travelled to Britain in 1881. In contrast to the usual complaints about the Canal's monotony, Chaudhuri revealed himself to be highly impressed by the 'sight of small but beautiful telegraph-stations surrounded by romantic gardens on the sandy coast ... which separates Africa from Arabia'; as a Christian missionary, he was extremely interested in the biblical heritage of the land he was viewing. Strikingly, he noted not only the heat of the Red Sea – as many European travellers did – but also the 'severe cold' of the Mediterranean, which he found difficult to endure.[63] The Mediterranean marked the arrival in a new climate zone and in a new world, as Lala Baijnath briefly noted, referring to the roughness of the passage between Port Said and Crete: 'Leaving Port Said, you leave Asia behind; you are in European waters when you enter the Mediterranean.'[64]

Eastward travellers now complemented the depiction of the disorder-liness of Port Said, despite its straight streets, and the tediousness of the Canal passage with mention of the heat in the Red Sea.[65] With its rough landscape and the rising temperatures, the Red Sea area – besides marking the arrival in a new world and a distancing from Europe – signalled, perhaps, that nature had not quite been overcome by technology.[66] The steamer's European passengers and crew changed into white suits, trop-ical helmets and the like, and sociabilities were reconfigured. By now, acquaintance with other Europeans on board would have become easier and 'sports during the day & dances at night' commenced relieving the stiffness and monotony of European etiquette.[67] Travellers started to lose

[61] MacMillan, *Women of the Raj*, pp. 21, 23; Deussen, *Erinnerungen an Indien*, p. 12; for advice on appropriate clothing, see Murray, *A Handbook for Travellers in India and Ceylon* (7th revised edn.), p. xvi.

[62] For the traditional fancy dress party, see, for instance, OIOC, Mss Eur/B2355: Memoirs of Colonel Ross vol. 5, 1921–24, p. 93.

[63] Choudry, *British Experiences*, pp. i–ii.   [64] Baijnath, *England and India*, p. 4.

[65] See, for instance, OIOC, Mss Eur/C739, Part of letter from John Wilberforce Cassels on his way to India, November or December 1879.

[66] For a contrast between the 'unique and grand' scenery of the Red Sea and the dullness of the Suez Canal landscape, see Dall, *From Calcutta to London by the Suez Canal*, p. 3.

[67] OIOC, Mss Eur/B2351: Memoirs of Colonel Ross vol. 1, 1869–1901, p. 84; see also Women's Library, London, Philippa Strachey: Ralph Strachey to Philippa Strachey, S. S. Sutlej, 19 October 1892.

their inhibitions and sleep on deck wearing pyjamas and covering themselves only with a sheet, as some descriptions noted in detail, and a general
apathy took hold.[68] At the same time, hierarchies between European and
non-European passengers remained very tangible. The Bengali Hindu
reformer, P. C. Mozoomdar, travelling to Britain in 1884, was given a very
bad cabin and was avoided by everyone, 'like a ghost let loose from
another world'. He was left to listen to conversations of the colonial
officials returning home, which all too often seemed to him to be absurd
distortions of the realities in his country.[69]

The changed atmosphere in the Red Sea is reflected in the account of
John Russell Young, a travelling companion of Ulysses S. Grant (the former
American president had embarked on a two-year trip around the world after
the end of his second term), describing at length how both the ladies and the
men changed dress once past the Canal and particularly pointing out the
Indian-style helmets they bought in Suez.[70] In order to 'kill time', the men
wagered on not shaving until reaching home with anyone touching a razor
having to pay the others a penalty. Young also described an intense fatigue
that seemed to take over in the Red Sea: he tried to read some of the large
amount of literature he had brought with him (including guidebooks but
also encyclopaedias, almanacs and old newspapers) and follow the study
plan he had laid out for himself between the different ports of call, yet he
confessed that all his 'useful books' had stayed in the cabin.[71]

The passage from east to west also came to mark a personal transition for
many travellers. Once past Suez, only a few passengers actually managed to
work on board, with the companions of another politician, Paul Bert, who
was on his way to take up the position of general resident of the French
Republic in Annam and Tonkin in 1886, definitely represented an exception, with him and his entourage working during the entire passage.[72]
However, in line with the transformative aspect of the *rite de passage*, some
colonial travellers found the passage especially conducive to reflecting upon
their lives: the British officer Sir Francis Edward Younghusband used the
passage between Port Said and Bombay to write about his 'purpose in life',
deciding to reform himself and to quit the Indian administration.[73]

---

[68] OIOC, Mss Eur/C739: Part of letter from John Wilberforce Cassels on his way to India,
November or December 1879; see also Deussen, *Erinnerungen an Indien*, pp. 12–13;
Treves, *The Other Side of the Lantern*, p. 25; Steel, 'Women, Men and the Southern
Octopus'.
[69] Mozoomdar, *Sketches of a Tour Round the World*, pp. 1–7, at p. 7.
[70] Young, *Around the World with General Grant*, p. 592.   [71] Ibid., p. 594.
[72] Chailley, *Paul Bert au Tonkin*, p. 14.
[73] OIOC, Mss Eur/F197/278 Younghusband Collection: On board ship between Port Said
and Bombay, and at Sialkot: Notes on 'My Religion' and 'My Purpose in Life'. December
1908–March 1909.

A plethora of travelogues illustrate the Canal as a moment of personal reflection and of transition. What is more, voyagers in both directions also voiced a view of the Canal, not as a meeting point standing for global connections, but rather as an east–west border where differences between the worlds were in fact highlighted and not overcome. As the above-cited voices make clear, the concept of the Suez Canal as a global in-between space had two principal facets: first, the harbour town of Port Said especially brought differences between its variegated and transient population to the fore; secondly, the passage through the Canal and through the Red Sea served, as suggested, as a personal *rite de passage* between Europe and Asia and vice versa, often coupled with experiences of deceleration markedly contrasted with (and perhaps only created by) the expectations of acceleration that came with global travel.

Imperial space

The spatial imaginations connected with the passage through the Canal cannot be detached from the imperial realities manifest in the last third of the nineteenth century. Over the first 20 years of the Canal's operation, the universal vision of the unification of the globe repeated again and again at the opening ceremonies and thereafter was frequently overlaid by an imperial conception of global space. As a hub for the dispersion of colonial personnel, the Suez Canal moved to the centre of imperial interests. Shared travel experiences, such as the sojourn in Port Said, also resulted in the perception of a more closely integrated imperial space.[74] What is more, following the Canal's opening, it emerged as a place of imperial competition and overlapping political responsibilities. In the next decades Britain consolidated its position at the top of inter-imperial hierarchies, the Canal becoming, despite de Lesseps' statue in Port Said, a de facto British *lieu de mémoire*.[75] The theme of global unification was reconciled with the idea of the Canal as an in-between space between Orient and Occident by envisioning it as a colonial marker rather than as an external boundary. Especially from the British perspective, the Canal thus became an internal threshold between different parts of a single imperial space. Yet the Canal as imperial space also became a place of imperial competition, as the following section will show.

---

[74] For the traffic between metropole and colony, see Rudyard Kipling's poem 'The Exiles' Line' (*Rudyard Kipling's Verse*, pp. 187–9).

[75] Sengupta (ed.), *Memory, History, and Colonialism.*

Threshold between metropole and colony

In travel guides geared towards colonial travellers, such as Edmund Hull's *The European in India; or, Anglo-Indian's Vade-Mecum*, published in 1874, the Red Sea was not only described in the manner of Ulysses Grant's companion, as a zone too hot to do anything useful, it was also directly defined as a threshold between Britain and its colonial dominions, a perilous transitional space that had to be overcome in order to return to safe waters. In line with the pathologisation of other, often tropical, regions of the world, the Red Sea became a stretch particularly dangerous for European travellers, where:

many a poor debilitated Anglo-Indian has found a last resting-place beneath its waters, ere he could reach the mother country in whose native air he had hoped to regain health and strength. Others, again, have sunk after having survived the actual duration of this part of the journey, in consequence of the increased debility it has brought about. Even hale men have been known to die in the berths, from apoplexy, caused by Red Sea heat.[76]

The Red Sea as a transitional and possibly deadly zone before regaining Europe did not only figure in Hull's *Vade-Mecum*, but, most famously, in E. M. Forster's novel *A Passage to India*. While for Forster's heroine Adela Quested, the passage through the Canal is a cathartic experience where the 'clean sands, heaped on each side of the canal, seemed to wipe off everything that was difficult and equivocal', Mrs Moore dies before reaching the Suez Canal. The narrator summarises: 'Somewhere about Suez there is always a social change: the arrangements of Asia weaken and those of Europe begin to be felt, and during the transition Mrs. Moore was shaken off.'[77]

The Red Sea signified just such a 'last danger' before regaining Europe for French authors as well – for example in the account of the journalist Paul Bonnetain, writing for the newspaper *Le Figaro*, who evoked the image of a 'rosary of cadavers' from Singapore via Ceylon and the Indian Ocean to the Red Sea, with the deaths multiplying the nearer one came to France, as if the joy of regaining their homeland was too much for those weakened from the Indochinese climate.[78] Other descriptions of the sea passage were more scientifically inclined, arguing that it was not the heat (although it apparently could reach 50° C in the shade) but rather the composition of the air that made people suffocate, thus causing the death

[76] Hull, *The European in India*, p. 32.   [77] Forster, *A Passage to India*, pp. 265, 256.
[78] Bonnetain, *Au Tonkin*, p. 8.

of so many of the sick returnees of Indochina just before reaching their native soil.[79]

Fear of the Red Sea could, of course, be inflated, something Edmund Hull knew well stating that the heat of the Red Sea was greater in anticipation, fostered by travel descriptions and narratives of the kind quoted above, and should be met with a 'cheerful spirit'.[80] George Nathaniel Curzon, future viceroy of India and a prototypical British Empire figure, underlined this attitude and illustrated to what extent travel descriptions propagated specific images of the passage before one had even undertaken it. During his first trip through the Canal and the Red Sea, on the occasion of his journey around the world in 1887, he observed that he had constantly read so many frightening descriptions of the Red Sea stressing the heat and all of its consequences, that he was quite worried when first entering 'these fatal waters'.[81] Yet he went on to note his astonishment, when the temperature was actually quite cool with only a few co-passengers around him being seasick. While for many routinely travelling on behalf of the British Empire, the Canal and the Red Sea represented an internal threshold between different parts of the Empire, for Curzon, it seemed to be just another station in a journey through quasi-British waters.

Highway of Empire

Travellers of different nationalities noted that past Suez, British domination was visible in every port town they visited. During his passage through the Red Sea, the French journalist Bourde perceived this British supremacy with some bitterness, noting that past Egypt, his country ceased to exist: 'From Suez to San Francisco, with the exception of Indochina, we will find everywhere but the English race.'[82] Australian women embarked for London perceived their journey as an encounter with various sites that bound the British Empire together.[83] And Murray's *Handbook for Travellers in India and Ceylon* of 1892 noted that for an Englishman a trip to India was no longer a big deal and did not require any special preparation as it only represented the passage 'from one portion of the British Empire to another'.[84] Some British travellers were somewhat disappointed by the familiarity that had now become associated with

---

[79] Bousquet, *Le Japon de nos jours et les échelles de l'Extrême Orient*, vol. 2, p. 449.
[80] Hull, *The European in India*, p. 34.
[81] OIOC, Mss Eur/F111/104 Curzon Collection: Diary Journey around the World 1887–88, vol. 3, p. 178.
[82] Bourde, *De Paris au Tonkin*, p. 23. For German perspectives of the passage, see Pesek, 'Von Europa nach Afrika'.
[83] Woollacott, '"All This is the Empire, I Told Myself"'.
[84] Murray, *A Handbook for Travellers in India and Ceylon*, p. xv.

the journey, only a few decades after the Canal had opened. The young Colonial Office official, E. J. Harding, for example, stressed the 'extraordinary "Britishness" of this particular route' opting for 'the Imperial Piccadilly' as a suitable nickname, as at any port the British would feel at home and what is more were able to buy all they could wish for, such as 'Kodak films, Whisky, Picture Postcards and other British delights'.[85] Yet besides the goods on offer, the Britishness of the Canal could also take a more substantial form.

Many debates reverberated around the question of the British domination of the Suez Canal. Between 1871 and 1895, 70 to 80 per cent of the Canal's tonnage travelled under the British flag.[86] Of course the British dominance did not go uncontested. Still, in those years the metaphor of the 'highway of empire' emerged as the Canal's predominant description, replacing the more universal images of the key, hyphen, or silver gate between east and west, mentioned earlier.[87] There were other, similarly expressive images hinting at the role of the Canal in imperial geography. An edition of the medical journal *The Lancet* of 17 December 1892, chose the simile of the wasp's waist between England as the head and thorax and India as the abdomen.[88] Otto von Bismarck is reported to have called the Canal the backbone of the British Empire.[89] When Nasser announced that he was nationalising the Suez Canal Company, Anthony Eden chose yet another bodily metaphor, calling the Canal Britain's 'windpipe'.[90] Bodily metaphors such as the lifeline, the backbone and the waist defined the Canal as an inherent part of the British imperial organism, not as a boundary between two worlds, thus transforming it into an 'emotionally charged symbol, summing up an empire and its ethos'.[91]

If these expressions marked the Canal powerfully as part of British (although not *exclusively* British) imperial infrastructure and body politic, it remained an important juncture between life in the metropole and life in the colony. Those moving to and coming from the colonies met here and fathers who retired from service in India passed their sons on their way to take up their colonial stations.[92] Those returning from the 'East' symbolically threw their topis into the Mediterranean upon leaving the Canal, signifying their departure from the colonial realm with

---

[85] Quoted in Pearson, *The Indian Ocean*, p. 232.
[86] Farnie, *East and West of Suez*, p. 751.
[87] See Farnie, *East and West of Suez*, part III; Simmons, *Passionate Pilgrims*, p. 177.
[88] *The Lancet*, 17 December 1892, quoted in Watts, 'From Rapid Change to Stasis', 337–8, at 337f.
[89] Simmons, *Passionate Pilgrims*, p. 178.
[90] Verbeek, *Decision-making in Great Britain during the Suez Crisis*, p. 84.
[91] Simmons, *Passionate Pilgrims*, p. 191.   [92] Farnie, *East and West of Suez*, p. 390.

its clear hierarchies.[93] The encounter with returning ships, according to Bourde often resembling warships on the morning after a battle and peopled by those defeated by the hot climate, fevers and dysentery, furthermore produced premonitions on the part of those entering the colonial realm 'east of Suez' for the first time.[94] In such encounters the difference between those voyaging as a matter of routine, and those leaving Europe for the first time, became particularly evident.[95]

In the context of an ever more integrated imperial space, the complex meanings of home and away moved into the foreground. In *Wanderings and Wooings East of Suez*, a popular novel by Ethel Boverton Redwood, presenting the adventures of a young girl 'in the East', an outward-bound steamer passes by a homeward-bound steamer waiting in one of the Canal's stations. The author captures the ambivalence of the scene and the tension between 'home' and 'away' that the Canal passage could represent:

Many relapsed into a profound melancholy at the sight of the cheering crowd that thronged the decks of the Nord-Deutscher Lloyd. A little bride's eyes filled with tears as she clung to her husband's arm. A French newly-married couple on their way to New Caledonia for five years, openly wiped their tears from their cheeks. Suddenly a voice from the deck of the homeward-bound vessel rang out with startling distinctness in the clear air: 'Any one going to Colombo?' A fair-haired boy shouted back, 'Yes, I am.' 'Then give my love to the sweetest place on God's earth', the voice replied, 'the place where I'd choose to live and die!' 'Ah, but you're going home!' cried the fair-haired boy who had left his people for the first time.[96]

The scene – taking place on a German steamer and mentioning not only British but also French colonial travellers – highlights the fundamentally 'trans-imperial' nature of this imperial relay station. Yet the imperial geography that is presented in the dialogue between the person on the homebound vessel and the boy proceeding to Colombo clearly carries a British stamp, shedding light on the ambivalent relationship between 'home' and 'away' in the colonial context – with the Canal as an equally ambivalent yet clearly imperially marked intermediary space.

Media in motion

The situation captured by Redwood underlines the very limited perspective of many passengers, framed by the view from the steamer that carried them on familiar ground through alien lands. These limitations were often

---

[93] MacMillan, *Women of the Raj*, p. 234.   [94] Bourde, *De Paris au Tonkin*, p. 19.
[95] See General de Beylié depicting his eighteenth voyage: *Journal de voyage en Orient et en Extrême Orient*, p. 5.
[96] Redwood, *Wanderings and Wooings East of Suez*, pp. 30–1.

reinforced by previous exposure to standard descriptions of the journey they were now undertaking. The various descriptions of the passage between the Mediterranean and the Indian Ocean reveal a repetition of similar images and metaphors, different media producing both a set of preconceived expectations (which could well be misleading, as Curzon's comment on the Red Sea exemplifies) and of uniform reactions, thus putting 'space on the map'. E. M. Forster expressed this phenomenon with reference to the visual arts, stating that 'the East has been so painted that nothing was new. It was like sailing through the Royal Academy'.[97]

In the travelogues, Port Said and the Suez Canal appeared as a space carrying simultaneously the universalising impetus of the Saint-Simonians and the feature of a cosmopolitan, heterogeneous in-between space representing for many the personal passage between metropole and colony. However, it was not only the passengers in motion who were linking this clearly defined space with the four corners of the world: besides serving the circulation of passengers and goods, the Canal also carried different media transporting its increasingly preset image to many places in Europe and elsewhere. Four such media are highlighted in the following: literature, guidebooks, photographs and postcards.

Books: guides and fiction

Guidebooks, such as Edmund Hull's *Vade-Mecum*, mentioned above, played an important part in standardising travel experiences and shaping the travellers' expectations before leaving.[98] They influenced the itineraries and actions of thousands of travellers. Then, as now, possessing the same guidebook often meant following the same routes and staying in the same hotels. Egypt had been a standard tourist destination since the early nineteenth century; between 1837 and 1842 such a large amount of books on Egypt were published that, for the artist W. H. Bartlett, writing in 1845, adding one more risked appearing 'like a piece of presumption'.[99] Correspondingly, Murray's guidebook assured its readers in 1891 that 'year by year travelling in Egypt becomes more easy, and elaborate preparations are less necessary'.[100]

---

[97] Quoted in Pearson, *Indian Ocean*, p. 239. See also Urry, *The Tourist Gaze*.
[98] More generally on guidebooks, see Parsons, *Worth the Detour*; Palmowski, 'Travels with Baedeker'; Mackenzie, 'Empires of Travel'.
[99] Quoted in Gregory, 'Scripting Egypt', p. 114.
[100] Murray, 'Preface to the Eighth Edition', *A Handbook for Travellers in Lower and Upper Egypt* (8th revised edn.), p. 3. There were also specific guidebooks on the Canal, such as Bernard and Tissot, *Itinéraires pour l'isthme de Suez et les grandes villes d'Egypte*.

The commercialisation of Egypt as a tourist destination reached a peak with the arrival on the scene of Thomas Cook's organised tourist excursions. Launched in 1869, his packaged trips paralleled the opening of the Canal and were an instant and significant contribution to the standardisation of the travel experience.[101] Thomas Cook's guidebook for India, Burma and Ceylon explained that on arrival in Port Said a uniformed Thomas Cook employee would board the steamer and at the charge of 6 pence per person would lead them to the shore.[102] In the Thomas Cook office, just next to Port Said's landing station, passengers could write letters, send telegrams, or read. Existing with similar features all around the globe, the Thomas Cook office was a global locality of a special kind, meaning that a European passenger could be certain to find a familiar location while away.

The standard guidebooks – above all Murray, Baedeker, Guide Bleu and Hachette – contained all kinds of practical information, such as the time (Port Said was two hours and nine minutes before Greenwich), how to dress and which hotels to choose. They also provided a city map pointing to all the institutions that could be important for western travellers. Of course they also contained sightseeing information. Emphasising the antique sights, both Baedeker and Murray's guidebooks still suggested a tour of the isthmus. However, they were not impressed with the cities and tried to circumvent them as far as possible. Still, Baedeker's Port Said map (Figure 3) indicates the guidebooks' function to standardise travel experiences by providing a list of hotels and other institutions catering for tourists.

Yet, passengers not only brought guidebooks on their journey but also novels and other light reading, such as Redwood's *Wanderings and Wooings East of Suez* quoted above. Often, passengers indulged in travel narratives recounting the journey that they were about to undertake. Joseph Conrad commented snidely on the fashion for travel narratives at full bloom in the 1880s and 1890s and their 'parrot-like remarks'.[103]

Arguably the most influential author depicting the Canal passage was Rudyard Kipling – himself of Anglo-Indian origins. Although many descriptions of Port Said and the Canal's function as an east-west boundary preceded Kipling's writing on this theme in the 1890s, Kipling was the most widely read author and uniquely eloquent in his portrait of Port Said as an ambivalent meeting point.[104] In line with the statements mentioned above, in his early novel, *The Light That Failed* (1891), one could read that '[t]here is iniquity in many parts of the world and vice in

---

[101] See Hunter, 'Tourism and Empire'; Brendon, *Thomas Cook*; Withey, *Grand Tours and Cook's Tours*.

[102] Thomas Cook & Son, *India, Burma and Ceylon*, p. 30.

[103] Conrad, 'Preface', p. xiii.   [104] Cf. Farnie, *East and West of Suez*, pp. 386–91.

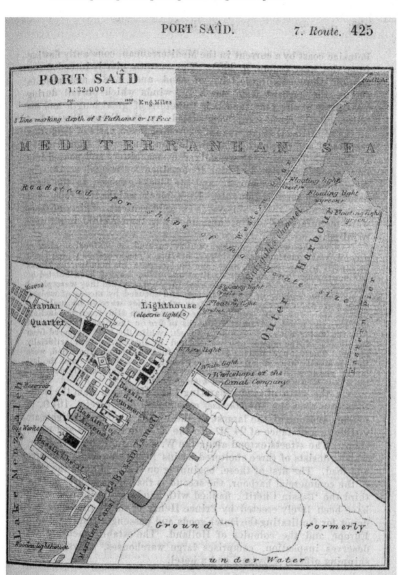

Figure 3 Map of Port Said: Karl Baedeker, *Egypt: Handbook for Travellers* (Leipzig: Karl Baedeker; London: Dulau and Co., 1878), p. 425.

all, but the concentrated essence of all the iniquities and all the vices in all the continents finds itself at Port Said'.[105] Kipling took up the same theme in the story 'Pambé Serang', claiming in both texts that at Port Said one could meet everyone one had ever known as everyone passed through this town sooner or later.[106] In the quote at the beginning of this chapter, he identified the Suez Canal Company's garden in Port Said as the 'dreadful and exact division between East and West'.[107] The theme of Suez as the boundary between two worlds was perhaps most famously voiced in the poem 'Mandalay':

> Ship me somewheres east of Suez, where the best is like the worst,
> Where there aren't no Ten Commandments an' a man can raise a
> thirst.[108]

Kipling thus repeatedly referred to an interconnected imperial space structured by internal thresholds; movement through the Canal served as an initiation into imperial life with its distinct set of rules, hence as a *rite de passage* in a literal sense.[109]

In the decades following the 1890s, Kipling's 'east of Suez' became a stock phrase. Many travel accounts referred directly to Kipling. US Consul General to Egypt, Frederic Courtland Penfield, entitled his own travel descriptions *Wanderings East of Suez*, placing a line by Kipling on his book's title page, and added to the abundance of Canal-analogies by perceiving the Canal not only as a connection or a 'universal artery of travel' but also as a boundary, or rather as 'the world's turnstile'.[110] Other authors, such as S. Parnell Kerr, while less directly 'Kiplingesque', still articulated the same basic themes of the meeting-point between east and west and the gateway to the 'enchanted realms of the East' as well as referring to its depravity and cosmopolitanism.[111]

Yet other authors did not detect any traces of the Orient and its promises, as with Frederick Treves who had the sensation of not having left Great Britain at all. Some parts of Port Said reminded him of the middle-class neighbourhood of any Lancashire town, others, such as the Arab quarter, of 'some sort of "native street" in a London

---

[105] Kipling, *The Light That Failed*, p. 44–5.
[106] See ibid.; Kipling 'The Limitations of Pambé Serang', p. 347.
[107] Kipling, 'A Return to the East', p. 244.
[108] Kipling, 'Mandalay', *Rudyard Kipling's Verse*, pp. 476–8.
[109] See Farnie, *East and West of Suez*, p. 390.
[110] Courtland Penfield, *Wanderings East of Suez in Ceylon, India, China and Japan*, title page, pp. 3, 13. Rachel Humphreys also paid explicit tribute to Kipling citing 'Mandalay' in her first chapter entitled 'Through the Eastern Gateway': Humphreys, *Travels East of Suez*, p. 7.
[111] Kerr, *From Charing Cross to Delhi*, p. 22.

exhibition'.[112] Pointing to yet another kind of global locality, Treves' observation illustrates the wide-reaching echo of world exhibitions in the creation of preconceptions as well as putting his finger on the artificiality of Port Said that had struck many before him.[113]

Novels like Redwood's *Wanderings and Wooings East of Suez* were written to ease the tediousness of the voyage and to entertain those who stayed at home with dreams of distant places.[114] Such light literature certainly had its share in the propagation of the pertinent images. In Redwood's novel, the tribute to Kipling once again was not only apparent in the title but also on the cover page and at the beginning of the first chapter. Both the travel guides that travellers carried with them and the mushrooming genre of travel writing, which many would read as preparation for the voyage or as entertainment during the ship's passage, were thus put into motion and circulated between Europe and the places they described – as objects travelling with their readers but also in terms of the remarkably repetitive ideas and imagery they contained, called by Derek Gregory the 'citationary structure' of Orientalism.[115]

Pictures: photographs and postcards

Ethel Boverton Redwood's heroine Carol's arrival at Port Said reiterates much of what has been developed in this chapter:

The first sight of the mysterious East! Will the traveller ever forget the thrill with which he sees before him, for the first time, the stretch of sandy desert, the camels against the sky-line, the white mosques gleaming under the fierce rays of the sun? The ship was approaching Port Said. Carol leant eagerly over the rail, and strained her eyes for a glimpse of the town. When at last it came into view, she felt a pang of disappointment – almost of disillusionment. Along the quay stretched a line of low, dingy buildings, grey-roofed, and plastered with English advertisements. Dirty coal-barges rocked the harbour; the dust from them rose up and darkened the sky. She raised her kodak apathetically and took a snapshot.[116]

By the time Redwood was writing, many real passengers would have replicated Carol's snapshot of Port Said from the sea. While the texts surveyed in this chapter were crucial in shaping travellers' expectations, visual material became ever more widely disseminated as well. Between the opening of the Canal and the First World War, photographs acquired

[112] Treves, *The Other Side of the Lantern*, pp. 12–14.
[113] See Mitchell, *Colonizing Egypt*, pp. 1–33 on the impetus and effects of such exhibitions. See also Geppert, *Fleeting Cities*.
[114] See Stieg, 'Indian Romances'.   [115] Gregory, 'Scripting Egypt', p. 119.
[116] Redwood, *Wanderings and Wooings East of Suez*, p. 21.

a more and more important role; they revolutionised the diffusion of standard images, and correspondingly of expectations nurtured before embarkation. During the Canal's construction, Europeans were already being exposed to etchings and lithographs of the site published in newspapers.[117] However, photographs became increasingly prevalent, changing ideas of authenticity and distance. Early portrait photography had largely been based in Europe, but as soon as equipment and techniques permitted, photographers travelled abroad in search of new impressions. Egypt became a favourite destination for photographers, such as Francis Frith, who took countless pictures of the monuments along the Nile from Cairo to Abu Simbel.[118]

In the first decades after 1869, the passengers themselves did not take their own photographs. Reliance on studios meant that certain views and perspectives were reproduced again and again. The studios particularly active in photographing the Suez Canal and Port Said were those of Hippolyte Arnoux and the Greek Zangaki brothers. If the work of the two Zangaki brothers (working between the 1870s and the turn of the century) went beyond the Canal itself, Hippolyte Arnoux made the Canal his central site.[119] French by origin, Arnoux was a Port Said resident, his studio being situated on the main square, the *Place des Consuls*. He documented the last years of the construction work with the help of a floating studio and was particularly interested in the mechanical dredgers and other machinery while also developing stereographs of Egyptian types and costumes.[120] Arnoux thus combined two interests prevalent in many written Canal descriptions: the modern engineering achievement and the search of the 'exotic' and 'oriental'.

The photographs by Arnoux and others record Port Said's gradual development during the 1870s. In a single album, that travellers would fill with images they had bought at their various stops, one can find the same shot taken during different construction stages, as different views from the same perspective were available simultaneously, reflecting the construction of the city from scratch.[121] Overall, the motifs were extremely repetitive, showing the Canal's Port Said entrance, the main

---

[117] See, for instance, FAL, Harvard Semitic Museum, HSM.83:005:005/AKP 128.13: *La construction du canal de Suez 1859–1869: Vues retrospectives*.

[118] See Nickel, *Francis Frith in Egypt and Palestine*; Bull and Lorimer, *Up the Nile*; Perez, *Focus East*; Golia, *Photography and Egypt*.

[119] See Perez, *Focus East*, p. 233.

[120] Arnoux, *Photographe de l'union des mers*; ANMT 1995060/1491–1499: numerous photographs by Hippolyte Arnoux; Perez, *Focus East*, p. 127.

[121] See for instance FAL, Harvard Semitic Museum Photographic Archives General, Egypt Box VI Album.

Figure 4 'Port Said: Rue du Commerce', photograph probably by Hippolyte Arnoux, details by the author.

building of the Suez Canal Company with its distinctive domes (by far the most impressive building in Port Said), specific steamers in the Canal and so forth. The different stations of the Canal passage, the Khedive's palace and de Lesseps' chalet in Ismailia were other favourite themes. Other photographs highlighted the multilingual street signs and rendered the variegated population on the streets as seen in Figure 4.

Photographs such as the one shown above formed an important documentary and promotional medium for the company. Famous visitors received albums; these varied in elaborateness according to the importance of the visitor. But the company was not alone in producing such albums: photographers accompanying royal voyages extensively covered all stations, framing their documentation in representative ways. An elaborate and oversized leather-bound volume recording the Prince of Wales' journey in 1875–76, and containing several pictures of the Canal, provides a good example.[122] Either at the beginning or at the end of the journey – depending on the travellers' route – Port Said and the Canal often figured in private albums immortalising the Grand Tour to Egypt. With the albums being shown to friends and relatives once back at home, they formed a powerful vehicle for putting in motion certain standard images of the Canal and Port Said and of other places on the tourists' favourite routes.

As the two decades surveyed here drew to a close, travellers could shoot their own photographs and did not anymore have to rely on pictures of professional photographers. From the 1890s onward, ordinary passengers increasingly brought their personal cameras. Meanwhile the Eastman Kodak Company had developed methods of making photographic dry plates rather than plates coated with fresh chemicals, as had been the rule before 1880. In 1888 George Eastman introduced the Kodak camera, the first simple, affordable and portable camera.[123] The birth of the snapshot was announced in the 1892 catalogue with the slogan: 'You press the button, we do the rest.'[124] However, even though more and more travellers were taking their own photographs, they often chose motifs very similar to those already in circulation – with the notable difference that they could now position themselves in the centre of the image. These photographs circulated in albums shown to large or small audiences and in letters sent home.

---

[122] FAL, Photographs collected during the Royal Trip to India by E. G. H. HMS Serapis 1875-6.
[123] In 1892, the prices still ranged from $6 to $25; see *Kodak Catalogue*.   [124] Ibid., p. 65.

Yet there were also pictures that were even more explicitly meant for circulation. In a roughly parallel development to the ensuing rapid increase in self-made photographs, picture postcards had begun to come into fashion, starting in the 1870s. Postcards led to a stronger association of certain geographical places with specific iconic sites – in the Canal Region, with, for instance, de Lesseps' statue and the company head-quarters.[125] The early picture postcards were much more about the photograph than about the text – there was no space available for a personal note on the back, the greetings and even the stamps often being placed on the picture side. Not only the images but also the cards' short texts were therefore often highly standardised.

A good example is provided by Grand Duke Ernst Ludwig of Hesse, who sent three postcards to his daughter from Port Said and the Canal in 1902 (Figure 5). The English, French and German subtitles under the images show how the emerging tourist market was catering for different passengers. In Port Said, postcard vendors came on board selling booklets of postcards

Figure 5 Postcards of Grand Duke Ernst Ludwig of Hesse on his trip to India 1902–03.

[125] For – often eclectic – postcard collections, see, among others, OIOC, CCIMP, CAOM, FAL, AFL. See also Patterson, 'Postcards from the Raj'; Alloula, *The Colonial Harem*.

Figure 5 (*cont.*)

Figure 5 (*cont.*)

Figure 6 Isaac Behar, *Souvenir de Port-Said: 24 vues,* booklet of postcards.

like the one reproduced here (Figure 6). On the Canal postcards, Egyptians frequently featured in the foreground contrasting tradition and technology. The cards often also depicted 'oriental women', in clear reference to Port Said's ambivalent moral status.

The diffusion of standardised images of the Suez Canal provided those who might never pass through the Canal themselves with certain associations of 'Suez' and 'east of Suez'. The sending of postcards and letters also represented a new form of structuring space. While guidebooks and photographs purchased for albums travelled with their owners, postcards almost always took the opposite trajectory, returning to where the passenger had come from.

These trajectories became continuously cheaper and faster: in September 1888 the *Phare de Port-Saïd et du canal de Suez,* one of the town's main newspapers, reported under the title 'Le tour du monde' that a Londoner had sent a postcard via Brindisi and Suez to Hong Kong with the request that it be returned to London via San Francisco and New York. The card had taken 70 days to round the globe, 40 days less than ten years earlier, and the journey had only cost 35 centimes or three-and-a-half pence.[126] The

---

[126] ANMT 1995060/1524: 'Le tour du monde', *Le Phare de Port-Saïd et du canal de Suez* 22 September 1888.

practice of writing letters on board or postcards in ports of call was thus more than a way to shorten the time of the passage – in an age of globalisation it was an increasingly cheap way of bridging the growing distance between the places one had left and those one was hoping to reach.

By 1890 the possibility of staying in touch with home – in an era in which postal services had become less expensive and in which, in urgent cases, telegrams could connect travellers with home in almost no time at all – contributed to a changing perception of a denser or more closely interconnected global space. Ralph Strachey travelling in 1906 put the distinction in speed between the different media in a nutshell, writing from Port Said upon hearing the news of a case of illness in the family: 'if I get a favourable telegram at Suez I shall feel much easier as your letters are now five days old'.[127] The speed and affordability of staying in touch thus redefined what it meant to be away, travellers not only being able to mail messages home but also to hear from relatives during their journey. In this respect, Port Said and Suez were points of transhipment where letters could be both posted and collected, illustrating the interlocking of different technologies at such nodal points. In fact they were the last contact points before the Indian Ocean crossing when one would truly be without news. Hence on a journey to Asia, the municipal building officer of Berlin, James Hobrecht, complained that he had not received any letters in Suez – as no ship was able to travel faster than his own, he would not hear from his relatives for four or five weeks.[128] This feature of Port Said as a last stop before exiting Europe will be reflected in later chapters, when it came to reaching political decision-makers or tracking down suspects or criminals before they were dispersed into the Indian Ocean world.

After the first two decades of the Canal's operation, global space was perceived as having shrunk considerably because of the circulation of postcards, the possession of the same or similar guidebooks, and the existence of specific global localities, such as Thomas Cook offices. Yet James Hobrecht's objection – just as in the frequent remarks regarding the slowness of the Canal passage – point to the resentment that arose when the global connections belied their promises and to the perception of acceleration as a double-edged sword, with the Suez Canal itself figuring at the same time as global accelerator and retardant. The many different metaphors connected to the Canal and to Port Said – the key, the hyphen,

---

[127] Women's Library, Philippa Strachey: Ralph Strachey to Philippa Strachey, SS Marmora, Suez Canal, 17 October 1906.

[128] Hobrecht, '. . . Dschunken, Böte, Dampfer zogen hierhin, dorthin, das war nicht die kleine, – es war die weite, weite Welt, an deren Rand ich stand. . .', p. 35.

the caravanserai, to mention just a few – point to the difficulty in locating Port Said between Europe and Asia but also to the increasing and increasingly fast circulation of images and descriptions. Yet if this global imagination was more and more standardised, Port Said and the Canal could combine the three conceptions of the global developed above: a space symbolising the unification of the globe and the boundary between east and west, a location of personal transition and heterogeneous coexistence of the whole world in one place and a location of imperial hegemony and competition. If the idea of a global space connected by infrastructures, such as postal services and regular steam lines and the increasingly standardised behaviours in the social space of the steamship, had become firmly established by the 1890s, at least (but not only) for British travellers it carried tangible imperial features, even if they sometimes came in the guise of an explicitly universal rhetoric. This politicisation of the real or imaginary global landscape of an imperial relay station translated into concrete and conflict-laden questions of governance and international standardisation that will be discussed in the next chapter.

2 Regimes of passage and troops in the Canal Zone

> The isthmus cut becomes a straight, a battle-field. A single Bosphorus has hitherto sufficed for the troubles of the world; you have created a second much more important one. In case of naval war it would be of supreme interest, the point for the occupation of which the whole world would struggle to be first. You have marked the field of the great battles of the future.[1]

When Ferdinand de Lesseps was received at the *Académie Française* on 23 April 1885, Ernest Renan is reported to have expressed the sentiments quoted above. And he was right, at least to a certain extent: during the First World War, the Canal Zone would indeed be turned into a battle-field staffed by colonial troops drawn from around the world. In 1926, a memorial for the Indian soldiers who died during the Sinai campaigns was unveiled at Port Tawfiq on the eastern side of the Canal.[2] The 'highway of empire' was thus turned more powerfully and explicitly into a British *lieu de mémoire*.

Yet during the First World War the Suez Canal was not only a place of fighting, but also a place of passage. Large numbers of troops passed through it to their arenas of fighting or spent some time in hospitals and garrisons in the Canal Zone waiting to be transferred to the front or home.[3] During the period under scrutiny in this book, it was already a military place: not so much in terms of fighting, as Renan had implied, but it was certainly militarised, with British army garrisons having been stationed there since 1882, after the British occupation of Egypt. What is more, it became a place of passage for many European troops, en route to their colonial stations, who shared with their civilian counterparts the fashioning of the Canal as a point of transition between home and away. It thus became a location where empires observed each other and where imperial interests were concentrated.

---

[1] (Ernest) Renan, quoted in Cameron, *Egypt in the Nineteenth Century*, p. 236.
[2] OIOC, IOR, L/PO/4/7: Unveiling of Indian War Memorial at Port Tewfik, Egypt.
[3] Huber, 'Connecting Colonial Seas', esp. 148–51.

72

Coming back to Renan once more: even if, in the perhaps slightly over-stated word of a journalist, the competition concerning the 'most important strategic position of the globe'[4] did not always take military forms, control over the Canal was one of the salient political questions of the time. The connection figuring so prominently on the mental maps of travellers also required concrete governance. In line with the ambivalent perceptions of globality traced in Chapter 1, the question whether the Canal was an imperial Piccadilly or a universal road also had implications for its political configuration. Hence the imagination of the Canal as universal or imperial was to a certain extent mirrored in questions of its rulemaking.

The Canal Zone was characterised by an extremely complex – and brand-new – power structure. The global and the local as well as several levels in between were tightly enmeshed in its regime. On the one hand this locality, run by a private company, concentrated imperial interests and functioned as a lynchpin in larger visions of empire. On the other there were recurrent attempts to find an international solution to the problem of securing the waterway's neutrality and thus enabling perpetual mobility at this location. Like other international zones such as Tangier in the inter-war period, the Suez Canal Region formed an extraterritorial locus of experimental rule-making where individuals fell under different legislations and where, at a time of nation states and the consolidation of colonial boundaries, sover-eignty and geography were remarkably incongruent. Charles Maier and others have argued that territoriality became a key feature in the 'modern era'. But in the same period new transportation networks also created zones of extraterritoriality characterised by overlapping and competing sovereign-ties, such as the one analysed here.[5] The Suez Canal was thus turned into an arena in which the 'rules of globalisation' were drafted and redrafted.

The debates regarding the regulation of troops in the Canal Zone at times of peace and war culminated in the 1888 convention on the Suez Canal. These debates point to the different scales and levels of interna-tional law and its limits. We will thus move in this chapter from the perception of space to its political organisation. Focusing on the regula-tions concerning the movement of people, and particularly on one form of mobility, the movement of troops, the discussion will present the actors involved in keeping the wheels of imperial infrastructure turning, while concurrently shedding light on the precariousness of these arrangements.[6]

---

[4] See ANMT, 10995060/1031: *Echo de finances*, 4 August 1872.
[5] Maier, 'Consigning the Twentieth Century to History'.
[6] On the history and ethnography of infrastructure see van Laak, 'Infra-Strukturgeschichte'; Leigh Star, 'The Ethnography of Infrastructure'; Huber, 'Highway of the British Empire?'; Guldi, *Roads to Power*; Engels and Obertreis, 'Infrastrukturen der Moderne'.

Taking the re-routing of the British-Indian troop service through the Suez Canal in the early 1870s as our starting point we will follow developments up to the Second French Madagascar expedition in the mid 1890s, which has been chosen as a typical imperial endeavour conducted through the Canal. As well as using the Canal as a transportation artery between the colonies and Europe, troops also played a part in the Canal's governance, for example, in the 1882 British military intervention in Egypt. Largely undertaken by the British Indian Army, this intervention underlined the urgency of the question of neutrality at times of peace and war. In its aftermath the Canal also became a hub for the circulation of strategic information regarding troop transports to the four corners of the world. Troop transports furthermore add another facet to the tension of acceleration and deceleration: While it was in the interests of the empires to accelerate their own troop transports, others were interested in controlling and monitoring them, relying in turn on rapid information transfers, extending the question of slowness and speed – as seen at the end of the last chapter – to the area of global information management.

In the following, the complicated institutionalisation of globalisation will first be assessed in an analysis of the changes in the de jure structure of the Canal between its opening and the 1888 convention of Constantinople, illustrating the entanglement of imperial interests, private companies and international negotiations. Here developments between the first decade of the Canal traffic, marked by experimentation, the impact of the 1882 British occupation of Egypt and the ensuing stabilisation can be clearly shown. Then the *de facto* governance of the Canal will be assessed with emphasis on the role of consulates in the regulation of troop transports through the Canal. Three aspects will be foregrounded: organising the consulates, relaying information between outposts and metropoles and the practical transfer of troops. The last section of the chapter concentrates on specific imperial campaigns of the 1890s (singling out the conflicts in Madagascar, South Africa and China), which highlight the challenges and limits of global rulemaking and its relation to the logics and logistics of empire.

De jure: regulating the Canal passage

From its opening the Canal system was accompanied by discussions about the ownership and status of the Canal, discussions that became more pressing, when more and more troops were conveyed via the Canal. This situation of inter-imperial debate was exacerbated by the British military occupation of Egypt, adding stationary troops to those simply passing through the Canal, which moved the question of the 'ownership' of the Canal right to the centre of political and legal debates. In 1888 an international conference presented the 'neutrality', a complicated legal concept, as we shall see, of the Canal as a solution. In the following section these three phases will be reviewed – the early phase of experimentation and debate, the British occupation and the attempt to come to grips with the British presence in Egypt and its implications for the Canal Zone during the 1880s culminating in 1888.

The early years: experimentation and standardisation

In a conversation with his private secretary, Johann Peter Eckermann, in February 1827, Johann Wolfgang von Goethe demonstrated his awareness of the importance of infrastructural projects. When speaking about Alexander von Humboldt's travels, he mentioned the need to construct large waterways that would connect the Mexican Gulf and the Pacific, unite the Danube and the Rhine and cut through the Isthmus of Suez. He concluded that he would like 'to see the English in possession of a Suez canal'.[7]

During the building period, however, there was nothing British about the Canal; Napoleon III even fashioned the project as France's 'great national work'.[8] In any event, these conceptualisations along national lines remained an exception. Instead, commentators stressed the enterprise's universal and international character; the idea of a 'neutral passage', which would be taken up in the 1888 convention, had already been introduced in the agreement of 1854 when the undersigned parties agreed that the Canal should always be under the supervision of the Canal Company and open 'as a neutral passage for all merchant ships, traversing from one sea to the other, without any distinction, exclusion or preference of persons or nationalities'.[9]

Still, implicit national claims of ownership recurred. A month after the Canal's opening, the newspaper *Le Gaulois* stated that an international congress meeting in Egypt on that occasion had voiced the desire for the Canal's neutrality and the 'international colonisation' of the isthmus. However, just a few lines further on, the author abandoned this internationalism and exclaimed: 'La revolution française chez Mahomet!'[10] For its part, the Suez Canal Company also looked back to the French Revolution (or at least to its most famous formula), proclaiming that the

---

[7] Eckermann, *Gespräche mit Goethe in den letzten Jahren seines Lebens*, pp. 580–1.
[8] Napoleon III, *Discours de son Altesse Impériale le Prince Napoléon*, p. 7.
[9] Boutros-Ghali and Chlala, *Le canal de Suez*, p. 6.
[10] ANMT, 1995060/1026: *Le gaulois*, 19 December 1869.

Canal project had introduced and instituted the principles of liberty and equality as the very conditions of its existence.[11] In more careful phrasing G. L'Hôpital highlighted the different levels of responsibility, claiming that the Canal Company was of French origin yet working on foreign soil 'for the commerce of all countries and for the general progress of civilisation'.[12] Whether the Canal project's aim was to be internationality, neutrality, or else the propagation of the revolutionary principles of equality and liberty, and of civilisation in its more general sense, was thus a matter of much debate.

Despite the French initiation of the engineering project on the one hand and the Canal's international status (or 'international colonisation') on the other, referring to it as the 'highway of the British Empire' soon became commonplace. Now that the construction had been completed – albeit initially against British will – and now that the British had begun to use the Canal to staff their empire, they needed guarantees that it would always remain open. William Foster Vesey Fitzgerald laid stress on the Canal's civilising effects, arguing that as a result Egypt had become 'possessed of a modern interest', his government now having a right to demand from Egypt that the neutrality of the Canal be observed.[13] Despite the voicing of such confident opinions, the idea of British dominance over the Canal did not go uncontested, as we shall see. Hence contrary to Goethe's statement, the question of who was in control of the Canal emerged as being closely tied to the shifting international relations of the time.

In the early years of the Canal traffic, its rules were in flux and its use by troops and other passengers was far from clearly regulated. In fact, it was not even obvious who would use the Canal at all. In a report to the British Parliament of 1870, Captain Richards and Colonel Clarke of the British Navy indicated that the Suez Canal would provide the budding steam navigation with a new impetus. They predicted that the British troop service between Britain and India, ships of war on their way to China and the great steam lines carrying mail, passengers and merchandise would particularly benefit.[14] Despite the British boycott of the Canal during its early years, by the time the French occupied Madagascar in 1895, numerous imperial missions had been carried out through the

---

[11] Compagnie universelle du canal maritime de Suez, *Rapport à la commission d'enquête sur la perception du droit de passage des navires traversant le canal*, p. 5.

[12] Quai d'Orsay, Paris, Mémoires et documents, Egypte 15 sheet 22: G. L'Hôpital, Extrait de l'exposé des motifs du projet de loi tendant à autoriser la Compagnie du Canal maritime de Suez à faire une émission de titres remboursables avec lots par la voie du sort, 1868.

[13] Vesey Fitzgerald, *Egypt, India, and the Colonies*, pp. 2–3.

[14] Richards and Clarke, *Report on the Maritime Canal*; see also 'La vapeur, la voile, et le canal de Suez', *Le canal de Suez: Journal maritime et commercial*, 14 September 1871; 'Les derniers soupirs de la voile militaire', ibid., 7 December 1871.

Canal. By then, practices of imperial intervention and colonial rule had changed – not exclusively, but certainly in part – due to new technologies and infrastructures, such as those tied to the Suez Canal. 'High imperialism' depended crucially on the reliable interchange of goods, information and people, and particularly of troops.

In January 1869, the Khedive and the shipping company P&O had renewed their agreement for the overland transportation of troops. Two-and-a-half years later, in June 1871, the Secretary of State for India in council approved the use of the Canal route for British troop transports to India; the 'Indian Overland Troop Service' was transformed into the 'Indian Troop Service'.[15] Much more significant than the need to remove a word in the service's letterhead was, of course, the need for new arrangements regarding the supply of provisions and the Canal route's supervision. In 1871–72 the arrangements were adopted as an 'experimental measure' although without a change in the general rules – the only modification being that an officer stationed in Egypt would accompany every troop-transporting ship during the Canal passage in case some troops had to be landed.[16]

After the initial period of British boycott and scepticism, the Canal route thus quickly became more established. The British Ministry of Transport listed costs of provisioning and coaling, and the numbers of passengers and their status; it also investigated how to make troop transportation via the Canal cheaper, pointing to the attempt to render global transportation more cost-efficient. The Admiralty purchased land in Port Said for offices, and different agencies began registering and overseeing the Canal's operation.[17] Arrangements were developed to take care of soldiers who had to be left behind in Port Said on grounds of illness and to rapidly pass on information regarding any unforeseen occurrences.[18] New troop transporters started their regular return journeys between

---

[15] SHD, BB4/1492, *Sous-dossier chemin de fer égyptien*: Agreement made and ratified on the day and date underwritten between the undersigned acting respectively on behalf of his Highness Ismaïl Pacha, Kedeve [*sic*] of Egypt on the one part and the Peninsular and Oriental Steam Navigation Company of London on the other, 2 January 1869; TNA, MT 23/26: Passage of Indian Troop Ships through the Suez Canal, Secretary of State for India in Council to the Director of Transport Services, 9 June 1871; TNA, MT 23/27 for amended letterhead.

[16] TNA, MT 23/27: India Office (Major General Military Secretary) to the Director of Transport Services, 23 June 1871.

[17] OIOC, IOR L/MIL/7/5636: Military Collection 125, Land at Port Said: Purchase of the land by the Admiralty and the India Office in 1871.

[18] OIOC, IOR L/MIL/5/536: Indian Troop Service: numerical returns of units and individuals (giving names of officers and their families) embarking at Bombay or Karachi for Portsmouth, and at Simons Town, Durban, Malta, Port Said, Queenstown, Plymouth or Portsmouth for Bombay, 1879–1880; TNA, MT 23/41: Numbers of Troops, Wives and

Southampton and Bombay and other destinations.[19] In this manner, the Suez Canal developed into a halfway station for British troops: a place to receive their disembarkation orders and change their uniforms.[20] It provides us with an example of the professionalisation of the global movement of troops and provisions, at the same time highlighting the problems and conflicts related to such movements.

The Canal witnessed growing British appropriation, both by the sheer numbers of those using it and by the institutionalisation of British influence – but did this mean it was British? There were of course unresolved issues. On a practical level, the calculation of the Canal's fees proved a matter of debate. Furthermore, the troops contributed an additional unruly element to the transient population of Port Said that was already quite difficult to control. Yet above all, the status of the Canal itself remained unclear in the first few decades after its opening. What happened to it in times of war? And who carried the ultimate authority over it?

Rather than having the legal status of an international waterway or a strait, the Canal, although cutting through Egyptian territory, was owned and run by a private joint stock company. As an Egyptian enterprise, the *Compagnie universelle du canal de Suez* operated on the basis of the agreements issued first by the Egyptian Khedive and then ratified by the Ottoman sultan. However, as Egypt had no legislation applicable to joint stock companies, it was organised along French lines. But since not enough shares had been taken up, and in order to secure the building project, the Egyptian government agreed to buy the remaining shares; taking account of additional financial aid, the Egyptians would end up raising 1.3 billion francs in obligations and 600 million in floating debts between 1862 and 1873.[21]

Still the Suez Canal Company would not be financially profitable until 1875. In fact, in the first years of operation its financial situation looked rather gloomy as not enough ships were using the new route and many investments needed to smooth the transit were still pending.[22] Nevertheless the Canal quickly became a major strategic asset. But at the same time, not least of all due to the Canal project, bankruptcy was

Children Embarked at Bombay for England during Trooping Season, 1873–4; Memorandum as to Telegraphing Movements of Indian Troop Ships during Season 1873–4: orders to send telegrams after arrival in each port and particularly 'with any *important* or exceptional occurrence in passage of the Canal'; TNA, MT 23/25: Hospital Stoppages against a Soldier whilst a Patient in Victoria Hospital Suez.

[19]   See, for example, TNA, MT 23/25 and OIOC, IOR L/MIL/5/536 for provisioning.

[20]   OIOC, IOR L/MIL/17/4/563: Instructions for Guidance of Officers Arriving with British Troops at Bombay and Karachi 1905 and 1909.

[21]   Bonin, *Suez*, p. 13; Bonin, *History of the Suez Canal Company*; Piquet, *La Compagnie du canal de Suez*.

[22]   See Hansen and Tourk, 'The Profitability of the Suez Canal'; Bonin, *Suez*, pp. 29–32.

looming large in Egypt – a situation that forced the Khedive Isma'il to sell his shares in the Suez Canal Company.

In November 1875, Prime Minister Disraeli acted swiftly, using the help of Lionel de Rothschild and foregoing prior consent from parliament to buy Egypt's shares: a financial coup that has since attained legendary status.[23] As a result, the British government ended up with 44 per cent of the company's shares and could supply 10 of the 24 positions on its board of directors. Disraeli's acquisition of the shares provoked international concern. Looking back, Charles Lesage assessed the action as a move that both was financially profitable and led inevitably to the British occupation of Egypt.[24] Either way, Egypt's financial relief obtained through the sale of the shares was not more than momentary; in 1876, the Khedive was forced to accept both a *Caisse de la Dette* taking charge of the deficit and French and British supervision over the state budget, referred to as 'dual control'.[25]

It goes without saying that such measures far from settled the question of the Canal's neutrality. In fact, the increasing French and British involvement in Egypt's internal affairs meant that it became even more crucial to come to an arrangement guaranteeing free transit through the Canal. Both the unpredictable situation in Egypt and wars involving the Ottoman Empire could impede a transit process that had become so crucial to the British Empire. The Russo-Turkish War of 1877–78 brought to the fore the question of the Canal's neutrality, as the Ottoman troops did not hesitate to capture Russian mercantile vessels and men-of-war on their way through the Canal. They interpreted the neutrality prescribed in the 1856 *firmān* as 'granting equal right of passage to all merchantmen subject always to the right of the Sovereign to capture Enemies Vessels as in other Ports of the Empire'.[26] This practice obviously created concern on the part of the British government regarding its transportation links with India, reflected not only in official documents but also in private letters like that of Eliza Tabor, who was stationed in Allahabad with her husband and wrote to her mother: 'I hope this war will not interfere with the comfortable coming and going of people through the Suez Canal.'[27]

[23] Rothschild, *'You have it, Madam'*; Blake, *Disraeli*, pp. 582–7.
[24] Lesage, *L'invasion anglaise en Égypte*, p. 231.
[25] See Owen, *The Middle East in the World Economy*, pp. 122–52.
[26] TNA, FO 78/2632: Mr Vivian to Earl of Derby, 22 May 1877.
[27] TNA, FO 541/24: Captain Malcolm to Sir A. Milne, 19 September 1881 (expressing his fear that Russia could block the Canal route); Women's Library, Eliza Tabor: Eliza Tabor to her mother, 26 May 1877.

Following the Russo-Turkish War and the 1878 Congress of Berlin, the British government abandoned its non-interventionist strategy regarding the Ottoman Empire. In 1879, 10 years after hosting the Suez Canal's extravagant opening celebrations, Khedive Isma'il was deposed by an initiative of the British and French and replaced by his son Tawfiq. Isma'il's strategy of making his country 'European' had failed; his expensive investments in infrastructure had increased Egypt's debts and thus its dependency on western powers.

The British experiment with the appropriation of the Canal, on a political and financial level, was always accompanied by components of international negotiation. From the outset the smooth functioning of the Canal's traffic demanded international standardisation – again often with a British tinge. With the Suez Canal Company levying a fee of 10 francs per passenger and per ton of freight, the number of passengers had to be registered and the ship measurements categorised according to a common measure, which proved a rather complicated undertaking – a company report revealed that there were as many different tonnages as there were different maritime nations.[28] In line with its loyalties, the company opted for the use of French tonnage. In 1871, an international commission decided, however, that it would be best to take the British ton as a general unit; this was implemented in 1872 – a tribute to the call of 'Britannia rules the waves'. From now on, every ship had to carry papers with the gross tonnage noted according to British measurements; in the absence of such papers, agents of the Suez Canal Company would measure the ships themselves. While the use of a measurement unit might seem a trivial technical detail, the adoption of the British ton not only reflected the political hierarchies of the moment but also the Canal's shipping proportions, with British steamers representing the most important share.[29] The choice of measuring units thus reflected the global geography of power.[30] It is a good example of the drafting of the rules of globalisation at the lowest level, highlighting the role of empires in this process. Yet even if, here, the British Empire was successful, these rules cannot

---

[28] Compagnie universelle du canal maritime de Suez, *Rapport à la commission d'enquête sur la perception du droit de passage des navires traversant le canal*, p. 8.
[29] CCIMP, MR 4481, Navigation maritime: Canaux maritimes et tunnels sous-marins (1840–1998): Compagnie universelle du canal maritime de Suez président de la chambre de commerce de Marseille, 9 September 1871. See also Quai d'Orsay, Mémoires et documents, Egypte 17 sheets 8–9: Board of Trade, Memorandum Showing the Present State of Arrangement with Foreign Countries on the Admeasurement of Tonnage of Merchant Ships 18 August 1871, GehStA PK, I. HA Rep. 120 A IX Nr. 23 Bd. 12–16: Vermessung der Seeschiffe, 1873–1886.
[30] See, for instance, Geyer, 'One Language for the World'.

simply be equated with the rules of a single, in some domains hegemonic, empire, as the following example shows.

The intricacies of these processes of rulemaking found reflection not only in the use and rejection of certain units, but also, for instance, in the taxation of space on the steamship. The regulations and fees were codified in the Company's 'Règlement de navigation dans le canal maritime de Suez', which was distributed widely.[31] The fee of 10 francs per ton with a surcharge of 3 (later 2.50) francs was confirmed in a convention and approved by the Sublime Porte in 1877. There were also strict rules regarding what could be deducted from the fee, laid out in a decree of 1873 with crew lodgings and kitchens, for example, being exempt from taxation. The calculation of fees – particularly regarding warships transporting troops– was the subject of recurrent discussions.[32] Despite the British government's acquisition of the Canal shares, British ships still had to pay the Suez Canal Company's dues. Warships and troop transports were exempt from the surcharge; they paid only the standard fee of 10 francs per passenger and ton and 5 francs for every 3-to-12-year-old child. Along with stipulating dues, the regulations established the standard procedures that ships passing through the Canal had to follow. At the same time, the international Canal agreements also had to be made congruent with national and imperial regulations, such as the different merchant shipping acts in force in the British Empire – procedures that point to the intricacies of global standardisation. Furthermore, the regulations and transit dues turned the Canal into a control point where captains were obliged to provide the Canal Company with passenger lists or at least allow control of the number of people on board and the amount of cargo they transported.

The debates surrounding such regulations illustrate the range of actors involved in activities related to the Suez Canal. In this manner, they illustrate that in this context, rules of globalisation did not mean anything uniform or uniformly enforceable but rather a difficult process of negotiations and power relations. Tensions persisted between interests shared in the international framework and those of the individual imperial

---

[31] Compagnie universelle du canal maritime de Suez, *Exploitation, Transit des navires, Règlement de navigation etc.* Many archives contain the regulations, demonstrating how widely they were circulated and how often they were revised; see, for example, SHD, BB4/1448; Quai d'Orsay, Correspondence politique et commerciale nouvelle série 1897–1918, Egypte 40; Bundesarchiv, R 901/75677 Band 1 Schiffahrt Nr. 129.

[32] Such debates took place for instance in the British Parliament, see ANMT, 2000036/0360 Actes parlementaires relatifs au canal de Suez (Parliamentary Papers relating to the Suez Canal): registre en anglais (années 1876–1882); for the calculation of tonnage see also Öthalom, *Der Suezkanal*, pp. 54–6.

authorities. They also persisted between those subscribing to the concept of the Canal as a financially profitable enterprise, and others focused on its status as a perennially open waterway. Just like Renan had predicted, the Suez Canal was thus turned into a conflict zone where inter-imperial tensions could come to the fore, not only regarding minute procedural details such as the use of measurement units or the calculation of fees but also regarding larger issues such as the integration of Egypt into one empire or the other.

The British occupation of 1882: an Egyptian and a global event

Thus far the Canal towns, and particularly Port Said, have been depicted as being connected more closely to the origins and destinations of the passing steamers than to the Egyptian interior. Indeed Port Said represented a 'link in the maritime chain joining Great Britain with its Asian and Pacific possessions' while at the same time integration into the Egyptian railway system, for example, was slow to develop.[33] However, the uprising of 1882 and its prologue integrated the Canal into the broader narrative of Egyptian history. In the Canal towns, as in other Egyptian cities, attacks against Europeans reflected a backlash against international dominance.[34] The following British occupation shifted the power balance and made the question of the internationality, neutrality or Britishness of the Canal a most pressing question.

The backdrop to the unrests leading to occupation was complex, with economic competition, social restructuring, fear of political dominance and religious sentiment all playing their part. The discontent gained its central manifestation in the movement led by the army officer, and later Minister of War, Ahmad 'Urabi.[35] In 1881, this broader movement found local expression in the Egyptian garrisons of Suez in a case of self-administered justice undertaken in 'Urabi's name, with several soldiers holding the governor captive for a day after the murder of one of their own. Even though it turned out later that not a European but a Bedouin had killed the soldier, the consul reported that 100 men came to the Government House to riot 'with drawn swords'. He raised attention to the problems that occurred if Egyptian soldiers rose up against their own officers and were thus 'allowed to take the law into their own hands in this way'.[36]

---

[33] Perkins, *Port Sudan*, p. 12; Modelski, *Port Said Revisited*, p. 57.
[34] For an earlier riot in Port Said, see Cole, *Colonialism and Revolution in the Middle East*, pp. 201–2; see also more generally Cole, 'Of Crowds and Empires'.
[35] See Schölch, *Ägypten den Ägyptern!*.
[36] TNA, FO 78/3334, sheets 119 ff.: Report Consul West, Suez, 18 December 1881.

The ensuing riots in Alexandria and the rebellion of 'Urabi in June 1882 provided a pretext for Britain to intervene militarily, the argument being that the lives of Europeans in Egypt were no longer secure and that the khedival government had to be stabilised.[37] In line with the 'dual control' already in place, Britain and France initially opted for joint intervention, although in the end France did not participate in the bombardment of Alexandria on 11 July 1882 granting Britain free hand in Egypt. As in the case of the British purchase of the Canal Company shares, French commentators would look back on this withdrawal in anything but enthusiastic terms.[38]

The invasion that followed the attack on Alexandria was executed through the Suez Canal against the opposition of Ferdinand de Lesseps who dreaded British intervention in the Canal Zone. On 2 August a proclamation was issued to the Egyptian inhabitants of Suez affirming British occupation in the name of the Khedive and asking them to behave in an orderly manner, because, in the case of 'any molestation of British Subjects or of any other foreign European subject', repressive measures would be taken. The proclamation furthermore asserted that the 'rumours spread by the Rebel Arabi Pasha' according to which the British were in Egypt in order to murder the Muslim population were not true at all and that they had come 'to restore order and peace to your country and wish to be your friends'.[39]

The fighting culminated in the Battle of Tel el-Kebir, close to the Suez Canal, on 13 September 1882. Henry Villiers-Stuart, a British member of parliament sent by the government to report on conditions in Egypt, visited the battlefield three months later, finding human body parts as well as dead horses and camels scattered around, fostering his vivid re-imagination of the battle.[40] Following the defeat of 'Urabi's troops, the British army occupied all of Egypt. Despite the British government first defining the occupation as provisional, its victory at Tel el-Kebir resulted in the presence of British soldiers in Egypt until 1954.

With the main locations of fighting being in close proximity to the Canal, the uprisings of the late 1870s and early 1880s and the British

---

[37] For a report on the Alexandria riots, see TNA, FO 78/3462: Telegram Calvert to Earl of Granville, 11 June 1882.

[38] See '1882: Souvenirs d'un Port-Saïdien', *Revue internationale d'Egypte* II/1, p. 7; Aubin, *Les Anglais aux Indes et en Egypte*, p. x. Other powers also worried about the fate of their nationals in the wake of a conflict between Egypt and the western powers: see, for example, Schmidt, *Through the Legation Window*, p. 147, n. 9.

[39] TNA, FO 78/3462: Proclamation by Admiral Sir William Nathan Wrighte Hewett to the Inhabitants of Suez being Egyptian Subjects, 2 August 1882.

[40] Villiers-Stuart, *Egypt after the War*, pp. 85–7.

invasion tied the Canal's history back into the national history of Egypt; at the same time, the events also had more immediate 'mobile' reverberations of both a local and a global nature. European residents of Egypt who feared assaults tried to leave the country, often via Port Said. With postal communications between Alexandria and Port Said being interrupted, on 9 July 1882 the British Consul at Port Said received orders from Cairo to embark all British subjects on the following day if at all possible. Following this injunction, and in order to escape impending violence, many Europeans (particularly of British, French, Italian, Greek, German and Austrian origin) retreated to the ships lying in the harbour of Port Said.[41] The 'troubles' also created financial difficulties: the consulate had given free passages to about 170 British subjects without keeping proper books and lists. As the number was greater than agreed by the government, the consulate could only reclaim its expenses after much justificatory effort.[42]

On a global scale, as news of the British occupation spread, empires other than the British started to fear the obstruction of *their* highway of empire illustrating that the occupation was not only a local but also a global event. On 28 and 29 June 1882, when the situation was about to escalate, two telegrams from the French Consul at Singapore to the governor of Cochinchina reported the consul's fear of the Canal's obstruction and of 'almost universal panic' in Egypt, with 20,000 British troops ready to embark for the country and the Egyptian troops occupying the Canal and about to dynamite it.[43] Later in July the French Vice Consul in Aden indicated to the governor of Cochinchina that he had sent a telegram to the governor of Saigon confirming free passage through the Canal after the attack on two British steamers by Egyptian soldiers.[44]

At the same time, complementing this dread at the interruption of Canal services, another worry loomed large in the mind of those dependent on global shipping connections: the possibility of epidemic disease outbreaks. The French argued that there were cases of cholera in Calcutta

---

[41] TNA, FO 78/3462: Consulate Port Said to Earl Granville, 17 July 1882.

[42] TNA, FO 78/3586, sheets 57–8: Baker to Earl Granville Foreign Office, Port Said, 30 November 1884. See also TNA, FO 78/3467: Draft Foreign Office to Consul Wallis, 9 August 1882 – instruction to 'furnish H. L. with a detailed list of the 105 British subjects who … you provided with free passages to Malta by the SS "Finchley"'. The French officials faced similar demands; see Quai d'Orsay, Affaires diverses politiques 1815–1896, Tome IV, Egypte 7, Sous-dossier rapatriement des nationaux français en Egypte; Sous-dossier réfugiés français venant d'Egypte.

[43] ANOM, Indochine GGI 14277: Consul de France à Singapour au gouverneur Cochinchine, Informations sur la guerre anglo-égyptienne – attaque du canal de Suez par les troupes égyptiennes 5 July 1882.

[44] ANOM, Indochine GGI 14212: Consul de France à Aden au gouverneur Cochinchine. Informations sur l'obstruction du canal de Suez 1882: Aden, 19 July 1882.

and Bombay justifying full-length observation and the quarantine of troop ships coming from India. The British denied this in order to enable rapid troop movements, hindering the observation of their Indian Army rushing to Egypt within a mere 24 hours.[45] This second global worry thus resulted, ironically, not from the Canal's closure but from its uncontrolled openness. It also showed how the openness of the Canal, particularly in times of a regional conflict, could become a matter of inter-imperial negotiating.

In August, the offices of the Canal Company were briefly occupied, the Canal traffic thus being suspended for a short period. Journalist Étienne Fabre targeted this interruption of traffic and communication, highlighting once again the importance of the Canal Zone as a crossroads of different global technologies, but also as an easily corruptible weak point in world-wide information transfers. He stated that the first act of the British author-ities upon arrival in Port Said had been to order the suppression of all transit of commercial ships. In Suez they had apparently sawn off a telegraph pole and had thus put a stop on all communications between Europe and Asia. Fabre went on to describe the anger of the British inhabitants of Mauritius who blamed the Egyptian Muslims for the disturbance of the telegraphic connection. He concluded that it was not 'Muslim fanatism' but 'British civilisation' that had interrupted the navigation between the two seas and cut the connection.[46] It would thus appear that the first concern of Britain's competitors was not so much the control of Egypt but the maintenance of the free flow of communication.

In another article, entitled 'The Suez Canal and Free Trade', Fabre described how the British free-trade policies, enforced for half a century, had always been ambiguous. However, the journalist indicated that after the Canal's opening, Britain could no longer have a monopoly with France, Italy and Spain also wishing to participate in this system of laissez-faire. He concluded that of the 'revolutions produced by the piercing of the Isthmus of Suez, this would not be the least curious'.[47] The suspension of the Canal traffic was thus for Britain's rivals a welcome occasion to internationally criticise the double standards of laissez-faire only where it suited British interests. These comments show how the acceleration of travelling and information transfer associated

---

[45] Quai d'Orsay, Affaires diverses politiques 1815–1896, Tome IV, Egypte 7, Sous-dossier précautions sanitaires à l'occasion de l'envoi des troupes anglaises de l'Inde en Egypte.

[46] ANMT, 1995060/1046: Étienne Fabre, 'Les Anglais jugés par eux-mêmes', Le télégraphe, 9 September 1882. For the 1882–83 interruption of the telegraph line, see Wenzlhuemer, *Connecting the Nineteenth-Century World*, p. 102.

[47] ANMT, 1995060/1046: Étienne Fabre, 'Le canal de Suez et le libre-échange', Le télégraphe, 23 November 1882.

with the Canal could be perceived as politically contingent and unevenly applicable. They also illustrate that the British occupation and the attempts of global rulemaking along imperial lines did not end the haggling over the status of the Canal. On the contrary, the question of the perennial openness of the Canal was now, at least for powers other than the British, more pressing than ever.

After 1882: imperial competition and international agreements

The British occupation of Egypt did not change the nominal affiliation of the country to the Ottoman Empire. Yet it did create a very complex political situation. Although its wider impact upon the history of colonisation, particularly upon the so-called 'Scramble for Africa', is still debated, the occupation certainly made an international agreement guaranteeing free passage through the Canal the order of the day. For most contemporaries it was clear that the answer had to be found at an international conference. These international conferences, which will be analysed in some detail in what follows, were in themselves global microcosms of a special kind, echoing many other internationalist meetings of the period. [48]

That the question of the Canal's status was a pressing one is illustrated by the fact that on 19 September 1882, only four days after the battle of Tel el-Kebir, a confidential meeting took place in the British War Office regarding the Canal's neutralisation. The report of the 'Committee appointed to consider certain Questions relating to the future Administration of Egypt' was printed in October 1882, assessing the best way of dealing with the Suez Canal question with specific attention to the interests of Great Britain in case of a war between the great powers. It concluded that the Canal formed part of Egyptian waters and therefore international law proscribed that no hostile action could be undertaken in the Canal unless the power undertaking it was at war with the Ottoman Empire. [49]

There were, however, differing views in Britain regarding the meaning of neutrality. Some observers held the opinion that now, even more so than after the purchase of the shares, Britain should not pay any Canal fees. The journalist Edward Dicey put it bluntly: 'It is England's manifest destiny to become mistress of the Canal as she has already become

---

[48] See, for instance, Geyer and Paulmann (eds.), *Mechanics of Internationalism*.

[49] OIOC Mss Eur/D604/10: Report of the Committee appointed to consider certain questions relating to the future administration of Egypt. Printed 20 October 1882.

mistress of Egypt.'[50] Thomas J. Lawrence, a professor of international law at Cambridge University and advocate of unhindered global traffic, connected the Canal explicitly to the wider world and stated that the British control over the seas had gradually decreased and that the *mare liberum* concept had replaced the idea of a *mare clausum* – with the exception of some narrow straits however, where 'the old exclusive ideas still lingered'. Lawrence was not in favour of neutrality, which in his interpretation meant that belligerent troops would be denied any passage through the Canal at all. Rather he argued that the Suez Canal should be treated like an extension of the sea and that the fees should be abolished altogether.[51] Other British commentators even called for the construction of a second, all-British canal.[52]

In order to come to grips with the situation, two international conferences were convened. The Suez Canal conferences of 1885 and 1888 shared elements with the numerous other internationalist endeavours taking place during the same period: endeavours couched in the rhetoric of universalism and cooperation, yet often serving as a stage for the competing powers to demonstrate their predominance. Furthermore they brought the nexus between imperial and internationalist ambitions into the open, culminating in tensions between the ideas of free movement and controls.

Between 30 March and 13 June 1885, a first conference to settle the affair of the Canal's status took place in Paris.[53] Among the participants was the French Prime Minister and Minister of Foreign Affairs, Jules Ferry, a fervent advocate of French colonialism, who was deposed over the continuing conflict with China and the expense caused by his imperial ambitions as the conference was in motion. Just before his deposition, he delivered a talk resounding with the universalism of the Canal's opening ceremonies of 1869. He placed the aims of the conference in a direct relationship with colonial projects and more specifically with the Berlin conference held some months earlier: 'You have been called to add one more stone to the new edifice that a peaceful and far-sighted Europe is striving to construct in order to take shelter from the violent and fruitless competitions of which the past is full, and to subject the universal and in some way irresistible movement of colonial expansion, which at this hour

---

[50] Dicey, 'Why not Purchase the Suez Canal?', p. 655.
[51] Lawrence, *Essays on Some Disputed Questions*, esp. pp. 44–5.
[52] See, for instance, Caird Library, P&O/17/1&3: The Second Suez Canal. Deputation from the Associated Chambers of Commerce to the Chancellor of the Exchequer, President of the Board of Trade, 13 July 1883.
[53] See Farnie, *East and West of Suez*, pp. 328–31.

carries away the activity of all nations, to precise and legal rules.'[54] According to Ferry, the Canal had a universal, European, humanitarian, peaceful, civilisational, colonial and international character, and in his view all of these adjectives carried fairly similar meanings.

After long debates, the conference ended without compromise as the British Foreign Secretary proposed a convention stipulating that the passage through the Canal should always be free and unhindered, yet the delegates of France, Russia, Germany and Austria-Hungary demanded the establishment of an international control commission, something that Britain, in turn, found unacceptable. The conference needs to be assessed in connection with the Berlin conference on Africa and the international sanitary conference in Rome where Britain equally maintained an isolated position and was able to disrupt the attempt to come to an international accord.

In 1888 there was another attempt to arrive at an agreement, this time at a conference in Constantinople with delegates from France, Germany, Austria-Hungary, Spain, Great Britain, Italy, the Netherlands, Russia and the Ottoman Empire. The result of this meeting was a convention according to which the Canal should always be open and freely navigable in times of both peace and war; in wartime, however, troop ships should only be allowed to take limited amounts of provisions into the Canal Zone and were permitted to neither embark nor disembark any troops or ammunition.[55] That said the agreement was decisively weakened by the fact that Britain only signed it with the caveat that the rules could be suspended should they limit the freedom of the British occupying powers in Egypt. This restriction remained in place until 1904 when, through the *Entente Cordiale*, France approved the British occupation of Egypt, receiving a free hand in Morocco in exchange. Even after conclusion of the *Entente Cordiale*, Britain nevertheless continued to sabotage the international control commission's annual meetings.[56]

After 1888, in the shadow of international disputes, Egypt would itself try to reappropriate the Canal. On different occasions petitions called on the Khedive to stand against foreign domination, particularly in 1909

---

[54] *Archives diplomatiques: Recueil mensuel international de diplomatie et d'histoire*, p. 122; for a fuller collection of the conference protocols, see also Quai d'Orsay, Mémoires et documents Egypte 16 1885: Protocoles de la souscommission pour réglementer le libre usage du canal de Suez.

[55] For the full text of the convention, see Boutros-Ghali and Chlala, *Le Canal de Suez*, pp. 16–19.

[56] See ibid., p. 19; Eschelbacher Lapidoth, *The Red Sea and the Gulf of Aden*, p. 158; Piquet, 'The Suez Company's Concession in Egypt', 118. See also CADN, Le Caire 285: Régime international et conventions politiques 1885–1940.

when the profits of the Canal were under discussion.[57] Although representing an enduring decision in the international arena, the 1888 solution did not remedy the problem of British dominance or clarify the status of the Canal. The ambiguity regarding the Canal status was underlined by the sheer number of legal dissertations written in the agreement's wake and by numerous conflicts when the agreement was compromised.[58] The 1888 agreement thus on the one hand strengthened the rhetoric of the internationality and neutrality of the Canal. On the other it showed the weakness of such international agreements. Whether they signified rules of globalisation, or whether global rulemaking was effectuated in a practical sense regarding, for instance, the carrying through of troop transports, will be assessed in the second part of this chapter.

De facto: administrating troop transports

The Suez Canal's de jure structure was intricate, yet its de facto governance was also ambiguous. For instance, the question of who was in charge of troops passing through the waterway resulted in a variety of answers: on board the ship traversing the Canal, the captain had supreme authority, while in the harbour towns the Egyptian governor of the Suez Canal District, the Suez Canal Company and the European consuls as well as (in the case of British troops) the commanding officer of the local garrison shared authority over those moving through. The following takes the debates regarding the neutrality of the Canal passage (which also hinged on questions of troop transports and the status of the Canal in times of war) to the practical level of how the troop transports were organised and supervised. In the following part, first the consulates of Port Said and Suez will be analysed as imperial relays. Then the consulates' crucial importance as information hubs sending intelligence to the political centres will be highlighted. Finally, one specific campaign, the French Madagascar campaign, will serve to come closer to the troops and their experience of the Canal passage, assessing whether and how it differed from those *rites de passage* of other colonial travellers whom we have encountered in the last chapter.

---

[57] See DWQ, '*Ābdīn* 243, 0069/004756 for petitions and telegrams. For protests against the renewal of the concessions see also CADN, Le Caire 284: Canal de Suez. Renouvellement de la concession du canal 1909–1937.

[58] See, for instance, Jacobs, *Die Schiffahrtsfreiheit im Suezkanal*; Dedreux, *Der Suezkanal im internationalen Rechte unter Berücksichtigung seiner Vorgeschichte*; Yeghen, *Le canal de Suez et la réglementation internationale des canaux interocéaniques*; Moussa, *Essay sur le canal de Suez*; Obieta, *The International Status of the Suez Canal*.

Organisations on the ground: the consulates of Port Said and Suez

The establishment and running of consulates represents a particularly good case study for global organisation and local problems of implementation. The following analysis of the French and British consulates of Port Said adds to the research on the Middle Eastern consulates more generally, interpreting them as important institutions in organising globalisation practically and on the ground.[59]

Although issues regarding tonnage and fees and the Canal passage itself gradually became standardised during the 1870s and 1880s, difficulties persisted involving the regulation of ships and the policing of the Canal towns.[60] On board the troop transporters various matters could hinder the smooth running of the intra-imperial connection, ranging from individual illness or death, fights and petty crimes on board to identifying specific travellers. Other problems could emerge while the troop ship was in the harbour such as soldiers having to stay behind in hospital, getting into fights in town, or losing all their money in one of Port Said's gambling dens.[61] Guidebooks catering for imperial travellers, in this case bound for Indochina, warned soldiers not to enter cafes or music halls at all, as they were always also places for gaming.[62] But trouble could loom even if the troops did not step on land in Port Said, with officers accompanying the troops being given specific instructions stipulating that at Port Said petty officers should be on duty on the troop decks to hinder the smuggling of liquor and other goods through the portholes.[63]

Despite the Canal's ambiguous status – on the one hand managed by a private company, on the other hand with international or neutral status, albeit without a treaty until 1888 – the Egyptian police were in charge of the area as fixed in a convention of 1866.[64] As soon as a foreign subject was involved however, the relevant consulate took over. All around the

---

[59] See Berchtold, *Recht und Gerechtigkeit in der Konsulargerichtsbarkeit*; Hanley, *Foreignness and Localness in Alexandria.*

[60] See, for example, ANMT, 1995060/1476: Compagnie universelle du canal maritime de Suez, Circulaire 'Inhumations clandestines dans les berges du canal', no date; ANMT, 1995060/1478 Police du canal en Egypte 1877–1930: letters concerning an alleged conspiracy to blow up the Canal in 1877.

[61] The French consular files contain references to many incidents involving troops: see, for example, CADN, Port Said 16 and Port Said 17 for various requests to identify soldiers or death notices; CADN, Port Said 47 for fights on board, arrests etc. Of course similar cases took place among the British troops, see, for instance, TNA, MT 23/44; MT 23/48.

[62] *Annuaire général de l'Indochine 1909*, p. 166.

[63] OIOC, L/MIL/17/4/563: *Instructions for Guidance of Officers Arriving with British Troops at Bombay and Karachi* (Bombay: British India Press, 1909), p. 9.

[64] ANMT, 1995060/1478: Convention du 22 février 1866, Article neuvième.

Ottoman Empire, the consuls had a specifically authoritative role. It was not only in Egypt that the capitulations, originating in the early modern period, exempted European residents from local taxation and placed them under their own consular jurisdiction alone.[65] In the second half of the nineteenth century, the influx of international residents into Egypt resulted in a call for a review of the inefficient system of 17 coexisting consular courts. Hence in 1869 the minister, Nubar Pasha, had appointed an international commission for the system's reform and in 1876 mixed courts were introduced to take care of all cases involving people with more than one nationality.[66] However, the consuls still maintained their function of mitigating conflict and presiding over many court cases. Travel guides, such as the 1885 Baedeker, thus duly recommended that travellers to the 'east' 'should take the earliest possible opportunity of entering into friendly relations with these most useful officials'.[67]

They were of even greater importance in a town like Port Said, with its particularly international population. In the 1870s, the responsibilities of those directing the newly founded consulates in the Canal Zone were still up for debate, even if Port Said quickly emerged as the most important consulate in the region. Charles Perceval, first vice consul and then consul at Port Said complained about understaffing and the 'important and multifarious' tasks involved in dealing with the shipping – an urgent matter as the Canal passage was not to be delayed. He consequently requested that the vice consul also be equipped with signatory powers in order to share the workload more equally. To add to this, he also had to entertain passengers recommended to him. In general the cost of living in Port Said, where even fresh water had to be purchased and imported from Ismailia, was relatively high, the consulate thus being obliged to ask for a more ample budget.[68] After the 1882 occupation of Egypt, the British consulates became more important as local actors of the occupying power, managing proceedings on the ground as well as providing London with crucial and time-sensitive information.

---

[65] See Martens, *Das Consularwesen und die Consularjurisdiction im Orient*; Piggot, *Exterritoriality*; Tarring, *British Consular Jurisdiction in the East*; Scott, *The Law Affecting Foreigners in Egypt*; Homsy, *Les capitulations*.

[66] See Brinton, *The Mixed Courts of Egypt*; also ANMT, 1995060/0941: *Les capitulations et la réforme judiciaire en Egypte* (Paris: Imprimerie Centrale des Chemins de Fer A. Chaix et Cie, 1867).

[67] Baedeker, *Egypt: Handbook for Travellers. Part First* (1885), p. 6.

[68] TNA, FO 78/2509: Consulate Port Said to Earl of Derby, 4 February 1876; TNA, FO 78/3011: Consul Wolff to Marquis of Salisbury, 30 August 1879; TNA, FO 78/2409: Foreign Office to Perceval, 4 January 1875 about inadequacy of consular residence in Port Said.

Perceval's approach to his situation was quite typical: the consuls frequently complained about living conditions in Port Said, often in order to justify leaves of absence or pay rises. Health problems were recurrent, the climate usually being blamed. We thus find Consul West going on leave to the Alps in 1884 suffering 'from General debility and great nervous exhaustion due to a prolonged residence in tropical climate'.[69] Equally frequent were problems of management and staffing. There were occasions of financial misappropriation and of employees who failed their examinations: Vice Consul Wolff, for instance, repeatedly failed the tests in arithmetic and Italian prescribed by the Foreign Office.[70] Organisational issues such as the appointments of consuls and staffing of the consulate, leaves of absence, yearly allowances and an appropriate building for the consulate thus formed a significant part of the consular correspondence together with reports of noteworthy incidents at Port Said and justifications of expenses.

Besides illustrating Port Said's complex extraterritorial and international situation, the consulate proceedings therefore demonstrate the practical problems that emerged from the effort to form a closely-knit network of communication between London and its outposts. The wider framework of this effort was a process through which the global system of consulates increasingly developed into long arms of empire responsible for conveying information to London or Paris and ushering their own troops as quickly as possible through their sphere of responsibility.

Even after the British consulate in Port Said had left its infancy, there were persistent managerial problems. These became the focus of attention when the British agent and Consul General, Evelyn Baring, from 1892 Lord Cromer, began to keep closer track of Egypt's consular services.[71] In the wake of several cases of bad administration and of misappropriation of funds, Baring and his staff repeatedly expressed their outrage at the 'disgraceful way in which the accounts were kept' and at the high expenses and inefficient running of Port Said's consulate.[72] In response, Consul Burrell called for both a prison for the consulate (something the French

---

[69] TNA, FO 78/3831, sheet 194: Medical certificate Suez, 25 July 1885; see also TNA, FO 78/4250: Consul Burrell to Salisbury, 1 September 1889.

[70] See TNA, FO 78/2509: Consulate Port Said to Foreign Office, 23 December 1876; TNA, FO 78/3334: correspondence about Vice Consul Wolff and his failure in the exams. For Wolff the dramatic situation of 1882 also had advantages: 'in view of the unfavourable opportunities for your studies afforded by the recent disturbed condition of Affairs at Port Said' he could postpone his arithmetic exam once again (TNA, FO 78/3586, sheet 80).

[71] See Owen, *Lord Cromer*, pp. 183–260.

[72] TNA, FO 78/4330: Report to Sir E. Baring, 6 January 1885; TNA, FO 78/3702, sheet 95: Report on Port Said Consulate, February 1884.

consulate possessed) and a greatly expanded staff. He furnished a list of 13 different positions, ranging from janissaries, bookkeepers and an honorary dragoman to a surgeon, an assistant jailer and a cook. In order to pay the new employees, he indicated that he clearly needed a much higher allowance, as the tasks at Port Said were 'far more pressing than at any other Consulate in the East'.[73] According to Burrell, this was even more the case after the Canal's opening for night traffic in 1887, the consul or his deputies now having to attend to business at any time of day or night in order to avoid traffic delays.[74]

Alongside many smaller complaints filed against the consulate by passers-by, more spectacular cases of mismanagement also occurred. While they represent very specific cases, they link Port Said to the wider world, both because several locations were involved – specifically London, Port Said, Cairo and Aden – and because they point to the problem of controlling a consular system that was spinning its web across the globe. When Consul Burrell fell ill in 1887, he appointed a certain Anthony Falanga, formerly chief clerk of the consulate, as pro-consul without prior Foreign Office authorisation.[75] Six years later, Falanga was found guilty of appropriating stamps and fees during night shifts, removing stamps from old files and re-using them while destroying the documents from which they were taken. On learning this, Foreign Secretary Rosebery advised that Falanga be tried in Egypt rather than in England where it would create much more of a scandal. Yet before any trial could commence, Falanga escaped from the Canal Zone, but was soon tracked down in Aden, where he died some days later of a stroke.[76]

These problems at the consulate highlight the precariousness of the rules and regulations as they were devised at international conferences and through different agencies of empire, not only when looking at the interlocking of these different agencies, but also when taking the local level of implementation into account, which was difficult to control and oversee. The enactment of such rules thus crucially depended on trustworthy

---

[73] TNA, FO 3702, sheets 96 ff.: Burrell to Sir Evelyn Baring, 31 January 1884.
[74] TNA, FO 78/4154: Burrell to Salisbury, Port Said, 17 January 1888; see also TNA, FO 78/4461: Consul Gould to Salisbury, Port Said, 7 March 1892.
[75] TNA, FO 78/4064: Consul Burrell to Marquis of Salisbury, Port Said, 30 June 1887.
[76] TNA, FO 78/4521: Extensive correspondence about Falanga's case; see sheet 71 for avoidance of prosecution in England; sheet 82: F.O. Draft Consul Gould, 2 May 1893; sheets 119 f.: Gould to Rosebery, 27 February 1893; sheet 159: Telegram 16 May 1893 concerning Falanga's arrest in Aden; sheet 182: Telegram 12 June 1893 reporting Falanga's death. Much of the blame for Falanga's flight fell back on Consul Gould who had shielded the suspect for some time out of compassion for his complicated familial situation.

local staff for instance for the collection of information about troops and armaments of other empires and for catering for the rapid transit of the troops of their own nationality or empire.

Information transfers: procuring and relaying intelligence

Despite internal problems that illustrate the difficulty of supervising the consulates from afar, the role of the consuls in Port Said was crucial. They were not only vital for the smooth working of imperial infrastructure – assisting the shipmasters with the necessary paperwork and, for instance, taking care of soldiers who could not travel on – they also handled and transmitted critical data. As a telegraphic hub and chokepoint, Port Said was thus a relay station for both infrastructure and imperial flows of information.[77] For one thing, there was information related to shipping and navigation – with the increasing need to set timetables it was all the more important to know about possible interruptions in advance. In Port Said, captains were supplied with updates concerning hazards in the Indian Ocean.[78] At the same time, the consuls served as mediators of political or personal information from London or Paris to specific persons in transit to their colonial stations. In 1884, Lord Granville, British Foreign Secretary, had to reach General Gordon, on his way to Khartoum to combat the Mahdi Uprising. As Gordon's steamer stopped in Port Said, this was Granville's last and only chance for contact.[79]

More frequently, Port Said officials collected information bound for London, Paris, or other European capitals. One recurrent theme was the implementation of the 1888 convention. Sometimes a perceived breach of the convention turned out to be a false alarm. In 1893, British marines were landed from a British man-of-war in Port Said. Before the event there had already been an exchange between French and British officials concerning whether this contravened Article 5 of the Suez Canal Convention with the conclusion that it did not as the landing took place in peacetime.[80] Such cases became more controversial in times of war. During the Russo-Japanese war (1904–05), to cite a later example, the

---

[77] For the role of telegraphy in diplomacy, see above, p. 10; see also Barak, *On Time.*
[78] In 1883, for example, they were notified about a volcanic eruption in the Sunda Straits that had left lighthouses destroyed (TNA, FO 78/3586, sheet 140: Telegram from Consul Rio to Consul Port Said, 1883, no date).
[79] TNA, FO 78/3702, sheet 67: F.O. Draft Telegram Consul Burrell, Port Said, 21 January 1884.
[80] Quai d'Orsay, Affaires diverses politiques 1815–1896, Tome IV, Egypte 20, Sous-dossier 4 débarquement des marins anglais à Port Said lors de l'inauguration du chemin de fer.

Russian Consul in Cairo expressed his fears to his French counterpart that the British in charge of Egypt would not secure the Canal's neutrality. The French Consul reported that his Russian colleague had indicated to him that so far he had always had a good rapport with the Egyptian Minister of Foreign Affairs and with Lord Cromer, but was worried about what could happen in the case of a deterioration of British-Russian relations.[81] The two men agreed that the lack of an international commission to survey the Canal's neutrality meant that the 1888 convention could not be enforced.

Yet the supervisory function of the consuls was not primarily related to the 1888 convention, but more generally to the gathering, processing and forwarding of reliable information about troop transports. As all the troop ships had to stop at this harbour in order to fill out the relevant paperwork for the Canal Company and to take coal, Port Said emerged as a central location for this process: 'one of the regular and most important daily duties of the Shipping Department of this Consulate is the careful preparation of the weekly return of the movement of all Foreign War Vessels at Port Said'.[82] This was a place where the origins, passage and destination of ships and the number of troops and weapons they carried could be precisely assessed. The geopolitical importance of the Suez Canal for military strategists becomes obvious when one looks at the telegrams meticulously noting this information. The Suez Canal developed into a space where powers could monitor each other. The shifting of troops was an important indicator of imperial strategy, Port Said thus emerging as a barometer of imperial competition and as a kaleidoscope of global information gathering.

No example is better suited to illustrate this global information collection than troop surveillance on different levels. Consuls were already informing their superiors about the number of ships passing this strategic position a good decade before 1888.[83] Many Russian troop ships figured on their lists; these ships navigated the new route between Odessa and Vladivostok, often carrying large numbers of soldiers, occasionally complemented by settlers.[84] After the Russian lease of Port Arthur, the staffing of the Russian garrison

---

[81] Quai d'Orsay, Correspondance politique et commerciale nouvelle série 1897–1918, Egypte 38: Le ministre de France au Caire au ministre des Affaires étrangères, Cairo, 6 March 1904.

[82] TNA, FO 78/4963: Consulate Port Said to Marquis of Salisbury, 5 March 1898.

[83] See TNA, FO 78/2639: quarterly returns of ships of war 1877; TNA, FO 78/2863: individual reports of troop ships 1878; for later, by then weekly, reports see TNA, FO 78/4317. The French consuls similarly informed the ministries in Paris of movements of warships, often sending their reports via the consulate in Cairo.

[84] See, for example, TNA, FO 78/4583: a large number of ships were transferred from Odessa to Vladivostok or China during the war between Japan and China in 1894, with the telegrams always indicating the type of ship and the number of soldiers on board.

was effectuated via the Canal. Alongside the Russian troop transports, many Ottoman ships brought reinforcements to unruly Yemen – sometimes carrying well over 2,000 men on a single ship and all listed meticulously in tables of the British consuls with general numbers from 1891 to 1903 given as 121,000 troops embarking for 'Arabia' and 59,000 returning.[85] Dutch cruisers made their way to Batavia, British torpedo ships to Hong Kong. A British steamship with 50,000 rifles and a million cartridges sailed through the Canal to Queensland, Australia. American steamers were registered en route to the Philippines. While in 1900 the French vessel *Alexander* transported 2,000 soldiers to Diego Suarez, the French base in Madagascar, three German ships transported 3,931 troops to Dagu in order to participate in the response to the Boxer Rebellion and an Austrian cruiser journeyed to Polynesia on a scientific expedition.[86] This potpourri illustrates how the Canal became a nodal point where a dispersed imperial geography was concentrated albeit for a short time only. This function became even more crucial as the century drew to a close and the German, French and British empires increasingly entered a weapon race.

Despite the importance of a trustworthy, tightly knit information infrastructure, there were discussions about the cost-benefit ratio it involved. In 1898 Consul Cameron sent some 53 telegrams at a cost of approximately 70 pounds to London. In the following year, the Foreign Office informed him that '[i]t is considered that for the future it will be sufficient if you will telegraph only important intelligence using your discretion in the matter. You should however take care to enter all movements of Russian Volunteer steamers in your weekly reports to the Admiralty.'[87] The media and thus the speed of information transfer was therefore up for debate in a time where this speed had a considerable price.

Sometimes it was difficult to gather the required information, as certain captains refused to let the consuls know how many soldiers they were transporting.[88] It was particularly problematic to secure trustworthy data

---

[85] TNA, FO 78/5308: Consulate to Foreign Office, Port Said, 3 March 1903; see also TNA, FO 78/5436: Telegram Consul Cameron to F.O., Port Said, 14 May 1905: 'Turkish transport Les Andes with 2553 troops left for Hodeidah'.

[86] CADN, Port Said 108: Telegram 13 February 1895; Quai d'Orsay, Correspondance politique et commerciale nouvelle série 1897–1918, Egypte 110: Consul Port Said au ministre des Affaires étrangères, Delcassé, 14 February 1899, 13 September 1900, 22 October 1900; TNA, FO 2/376, sheet 430: Telegram 27 February 1900.

[87] TNA, FO 78/5036: Consul Port Said to Mr Crowe, 6 January 1899; F.O. Draft Consul Cameron January 1899.

[88] See TNA, FO 78/2863: Consul West to Secretary of State for Foreign Affairs, Suez, 19 July 1878; see also Quai d'Orsay, Correspondance politique et commerciale nouvelle série 1897–1918, Egypte 110: Le ministre de la Guerre au ministre des Affaires étrangères, Paris, 20 June 1902.

Figure 7 'From Europe to the Far East: In the Suez Canal. Russian Armed Cruisers Conveying Troops to Port Arthur: Men Saluting and Cheering Each Other', *The Graphic*, 7 May 1898.

in the highly charged context of the South African War. When the German East Africa steamer, *Kanzler*, left for Natal in January 1900, carrying 140 passengers for various ports, including 20 Dutch Red Cross officers for Lourenço Marques (now Maputo in Mozambique), the consul stated that he believed them to be 'genuine medical men'. However, the captain refused to give any information concerning the other passengers or to hand over the passenger list.[89]

In the context of the South African War, the British were particularly worried about the transportation of ammunition. Highlighting the ambiguous role of Germany in the South African War, in a telegram dated 16 January 1900, Consul Cameron reported that the captain of the German steamer, *König*, had openly boasted that in the last four years his ship alone

[89] TNA, FO 2/376, sheet 438: Telegram Consul Cameron, Port Said, 8 January 1900 and ibid., sheets 440 ff.: Consul Cameron to F.O., Port Said, 8 January 1900.

Figure 8 'Soudanese Soldiers in the Canal', no photographer, no date.

'had taken enough munitions of war to Delagoa Bay to last the Transvaal for ever'. He concluded that the German East Africa Line was full of Boers and their European friends and that it did not conceal its sympathies.[90] In such situations, the consulate received its vital information from other passengers rather than from the captain. In this specific case a certain Mr E. Cecil, a member of the British Parliament and a passenger on the *König*, disclosed that two 'Transvaal spies' named Rooth and Michel were on board and might disembark at Naples.[91] In order to gain more extensive information, there were also attempts at active spying – Lord Cromer, for instance, made arrangements to place a German-speaking agent on a German ship at Port Said.[92]

The consul at Port Said complained that sometimes not only the captains proved uncooperative but also the coal merchants who were asked about information on certain ships for which they were providing

[90] TNA, FO 2/376, sheet 447: Telegram Consul Cameron, Port Said, 16 January 1900.
[91] TNA, FO 2/376, sheet 446: Telegram Consul Cameron, Port Said, 15 January 1900.
[92] TNA, FO 2/376, sheet 350: Telegram Lord Cromer, Cairo, 2 January 1900.

coal. He pointed to a tension developing far from home and in a particularly global place marked by private companies and their interests, regarding loyalties for Great Britain and for the companies they were working for. He indicated to the Foreign Office in London that the Maltese and at least a 'large portion' of the Greeks and Levantines proved 'intensely loyal to England'; yet, there were British employees in French firms or in British firms involved in the coaling of foreign vessels 'who take pride in confining their loyalty to their firm in opposition to their country'.[93]

In slight contradiction to his earlier statement, when 'a gentleman from Brazil with a Levantine Name', Dimitri Sfezzo, local manager of the British Coaling Company Cory, stated that he knew nothing of a cargo of gunpowder to Zanzibar and Mozambique, the perturbed consul reported that such an answer would not have been given by a British shipping and coaling agent; he concluded that 'Senhor Sfezzo is a foreigner and a stranger unacquainted with the East' – pointing once again to the sometimes paradoxical conception of home and away, foreigner and resident in a global locality such as Port Said.[94] These incidences illustrating the obstacles of a smooth acquisition of intelligence furthermore highlight that, by 1900, the Canal had become not only a crucial infrastructure for the transportation of troops but also for the acceleration and deceleration of strategic information.

Imperial interventions: the Madagascar expedition

Of course, the consuls not only provided information on foreign troops but also administered the transfer of soldiers of their own nationality or imperial allegiance. Following the Berlin conference of 1884, large parts of Africa came under colonial rule. Britain and Germany established colonies in East Africa; France and the Netherlands expanded their rule in South East Asia. Many of these operations, as well as the Russian colonisation and settlement of Siberia, at least in its eastern part, and the Ottoman attempt to control its possessions on the Arab Peninsula, necessitating the transfer of large numbers of troops between Constantinople and the eastern rims of its empire, were managed via the Suez Canal.

The transportation of troops not only engendered the need for trustworthy information to reach Europe's capitals, on the local level it also

---

[93] TNA, FO 2/376, sheet 441: Consul Cameron to Marquis of Salisbury, Port Said, 8 January 1900.

[94] TNA, FO 2/376, sheets 444–5: Consul Cameron to Marquis of Salisbury, Port Said, 13 January 1900.

meant a potential for conflict between the Canal Company and the relevant imperial powers. Sometimes the number of troops on paper did not correspond to the number counted by the Canal agents.[95] In 1901, the Ottoman government sued the Canal Company in the Cairo courts for the 10 franc per head charge on Turkish troops in transit. According to an author writing in the *Shipping Gazette*, the Ottoman Porte 'contends that troops are in no sense of the word passengers, but can be likened much rather to heads of cattle exported for slaughter or other cargo'. There were about 45,000 Ottoman troops stationed east of Suez, one-third being exchanged annually resulting in a yearly payment of 30,000 francs by the Ottomans to the Canal Company. Although the Russian contribution was more irregular, there were also large numbers of Russian troops shipped back and forth, mainly between Odessa and Vladivostok, obviously with a clear increase in times of conflict, such as during the Russo-Japanese War.[96]

Of course, the consuls not only provided information on foreign troops but also administered the transfer of soldiers of their own nationality or imperial allegiance, trying to usher them through the Canal Zone as quickly as possible. A look at the usage of the Canal during the Madagascar campaign serves as a good example of its function as a relay station for the management of troops between home and abroad. France had extended its influence in Madagascar since the early 1880s, establishing a settlement at Diego Suarez without, however, placing the whole island under colonial rule. In 1890, the British acknowledged Madagascar as a French protectorate. Nevertheless, the Madagascan army commander and prime minister, Rainilaiarivony, refused to accept French rule. Five years later, in January 1895, French troops therefore landed in Madagascar, occupying the capital of Antananarivo in September of that year.[97] Focusing on the use of the Suez Canal in relation to this conflict, the 1895 French Madagascar expedition highlights many aspects of imperial infrastructure: the provisioning of food, fuel and seamen discussed in greater detail in the following chapter, as well as furnishing aid for diseased soldiers and the organisation of relief.

---

[95] See, for instance, ANMT, 1995060/4993: Chef du service du transit au Prince d'Arenberg, 22 October 1900, reporting that the Ottoman troop ship *Babel* had declared 700 military passengers, yet during a check, agents of the Suez Canal Company had counted 996 persons on board.

[96] ANMT, 1995060/4993: 'Dues on Troops in the Suez Canal', *Shipping Gazette*, 17 April 1901.

[97] For the larger context, see Campbell, *An Economic History of Imperial Madagascar*, esp. pp. 305–39.

The troops designated for Madagascar frequently moved there from Algeria via Toulon, the main military port in France. The French Consul in Port Said had to inform Paris about the passage of ships and the state of health of the soldiers, and indicate if something unforeseen had occurred. Sometimes problems arose with specific steamers pointing to the shortcut of the Canal as potential retardant, as was the case with the *Château-Yquem* on its return from Madagascar when the superintendent of the troop transporter was found dead in his cabin and, in addition, the ship was stuck in the Canal for several days and the possibility of desertion was feared. Because of the high temperatures, 800 troops had to be evacuated. After two days the ship could depart with an upbeat final assessment: 'Material and moral condition of the men excellent.'[98] The case of the *Château-Yquem* illustrates that not only disease but also desertion were problems that could diminish the troops even before their arrival at the destination where they were to be employed. A 'native' engaged as an ancillary conveyor for the Madagascar campaign abandoned the *Massilia* at Port Said profiting from the coaling procedures. The consul filed his personal description, including the *zabība* on his forehead which characterised him as pious Muslim.[99] Similar incidents of course also took place on other occasions, for instance in 1900 when 14 French legionaries left their ship during the Canal passage by swimming.[100] In order to prevent such problems, the ships returning to France or to Algeria should, the Minister of the Navy indicated, avoid contact with the Egyptian harbours altogether if at all possible.[101]

During the return journey, cases of disease and death were frequent. If someone died on board, his burial had to be organised by the consul and his belongings returned to France.[102] There were also leaks of information: in October 1895 the press published the names of those soldiers who had died during return transportation on board the *Shamrock* before the

---

[98] CADN, Port Said 85: various telegrams concerning the situation of the *Château-Yquem*. The file also contains regular information about ships passing through without specific incident.

[99] CADN, Port Said 85: Copie d'une lettre adressée au vice consul de France à Suez par le chef d'escadron Henry, commandant le groupe des batteries d'artillerie de la Marine, commandant à bord du *Massilia*, Canal de Suez, 1 May 1895.

[100] CCIMP, Messageries Maritimes (Rapports de Voyages) 241, Guadiana (1888–1907): Ligne de Chine commerciale, Voyage N° 13, Marseilles, 15 November 1900.

[101] CADN, Port Said 85: Ministre de la Marine au consul de France à Port-Saïd, Paris, 31 October 1895.

[102] See, for instance, CADN, Port Said 62: Telegram Port Said, 14 October 1895 – burial of four soldiers repatriated from Madagascar; see also CADN, Port Said 16: Consul Port Said au commissaire chef du service colonial à Marseille, 21 December 1898 – concerning the belongings of a colonial official who died in Port Said.

families could be informed by the French Navy. The Minister of War then clarified the procedures: lists had to be dispatched to the War Ministry, along with all information regarding deceased soldiers, and all precautions had to be taken to avoid journalists getting hold of any information relating to deaths on board.[103] The treatment of deaths on board indicates the attempt to channel not only mobility but also information: in an age of faster news transfer it became crucial to control such informational flows. The various incidences enumerated above also show the limits of speeding up troop transports and the obstacles they could encounter.

As indicated, catering for diseased soldiers and providing relief also formed part of the work of an imperial relay station. Even if the sources on this relief provision are scant, they give us insight into the internationalist (on the part of the Red Cross) but also patriotic impetus of alleviating the suffering of soldiers. The reports of the returning troop ships reveal that the health of the soldiers repatriated from Madagascar was often less than ideal. The Port Said committee of the French section of the Red Cross was founded in order to help the 'refugees of Madagascar' of the years 1886, 1892 and 1894–97. Besides the Red Cross, other benevolent associations at Port Said included the *Dames françaises* and the *Société française de secours aux blessés militaires*.[104] The documentation of these organisations in the consular files contains less information about the soldiers themselves than about their provision with money, food and tobacco. The goods on offer included French newspapers, different types of clothing as well as food and drink, particularly sweets such as jam, chocolate, condensed milk, Bordeaux wine and – interestingly enough – 'Coca-Kola'. Cigarettes, cigars and pipes were also provided, as well as games. Over the course of the years, the provision of support became more standardised, a development expressed materially in the, by then, printed forms indicating relief supplies and their recipients.[105]

In 1897, after the end of the Madagascar campaign, Port Said resumed its normal function for French military transports. At one point, General Gallieni, by then governor general in Madagascar, wrote to the French Consul in Port Said to gather some information relevant for the now regular colonial traffic to Madagascar, because he was assembling a guidebook for travellers and colonisers embarking to Madagascar. As we have

---

[103] CADN, Port Said 85: Ministre de la Marine au vice admiral commandant en chef, préfet maritime à Toulon, Paris, 12 October 1895.

[104] CADN, Port Said 155: Croix-rouge française: Création du comité à Port-Saïd en faveur des réfugiés de Madagascar (1886, 1892, 1894–1897).

[105] See CADN, Port Said 155: Association des dames françaises, Sous-comité de Port Said, Relevé, détaillé par bateau, des secours distribués aux malades et convalescents de passage à Port Said de 21 Janvier au 20 Décembre 1896.

seen, similar guides had already been published for colonial voyagers to Indochina, among other areas, the consul at Port Said always receiving a copy.[106] In his reply, the consul followed the guides that were already in circulation pointing to the scheduled departures of the *Messageries Maritimes* and other companies serving East Africa and detailing the principal hotels, the local transportation and the shopping opportunities. He also noted the 'French circle' that had now been formed in Port Said to serve both civil and military French travellers. Again he warned that his compatriots, and above all militaries, should avoid developing the habit of visiting the roulette in the 'Eldorado', a gambling hall disguised as music cafe and owned by Greek nationals.[107] The transportation of troops thus became once again a routine endeavour with Port Said offering its characteristic dangers and temptations.

Isma'il had hoped that the construction of the Canal would make Egypt European. Instead the waterway's increasingly important role in colonial projects 'east of Suez' went hand in hand with an internal colonisation of the Canal Zone that accompanied informal British rule in Egypt but clearly differed from it. The example of troops shows well how the Suez Canal came to be a tool of acceleration and deceleration. It was in the best interest of empires to have their troops relocated as quickly as possible in order to avoid shortages in their colonial possessions, showing how the distinction between troops and other forms of mobility was made at this locality. At the same time as troop transports were to be sped up, the transfer of men and weapons of other powers could be assessed here, as everyone had to go slower and submit to certain controls and checks. What is more, sometimes speed in terms of the transmission of news via telegraph was too expensive. Speed was thus an asset that was to be applied discriminately.

As this allotment of speed shows, the example of the Suez Canal reaches far beyond the locality itself – not only in terms of the connections that were served by it but also in terms of local experimentation with a global set of regulations. A survey of the governance of Port Said, both de jure and de facto, underlines the wide range of agents sharing sovereignty in this region – among others the international shareholders' Suez Canal Company, the delegates at the conferences, the occupying powers, the consuls, the captains and so forth. Such a survey sheds light on the shifting geographies of empire marked out by the development of new spaces of

---

[106] See CADN, Port Said 16: Indochine française, Direction de l'intérieur au consul Port Said, 10 March 1878, Envoi de l'annuaire de la Cochinchine (année 1878).
[107] CADN, Port Said 16: Consul Port Said au général Gallieni, commandant le corps d'occupation et résident général de France à Madagascar, 28 September 1897.

interaction. These geographies converged in several strategic 'choke-points', which were both crucial to tying the territories together and sensitive points of possible interruption. They represented not only inter-faces between the global and the local (as illustrated in the interpretation of the occupation of Egypt and the Canal Zone as a 'global event') but were also spaces where the diplomatic realm, in its old-fashioned sense, collided with colonial discourses and new arenas of internationalism. This led to a need for new rules, or at least for new forms of accommodation, such as international conventions, whose enforcement was not always easy. In a newly constructed location such as the Suez Canal, this dynamic played out in a particularly intense form. The Canal thus emerged as a location of connection but also of congestion; instead of being a smooth highway of empire, it developed into a turnstile where passengers observed the slowness of their own passage through a contested space of slow decision-making and constant concern for imperial governments.

In this process the extraterritorial location of the Canal emerged as a 'laboratory of rulemaking' centring on different spaces – the harbour of Port Said, the troop ships or the consulates as arms of empire and relays of information. These spaces also pointed to the tensions between interna-tional and imperial orders as well as to the limits of these rules and regulations – be it in terms of the problems in gathering information or in securing the passage of soldiers without any side effects of desertion or unruly behaviour. The difficulties of the creation and application of a uniform 'regime of passage' show that not only the images of the global assessed in the first chapter but also its regulation were not at all straight-forward. As an infrastructural hub, the Canal was furthermore marked not only by the tension between international and (British) imperial claims, but also by the role of private companies, which will be the theme of the following chapter.

3   Companies and workers

Some people contend that Lord Cromer is the actual Khedive of Egypt, while others hold to the primacy and potency of Abbas II. But the best-informed persons all recognize that the real Khedive of Egypt is the firm of Thomas Cook & Son. It was they that carried the British troops to Dongola, and it is they who would have carried the English soldiers to the deliverance of Khartoum and the rescue of Gordon, and have got them there on time, if Mr. Gladstone's government had only been wise enough to buy its Gordon-rescue and Khartoum-relief expedition-tickets at their office.[1]

In the description of his round-the-world trip, the American traveller John Henry Barrows chose Thomas Cook's travel agency, encountered in the first chapter, as an example to highlight the nexus between political involvement in Egypt and the role of private companies, which were central to the workings of imperial infrastructure. The troop transportations through the Suez Canal, which came into view in the preceding chapter, not only depended on political organisation, but also relied on commercial enterprises for shipping and the provision of food, fuel and seamen. In the Suez Canal Region, the interdependent political actors and commercial companies were closely enmeshed. As the above quotation illustrates – obviously taking a slightly ironic tone – in Egypt's complicated political situation, it was even plausible to argue that private actors carried more authority than official ones. Private companies emerged as an important factor in the shaping and application of the 'regimes of passage' analysed in the last chapter.

Yet in the commercial realm of the Canal Zone, not only the globally active companies, like the shipping companies, or companies with a global shareholder community behind them, like the Canal Company, but also the mobile workers, drawn from various regions, added to the sense of the Canal as a global locality. Consuls, colonial administrators and troops were not the only ones who travelled for work. They were complemented

[1] Barrows, *A World-Pilgrimage*, p. 315.

105

by highly mobile workforces concentrated in the region, such as shipping crews, coal heavers and Canal workers. Whereas in the last chapter, the integration of the Suez Canal into global networks of politics and military strategy was emphasised, integration into the region (i.e. the Eastern Mediterranean) mattered equally as soon as workers had to be hired. Diplomats, workers and other people as well as objects of all kinds were drawn to this newly created space in the desert as to a magnet. In addition to the movement of people *through* the Canal, the movement of people *to* the Canal therefore deserves further attention.

This movement of people, but also of provisions and coal, to the Canal could be a considerable undertaking, pointing to the complexity of global and imperial infrastructures. Infrastructures, which are often invisible and taken for granted, are concentrated and become apparent in locations such as the Suez Canal, especially when problems compromise smooth communication, whether by high traffic volumes, controls, or accidents. At the harbour towns of the Canal, passengers changed ship and experienced waiting times before their steamers could proceed, while coal and provisions were provided and crews were hired. This facet of the Canal did not only leave its imprint on the spatial imagination of travellers. It also illustrated that the smooth transit through such an infrastructural relay station depended on a wide variety of factors: international agreements and diplomacy attempted to secure free movement in times of peace and war; coal and seamen had to be shifted globally so that the right amount of both was available at Port Said at any one time to avoid not only shortages but also oversupply, which would increase the costs of storage and the support of seamen; and workers had to be kept minimally content in order to avoid the threat of strike and sabotage.

Adding a further tile to the mosaic of mobilities in the Canal Zone and contributing to the thriving field of global labour history, this chapter acquaints us with the workers who populated this particular space.[2] These workers were crucial to the acceleration (or deceleration) that the Canal provided while they themselves moved voluntarily or involuntarily or, on the contrary, were prevented from moving. Looking in turn at the Canal Company, the coaling firms and then the shipping lines operating in the Canal, the mobility of workers and workers' grievances are thus at the centre of the chapter, using concepts of free and forced mobility (and their political imperatives) and paying attention to categories such as race and nationality, which played a crucial role in the treatment of workers and their mobility.

---

[2] On global labour history see van der Linden, *Workers of the World*; Andreas Eckert, 'What is Global Labour History Good For'.

Canal workers and the Canal Company

The Suez Canal Company was fundamental to the creation but of course also the daily operation of the Canal. This became particularly obvious when it came to the relationship of the Canal Company and the realm of politics, to the relationship between the Canal Company and its customers and to the relationship between the Canal Company and its workers and their grievances, three fields that will be reviewed in turn in the following sections of this chapter.

The Canal Company, local politics and international customers

The *Compagnie universelle du canal maritime de Suez* has been called a 'state in the state'.[3] It was an Egyptian joint stock company, largely organised according to French models, yet at the same time international in terms of its origin and shareholders' community. More recently, the company has received the interest of Hubert Bonin, former employee of the company, and Caroline Piquet.[4] In their works they meticulously note the legal and political development of the Canal Company, its organisational structure, as well as the relationship with the workers. In the following we can therefore content ourselves with specific spotlights shedding light on the issue of rulemaking and rulebreaking, forming the centre of this chapter.

Due to its ambivalent status, shifting between its submission under Egyptian law, French involvement and international (particularly British) shareholding, the Canal Company's relations both to the local government of the Canal Zone and to the British power were far from unproblematic, pointing to the variety of actors involved in the 'rules of globalisation' as developed in the last chapter. More than once, conflicts between the company and the governor of the Suez Canal Region erupted, often regarding the question of who had to pay for certain improvements such as repairs of parts of the Arabic neighbourhood after a fire in 1884 or the construction of a new hospital.[5] Also there were recurrent petitions by the inhabitants of the Canal

[3] See Piquet, *La Compagnie du canal de Suez*, p. 19.
[4] Bonin, *History of the Suez Canal Company*; Piquet, *La Compagnie du canal de Suez*.
[5] See DWQ, Majlis al-Wuzarā', Qanāt al-Suways 2, 0075–017015: Gouvernorat général de l'isthme de Suez au conseiller financier, Port Said, 18 May 1884 (about the fire in Port Said); DWQ, Majlis al-Wuzarā', Qanāt al-Suways 5, 0075–017038: Ministère des Finances au président du Conseil des ministres Le Caire, 16 March 1887.

Zone for a fairer distribution of the company's profits.[6] At other occasions
the Suez Canal Company was accused of avoiding Egyptian tax payments.
In January 1887, for instance, it had to appear in a court case concerning the
import of conveyors produced in Britain and used in the Canal to transport
silt, which dredgers were constantly extracting, to the sea.[7]

The relationship between the Suez Canal Company and the British
occupational forces was also ambiguous. After 1882, the company opened
an office in London and let some of its buildings to the troops stationed in
the Canal Zone, yet it remained sovereign concerning the management of
the Canal itself. At the same time, the British paid strict attention to ensure
that the company did not exert any political influence.[8] De Lesseps
reported that the British consulate and, following this model, several
other consulates had discouraged their nationals from voicing complaints
against the company concerning the operation of the Canal via the French
consulate, in order to try to keep the spheres of French politics and the
commercial realm of the Canal Company as separate as possible.[9]

This short insight into the relationships of the Suez Canal Company
with the different agencies in power in Port Said, particularly the Egyptian
government, the British occupational force and the French representatives, already shows that in the Suez Canal Region, private and public
interests were closely enmeshed. That this enmeshment was not always
frictionless is easy to imagine. The relationship between the Canal
Company and the ships using its services could be equally problematic,
as the following section will show.

The Suez Canal Company had to avoid frictions in its relations with the
political actors in charge in the Canal Zone, as what mattered most to
those navigating through the Canal was the smooth and rapid functioning
of the infrastructure. During the early years, the traffic was marked by
minor and major accidents – as noted in the introduction, the Empress
Eugénie had been in tears during the first passage through the very narrow
Canal. After the beginning of regular traffic, many reports noted the
difficult navigation. An account of 1870 stated that at no point did the

---

[6] DWQ, Majlis al-Wuzarā', Qanāt al-Suways 2, 0075–017013: Agreement regarding the
profits of the Canal, 1909; DWQ, 'Ābdīn 243, 0069-004756 for petitions and telegrams.
[7] DWQ, Majlis al-Wuzarā', Qanāt al-Suways 5, 0075–017042: Cour d'appel d'Alexandrie.
Audience du 19 janvier 1887. Conclusions pour la direction générale des douanes
égyptiennes contre la Compagnie du canal de Suez. Réponse à la note adverse
(Alexandria: Typo-Lithographie Lagudakis & Falco, 1887).
[8] Piquet, 'The Suez Company's Concession in Egypt', 118.
[9] ANMT, 1995060/0941: Ferdinand de Lesseps, 'Note sur la situation des Français en
Égypte à l'égard des indigènes et des étrangers dans le cas où l'Assemblée nationale
repousserait le projet de réforme judiciaire', Paris, 7 June 1875.

depth exceed even 7 metres.[10] The lists of the French naval station in
Egypt and local newspapers mentioned that numerous ships ran aground
during the passage.[11]

Even after the Canal traffic had been well established, many passengers
made suggestions about how the Company could improve its working.
During his tour around the world in 1878–79, the self-made man, Andrew
Carnegie, watched the steamers crawling slowly through the Canal (taking
up to four days to 'squeeze through') from the windows of the railway
carriage carrying him to Cairo. He observed in his travel notes that the
traffic could have been doubled at any point by lining the shores with
electric lights to enable night passage. Furthermore, he believed that the
Canal had to be widened in order to allow two-way traffic. Others proposed that the Canal should serve one direction at night and the other
during the day.[12] A famous imperial careerist, George Nathaniel Curzon,
stated some four years later that the waterway required enlargement.[13] By
then, night traffic had been introduced and construction work had begun
to expand the Canal. Despite the fact that the Canal Company had to keep
the intruding desert sand from blocking the Canal on a constant basis, it
gradually increased in depth to 9 metres and in width to 37.[14]

The Company employees that passengers and captains traversing the
Canal came into closest contact with were the pilots employed by the Suez
Canal Company to ensure the secure navigation of the large steamers
through the narrow Canal. To take pilots on board was one of the many
obligations that was intended to guarantee a smooth transit – turning the
Canal into a highly regulated and supervised space.[15] Other rules
included, for instance, maximum speed, the prohibition of overloading
the deck with coal and merchandise and of throwing any objects whatsoever into the Canal. Some pilots preferred the traffic at night, as there

---

[10] SHD, BB4/1492: Compagnie universelle du canal maritime de Suez, Note pour
l'amirauté anglaise: Situation du canal maritime de Suez au 1er décembre 1870.

[11] SHD, BB4/1492: Station navale d'Egypte, Rapports sur les bâtiments transitaires 1870;
ANMT, 1995060/1027 sheet 199: *La finance*, 28 April 1870, *La revue financière*, 28 April
1870; sheet 240: *La sûreté financière*, 22 May 1870.

[12] Carnegie, *Round the World*, pp. 263–4; Villiers-Stuart, *Egypt after the War*, p. 486.

[13] OIOC, Mss Eur/F111/104 Curzon Collection: Diary Journey Around the World 1887–
88, vol. 3, pp. 184–5.

[14] DWQ, Majlis al-Wuzarā', Qanāt al-Suways 5, 0075–017035: Note concernant le licenciement des ouvriers embauchés par la Compagnie du canal de Suez pour l'exécution des
travaux d'amélioration du canal.

[15] The 'Règlement de navigation' can be found in many different archives and compilations,
pointing to its wide circulation; see also advisory books for captains, such as Taylor, *The
India Directory*, pp. 25–6: 'Regulations for the Navigation of the Suez Maritime Canal'.

were fewer local boats that could obstruct the passage.[16] Collisions became rarer as pilots assisted the passage, yet some spectacular accidents could not be prevented, such as that of the *Chatham*, which had to be blown up in the Canal under considerable media attention with a special train conveying newspaper correspondents to the scene in 1905.[17]

Certain shipmasters were not pleased about giving up the authority over their ship during the passage. The commander of the *Messageries Maritimes* steamer, *Meï-Kong*, for example, complained about a pilot called Vaulpré who was a 'bad manoeuvrer, lacking *coup d'œil* and self-control, filled with vanity'.[18] Sometimes the pilots were even accused of having caused an accident themselves through their bad advice, as in the case of the *Britannia*, on which Indologist Paul Deussen was travelling.[19] Henry Villiers-Stuart on the other hand preferred the French pilots to their superiors in the Canal Company. He spent some time on a French pilot launch and noted, with no small amount of jingoism and illustrating the inter-imperial tensions concentrated in the Canal Zone as well as the French image of the Company in the eyes of the British, that he regretted that the French officials of the Company lacked the French pilots' 'bonhomie'. In a generalising manner he concluded that the 'estimable qualities' of French people in their private lives became unbearable once they had official posts of some authority. He attributed much of British criticism of the Canal and de Lesseps – going as far as proposing the construction of a second all-British canal – to this, in his eyes, typically French behaviour.[20]

These spotlights on the perception of shipmasters regarding the general management of the Canal and, more particularly, the pilots coming on board the ship show the competition and conflicts that could arise if two hierarchical systems – the Canal Company and the steamship – intersected. Yet the hierarchies within one of these systems itself could also be upset as the next section of this chapter on Canal workers' movements and its final section dealing with unruly seamen will show.

---

[16] See Parfond, *Pilotes de Suez*, p. 133.

[17] 'The Wreck of the Chatham', *The Times*, 25 September 1905, p. 10; 'The Suez Canal: The Chatham Blown Up', *The Times*, 29 September 1905, p. 4; 'The Suez Canal: The Blowing Up of the Chatham', *The Times*, 30 September 1905, p. 5. See also Compagnie universelle du canal maritime de Suez, *Accident du 'Chatham'*, September 1905.

[18] CCIMP, Messageries Maritimes 362, Meï-Kong (1871–1876): Captain Meï-Kong au directeur Messageries Maritimes, Marseilles, 4 April 1872. See also CADN, Port Said 38: Agent chargé du contentieux de la Compagnie du canal de Suez à M. Monge, gérant du consulat de France à Port Said, Port Said, 13 May 1874 concerning a steamer which refused to take a pilot on board.

[19] Deussen, *Erinnerungen an Indien*, pp. 235–6.

[20] Villiers-Stuart, *Egypt after the War*, pp. 488–9.

The Canal Company and workers' movements

Despite the increasing mechanisation of the Canal work during and after the construction period, infrastructures were not (and are not) unmanned. The Suez Canal Company employed many workers of different nationalities, which were integrated into a hierarchical pattern.[21] The upper echelons were most often filled with European engineers; Greeks and other Levantines occupied a middle ground. Finally Egyptian workers executed the more menial tasks. The Canal Company thus fostered a large amount of mobility and tapped into the flows of Eastern Mediterranean labour circulation.[22]

Much more problematic for the daily operation of the Canal than the ability, both practical and social, of the pilots encountered in the previous section of this chapter or those globally active, often French-trained, engineers in the higher echelons of the Canal Company, were its more menial workers, particularly those operating the huge dredgers on the sides of the Canal. Even after the improvements mentioned above, dredgers had to work continuously to keep the intruding desert sand from blocking the Canal. They were an apt representation of the Canal's technological triumph and fascinated many travellers. However, the subjugation of nature did not proceed without accidents. In 1885, a dredger that was touched by a passing ship collapsed into the Canal, interrupting navigation for 10 days and producing a jam of 123 waiting ships until it could be blown up and removed.[23] Such stoppages showed the workers operating the machines that they commanded a significant negotiating power. The photograph by one of the Zangaki Brothers (Figure 9) highlights the sheer size of the dredgers, yet it also pays clear tribute to the workers posing on top of the machines they are handling.

Animosities between captains and individual pilots were not the only source of complaint. In addition, certain groups among the Canal Company workers became stereotyped as perennial troublemakers, with Greeks and Maltese enjoying a particularly dubious reputation. During the building period, the Canal had already grown into a place that was not easy to control and the construction supervisors had to deal with

---

[21] For the representation of different nationalities among the Canal Company personnel, see CADN, Le Caire 284, Compagnie du canal (1892–1940): personnel (1892–1940).

[22] Piquet, *La Compagnie du canal de Suez*, pp. 248–58.

[23] See *Hippolyte Arnoux: photographe de l'union des mers*; for a similar case, see Caird Library, P&O/17/1&3: Suez Canal Company v. P&O Steam Navigation Company, The 'Travancore', Statement of Case for the Defence.

Figure 9 'Dredger *Derocheuse*', photograph by the Zangaki Brothers.

murders and other criminal acts on the building sites. The workers on the dredgers were seen as being the most prone to strike and rebellion.[24]

After the completion of the Canal, parts of the workforce behaved in an unruly manner. One of the main problems at this stage was that some workers did not want to leave the site once the building work had been finished. In his *Voyage pittoresque*, published in 1869, Marius Fontane described one of the building sites on the Canal bank that seemed a particularly strange global locality. Seamen and workers of different countries had set up camp here, forming a motley population of many different ethnic communities. According to Fontane, in contrast to other well-organised building sites in the Canal Zone, here, doubtful groups of unemployed workers lingered and played dice.[25] Fontane was thus already referring to those people in a state of limbo who had been drawn

[24] See ANMT, 1995060/3601; ANMT, 1995060/3602; ANMT, 1995060/3603.
[25] Fontane, *Voyage pittoresque*, pp. 30–1.

to the former desert strip, which by then had become a waiting room for all kinds of individuals.

The unruliness of the workers continued once the Canal was opened. In March 1870, fights between Greeks and the local authorities resulted in the shooting of the vice governor. In reports to Ferdinand de Lesseps, the agitations were explained with direct reference to large numbers of former workers refusing to leave the building sites. Having spent all their savings, they found themselves in dire straits and were ready to do anything to support themselves, leading to a higher frequency of soliciting and of theft. Yet, according to the report, the local authorities were not taking any necessary measures and even graver disorder was feared.[26] Although the 1870s were calmer than expected, a conflict in Port Tawfiq between Greeks and Berbers in 1885 once again triggered debate about the policing of these newly constructed towns. Representatives of the Suez Canal Company voiced the opinion that, as the camp was exclusively composed of people paid by the company, the company should also be responsible for its security and policing. The Canal Company's agent, Rouville, however recommended that rather than establishing a local police force it would be more useful to set an example by punishing a single person with particular severity.[27] Hence, such incidents raised not only questions of how to dispose of former workers but also, more generally, how the Canal Zone was to be controlled more efficiently.

In the 1880s and 1890s, labour movements in Port Said became increasingly organised, culminating in the creation of a workers' union in Port Said in 1893 after a number of, sometimes violent, strikes.[28] The amelioration works of 1886, which were to deepen and broaden the Canal, necessitated the hiring of additional personnel. As these works were completed, labour unrest grew more frequent and more forceful. In 1891 similar troubles occurred. The head engineer reported that he had received petitions from some workers demanding that the company include them in the allocation of bonuses accorded to other personnel involved in the enlargement.[29]

---

[26] ANMT, 1995060/1477: Le chef du service du domaine au président de la Compagnie, Paris, Ismailia, 3 March 1870.

[27] ANMT, 1995060/1477: Comité de direction, Séance du 23 juillet 1885; Le chef du service du domaine à M. Ferdinand de Lesseps, Ismailia, 8 July 1885.

[28] Piquet, *La Compagnie du canal de Suez*, pp. 315–24.

[29] Quai d'Orsay, Affaires diverses politiques 1815–1896, Tome IV, Egypte 19, Sous-dossier conflit entre la Cie de Suez et les ouvriers 1891: L'ingénieur en chef au ministère des affaires étrangères, Paris, 26 June 1891.

In 1892, when most of the work was accomplished, the company decided to reduce the overall workforce and to lay off 420 workers of different nationalities. The figures point to the composition of the workforce as well as to the disproportionately large number of Egyptians and Greeks that were made redundant. The company argued that the laid-off workers were treated in the most just, humane and benevolent manner possible.[30] They would receive compensation equivalent to the salary of 15 workdays per year spent in the service of the company and they would be repatriated without any additional payment. This measure was largely in the interest of the company, because, in parallel to the years that followed the completion of the Canal, it was particularly valuable to them to ensure that the workers who had been drawn to the Canal and were now to be discarded, would leave the Canal Zone as quickly as possible.

In 1893, labour protests about working conditions were rekindled and connected to international contexts. This time, the strikers threatened to sabotage the Canal by destroying the dredgers and forcing them into the Canal so as to block the waterway. This threat enabled them to attract international attention, as shipping companies and captains were worried about any obstruction to the smooth course of Canal traffic.[31] The Canal Company received several petitions and the strike leaders, Emmanuel Limbéris and Kanakis Diakenandreas, travelled to Paris to submit their complaints to the Ministry of Foreign Affairs. Their appeal was based on the special role of France in relation to the Company, highlighting an amalgamation of the Company's interests and French politics, which the British had wanted to avoid.[32]

As a reaction to the strikes, in an article published in the *Bulletin décadaire*, the company defended itself by stressing the mobile nature of the workforce: the workers had come spontaneously from Greece, Italy, or Dalmatia asking for work and the Company had not done anything to attract them. According to this depiction, the Canal had a strong force of attraction that radiated in a wide circle and exerted a pull on workers from the whole of the Mediterranean basin. The article went on to praise the

---

[30] DWQ, Majlis al-Wuzarā', Qanāt al-Suways 5, 0075–017035: Note concernant le licenciement des ouvriers embauchés par la Compagnie du canal de Suez pour l'exécution des travaux d'amélioration du Canal.
[31] Quai d'Orsay, Affaires diverses politiques 1815–1896, Tome IV, Egypte 20, Série B Carton 16: 'Grève imminent à Suez', *La libre parole*, 8 October 1893.
[32] Quai d'Orsay, Affaires diverses politiques 1815–1896, Tome IV, Egypte 20, Série B Carton 16: MM. Emmanuel Limbéris et Kanakis Diakandreas délégués des ouvriers du canal de Suez au ministre des Affaires étrangères, Paris, 18 October 1893; Ministère des Affaires étrangères à Guichard, sénateur, président du Conseil d'administration de la Compagnie de Suez, Paris, 7 October 1893.

Suez Canal Company, stating that there was no other company in the whole world (once again pointing to the characteristic of the Canal Company as playing in the same league as other global companies) that behaved as paternally and as generously towards its workers.[33]

In the following year, an envoy reported to the advisory council of the Suez Canal Company in London that about 60 workers, consisting of seamen and stokers employed on the dredgers, had left their posts and declared that they would only return if the company assured them 10 months of paid work per year as it did to workers in other sections of the Company. The envoy referred directly to the workers' origins, stating that the Greeks were responsible for the labour dispute. According to him they were incorrigible and stuck to their demands, whereas workers of other nationalities – some Italians and French, as well as one Belgian – who claimed to have only followed the strike movement because of the intimidations and threats of the Greek leaders, had changed their minds quickly and had returned to work without upholding their demands.[34]

One answer to labour movements was deportation. The strikes of 1894 grew more violent, as the wives of the Greek workers apparently grouped together, and the Company feared that the strike would spread further. To prevent this, some of the workers were expelled to Greece.[35] From the Company's perspective, the only solution to bring this unruly group of mobile workers into line was thus to threaten them with forced mobility: if the workers remained disobedient, they would face repatriation to their countries of origin. This could be particularly problematic in the case of Greek workers, who did not always originate from Greece but from various locations in the Ottoman Empire or belonged to a mobile workforce seeking employment at the large building sites, such as the railway constructions, of the period.

Even though Evelyn Baring travelled to Port Said to assess the situation, and despite the fact that the unrest culminated in the killing of the French chief engineer, the Company still decided to downplay the event, arguing that the strikes would not have had the same echo in France without the assassination of the engineer, which had furthermore taken place in Ismailia where the workers otherwise had remained 'perfectly quiet'.[36]

---

[33] Quai d'Orsay, Affaires diverses politiques 1815–1896, Tome IV, Egypte 20, Série B Carton 16: *Bulletin décadaire* n° 786, 22 October 1893.

[34] ANMT, 1995060/0159: Grève des dragueurs de Port-Said, Note envoyée à Londres pour le comité consultatif du 28 septembre 1894.

[35] CADN, Le Caire 485, Sous-dossier grève de Port-Saïd – Canal de Suez – 1894: Déchiffrement, Port Said, 3 October 1894; Dipl. Paris, Cairo, 12 October 1894.

[36] Quai d'Orsay, Affaires diverses politiques 1815–1896, Tome IV, Egypte 21, Sous-dossier grèves de Port-Saïd 1894: *Bulletin décadaire*, 22 October 1894.

In 1898, however, the Canal workers went on strike again and the French Consul at Port Said, Léon-Vincent-Auguste Hugonnet, informed Georges Cogordan, Consul General of France in Egypt, of the 'state of exasperation' of the Canal workers, who had been made redundant, and of death threats that had been voiced against the directors of the relevant sections. He announced that he wished to leave his position as soon as possible.[37]

The frequent strikes of the Canal workers shed light on a particularly active labour force that was increasingly aware of its negotiating power. The attention that the agents of global transportation networks, such as shipping companies (often with their headquarters in faraway places), paid to the labour movements are a clear indication of the importance that was by now attributed to the smooth transit through the Canal. The strikes also reveal the international character of the workforce and, what is more, the frequent reference to this international composition.[38] Furthermore, the strikes were always connected explicitly to mobility. This found reflection in the attempts of the workers to lobby for their rights in faraway places, such as Paris, but also in the responses of the Canal Company, which was prepared to use forced mobility as a last resort.

Coal heavers and coaling houses

Coal was crucial for keeping the Suez Canal as the artery of empire pulsing. In the decades after 1869, Port Said developed into a large-scale relay station of coal and other supplies. The provision of sufficient and affordable fuel was an essential element in the connection of faraway places. The functioning of infrastructure thus did not only consist of the passage through the Canal and the workers who sustained it – specific goods, primarily coal, had to be brought to the edges of the Canal too and necessitated a whole chain of interactions to get there.

With the exception of some men-of-war, whose depth of draught prevented them from taking on heavy coal before passing through the Suez Canal, few ships bunkered coal in Suez – it was Port Said that became the central coaling station of the region: of the 1,697 ships that had passed the Canal in 1890 from north to south, 1,557 had taken 487,572 tons of coal

---

[37] Quai d'Orsay, Correspondance politique et commerciale, nouvelle série 1897–1918, Egypte 37, M. Hugonnet, consul de France à Port-Saïd à M. Cogordan, ministre plénipotentiaire chargé de l'agence et consul général de France en Egypte, Port Said, 26 March 1898.

[38] In terms of the international composition of the labour force, the situation on the building site of the Panama Canal was comparable. See Greene, 'Spaniards on the Silver Roll'.

in Port Said.[39] In 1899, the quantity of coal transhipped in Port Said exceeded a million tons for the first time. The largest amount reached Port Said from Britain, most of it from South Wales, with some coal from the Tyne district around Newcastle. By the beginning of the twentieth century, small amounts of coal were also imported from Westphalia via Rotterdam, and, during a railway strike, from the USA. These various origins illustrate that coal was a global commodity in the literal sense of the word.[40] Together with Aden, Port Said thus became the largest coaling station in the world, catering for almost all ships transiting to and from Asia and East Africa.[41] The following section first looks at coaling at Port Said shedding light on both the companies and the workers involved in the process. It then turns to the perceptions of this process by passengers before looking at problems that could arise, particularly strike movements that can be analysed in parallel to the Canal workers' upheavals.

Coaling at Port Said

The structure of the coaling companies highlights the ambivalence between free markets and monopolisation, as any new coaling company had to be officially recognised. In the late nineteenth century Port Said accommodated four coaling companies. Two of them were French and two British; in 1901 a German company was set up to serve the increasing number of German ships.[42]

The price of coal was a constant source of worry for the shipping business. Some months before the approval of the Canal route as the main trajectory of troop transportation to India, the captain of the troop ship *Jumna* argued that as the British troop ships would provide a large income to the Canal Company, at least the coal should be transportable free of duties.[43] The engineer Paul Borde phrased the issue even more clearly in terms of free trade. He noted that in his writings de Lesseps was clearly a proponent of economic liberalism. And if that were the case then de Lesseps would have to detest excessive taxation. Borde agreed that a shorter route to the Far East had to be paid for, yet at a moment when

---

[39] Murray, *A Handbook for Travellers in Lower and Upper Egypt, Part I* (1891), p. 305.

[40] TNA, FO 78/5372. British Consulate, Port Said, 21 January 1904, Suez Canal District Answers to Questions for British Consuls.

[41] TNA, FO 78/2509: Consul Perceval to Earl of Derby, Port Said, 4 February 1876.

[42] CADN, Port Said 82: Création d'un dépôt de charbon allemand à Port Said (26 juillet 1901–27 février 1903); see also OIOC, IOR, R/20/E/164 about a coaling company to be set up in Perim.

[43] TNA, MT 23/26: Extract of a letter from the captain of HMS *Jumna*, 3 March 1871.

'free trade is becoming a necessity of our times' and when all (at least all fiscal) barriers on the borders should be lowered, a tax of 10 francs on every ton of coal seemed disproportionate. After all, steam was the motor of the Navy and the basis of the Suez Canal Company's prosperity.[44]

Ideally the provision of coal would be both cheap and reliable. Captains responsible for troop transports received the order to save fuel so as to keep expenses low and the use of coal was carefully tracked.[45] Yet despite the Canal Company's fees, and the monopoly of the Canal's four coaling firms, the competition between the English and French (and later the German) firms still meant that coal was cheaper in Port Said than in other ports.[46] Therefore British troop transports were encouraged to stock up on coal here in order to buy less in Bombay.[47] Also, by 1873, the method of how to determine the quality of the coal that was loaded was already being discussed, pointing to the standardisation of all matters connected with the global transport system. All captains of Her Majesty's troop ships were requested to check the quality of the coal when the lighter was still alongside the ship.[48] Finally it was crucial to guarantee the secure provision of coal, even – or especially – in times of war. During the Russo-Turkish War, the Russian Consul General in London granted vessels carrying coal from the United Kingdom to Port Said a special protection against seizure by Russian cruisers in order to keep the traffic through the Canal uninterrupted.[49]

And it was not only the price of coal, its supply, or its quality that were a matter of concern but also the act of loading it. After the opening of the Canal, manual labour to load and unload coal was in demand. As a result, between one and three thousand coal heavers gathered in Port Said. Due to the efficient organisation of this large workforce, Port Said developed into not only one of the largest but also one of the fastest coaling stations in the world. As the largely French- and English-speaking coaling companies were unable to communicate with the coal heavers directly, they employed sheikhs as heads of the coal heavers' guilds who in turn hired and paid the coal heavers. In order to guarantee the speedy loading, the companies thus had to rely on both trustworthy

---

[44] Borde, *L'isthme de Suez*, ch. 8: 'Les charbons par le canal de Suez', at p. 91.

[45] TNA, MT 23/52: Coal supplies for Indian Troop Ships Season 1875–6.

[46] TNA, FO 78/3334, sheet 147: Report on the Trade, Commerce and Navigation at Suez for the Year 1880.

[47] TNA, MT 23/153, Indian Troop Service, Sailing Orders – Southampton to Bombay and back, paragraph 7.

[48] TNA, MT 23/45: Procedure for Determining Quality of Coal supplied by Contractors at Port Said, Admiralty, 3 December 1873.

[49] TNA, FO 881/3306: Certificates of Protection of Vessels with Coal Proceeding to the Suez Canal, Extract from the *London Gazette*, 24 August 1877.

middlemen and seasonal workers, mainly from Upper Egypt, willing to temporarily move to Port Said. The procedure of coal heaving was made increasingly efficient not least through the introduction of the telephone shortly after 1900. During their stay in Port Said the coal heavers dwelt in the so-called Arab quarters. The coal heavers' guilds were soon subdivided into contracting teams, each headed by a chief. As soon as a ship arrived from the Mediterranean or through the Canal, the sheikhs were informed of the ship's demands by telephone. The sheikhs then sent out men who were employed by the coaling companies to fetch the coal heavers in their domiciles at any time of the day or night and to accompany them to the coaling barges. There the chiefs were already waiting to direct the barges towards the steamers and to oversee loading. This system enabled the loading of an average of 100 tons per hour.[50]

Like the workers of the Suez Canal Company, observers often described the coal heavers as being an especially mobile workforce. This mobility could carry different meanings. In line with the negative stereotypes associated with certain sections of Canal workers, and referring to a discourse critical of constant mobility or 'vagrancy' developing in Europe, the local newspaper *Phare de Port-Saïd* called the sheikhs 'vagabonds' and the coal heavers themselves a 'drifting population of unemployed with which the Arabic town is teeming'.[51] When, during the First World War, French officials wanted to recruit Arab labourers for war-related employment in Marseilles, the French Consul at Port Said wrote to his superior in Cairo that the coal heavers of Port Said would be the best choice as they were particularly easy to move, because they were from Upper Egypt and thus were used to living far away from their homes.[52] According to this opinion, the primary mobility of the coal heavers consequently made them easily moveable to any other place of action. In this case, mobility, which was deemed so suspect, could also become an asset for companies and governments.

Passengers and coal heavers

The procedure of coaling was not a purely technical undertaking that was of interest only to the shipping companies. Watching the coal heavers amazed or disgusted many western travellers; they became one of the

[50] *Annuaire général de l'Indochine 1909*, p. 167.
[51] CADN, Port Said 82: *Le phare de Port-Saïd et du canal de Suez*, 21 May 1894, p. 1.
[52] CADN, Port Said 82: Le consul de France à Port Said à A. Defrance, ministre de France en Egypte Le Caire, Port Said, 30 June 1915.

sights of Port Said noted in almost every travel diary. As seen in connection with the depictions of Port Said and the Canal, the descriptions of coal heaving always contained the same elements – the barges, the coal heavers, their chants or shouts and the dust – and were heavily marked by racial stereotyping. Traveller Helen Caddick was most fascinated by the speed of this 'fastest Coaling Station in the world' where 300 men were able to load 1,200 tons of coal on a steamer in only five hours. She highlighted the curious fact that all of the coal was imported from Newcastle, pinpointing a further global connection, alongside the passengers, workers and postcards moving between the continents.[53]

Writer S. Parnell Kerr described the night-time coaling as an almost surrealistic scene, referring to the coal heavers as 'hurrying, demon-like figures', 'manikins' or 'little demons' whose work was accompanied by shouts and a 'babel of noise'.[54] Surgeon Frederick Treves, travelling in 1904, agreed that the night-time coaling scene 'is one of the sights of the world, and would have fired the heart of Dante', during the day however it was 'a pageant which could be of interest only to a dust contractor'. He was aware of the fact that the scene had been described many times, but he still had to express how unindividual the workers in charge of the coaling seemed to him:

The stream of basket carriers might be coming out from the crater of a volcano, and it is a matter of wonder that they are neither charred nor smothered. They are all so much alike that the procession on the plank may be made up of one toiling man multiplied a thousand times.[55]

The descriptions of the coal heavers once again point to the repetitiveness that emerges from a comparison of travelogues. The coal heavers were perceived as being so typical of Port Said, that they even formed a popular motif of postcards or snapshots taken from the ship's railings (Figure 10). The particular attention that passengers gave to the coal heavers might be explained by the fact that there was just not much to see at Port Said. But it also points to the fascination of steam technology. This fascination was reflected by some depictions explicitly ridding the coal heavers of all individuality and reducing them to a trope of their repetitive, almost mechanical work. Furthermore, and perhaps most importantly, coal

---

[53] Caddick, *Travel Diaries of Helen Caddick*, p. 14. See also Paterson, *Reminiscences of a Skipper's Wife*, pp. 45–6.

[54] Kerr, *From Charing Cross to Delhi*, pp. 29, 32. The coaling procedures were also taken up in fictional texts. See, for example, Macdonald, *The Great White Chief*, p. 32; Redwood, *Wanderings and Wooings East of Suez*, pp. 21–2.

[55] Treves, *The Other Side of the Lantern*, pp. 16–18.

Figure 10 'SS *Caledonia* Coaling at Port Said 1912', photograph by Kathleen Davidson travelling to India.

heavers were one of the first 'exotic encounters' on the journey that European passengers could report back home.

Coal heavers on strike

Even the efficient coal-loading system of Port Said that impressed many travellers was occasionally interrupted. For one there was the unruliness of individual coal heavers and the theft of coal.[56] Yet organised labour movements, like those of the Canal Company workers, were much more worrisome for those involved in the shipping business than such one-off events. The strikes of the coal heavers of the 1880s and 1890s – closely connected to the unrest of the Canal workers – hold an iconic place in Middle Eastern historiography as the 'first indigenous group of Egyptian workers to go on strike for higher wages'.[57] In contributions concerned

---

[56] For thefts of coal, see, for example, CADN, Port Said 82: Agence et consulat général de France en Egypte à M. Lappont, consul de France à Port-Saïd, Cairo, 16 June 1905: 'la pêche illégale du charbon'; TNA, FO 846/5, p. 4: court case against Antonio Schembri accused of stealing coal and sentenced to three months' imprisonment, 27 April 1881.

[57] Chalcraft, 'The Coal Heavers of Port Sa'id', 110. See also Beinin and Lockman, *Workers on the Nile*, pp. 23, 27–31.

with the strikes, the organisation of the workers has been found to be particularly noteworthy. However, these events also point to the precariousness of new infrastructures. Even if during this period the Canal was never sabotaged completely, the strikes of the coal heavers (and of the Canal workers for that matter) highlighted the transportation system's fragility.

The labour disputes not only raised questions concerning the responsibility of private companies and the government of Port Said. They also reverberated more broadly, engendering worries that the smooth transit through the Canal could be interrupted. It was debated as to how far they were related to events within Egypt or even larger-scale phenomena, or whether they were purely local issues. The captain of the French frigate, *Ponty*, addressed the highest authority, the Minister of the Navy himself, to express his opinion concerning this matter. For him, it was clear that the political issues always at stake in Egypt were at the root of the strike movement. The British had only instrumentalised the movement, the captain was certain, so that it fit their political goals and interests.[58] Be that as it may, the shipping companies' captains quickly became very anxious about this complication in the global transportation networks pressing for the fulfilment of the strikers' demands. The local strikes were thus politicised not only on a British-Egyptian level but also on that of international companies and inter-imperial rivalries.

The strikes in Port Said also exerted influence 'east of Suez' pointing to growing global interconnectedness as they led to the sudden increase in the demand for coal and consequently for workers at the coaling stations of Aden and Perim in the Red Sea. The office of the *Messageries Maritimes* in Aden constantly employed about 80 Arabs and every two months additionally 150 to 200 Arab 'coolies' to discharge the coal that was bunkered there. Here racial stereotypes came to play an important part, as the Arab workers were chosen, because, as it was stated, Somalis who were also available were 'not robust enough' for such hard work.[59] However, the situation was more complicated on the small island of Perim as the local coaling station reported that during a later strike in Port Said, they had to hire 118 additional men from Aden. The manager concluded that there always was a large 'floating population' in Aden from which the coaling agents could simply 'pick up what native labour is required as it comes along'.[60] These

---

[58] Quai d'Orsay, Affaires diverses politiques 1815–1896, Tome IV, Égypte 21, Sous-dossier Grève de Port-Saïd, Grève des portefaix charbonniers: Le capitaine de la frégate *Ponty*, commandant le croiseur *Cosmao* au Ministre de la Marine, Port Said, 3 June 1894.

[59] OIOC, IOR R/20/A/2583, sheet 83: L'agent des Messageries Maritimes au gouverneur de la Française des Somalis, Djibouti, 16 December 1907.

[60] Ibid., sheet 99: Managing Agent Perim Coal Company to Assistant President Perim, no date.

and similar expressions voiced by agents and shipmasters involved in different parts of the coaling process illustrate the racial discrimination of certain
groups but also the emphasis on the mobility of the workers not only in Port
Said but also in other harbours such as Aden and Perim.

Both the strikes of the coal heavers and of the Canal Company workers
show that Port Said's function as an 'imperial relay station' implied that
local conflicts had far-reaching effects as captains of several shipping companies stepped in on the side of the coal heavers, and the Canal workers'
leaders travelled as far as Paris for more effective petitioning. Also, the
workers related to the business of mobility were often mobile themselves.
In the European perceptions, their own mobility often meant an increase in
their claims on commerce and colonisation. The menial workers' mobility,
however, made them rootless and disposable. If these workers were central
to the acceleration viewed so favourably by many contemporaries, their *own*
mobility was to be channelled, meaning at times deceleration or stand-still,
and at times forced mobility or deportation.

Seamen and shipping lines

The conditions of workers in Port Said reveal the intricate legal and
economic situation of the town. They also reveal its role as a hinge
between sea and land, where transgressions of hierarchy on the part of a
mobile workforce were frequent. Even if these hierarchies consisted of
various levels, they were most often structured along imperial lines, often
with racial undertones. Beyond the workers and their condition, the
competition between different shipping companies as well as both naval
and civilian steamships themselves, representing a very rigid organisation,
which was often contrasted with the unruliness of the port town, became a
symbol of imperial rivalries and hierarchies in more than one sense. What
is more, seamen on board the steamships represented mobile workers par
excellence.[61] They are therefore covered in considerable detail in the last
and longest part of this chapter.

In the following we will first look more generally at the treatment of
seamen in the steamship's microcosm before analysing the function of
Port Said and the Canal in the switching of crews and dealing with sick
seamen. In this context, just as in the context of troop transports, together
with the private shipping companies, the consulates occupied a central
role. As seamen often ran into trouble once in the harbour, they were also

---

[61] Seamen have recently emerged as a thriving field of research; see, for instance,
Kennerley, 'Stoking the Boilers'; Hyslop, 'Steamship Empire'; Fink, *Sweatshops at Sea*;
Balachandran, *Globalizing Labour?*.

frequently sued at the consular courts, whose proceedings represent a valuable source to find out about this mobile group. Also, just like in the organisation of the coal heavers, middlemen were central to keeping the global and imperial infrastructure working. The case of the seamen thus points to the intricacies of an imperial relay station, shedding light on the institutionalisation of global processes, but also their limits and problems, in this case mainly connected not so much to organised strike movements but to the unruly behaviour of individual seamen.

The social space of the steamship: empire in microcosm

With its division into several classes of passengers and different categories of workers, a steamship could be seen as an ideal representation of empire in microcosm, as a traveller in 1884 on his way to India put it, referring to 'that glorious British Empire of which we are here a small, moving, isolated fragment'.[62] This notion of the reproduction of imperial hierarchies within the bounded space of the ship emerged in the descriptions of several passengers, yet with quite different emphases. Ships were thus on the one hand global localities in carrying people of different nationality on (and under) their decks, on the other they carried the national or imperial characteristics of their origins around the globe.

The P&O ships became particularly closely linked to the British Empire. Not only due to their role as connectors between the British Isles and the colonies, but also because of their dependence on government contracts and subsidies, they became 'flagships of imperialism'.[63] In his poem, 'The Exiles' Line', of 1890, Rudyard Kipling emphasised the task of P&O in connecting the 'wheel of Empire'.[64] Besides the fact that the ships tied the various sites of empire together, many travellers on P&O steamers pointed to the imperial hierarchies dominant on board. American travellers were especially struck by the behaviour that British passengers showed once inside the ship. Andrew Carnegie contrasted the people one encountered in the Atlantic realm with those of the Indian Ocean world, idealising the American dream of flat hierarchies. The English, so he claimed, had a tendency to form a lot of different 'small cliques'. Whereas on an Atlantic steamer, the Americans were united by 'congenial tastes and education', in the case of the Indian Ocean British steamers, 'rank and position' played a crucial part and it was impossible to

---

[62] Edwin Arnold, quoted in Ewald, 'Crossers of the Sea', p. 81. For an analysis of the social space of the steamship, see Pietsch, 'A British Sea'.
[63] See the title of Harcourt, *Flagships of Imperialism*.
[64] Kipling, *Rudyard Kipling's Verse*, pp. 187–9.

introduce different people as 'miserable barriers of artificial distinction stood in the way'. He concluded: 'Vandy and I being republicans, not caring a rap about either birth or position, and without social status in England, seemed to be the only cosmopolitans on board.'[65]

The companion of the former US president, Ulysses Grant, also noted the hierarchical organisation of the steamer, which for him precisely mirrored imperial realities. Most of his co-passengers were Englishmen bound for India. When there was a muster one morning,

the ship's company fell into line, Hindoos, Mussulmans, Chinese, Egyptians, Nubians – it seemed as if all the nations of the Oriental world had been put under contribution in order that the good ship 'Venetia' should make her way from Suez to Bombay. The 'Venetia' is commanded by Englishmen and served by Orientals.[66]

Young's observation not only points to the multitude of different persons found on board; his enumeration of people of various origins assembled in one single space calls to mind the depictions of the city of Port Said presented in Chapter 1. However, in contrast to its straight streets and 'modern' appearance, Port Said was often described as disorderly and prone to infringements of all sorts. The ship represented the same diversity of human life but inserted into a rigid hierarchy.

As the quote of yet another American traveller, John Henry Barrows, cited at the very beginning of this chapter, made plain, the travel experience of many passengers was shaped by British companies such as Thomas Cook and P&O. Edmund Hull, in his *Vade-Mecum*, sang the praises of the latter, which, despite the competition that the Suez Canal had engendered, was outstanding in speed, punctuality, service and the outfit of the steamers.[67] Some French travellers were also impressed, comparing the meticulous service and particularly the 'Hindu stewarts, polite, silent, almost invisible' with the dereliction of the *Messageries Maritimes*.[68]

However there were also critics of British shipping, such as Paul Bourde, who stated with confident nationalism that in fact the British themselves preferred the French ships to the British ones 'escaping from the barbaric cooking of their compatriots'.[69] Some British travellers joined in the critical assessment of their countrymen's eating habits:

---

[65] Carnegie, *Round the World*, pp. 261–2.
[66] Young, *Around the World with General Grant*, p. 597. See also Barrows, *A World-Pilgrimage*, p. 321.
[67] Hull, *The European in India*, p. 25.
[68] Travelling in a later period: Carré, *Promenades dans trois continents*, p. 119.
[69] Bourde, *De Paris au Tonkin*, p. 4.

Isabel Burton wrote mockingly that the British 'want huge lumps of beef and mutton four times a day' and that they ate 'like locusts and drank the cellar dry almost before we got to Aden'.[70]

In contrast, the French *Messageries Maritimes* prided themselves on their superior culinary offer. The tickets comprised food and wine, for first class travellers other drinks such as grog, syrups and lemonade as well as beer, Marsala, Sherry and Cognac were provided.[71] Although the *Messageries Maritimes* had the reputation of catering well for their passengers' needs, some English travellers on the steamer line to Madagascar expressed their astonishment not finding any whisky on board. Others complained that Roquefort cheese was not served frequently enough.[72]

At the beginning of the twentieth century new competitors joined the world of shipping. Recently established German shipping lines, for example, started to offer lower prices than the *Messageries Maritimes* for journeys to Australia and the African coast.[73] The German government also began to follow the British and French example and to subsidise specific lines.[74] Politics and economics were thus closely intertwined in the business of global navigation.

Besides being representatives of their countries or empires of origin, the steamships were also places of racial hierarchies, which were most marked in relation to the Arab or African seamen on board, the 'lascars', who caught the amazement of many travellers. When Mark Twain travelled in 1895 from Sydney to Ceylon he saw a crew of indigenous seamen, so-called lascars, for the first time and was amazed by their 'oriental' dress and appearance:

White cotton petticoat and pants; barefoot; red shawl for belt; straw cap, brimless, on head, with red scarf wound around it; complexion a rich dark brown; short straight black hair; whiskers fine and silky; lustrous and intensely black.[75]

---

[70] Quoted in Pearson, *Indian Ocean*, p. 232. See also Mozoomdar, *Sketches of a Tour Round the World*, pp. 4–5; Barrows, *A World-Pilgrimage*, p. 322.

[71] AFL, 1997/002/5032: Messageries Maritimes, *Service des lignes au dela de Suez: Itineraires et tarifs* (Imprimerie centrale des chemins de fer, 1er mars 1889, n° 2).

[72] AFL, 1997/002/4455: Messageries Maritimes, Port Said, Rapport général de service, exercice 1891, chapitre 4 Trafic; CCIMP, Messageries Maritimes 302, Laos (1897–1907): Ligne de Chine, Voyage N° 14, Marseilles, 7 July 1901.

[73] AFL, 1997/002/4455: Messageries Maritimes, Port Said, Rapport général de service, exercice 1891, chapitre 4: Trafic. For the subsidy of mails carried through the Canal by P&O since 1874, see Harcourt, 'High Road to India'.

[74] Bundesarchiv, R/901/77477, Band 42: An die Botschaft der französischen Republik. Verbalnote, Berlin, 6 May 1912.

[75] Twain, *Following the Equator*, vol. 2, p. 11.

Where Twain stressed their exotic manifestation, which he coupled with certain character traits ('willing and obedient', 'go into hopeless panics when in danger'), the French traveller, Paul Bonnetain, who caught a glimpse of the stokers during their evening prayers, was slightly disappointed that they were dressed just like European workers, which formed a strong contrast to their behaviour and appearance otherwise.

What impressed Bonnetain most was the moment that the lascars disappeared back into the underworld of the ship. It almost seemed as if the moment of their simultaneous existence on deck seemed to have only made him aware of the fact that there was a second world on that very ship that was taking him across the oceans. He described the scene in some detail. A voice called them and they descended step by step to the very bottom of the ship, six meters under the sea, where a fire pointed toward the 'underworld of the engin', slowly disappearing until only their shadows were visible and far-away sounds indicated the stuffing of coal into the engines. Even the air that came out of the hole into which they had vanished was unbreathable and stifling.[76]

As in the case of some descriptions of the coal heaving procedures, Bonnetain stressed the de-individualisation (and perhaps de-humanisation) that came with the mechanically undertaken toil of the stokers.

The descent of the lascars into the ship's bowels points to their invisibility during the largest part of the journey. For many privileged travellers, it was thus not only the variegated crowds of Port Said that remained faceless. Yet the lascars were indispensable for the ships' working and played a particularly important part in the Suez Canal connecting the world of shipping east and west of Suez.

Racial stigmatisation

It is worth taking a closer look at the seamen and their work experiences. Obviously, ships were not only extremely hierarchical social spaces but also extremely hierarchical work environments. People moving equally fast on the same ship could represent very different mobilities, and accordingly receive very different treatment, which was in this case not differentiated in relation to the speed or the mode of conveyance but to the position and, importantly, the ethnic origin of the workers.

The demarcation line was particularly stringent between European and non-European crew members. Since the early nineteenth century, Asian seamen, or 'lascars', had found wide-ranging employment. In the age of

[76] Bonnetain, *Au Tonkin*, pp. 16–19, esp. p. 18.

steam navigation, which had added new professions to the world of seafaring, these sailors often occupied the posts of coal trimmers and stokers, particularly in the waters 'east of Suez'. They represented therefore not only the tail end of hierarchies on board but also worked under the harshest circumstances. The condition of Indian and Arab seamen is a good case in point to distinguish between sheer mobility and the freedom of movement. If the spatial mobility of lascars was expanded with the introduction of the steamship, their social mobility did not increase to a similar degree. Janet Ewald thus concluded that the introduction of steam made seamen more mobile than ever before extending their range of employment across the whole globe. At the same time their *social* mobility was increasingly restricted.[77]

Different racial stereotypes soon came to be associated with different groups of sailors. European seamen were suspected of being prone to drunkenness and disobedience, always ready to pick a fight, whereas Arab and Asian sailors were described as less intelligent, but more docile than the Europeans.[78] Racial stereotyping also figured when transgressions of hierarchy, such as the inappropriate contact between the crew and the passengers, were suspected. In the context of the transport of indentured labourers between the island of Saint Helena and Calcutta, the Crown Agents for the Colonies wrote to the Marine Department of the Board of Trade in 1894 that they needed advice on the use of 'Negro sailors' on 'Coolie Emigrant vessels'. They claimed that the latter had the 'tendency to molest and interfere with the female Emigrants' and repeated the guideline of the surgeons' superintendent not to employ 'Negroes' and 'Mulattos' on such ships.[79] The captains of the *Messageries Maritimes* voiced similar convictions concerning Chinese stokers, who, they claimed, were more difficult to supervise and were not used to obeying orders. They complained that, due to a shortage of staff, they had to employ Chinese as well as black seamen.[80]

The discrimination of non-European crew members also materialised in terms of their wages and their general treatment both on passenger and on troop steamships. Non-European stokers were first of all paid less than their European colleagues and usually received local currency in

[77] Ewald, 'Crossers of the Sea', p. 91; Steel, *Oceania Under Steam*, pp. 97–125: 'Labour, Race and Empire: Debating the "Lascar Question"'.

[78] Berneron-Couvenhes, 'Le personnel navigant les paquebots de la compagnie des Messageries Maritimes vers 1880–1900', p. 208. See also Ahuja, 'Die "Lenksamkeit" der "Lascars"', 326–30.

[79] OIOC, IOR L/PJ/6/382 file 1739: Crown Agents to Assistant Secretary, Marine Department, Board of Trade, Downing Street, 2 August 1894.

[80] CCIMP, Messageries Maritimes 362, Meï-Kong (1871–1876): Rapport général du voyage N° 12 de Marseille à Shanghai et retour, novembre 1871.

accordance with colonial wages.[81] Additionally, they were treated much worse than European members of the crew, as the following episode illustrates. The Resident Transport Officer Hull at the dockyards of Bombay wrote to the director of transport services of the Admiralty in 1871 stating that some ships had returned blankets which were so dirty 'as to leave no doubt that they had been issued for the use of the Natives'. The captain of the *Euphrates* responded to the accusation by saying that he had handed out 100 blankets, which had already been used by the troops he transported, to the indigenous stokers at the request of the ship's surgeon as it was very cold at Suez, at night falling to 1°C. They were, however, he stressed, 'carefully selected from those most soiled by the Troops'.[82] This individual example points to the routine mistreatment of lascars on board British troop transports, which most probably was also practised on other European steamships.

The optimising and economising of space on the ship also targeted the space reserved for lascars and points to the complications of imperial legislation. Not only did 'native seamen' on troop ships not receive blankets and other equipment necessary for minimal physical comfort, they were also assigned less space on the commercial steamships, an issue that continued to be the subject of haggling on the part of the shipping companies. P&O, for example, wanted to reduce the space assigned per 'native seaman', going so far as to argue that the more discriminatory 1876 Indian Act, rather than the 1894 British Merchant Shipping Act was applicable in the case of lascars. In 1901 the conflict culminated in a lawsuit.[83] P&O could not uphold its claim, yet the case still points to the issue of competing legislations in imperial contexts. The legalisation of differential treatment illustrates that in the decades after the opening of the Canal, the world of navigation had become more regulated, which in this case translated into increasing discrimination. Both the (mis)use of blankets for lascars and the haggling over space shows how minute details reveal the rules of globalisation which were very often about effectuating global connections at the lowest expenses possible. There were many attempts to circumvent these rules in order to reap larger

---

[81] For the difference in wages, see, for example, AFL, 1997/002/4474: Messageries Maritimes Suez, Rapport général de service, exercice 1882, personnel; for differential treatment see also TNA, MT 9/432: Mercantile Marine Office Dundee to the Assistant Secretary, Marine Department, Board of Trade, December 16, 1891; Ahuja, 'Die "Lenksamkeit" der "Lascars"', 347–9; Balachandran, 'Circulation through Seafaring'.

[82] TNA, MT 23/27: *HMS Euphrates* signed Captain (name not readable), Portsmouth, 21 June 1871.

[83] Caird Library, P&O/50/4: 'P&O Steam Navigation Company v. the King', *The Times*, 2 June 1901.

profits – in addition to 'rulemaking' the Canal Zone thus also became a space of 'rulebreaking'.

Switching crews in Port Said and Suez

No example provides a more telling illustration of the Canal's role as global and imperial relay station and infrastructural hub than the provision and switching of crews at this location marking the boundary between east and west. It became a logistical challenge of global dimensions to supply the right number of seamen at the right moment for commercial and military shipping. In the requests that shipmasters of troop ships sent to the consuls, seamen figured as part of the general furnishings, when they ordered, for instance, the provision of 260 tons of coal, 25 tons of fresh water, 4 live cattle, 200 kilos of hay and 56 Asian stokers.[84] What is more the harbour town of Port Said often witnessed unruly behaviour on the part of the seamen, when the hierarchical rules of the steamer were temporarily suspended.

In Port Said and Suez, sections of the shipping crews were often exchanged. Hence not only coal but also crews had to be allocated globally so that the right amount of stokers or coal trimmers was available in the right harbour at the right time. As in the case of coaling, speed and timing became increasingly important. Hubs like Port Said and Suez were places where seamen were looking for employment, were hired, or made redundant. On the one hand, Arab or Indian stokers were preferred for the journey through the Red Sea (in line with the racial stereotypes outlined above, captains claimed that they could cope better with the heat); on the other hand, there were increasingly tight regulations against introducing Asian seamen into Europe.[85] This meant that all-European crews had to sail west of Suez, while east of Suez, the right amount of lascars had be hired.

According to Rudyard Kipling, Port Said was also the linguistic boundary where the language of the stokers shifted from the idiom of the Levant to the 'Other Lingua Franca' in use all the way to the Kurile Islands northeast of Japan.[86] In order to reduce the linguistic gap between the Europeans

---

[84] CADN, Port Said 85: Telegram Amirauté Alger, commandant Amiral Charner à consul France, Port Said, 1 July 1900.

[85] TNA, MT 9/432: Board of Trade Marine Department, 16 December 1891– Report rel to Arab Seamen being placed on agreement which except so far as applied to them expires at Dundee and also as to Port Said Consul making it a condition in every case for Arab Seamen to be discharged at his Port; ibid.: Mercantile Marine Office Dundee to the Assistant Secretary, Marine Department, Board of Trade, 16 December 1891. For the increasingly tight regulations see Lane, 'The Political Imperatives of Bureaucracy and Empire'; Tabili, 'The Construction of Racial Difference in Twentieth-Century Britain'.

[86] Kipling, 'The Limitations of Pambé Serang', p. 344.

and the Asians working on board, especially if they were not employed as stokers but also on deck, dictionaries such as the *Lascari-Bât* (compiled by a commander at P&O) were published containing the most common vocabulary to command seamen in 'Lascari', a mixture of Arabic, Hindi and other Indian Ocean languages.[87] Still there were (as in the case of coal heavers) communication problems between the commanding Europeans and their workers who often had to be addressed through middlemen, adding to the multi-layered structure of employment patterns.

Such middlemen were necessary to make the global allocation of seamen work smoothly. The stokers were not hired directly by the captains, but by brokers who negotiated with the shipping companies or, in the case of military traffic, with the consuls.[88] The contract of 182 stokers employed between Port Said and Djibouti on four steamers of the French Navy in 1900 can serve as an illustration of employment procedures and working conditions. The contract and the lists, which contained Arab names only, were signed by the French consul and the leader of the stokers' corporation at Port Said, Mahamed El Isnaoui. The contract specified that the stokers would receive the first half of their pay in Port Said and the other half in Djibouti and that they were expected to participate in all the work related to the machinery, including its cleaning, before they left their position. They were submitted under the discipline on board and could be punished with imprisonment in the case of any insubordination or not fulfilling their duties. Each group of stokers was headed by a 'corporal', who was to supervise them and translate the orders and to be paid 20 francs more than the stokers (100 instead of 80). In the case of these state-employed stokers, the French government was responsible for their return to Port Said, for the payment of the quarantine fees and for a compensation of one franc for every day during which they were out of work.[89] This procedure points once again to the intricate intersection of the private and the public domain in the Suez Canal.

In the 1870s, British officials debated whether it was more profitable to employ European stokers on troop ships all the way to Asia in order to avoid the complicated switching of crews in Port Said and instead of having crews sent from Bombay to Suez and then make them wait there for the ship's arrival.[90] At the beginning it remained questionable as to whether enough Europeans could be found to take on these extremely hard and draining posts.[91] However, the director of transport reported

---

[87] Valentini, *Lascari-Bât*.   [88] See Lawless, 'The Role of Seamen's Agents'.
[89] CADN, Port Said 85: Contrat d'engagement de chauffeurs, 27 June 1900.
[90] TNA, MT 23/48: Military Secretary India Office to the Director of Transports, 19 June 1874.
[91] TNA, MT 23/44: Director of Transport, no date.

that the experiment of employing 16 additional European stokers 'in lieu of Natives' on board the troop transporter, *Crocodile*, proved successful. He thus asked for permission to employ the same number of stokers on the *Malabar*, which would save the expense of 'sending natives from Bombay to Suez' and have them wait there for a significant amount of time as well as make it possible 'to test the ability of Europeans to perform the duty of Coal Trimmers on the Indian side of Egypt'.[92]

Nonetheless, the idea of all-European crews remained a mere experiment. The prevailing opinion persisted that Asian stokers dealt with the heat in the Red Sea better (or that they were simply not in a position to complain). The captain of the *Guadiana* took up the climatic racial argument when he reported in 1900 that he had been lucky to replace 12 French sailors with 16 Arabs in Suez because of the extreme heat that they had encountered in the Red Sea.[93] Besides shedding light on ideologies of racism in the intricate imperial machinery, the exchange of seamen in Port Said also serves as example of the enactment of the 'rules of globalisation', as introduced in Chapter 2. As well as pointing to the fact that the lascar crews were distributed and redistributed globally, forming an integral part of the logistics of transportation, these discussions highlight the experimental character of the rules and regulations in place to deal with them.

Despite the experimentation with different forms of switching crews at Port Said, there were frequent disputes regarding the correct calculation of Suez Canal fees and attempts to evade payments. At times the ships were transporting lascars back to the port of origin and were still counting them as part of the crew in order to avoid the charges.[94] In 1889 an advisory committee was set up to debate the issue. The committee pointed to the lack of a legal limit to the number of crew members. They advised that the Canal Company should notify shipowners that they should consider 'Lascar crews brought from the East' as passengers and pay for them.[95]

Regardless of this clarification, there were still cases such as the *Arabia* passing unhindered in 1889 with a crew of 100 men.[96] The SS *Karamania*,

---

[92] TNA, MT 23/44: Director of Transport to M. A. Milne, 21 November 1873.

[93] CCIMP, Messageries Maritimes 241, Guadiana (1888–1907): Ligne de Chine commerciale, Voyage N° 13, Rapport général du voyage de Marseille à Haiphong et retour. Exercice 1900.

[94] ANMT, 1995060/4993 contains numerous such cases, mostly British steamers with Indian lascars, but also, for example, the German steamer *Kriemhild* with 13 Chinese stokers to be counted as members of the crew (Le chef du service du transit à J. Guichard, président de la Compagnie, Ismailia, 25 July 1895).

[95] ANMT, 1995060/4993: Extract from the minutes of the 'Comité consultatif', 1 August 1889; Extract from the minutes of the 'Comité consultatif', 27 September 1889.

[96] ANMT, 1995060/4993: Service du transit et de la navigation à Ferdinand de Lesseps, 16 August 1889.

however, carrying two crew-rolls, one containing 37 Europeans and the other 51 lascars, with the captain ready to admit that he planned to leave one of the crews in England, was charged for the lascars.[97] A similar case was documented in 1902 on the SS *Fulwell*. Here it was disputed whether the lascars were sleeping in the part of the steamer designated for the crew or whether they stayed in the taxed volume of the ship.[98] A further practice, also not always successful, was to pay the lascars half their wages during the time of the transport to the port of origin or until the transfer onto a new steamer.[99] This evasion of the payment of Canal fees for lascars points both to the need of making global connections as cost-efficient as possible referring to worldwide competition and to the breaking of the rules and regulations set up by international bodies such as conferences or companies.

The incorrect indication of the number of lascars transported on board a ship was only one of the problems that could occur. In many cases, the consuls had to be consulted as they often simultaneously served as naval agents and were involved in the discharge of seamen and in the provision of medical certificates for troop ships.[100] The archival material reveals that while regulations regarding seamen were made on a national or imperial basis the problems of their implementation become particularly obvious in the global locality of the Suez Canal. Despite the fact that the captains depended on the consuls to negotiate with the brokers providing the seamen, there were also many complaints regarding the insufficiency of the consular arrangements, their opening hours, the fees for certain services, or the slowness of the inspections regarding the discharge and transfer of native crews.[101] In the case of sick seamen, the consulate had to remain open until the issue was settled, otherwise, the 'shipping community' would protest.[102] These consular procedures were thus crucially connected to the speed or slowness associated with the Canal.

---

[97] ANMT, 1995060/4993: Chef du service du transit à Ferdinand de Lesseps, 21 May 1891.

[98] Ibid., Secrétariat, Note no. 3838, Présence de lascars dans les espaces de pont MM. Holt et Branfoot, SS *Fullwell*, Paris, 17 November 1902.

[99] See, for example, ANMT, 1995060/4993: Chef du service du transit à Ferdinand de Lesseps, Ismailia, 20 December 1888 concerning the SS *Indrani*.

[100] See, for example, TNA, FO 78/4461: Consul Gould Memo, 25 February 1892; TNA, FO 78/5036: British Consulate Port Said to Marquis of Salisbury, 29 June 1899; TNA, MT 23/232: 'Instructions for the British Consul as Naval Agent', 19 August 1909.

[101] See among others TNA, FO 78/2409: Consul Perceval to Earl of Derby, Dublin, 16 July 1875; TNA, FO 78/5165: F.O. Draft Consul Cameron, 21 February 1901; CADN, Port Said 120: Ministère des Affaires étrangères à M. Summaripa, consul de France à Port-Saïd, Paris, 10 August 1900.

[102] TNA, FO 78/4963: Cameron to Salisbury, Memorandum dealing with a protest made against this Consulate by Mr.Wilfried H. Dulcken, Royal Naval Reserve, Master SS *Clan Robertson*, 30 October 1898.

The troops and seamen both added a lot of work to the British consulate and made the consul complain, in 1884, that the French consulate carried much less of a burden as it was mainly responsible for employees of the Canal Company and 'of other respectable persons', whereas the British consulate constantly had to deal with 'troublesome Maltese', 'drunken and mutinous seamen' as well as 'crowds of Australian emigrants' and others who came to spend a few rowdy hours in Port Said. All of Port Said's consulates together did not apparently have the quantity of prisoners, seamen in hospital and in the boarding house that the British consulate had to deal with.[103] This large number of problematic cases that the British consulate was responsible for presented the flipside of British global imperial predominance.

The discharge of seamen on grounds of sickness proved particularly prone to conflict as the procedures to settle such cases were not clearly defined.[104] Once again these quandaries point to the standardisation of procedures and to processes of rulemaking, which steadily solidified in the first two decades of the Canal traffic. The shipping masters in charge of the troop transports often found that these procedures were taking too long and that the paperwork was too extensive. One captain complained that the paying and signing off of one 'sick native seaman' should not take more than half an hour. However, the consul retorted that this same captain had not treated his lascar with the humanity he deserved, as the seaman had been ill with diarrhoea (later diagnosed as typhoid fever). The consul pointed out that this same captain should have brought him in a cab and the vice consul would have sent him on to the hospital, writing on the form 'too ill to sign'. Referring to the racism with which captains were treating their subordinates, the consul stated that it was 'immaterial whether Khoozoo was an Englishman, a foreigner, or a "nativer"'. Also it was not important how much he was earning. The consul, went on to note, with astonishment, that, unlike other captains, the captain had not expressed a word of sympathy for his dying seaman. To him Khoozoo was merely 'one sick native seaman who has as wages six shillings and sixpence'.[105] Money was not completely beyond the consul however, who took care to note that the seaman who died that very night had caused an expense of over 4 pounds to the Board of Trade of the Government of

---

[103] TNA, FO 78/3702, sheets 106f.: Report Consulate Port Said to Sir Evelyn Baring, Port Said, 31 January 1884.

[104] TNA, FO 78/5036: Consul Cameron to Marquis of Salisbury, Port Said, 29 June 1899.

[105] TNA, FO 78/4963: Cameron to Salisbury, Memorandum dealing with a protest made against this Consulate by Mr. Wilfried H. Dulcken, Royal Naval Reserve, Master SS *Clan Robertson*, 30 October 1898.

India. The reference to the speed or slowness of the bureaucratic procedures at Port Said also points to the value of time in the acceleration and
deceleration of global mobility. What is more the treatment of Khoozoo
also points to the different value of mobile people intersecting in the Suez
Canal Region.

There were other occasions where the seamen themselves complained
about the treatment they received on board. In October 1898, the lascar,
Abdul-Hákim, jumped into the Canal and was rescued from drowning by
some boatmen. When brought to the police at Ismailia and then sent on to
Port Said, he criticised the treatment he had received from the overseer (or
Serang). He was sent back to Calcutta after 10 days 'having cost the
Government £ 1–19–6' with the consulate furthermore asking for a reward
for his rescuers.[106] Just as in the case of troop transportations, some problems on board thus had to be dealt with on land, such as disease, mutiny, or
if seamen ran into trouble during an outing at Port Said.

The court proceedings of the British consulate form a particularly
valuable source on the misbehaviour of seamen – both of the Navy and
the shipping companies – at Port Said. They are teeming with cases of
sailors convicted for drunkenness, unwillingness to work after a night out
in Port Said and other forms of licentious behaviour. The cases where
seamen of different origins, Maltese, South Asian, or Adenese, fell ill or
got into trouble, are particularly interesting, as they show how the competing sovereignties of the shipping companies and the captains, the
consulates as representatives not only of European states but also of global
empires, and finally Egypt as the territorial power, played out. Sometimes
the crime that was tried at the court consisted of violent behaviour on
board or fights with Greeks or Arabs in Port Said.[107] In other, very
frequent, cases the charge was desertion or refusal to work.[108] On rare
occasions, the seamen could cause the ship to miss its slot and thus create
a significant delay.[109] The refusal to work could take very different forms,
such as the simple wearing of female dress in the case of a Maltese seaman,
who argued that it was the day of carnival in Malta – he was subsequently
sentenced to 14 days' imprisonment. Others insulted their superiors or

---

[106] Ibid.; for a similar case see TNA, FO 78/5036: Draft Consul Cameron, 12 June 1899.
[107] See TNA, FO 846/3: Hadji Mahmoud v. A. Mitrovich, Charge of assault committed on
the evening of the 14th instant at the entrance to the Jardin Oriental on the Place de
Lesseps, 17 June 1875.
[108] See, for example, TNA, FO 846/3: 9 July 1874, 2.30 p.m. Harry Cook and Joseph Rosul
(?) charged with 'having deserted at the Port from the *SS Titan* on the 7th instant'; TNA,
FO 846/4: 22 February 1877, James W. Woods Master of *SS Kater*, of Whitley v. John
Lucas, Fireman. On drunkenness and refusal to do the work.
[109] TNA, FO 846/5, sheet 167: 18 April 1883 – four seamen charged with 'drunkenness and
wilful disobedience to lawful commands' cause detention of the ship.

other officials, using 'foul and abusive language' or 'striking and threatening several of the crew'.[110]

As the proceedings became more formalised, the standard phrasing of the offence was 'wilful disobedience to lawful commands'.[111] This was the case for a certain Richard Ruperty who had, according to his master, called him a 'son of a whore' and a 'god damned son of bitch' and threatened to stab him with a knife. Consequently (although he claimed to remember nothing) he was sentenced to eight weeks' imprisonment and costs.[112] In another case, seven seamen stated that they would rather go to prison than to go back on board and subsequently received a sentence of two months.[113] Many of the seamen appearing in court had British names, yet there were also lascars, such as Mohammed Nassim, who in August 1881 was charged with insolent behaviour and received one month in prison.[114]

The accused were almost invariably pronounced guilty, their sentences ranged from three days to two months, but the length of the conviction did not follow any recognisable pattern. On occasion a ship could not leave in time because of such problems of disobedience. In order to avoid compromising the times of departure, often those found guilty were only imprisoned until the ship was bound to leave Port Said and then had to pay an additional fine.[115] On other occasions, however, the mere use of insulting and threatening language could lead to five weeks' imprisonment.[116]

Even if we often only find out about seamen's experiences once they are in the hands of officials and if this legal material has to be reviewed very critically, the plethora of cases allows us to get a glimpse of the lives of seamen and their self-characterisations. What is more, it gives us details of the rulebreaking (in contrast to the difficult rulemaking highlighted in the preceding chapter) so often associated with the town of Port Said stereotyped as a space of disorder. Besides illustrating the hierarchy on board, and in turn the insubordination of seamen on the shore, the British (and French) consular court proceedings provide us with a clearer insight into the working conditions of seamen through individual cases, such as that of Joseph Zarar,

---

[110] See TNA, FO 846/4: sheets 5f., 12 February 1877; sheet 70, 30 January 1878; sheet 74, 25 March 1878. In more than one case the seamen stated that they did not remember what they had done as they had been drunk.

[111] See TNA, FO 846/5: sheet 13, 22 June 1881; sheet 24, 21 July 1881; sheet 39, 25 October 1881 and other cases.

[112] Ibid., sheet 189, 4 June 1883.

[113] Ibid., sheet 40, 25 October 1881. Sometimes, the seamen also complained about the food – see, for example, TNA, FO 846/5: sheet 57, 11 March 1882.

[114] Ibid., sheet 35, 9 August 1881.   [115] Ibid., sheet 99, 25 September 1882.

[116] Ibid., sheet 97, 11 September 1882.

a trimmer on board the *Jersey City* bound from Port Said to Java who died after the chief engineer had forced him back to work.[117]

This wealth of individual stories provides us with a clear picture of the unequal treatment that many lascars received on board. Their stories shed light on the differentiation and complexity of hierarchies, which did not exhaust itself in a mere division between Europeans and non-Europeans but included the differentiation of the stokers regarding their origin, for instance, or the special position of middlemen, negotiating between the European companies and their workers who also generally came from similar backgrounds. Racial categories and the position one occupied in an imperial hierarchy thus often corresponded with one another, yet in detailed and complex ways.

While the coal heavers and Canal workers connected the Canal Zone to the Levant region, seamen with their particularly global biographies related Port Said once again to the wider world. They contributed a large section of Port Said's transient and at times unruly population and made the town's role as a relay between the rules of the land and the rules of the sea most palpable. In *Heart of Darkness*, Joseph Conrad wrote that 'most seamen lead, if one may so express it, a sedentary life. Their minds are of the stay-at-home order, and their home is always with them – the ship; and so is their country – the sea'.[118] Taking Conrad's expression further, the harbour, this hinge between the land and the sea, was thus the space where seamen were most 'mobile'; it was also where the hierarchies of their home, the ship on the sea, ceased to be in force.

Port Said itself, as a private-interest governed space, dominated by international companies, did not, however, extensively profit from its geographical position. The busy harbour life and the constant passage of ships leaving for every imaginable destination did not mean that much profit remained once the steamers had departed. Even if the events of 1882 had integrated Port Said and the Canal Zone into the broader narrative of Egyptian history, the town was much more intricately connected to the European, Asian, African and Australian destinations it was serving than to Egypt itself.[119] After the introduction of night traffic on the Canal, the economic problems actually increased. The *Phare de Port-Saïd et du canal de Suez*, underlining that Port Said occupied a 'geographically privileged situation' concluded that 'electric light has carried a terrible blow to commerce which is now sluggish'.[120] If technological progress had led to the creation of Port Said, it had now reduced its economic opportunities.

[117] Ibid.: sheet 113, 30 September 1882.   [118] Conrad, *Heart of Darkness*, p. 5.
[119] Modelski, *Port Said Revisited*, p. 57.
[120] ANMT, 1995060/1524: *Le phare de Port-Saïd et du canal de Suez*, 27 June 1888.

The examples given above highlight not only the reliance on private companies for crucial services and their increasing competition (occasionally decided by the quality of the food that was served) but also the commercial basis for imperial rule. The Canal's position as an infrastructural relay, however, did not depend on its commercial success or failure alone, but consisted, for instance, in efficient coaling and transhipment and in the security of politically salient information (such as the shifting of troops) dispersed from this location. Furthermore, the three cases of global workforces mentioned show the intricacies of a global infrastructural relay station where the rules of private companies and of the outlets of governments had to be brought into line. What is more, the differentiation between various mobilities, often concentrated on one and the same steamship, became particularly obvious here, showing for instance that the mobility of workers or seamen did not mean free movement, but was often highly regulated.

Such a relay station was also particularly easily vulnerable to disruption. On the part of individual seamen, refusals to work were recurrent, and Canal and coal workers made frequent use of this disruptibility with strike movements radiating far beyond the location itself and bringing the Canal as a zone of acceleration (for instance when it came to the speed of coal-heaving) but also of possible deceleration further into relief. If the Canal became a space of standardisation and rulemaking on a global scale, it also became a locale of collective or individual rulebreaking. As a response, companies either opted for forced mobility (repatriating striking Greek workers for instance, some of whom had perhaps never lived in Greece proper) or forced non-mobility (as in the case of the frequent arrests of seamen) adding further political uses of mobility to those reviewed in earlier chapters.

These reactions also pointed to the fact that, at this location, several hierarchies interacted and sometimes collided – most explicitly the hierarchies of the ship and those of the Canal Company, which became obvious when pilots were taking command on board or when middlemen were necessary for the hiring of indigenous workers. Yet ideas of the racial hierarchies of workers and seamen, and of the categorisation of mobility along those lines, overarched these conflicts between the rules of the sea and the rules of the land. These ideologies were also deeply engrained in the vision of a civilising mission, a concept that will be further explored in the second part of this book.

Part II

Frontier of the civilising mission: mobility regulation east of Suez 1880s–1900s

4 Bedouin and caravans

Der Menschengeist, der sich erhoben,
Bleibt nicht am Wüstenthore steh'n.
Da wo jetzt mühsam Karawanen
Die sandverwehten Straßen zieh'n,
Wird einstens stolz auf ehrnen Bahnen
Das Dampfroß seine Funken sprüh'n.
Da wo jetzt Sklavenketten klirren,
Wo Stumpfsinn herrscht und Grausamkeit,
Wird einst der Aar der Freiheit schwirren
Zum Morgenroth der neuen Zeit.[1]

Indigenous seamen on board the ships and coal heavers in Port Said provided European travellers with glimpses of the 'exotic'. Much less than contact or encounter, these perceptions often served to reinforce stereotypes rather than to challenge them. While both seamen and coal heavers formed an essential component of the imperial transportation nexus, the construction of the Suez Canal also engendered intersections with other mobilities that were not part and parcel of the Europeans' own movement. Bedouin and caravans could be spotted on the banks both of the Canal and the Red Sea, traditional dhows roamed between the African and Arabian coasts and pilgrims made their way to Mecca using a variety of vehicles for their strenuous journeys. While the focus of interest in Part I was the establishment of the Canal system, Part II emphasises interactions with other pre-existing desert and Red Sea mobilities. It explores the 'civilising mission' as it came to the fore between the 1880s and the 1900s when the period of experimentation in the Suez Canal proper had ebbed and its operations had been standardised.[2] Of course, the civilising mission was part of the

---

[1] Manzotti, Marenço and Stoltze, *Excelsior*, p. 42: 'The human spirit which has raised itself / Does not remain at the desert's gate. / Where caravans now arduously / Toil along roads covered with sand drifts / One day the iron horse / Will proudly spray sparks on the brazen tracks. / Where the chains of slaves now rattle, / Where apathy and cruelty rule / The eagle of freedom will one day soar / At the dawn of a new era.'
[2] See Barth and Osterhammel, *Zivilisierungsmissionen*, esp. pp. 363–425.

original Canal project, as surveyed in the introduction. Yet toward the turn of the century, channelling mobility came to mean more than attempts at standardisation down to the minute level of measuring units or the regulation of traffic with the aim of keeping certain movements free from obstruction, as seen in the first part of the book. It touched upon the distinction between 'modern' or 'civilised' and 'outdated' or 'traditional' mobilities and upon the question of the acceleration and deceleration of different forms of movement.

This connection between acceleration and deceleration can be demonstrated at global level as well as locally. The new infrastructures and the spatial rearrangements that went with them meant that certain regions were excluded from the business of mobility. In the case of the Suez Canal, the obvious example would be the route around the Cape of Good Hope, first charted by Vasco da Gama in 1497, and for some 270 years the main highway between Europe and Asia. The cities of Durban and Cape Town saw some decline following the opening of the Canal. The re-routing of global movements thus also necessarily disconnected other parts of the world.[3]

This simultaneous acceleration and deceleration also took place in the Canal itself or in close proximity to it. All three chapters of this part take a larger perspective moving at times east of Suez to the Hijaz or the Red Sea and then coming back to the Canal. In this manner they can show how the margin of civilisation was conceptualised as a moveable frontier, to be pushed eastwards from Suez. At the same time, the examples introduced in the following chapters also point to the ambivalences and internal contradictions of the civilising mission, which often, and somewhat paradoxically, relied on the very mobilities deemed backward and traditional. In the perception of European observers, the introduction of regular steamer lines into the Red Sea and the building of the Canal itself led to the juxtaposition of two ways of life, namely 'desert life' and 'industrial life'. These commentators often interpreted the former as timeless and unchanging, with the latter representing progress and advancement. The simultaneity of these two modes was something that many travellers commented on. After all, the Canal provided a comfortable environment for the consumption of one's very own vision of the desert, while sipping a cold drink on board the steamer. Frequently, their observations were phrased in the dialectic of civilisation and its absence, which was often coupled with a derogatory view on this 'outdated way of life'. But there were other attitudes as well, such as romantic idealisation of the desert, or an attempt to adopt a scientific approach to it.

---

[3] See Osterhammel and Petersson, *Geschichte der Globalisierung*, pp. 24, 41.

These different European approaches towards desert life also found their way into politics. In the following, such relationships between desert and Canal mobilities will come under scrutiny, tracing attempts to establish and increase 'modern' networks of control and supervision, and showing that the redirection of world traffic through the Egyptian desert and the Red Sea could also have a more indirect impact, such as growing interactions, new conflicts and attempts by various governments to strengthen their hold and control. At the same time, in order to set up new patterns of control, reliance on the specific skills and routes of desert dwellers often proved essential. Despite frequent comments by observers and despite the new restrictions and controls it faced, 'desert mobility' thus did not represent 'a bygone age' after all. The chapter moves – after introducing the role of the desert and its inhabitants in contemporary and often schematic European discourses on civilisation – to the deceleration of desert mobilities due to the Canal, to the growing governmental interference and to the resistance to this deceleration (both in close proximity to the Canal and further east of Suez). It then looks at those moments where the acceleration of Canal mobility relied on desert mobility, drawing out the tension between the hampering of movements, the resilience of 'traditional' forms of mobility and the reliance on 'traditional' skills.

Civilising mission

By the end of the nineteenth century, European engagement with arid regions had a long history.[4] Before the opening of the Canal, however, travellers had to make a concerted effort to be able to observe life in dry lands in person. The journey through the Canal allowed a glimpse of the desert from the steamer without any of this previous struggle, or without even having intended to see it at all. Instead, a view of the desert came as a supplement to every transcontinental ticket; Indologist Paul Deussen even witnessed a genuine Fata Morgana of a city floating over a lake while travelling on the Canal.[5] Three attitudes can be distinguished here: some reacted with a romantic fascination with one particular form of desert dwelling, i.e. nomadic life, equating it with ultimate freedom, which was explicitly contrasted with Western civilisation and all of its constraints; others adopted a specifically scientific or anthropological view and ventured to catalogue this 'exotic' form of life with all its specificities; others still voiced disgust or contempt.

---

[4] See, for example, Carruthers, *The Desert Route in India*.
[5] Deussen, *Erinnerungen an Indien*, p. 236.

Despising desert mobility

Even if all these attitudes towards the 'desert' were connected with the rhetoric of the civilising mission in one way or another, it was the most critical approach where this mission became most apparent. The language of late nineteenth-century believers in progress was obviously not one of civilisation approaching its limit, as the expression 'frontier of civilisation' chosen for this part of the book might imply; it was rather committed to a vision of linear progress and modernisation. The idea of 'uplifting mankind' was essentially temporal: those who were backward should rapidly be brought up to date.[6] However this idea also encompassed a spatial facet, as civilising missions did not only progress through time, but also carried the vision of an advance through space. It included the concept of a progressing frontier of civilisation, which delineated 'civilised' and 'uncivilised' forms of life and, in the case of the Suez Canal, crystallised into an interface between 'civilised' and 'uncivilised' forms of mobility.

Western European theatregoers had been introduced to the Suez Canal's participation in this endeavour of civilisation's spatial advance through the ballet *Excelsior* quoted at the beginning of this chapter. The Italian choreographer Luigi Manzotti's *Excelsior* was performed first in Milan in 1881, then moved to other European cities such as London in 1885 and to Frankfurt in 1891 on the occasion of the International Electro-Technical Exhibition. The ballet's plot tells the success story of civilisation at its best. It is the tale of a duel between the demon of darkness and the genius of light that helps progress and civilisation to their final victory. The first scenes take place in Europe featuring the invention of the steamship, the railway, electricity and the phonograph with each example highlighting the shrinking of space through the advance of technology. On every occasion, the demon of darkness attempts to impede the accomplishment of the new invention, yet at the last moment the genius of light always prevails.

The seventh scene finally ventures outside of Europe. Suddenly, the spectators find themselves transported to the desert, where the demon of darkness exclaims with firm conviction and with extreme pathos that here nature has piled up a wall that the genius of light will never storm, that this is the final boundary of culture, beyond which only violence and avidity rule.[7] The demon continues to praise the desert as the 'boundary of

---

[6] For Roosevelt's quote of 1899, see Osterhammel, "'The Great Work of Uplifting Mankind'", p. 363.

[7] Manzotti, Marenço and Stoltze, *Excelsior*, p. 41.

culture' and therefore as the final stronghold of his power: this is the territory where civilisation will never make any inroads. In the last part of his monologue he points to the indivisibility of civilisation, science and transportation. No explorer shall ever travel through these lands, no steamer shall disturb their silence and the railway shall never be carried to the 'dark continent'.[8]

Civilisation thus ends where steam transportation cannot enter – the desert is the ultimate frontier. However, as suspected, the genius of light – as a *deus ex machina* – intervenes and declares that the demon is mistaken; the transportation revolution will not stop at the edge of the desert and will conquer the 'dark continent' too. Soon the railway will replace the painfully slowly travelling caravans. Together with this technological advance, the personified freedom will liberate all slaves and herald a new era.[9] At this moment of the genius's declaration, the clouds part and the Suez Canal appears filled with the ships of all nations. Slaves are freed and civilisation, in the allegory of a young woman, is courted by England, China, Turkey and Spain, but does not want to belong to one single nation. A celebration follows, standing for the unification of all peoples through the connection afforded by transportation.

Clearly this culminating scene of *Excelsior* mirrors the vision of the Canal as a great unifier, propagated by the Saint-Simonians and by the official rhetoric of the Canal builders. In this interpretation, the Suez Canal is depicted as the outpost of civilisation, connected with the linear vision of unstoppable and irreversible progress, a vision present in the minds of many western travellers venturing on their journeys. The caravan, once the only possibility to cross the desert, now became an example of technological backwardness; the advance of civilisation in turn was equated with the expansive penetration of non-European spaces with European technology.[10]

Until the eighteenth century, the caravan was regarded as a complex form of social organisation and as a remarkable method of covering huge distances in a more or less controlled manner.[11] However, in the eyes of the authors of *Excelsior*, and most western beholders passing through the Suez Canal, this reputation had undoubtedly changed. The lack of spatial definition connected with nomadic life became a primary marker of backwardness for European intellectuals, such as Georg Simmel who

---

[8] Ibid., pp. 41–2.   [9] Ibid., p. 42; see also Brantlinger, 'Victorians and Africans'.
[10] See Austen, *Trans-Saharan Africa in World History*, pp. 118–38.
[11] See, for instance, Osterhammel, *Die Entzauberung Asiens*, pp. 123–4.

distinguished between the traffic linking western cities and the 'restless nomadic movement' of 'primitive' groups.[12]

Some observers literally abhorred the Bedouin and their apparent uncontrollable way of life. Kipling named the colonial officials constantly moving between Europe and Asia the 'gypsies of the East', yet most western travellers took great care to distinguish their travelling from nomadic or even 'gypsy-like' mobility.[13] In contrast to those venturing into the desert on expeditions and the like, one did not need to know how to ride a camel, find water or generally survive in the desert when standing behind the railings of a steamer. The observer and the desert, with all its presumed dangers, were in close proximity, but at the same time an unbridgeable gulf remained between them, not unlike that between a lion and a visitor to the zoo. For these travellers, the Canal was not a 'contact zone'; it was rather a zone of distancing, as Mary French Sheldon, an American explorer, exemplified in her travel narrative.[14] Her judgment from the steamer is an apt illustration of western arrogance and is worth quoting in detail:

We pass an Arab camel caravan, and for the first time saw women unveiled. One woman, whom I was scanning through my field glasses, prior to taking a snap-shot, glared at me, and with precipitation jerked up from the banks in her arms a quaint-looking little dog, cast a defiant glance towards me, as she discovered that she was the object of my observation, and tossed the little pet upon a camel's back into a saddle made like a nest with rugs and blankets, and covered it from my *evil eye*. This act accomplished, she rushed to the water's edge and followed the course of the slow-moving steamer, imprecated and railed at me in the most vehement manner – about what? – ah! ask the Arabs who heard. This caravan was bound for the Holy Land, and a set of more villainous-appearing land sharks I never beheld. Unclean, utterly miserable, degraded beings, knowing only a migratory life, in common with their camels and their vermin, devoid of principle, eking out a questionable existence by cunning, extortion, and mendicancy.[15]

The Canal, the steamer, the camera – powerful symbols of western technology and progress – are contrasted with the desert, the veil and the caravan itself, attributes connected to two forms of life described as utterly incompatible, but still encountering each other for a brief moment in the Suez Canal Zone. Mary French Sheldon distinguished the two modes of mobility – her own and that of the caravan – in a telling way. Often Western civilisation was described as mobile and progressive and the 'Orient' as immobile and stagnant, but for her, it seemed to be the other way around. She depicted herself almost as sedentary while the

---

[12] Simmel, 'Soziologie des Raumes (1903)', p. 230.
[13] Kipling, 'The Exiles Line' in *Rudyard Kipling's Verse*, p. 189.
[14] For the concept of the 'contact zone', see Pratt, *Imperial Eyes*, pp. 6–7
[15] French Sheldon, *Sultan to Sultan*, pp. 28–9.

objects of her observation knew 'only a migratory life'. Her perspective reminds us of Claude Lévi-Strauss' observation during his first journey to Latin America when he noted that being on a big ship 'was the opposite of "travel", in that the ship seemed to us not so much a means of transport as a place of residence, a home, in fact, before which Nature put on a new show every morning'.[16] Mary French Sheldon – on the Canal, on board a steamer, with a camera in hand – was on her own ground and it was the passing caravan that represented a strange and alien object. Her statements show clearly that mobility and modernity or civilisation were not always connected, on the contrary, a 'migratory life' of constant movement could also be understood as a sign of backwardness.

Science and classification

Although fashioning herself as scientific explorer, Mary French Sheldon did not bother to leave the ship, and was far from using any scientific vocabulary in her judgment of the caravan. Yet in the second half of the nineteenth century, there developed an emphatically scientific or anthropological perspective towards the different desert tribes. This ethnographic interest was in line with a more general trend towards recording and classification, based on the physiognomy of the observed – with methods such as measurements of skull, nose or height for example – on their geographical origins or on their historical trajectories.[17] In his 'Études sur le folklore Bédouin de l'Egypte', published in 1911 in the journal of the Egyptian Geographical Society, the ethnographer and author Ernst Klippel, for instance, provided a meticulous classification of the different groups and subgroups of Bedouin roaming the Egyptian territory, creating a list of 87 tribes in the Sinai region alone.[18]

This classificatory attempt also filtered through to representations designated for tourists. Many of those travellers who noted their impressions of Port Said stressed the variety of people they encountered; one even called it an 'ethnological museum'.[19] With numerous postcards featuring 'natives', some depictions went into considerable detail in their interest in classification. A map of the Suez Canal (Figure 11) included – besides different views of the Canal and its shore and portraits of

---

[16] Quoted in Cresswell, 'Introduction: Theorizing Place', p. 13.
[17] See, for example, Chantre, *Recherches anthropologiques dans l'Afrique Orientale*; Weill, *La presqu'île du Sinai*; Schwally, *Beiträge zur Kenntnis des Lebens der mohammedanischen Städter*.
[18] Klippel, 'Etudes sur le folklore Bédouin de l'Egypte'. On the Egyptian Geographical Society, Fogel, *Une société savante entre deux mondes*.
[19] See quote by Lala Baijnath on p. 46 above.

Figure 11 Map and photographs by Hippolyte Arnoux, details by the author.

Muhammad ʿAli, Saʿid, Ismaʿil, Tawfiq and Ferdinand de Lesseps – 12 images of different characters or 'types' found in the Canal Region with explicit reference to their supposedly distinct physiognomies. Next to several sheikhs and different categories of women, the collection presented four Bedouin from Mount Sinai, the region around Petra in today's Jordan, the ʿAtaqa mountains and Moses' Wells (both near Suez) with their alleged attires and weapons.

Romanticisation

Ethnographer Ernst Klippel did not limit himself to scientific categorisation however. He made no secret of his fascination with the desert and its inhabitants and even immersed himself in Bedouin life. After having lived in Cairo for 15 years as a conservationist, studying Arabic and spending weeks with the Bedouin, he travelled the deserts, pretending to be the son of a sheikh.[20] When he took the ship between Port Said and Beirut, prior to joining the Damascus caravan, he was exhilarated by the attention that he received from his fellow passengers. Especially the Greek, Italian, French and English ladies were ready to pamper the 'pretend' Bedouin.[21] Besides pointing to the fact that some Europeans readily perceived and treated the desert dwellers like children, Klippel also stressed the peculiarity of a 'seafaring Bedouin', a personification of two forms of mobility that were normally strictly separate.

Klippel was not the only one to travel in disguise with the Bedouin even if he took his engagement particularly far. There was an enduring fascination with the supposedly uncontrolled mobility of nomadic lifestyles, which, in opposition to the 'civilised world', maintained the association of unbound freedom. Notable Bedouin companions included Lady Hester Stanhope, Jane Digby and the famous Mecca traveller, Richard Burton.[22] Even among those who abstained from closer relationships with the Bedouin, a similar fascination for the freedom of the Bedouin lifestyle often endured, with travellers entirely sympathetic to the rejection of Bedouin to be forced under the 'yoke of the respectable, taxpaying, sermon-listening sedentariness'.[23] Regardless of earlier adventures with her husband Richard Burton, Isabel Burton still cherished the comfortable Canal journey. After a very positive account of the Canal as the last link in the 'great belt of trade' that held the modern world together, she expressed her delight about 'smelling the desert life' which reminded her of her old, adventurous life. When they reached al-Qantara she noted:

The scene is that of all Eastern pictures – the Nizam regular soldiers, and negroes, Bedawin draped in usual cloak and *kuffiyyeh*, and women in blue garments, not changed a hair since the day of Abraham, except that they now carry matchlocks instead of spears. ... A seedy *dahabiyyeh* rolls past us; it is a craft belonging to a bygone age and is hustled out of the way by the fussy high-pressure *mouche*, which carries the daily mails to Ismailiyyah. This was the pleasantest two days

---

[20] Klippel, *Wanderungen im Heiligen Lande*, p. vi.
[21] Klippel, *Unter Drusen, Kurden und Teufelsanbetern*, p. 10. See also Klippel, *Als Beduine zu den Teufelsanbetern*.
[22] See Simmons, *Passionate Pilgrims*; Ure, *In Search of Nomads*.
[23] See, for example, Budde, *Erfahrungen eines Hadschi*, p. 199.

imaginable, – like a river picnic; we read, wrote and lounged on the bridge, glass in hand, with the captain and the surly Maltese pilot.[24]

Despite her self-image as a hardy traveller of the desert, and contrary to those who found the Canal passage dull and boring, Isabel Burton seemed to enjoy the consumption of the stage-like scenery from the deck of the ship tremendously. Although the two women came to very different conclusions, like Mary French Sheldon, she looked at the panorama almost as if it were a painting or a postcard slowly passing through a picture frame.

Canal time and desert time

The three different approaches outlined above – contempt, classification and romanticisation – converged in one important facet: many of the travellers conceived their journey not only as a journey through space, but also as a journey through time. Isabel Burton referred twice to the different ages of her steamer and the people and modes of transportation she saw. She noted that the clothes of the Bedouin had not changed since 'the day of Abraham' – a reference to the unchanging nature of Bedouin life that was backed by anthropological and ethnographic publications of the time. On the Canal itself another encounter was even more directly couched in notions of temporal progress, as the small steamer carrying the mail to Ismailia outran a traditional sailing boat. Many other travel descriptions used the imagery of the static Orient and juxtaposed it with the acceleration brought about by steam navigation and the Canal. Again and again the desert was depicted as eternally unchanging.[25] Reverend John Henry Barrows, for instance, referred, just like Burton, to the biblical heritage of the region and imagined how surprised Joseph would have been to see the huge steamers (which were apparently carrying wheat to relieve the famine in India and were thus themselves part of the 'civilising mission') moving through the desert landscape.[26]

However, not everyone perceived the Canal as the epitome of novelty in an ancient landscape. As the famous surgeon Sir Frederick Treves made his way through the Canal, he restricted his version of time travel not just to the dichotomy of 'old desert' and 'new steamer', but took the Canal, the telegraph posts and the dredgers with workers from all around the Mediterranean, in short the entire artificial setting, back thousands of

---

[24] Burton, *A. E. I. Arabia Egypt India*, p. 66.
[25] See for instance Bourde, *De Paris au Tonkin*, p. 19.
[26] Barrows, *A World-Pilgrimage*, p. 316; see also OIOC, IOR, Mss Eur/C739: Letter from John Wilberforce Cassels on his way to India, November or December 1879; or the scene on the Canal in David Lean's film *Lawrence of Arabia* (1962).

years. For him, the Canal landscape looked just like the earth at the beginning of its very existence and the Canal itself did not appear artificial but rather like 'the first stream which trickled across the still warm earth'.[27]

Others retained the rhetoric of the civilising mission, concluding that the inhabitants of the shores of the Canal were ready for change. The American doctor, theosophist and spiritualist, James Martin Peebles, thought that the Arabs he saw had already lost their idyllic, prehistoric condition and were now 'the degenerate sons of Araby's better days' whose 'golden age' had passed. Suez did not appeal to him at all and he concluded that it was not astonishing that the Israelites had wanted to settle elsewhere. In line with the rhetoric of the civilising mission, he then credited de Lesseps for the fact that Egypt was now 'waking from the dreamy slumbers of weary centuries'. To him there was nothing romantic about the desert at all and he recommended an irrigation effort to transform it into arable land.[28]

In a similar vein, Père Charmetant, the French missionary on his way from Algiers to Zanzibar, was disenchanted by the boring Canal, but to an equal degree by the life on its coasts that consisted of a lone cameleer who had to restrain his animal after it had been frightened by the huge steamer (once again pointing to the clash of different forms of mobility) and some huts on the Canal's rim in the desert where a small number of Europeans lived just like Robinson Crusoe on his island. Like Isabel Burton, Charmetant pointed to the contrast between the two incompatible modes of conveyance, the camel and the machine, with the former being frightened by the simple passage of the latter. Also, by comparing the Canal workers to Robinson Crusoe, he likened the desert to uninhabited and uninhabitable terrain, thus deciding to ignore the life he actually encountered there. In the next breath – and in contrast to others who argued that the life of the Bedouin represented true freedom – he claimed that the Arabs would not want to live in this prison of sand and stones if they could choose otherwise. Rather than unbound freedom, in this view the desert came to represent the greatest possible confinement.[29]

In line with the more romantic vision of 'desert life', others pointed to the disruptive nature of western intervention and charged it with the 'degeneration' of the desert dwellers. As seen above, for Frederick Treves the Canal might have appeared ancient, but Port Said represented a new creation. Treves repeated the familiar story of Port Said as meeting

---

[27] Treves, *The Other Side of the Lantern*, p. 20.
[28] Peebles, *Around the World*, pp. 266, 269, 270.
[29] Charmetant, *D'Alger à Zanzibar*, pp. 12–13. See also McMahon, *A Journey with the Sun Around the World*, p. 175.

place of east and west, but with a remarkable twist: here the 'man from the desert' was drawn near 'Western civilisation' where he expected some benevolent uplifting, but on the contrary was degraded to a drunkard and coal heaver: 'The blessings of civilisation come to him in the guise of tinned meat, gin, and coal carrying, and he obtains doubtful advantage from these means of grace.'[30] For Treves, the civilising mission thus did not mean, as for many, linear progress, but rather linear degradation.

Whether travellers described the developments in the Suez Canal Zone in terms of linear progression to modernity, or in terms of the simultaneous existence of different eras, time was as recurrent a category as space, even making it into the travel guides: the Suez Canal itself was all about timetabling and avoiding delays. Even if it was often also associated with an unexpected and at times nerve-wracking slowness of movement, the Canal time was contrasted with the time of the population surrounding it, because, according to the 1898 Baedeker, one of the characteristic traits of the 'natives' was their alleged incapability of valuing time.[31] The juxtaposition of different mobilities, speeds and (alleged or actual) estimations of time pointed to the fact that – unlike Manzotti's ballet suggested – one form of mobility did not fully replace the other, but rather entered into a multi-layered coexistence. Consequently, the impact of the Canal traffic upon the arid regions surrounding it and the persistence of alternative modes of living deserve additional scrutiny.

Deceleration of 'desert mobilities'

If all three attitudes sketched out above connected the idea that caravans and Bedouin belonged to a bygone age, it is worth investigating the actual relationship between western influence, represented by the Canal, and the forms of mobility to be found on its shores. As will be seen in the next two sections, the new Canal did significantly restrict life on its shores, yet their relationship was of course more complex than a simple replacement of old ways of life with modern. It was marked by an awkward coexistence, resentments about dwindling opportunities and resistance to penetration. In what follows we will use different scales to investigate this deceleration of desert mobilities and the reactions to it, looking at the place on the Canal where the two modes of mobility intersected most closely at al-Qantara, at the Sinai and at the Hijaz where different attempts to make the arid regions governable – through scientific classification, political organisation and faster information transfer – became particularly visible.

[30] Treves, *The Other Side of the Lantern*, p. 15.
[31] Baedeker, *Egypt: Handbook for Travellers* (1898), p. xl.

The intersection of two global routes at al-Qantara

Contrary to the expectations of proponents of the civilising mission, brought to life in the ballet *Excelsior*, the new means of transportation did not totally replace older ones, but it did significantly hamper Bedouin mobility and slow down caravan trajectories.[32] The intersection of the land-based and the maritime routes was most conspicuous at al-Qantara, the point where the Suez Canal cut through the old caravan route between Cairo and Damascus (see Figure 2). To guarantee the continuation of the caravan a simple ferry service was installed which became the main crossing point.[33] The archives do not yield any extensive information as to how the crossing was organised; photographs give a clearer idea of the procedure as well as of the persons and animals that were ferried across.

In the photographs below (Figures 12 and 13), which illustrate the junction of the two world routes so vividly, the size of the caravans pictured crossing the Canal looks rather paltry, although the number of the animals shuttled across was still given as ranging from 100,000 animals in the first six months of 1864 to about 20,000 in 1869.[34] Even if the traversing caravan was steadily reduced in size, it still emblematically represented the boundary function of the Canal. Marius Fontane noted the Asiatic and African character of al-Qantara, which stood in contrast to the 'European' features of many other elements of the Canal.[35] He was joined by Ernst Klippel, who found the short journey in the pontoon only worth mentioning as it represented the passage between Asia and Africa.[36]

Despite the small size of the caravan, some were impressed by al-Qantara's geography of simultaneity, or stressed its continental scope as a passage between continents; others however lamented the decline of the caravan trade. In 1881, the adventurous Ludwig Salvator, Archduke of Austria, decided to venture along the old overland route between Egypt and Syria, which was replete with associations alluding to the journey of the Israelites and the flight of the Holy Family. This was easier said than done though, as the 'old highway, formerly so frequented by caravans, travellers, and pilgrims' was now 'deserted and forgotten'.[37] Salvator reported that even cattle-dealers now shipped their animals from the ports of Jaffa to

---

[32] See, for instance, Bourdon, 'Les "routes anciennes et les pistes"'.
[33] See Lewis, *Because I've Not Been There Before*, p. 26; Villiers-Stuart, *Egypt after the War*, p. 491.
[34] Bernard and Tissot, *Itinéraire pour l'isthme de Suez et les grandes villes d'Egypte*, p. 89; Fontane, *Voyage pittoresque*, p. 16.
[35] Fontane, *Voyage pittoresque*, p. 17.
[36] Klippel, *Als Beduine zu den Teufelsanbetern*, p. 25.
[37] Salvator, *The Caravan Route between Egypt and Syria*, p. viii.

Kantara. Kilomètre 45.

Bac des chameaux et navire en Transit.

Figure 12 'Al-Qantara Kilometre 45: Camel Ferry and Steamship in Transit', photograph by Hippolyte Arnoux.

Alexandria and only some camel-drivers were encountered on this 'once favourite route'. He therefore had to order a caravan of horses and mules from Jaffa to join him at al-Qantara and decided to travel there himself by boat. Once in the desert, the route from Egypt to Syria was now clearly marked by telegraph posts, which one simply had to follow and yet he 'soon began to enjoy that feeling of freedom which a boundless plain always inspires' while observing at the same time the large steamers 'majestically advancing to all appearance through a sea of sand'.[38] Henry Morton Stanley described al-Qantara, even more drastically than Ludwig Salvator, as a

[38] Ibid., pp. ix, 2.

Kantara. Kilomètre 44.

Pont des caravanes de Syrie.

Figure 13 'Al-Qantara Kilometre 44: Bridge for Syrian Caravans', photograph by Hippolyte Arnoux.

symbol of decline, because until recently the same spot had been the 'highway' of all caravans passing between Syria and Egypt. Before the opening of the Canal, cattle herds and 'long strings of camels bearing Egyptian and Syrian travellers' had passed this very location almost every day.[39] Thus for Salvator and Stanley, one world route clearly replaced another, even if one could wistfully try to recall the older one, as Salvator did.

Dwindling opportunities for desert dwellers

The simultaneity of desert and Canal made for striking impressions, even if the timelessness and immutability of 'desert life' were obviously largely

---

[39] Stanley, *My Early Travels and Adventures in America and Asia*, pp. 54–5.

fictitious. But the construction of the Suez Canal opened up new regions for some, and closed opportunities for movement for others. The caravan route between Egypt and Syria was cut in two; Bedouin territories were suddenly altogether inaccessible; certain trades, such as the supply of drinking water to Suez or the local organisation of pilgrim traffic had to adapt to the new conditions.

By the 1880s the structure of Egyptian society was still marked by a distinction between town dwellers, peasants (mainly living in proximity to the Nile or in the region of the Delta) and Bedouin tribes roaming the desert, but all three parts had undergone changes that predated the building of the Canal and the increasing European involvement in Egypt. It is certain that some areas of the country were more difficult to penetrate than others. Travellers' safety in the Sinai region, for instance, had time and time again been a source of concern.[40] Muhammad 'Ali had already attempted, albeit not too successfully, to bring the Bedouin tribes of the deserts and steppes and the Sinai Mountains under closer governmental control, not least in order to integrate them into military service and the fiscal system.[41] In line with colonial strategy elsewhere, the British occupational authorities opted for limited interference with the fabric of Egyptian society.[42] Nevertheless more and more Bedouin chose a sedentary lifestyle as the century came to a close.[43] In his study, Klippel gave the figure of 147,600 sedentary Bedouin in 1882 and contrasted it with 531,000 in 1897, attributing this development to the loss of income due to the transfer of the pilgrim traffic onto steamships and railways and to the incentives to settle since the reign of Muhammad 'Ali.[44]

Besides these reasons for abandoning nomadic life, there was of course a more broad-ranging reduction of opportunities that the caravan trade faced in the last decades of the nineteenth century. The discovery of the route around the Cape in the sixteenth century and the establishment of the Dutch and English East India Companies in the early seventeenth century had already had a destructive impact on the caravan trade.[45] The opening of the Canal led to the further weakening of the 'great desert route', since the transport of goods and the conveyance of pilgrims to

---

[40] On travel descriptions of the Sinai in the nineteenth century, see Rabinowitz, 'Themes in the Economy of the Bedouin of South Sinai'.

[41] See Tilt, *The Boat and the Caravan*, p. 229; Aharoni, *The Pasha's Bedouin*, pp. 186–207.

[42] Compare with more intense British involvement with Bedouin in the Mandate territories; see Falah, *The Role of the British Administration*, p. 3.

[43] This process also took place in other regions of the Middle East – see the contributions in Mundy and Musallam (eds.), *The Transformation of Nomadic Society in the Arab East*.

[44] Klippel, 'Etudes sur le Folklore Bédouin de l'Egypte', p. 19.

[45] Steensgard, *The Asian Trade Revolution of the Seventeenth Century*, p. 9.

Mecca shifted to large steamers. Formerly insignificant port cities began to flourish, with the caravan routes as well as the places connected to them going into decline. Gradually the importance of caravan centres was replaced by that of thriving port towns.[46]

Not only the caravans themselves but also those involved in supplying them with provisions and water at different stations or guarding the caravan during transit were affected by this decline. The small town of Suez was struck particularly severely. Many related the situation directly to increased foreign interference. In 1873, the British Consul at Suez, G. W. West, reported to the Secretary of State for Foreign Affairs that the 'natives' living on the shore of the Red Sea, including the population of Suez, saw themselves as being tied more closely to the Hijaz than to Egypt, that they showed respect to pilgrims and *ashrāf* only and that 'religious demonstrations caused by fanaticism' had been on the increase. Apart from the fresh water canal providing their town with potable water, the inhabitants of Suez felt that the recent developments had not benefited them but had led instead to increased taxation. The fact that the pilgrim traffic had now moved on board the steamers, rather than being led by inhabitants of Suez across the isthmus, which had been their most lucrative business, was especially painful and contributed to the perception of the 'advance of civilisation' as a set of inconveniences. Consul West went on to state that these innovations (including taxation, canals and steam naviga-tion) had undermined the initially positive feelings of the inhabitants of Suez towards foreigners and had led them to be more openly and more fanatically religious. In the rest of his report the consul, however, suddenly shied away from strong political statements and denied any political motive behind the reawakening of religion.[47] Even if the consul's report was certainly marked by his political mission as well as the expectations of the addressees, it still gives insight into the general perception that the Canal had brought disadvantages rather than progress to this part of the globe. It furthermore sheds light on the worries connected with religion and its anticolonial potential; a theme that will be explored further in Chapter 6.

Besides the declining opportunities for the Bedouin in the region of Suez, the Canal also cordoned off formerly contiguous territories on the African side of the isthmus that had belonged to the sphere of influence of specific Bedouin tribes.[48] In line with the civilising impetus, Isabel Burton assessed

[46] See Franck and Brownstone (eds.), *To the Ends of the Earth*, pp. 183–4; Rafeq, 'Damascus and the Pilgrim Caravan', pp. 130–43.
[47] TNA, FO 78/2288: Consul West to the Secretary of State for Foreign Affairs, Suez, 13 September 1873.
[48] Farnie, *East and West of Suez*, p. 148.

this result very positively, stating that the Canal – which according to her had also changed the climate, drawing a strong wind from the north carrying fogs and clouds – formed a 'grand line of defence on the Eastern frontier', specifically as a moat against the Bedouin.[49] Burton's geopolitical thinking might not have been alien to her period, but the idea that the Suez Canal represented a restriction of certain mobilities was certainly not part of the official rhetoric or the slogan, *Aperire Terram Gentibus*, on de Lesseps' statue. Yet it was true: the easing of mobility for a select few correlated with a restricted freedom of movement for others, as the example of those moving in the drylands surrounding the Canal made particularly obvious.

Resistance against European penetration on the Canal and east of Suez

In connection with the obstruction that the Canal system and European involvement more generally meant for the desert mobilities and, as mentioned in relation to the inclusion of Bedouin in the tax system, European penetration often encountered resistance. The romantic image of the Bedouin's freedom paralleled the perception of their uncontrollable nature. A few incidences clearly pinpointed the complicated relationship between Bedouin and the increased western presence in the regions 'east of Suez'. They also exemplified that desert mobility did not go into decline everywhere but sometimes stood up to the civilising mission. Where this desert mobility was perceived as a threat to western dominance it was nevertheless a very modern threat, as the Edward Henri Palmer murder case, described in some detail below, shows. This case furthermore illustrates the entanglement of imperial interests and scientific endeavours, which has already shone through in other sections of this chapter.

Several smaller conflicts also involved nomads. When the steamer *Meï Kong* of the *Messageries Maritimes* had an accident in 1877 close to Aden, for instance, it was reported that the hostile attitude of numerous 'natives' did not allow for any material to be saved.[50] Other events in closer proximity to the Canal corroborated the negative image of the Bedouin. In 1872 a certain Mr Perkins was found in the desert near Suez and died shortly after. Perkins had stayed for over two months in Suez, penniless and claiming that he was eventually bound for China. The circumstances of his death were so unclear that the investigation went up to the Secretary of State for Foreign Affairs, with the consul reassuring the Secretary that

---

[49] Burton, *A. E. I. Arabia Egypt India*, p. 65.
[50] Bois, *Le grand siècle des Messageries Maritimes*, p. 206.

the Mount Sinai Arabs did not usually 'ill use travellers' and that those roaming near Suez were 'of the most peaceful and unoffending nature'.[51]

Whereas the case of Perkins is illustrative of the fears and stereotypes attached to the Bedouin, there were other cases in which Bedouin involvement was undeniable. As early as 1869, the Orientalist Edward Henry Palmer undertook an expedition into the arid lands bordering the Suez Canal and came to very negative conclusions, criticising the widely held romantic image outlined above:

> I cannot expect respectable tax-paying Englishmen to enter with much appreciation into the Bedawín question, and I know the prejudice that exists, in this country particularly, against the extinction of a romantic and interesting race ... I must nevertheless state my belief that the 'noble savage' is a simple and unmitigated nuisance. To the Bedawí this applies even more forcibly still, for, wherever he goes, he brings with him ruin, violence, and neglect.[52]

After years of teaching as a professor in Cambridge, in 1882 Palmer ventured once again into the deserts of the Sinai. This time he travelled not with an academic but with a political mission to render some Bedouin tribes loyal during the British advance and secure their non-interference with the Suez Canal by distributing gold and the like, highlighting the very present importance of the Bedouin in current affairs. According to G. W. Murray's account, Mutayr, sheikh of the Safeiha tribe, presented himself to the expedition as the sheikh of all the al-Ahaywāt (one of the leading tribes of the region). After having gained Professor Palmer's confidence, he arranged for them to be kidnapped. Mutayr's son escaped with the gold and, as Mutayr refused to share the loot, the rest of the band murdered Professor Palmer and his company in order to blacken Mutayr's name with the future rulers of Egypt.[53] The investigations that ensued are illustrative of the difficulty of collecting trustworthy information, as several journeys were undertaken in order to gain a clearer insight regarding Palmer's fate.[54] After further attempts in September, West himself travelled to al-Tur in October in order to search, unsuccessfully, for the expedition.[55] Palmer's murder and the investigations that

---

[51] TNA, FO 78/2233: Consul West to Secretary of State, Suez, 2 November 1872.
[52] Palmer, *The Desert of the Exodus*, p. 297.   [53] Murray, *Sons of Ishmael*, pp. 250–1.
[54] TNA, FO 78/3462: Consul West to Principal Secretary of State for Foreign Affairs, 20 August 1882.
[55] TNA, FO 78/3462: extensive correspondence, see, for instance, West to F.O., 2 September 1882; West to F.O., 4 October 1882; West to Earl Granville, 23 October 1882; Telegram Consul West, 26 October 1882; West to Earl Granville, 4 December 1882. See also TNA, FO 78/3702: Correspondence concerning costs of search expeditions. The remains of Palmer were eventually recovered and buried in London's St Paul's Cathedral.

followed clearly demonstrate the British occupational power's difficulty in understanding the tribal structures of the Sinai and eliciting loyalty or gaining trustworthy information from them.

During the 1882 conflict, some Bedouin did in fact get involved on the side of the British. When Egyptian soldiers attacked two steamers proceeding through the Canal, the crew and passengers were protected by Bedouin intervention.[56] Just 13 years later, the Baedeker stated that the government had now successfully penetrated the wild territory of the Sinai, which was now safe for travellers.[57] The government could perhaps guarantee the safety of most travellers, however the khedival officials, as well as the occupational powers, were still struggling to bring the region under closer control and foster reliable collaboration.[58]

As the informal dealings with the Bedouin during 1882 proved, there had been a long-standing tradition of giving the Bedouin special treatment in order to ascertain their collaboration with the political authorities. They were, for example, exempt from military service in Egypt. Yet, since Muhammad 'Ali's army reforms, the census, which went hand in hand with military service, had been an efficient method of recording the population. Hence, in the case of the Bedouin, a different technique had to be employed for the cataloguing of the population. In order to gain more reliable information on them, the government attempted to create a register of all male Bedouin living in any part of Egypt where recruiting was practised.[59]

The British occupation also aimed at guaranteeing closer political penetration of the Sinai, while at the same time attempting to meddle with the internal affairs of the Bedouin as little as possible. In 1906, Lord Cromer sketched out how the Sinai could be more tightly controlled by placing the entire region under uniform military rule, with a British officer in charge as commander and Egyptian officers disseminated across the peninsula. Furthermore he aimed to establish closer supervision of the inhabitants of remote parts of the Sinai in order to bring them under any form of rules and regulations at all. In line with the rhetoric of the civilising mission, Cromer mocked the 'very primitive system' of the judicial services based on tribal customs, giving the example of a judge who apparently

---

[56] ANOM, GGI 14212: Consul de France à Aden au gouverneur Cochinchine, Aden, 19 July 1882.

[57] Baedeker, *Egypt: Handbook for Travellers* (1895), p. xx.

[58] DWQ, Majlis al-Wuzarā', Niẓārat al-Harbiyya 80075–014960: Comité des finances Le Caire, 18 Janvier 1894. Note au Conseil des ministres. See also DWQ, Majlis al-Wuzarā', Niẓārat al-Harbiyya 12.

[59] DWQ, Majlis al-Wuzarā', Niẓārat al-Harbiyya 80075–014958: Modification of Decree of 1885 regarding the exemption of Bedouin; ibid., 0075–014962: 'Law as to the Exemption of Beduins from Military Service'.

made decisions based on his dreams. Still he argued that even such arbitrary practices should not be interfered with more than necessary.[60] These incidents illustrate the sense of frustration among the Sinai nomads, but also the necessity that governments saw in controlling the inhabitants of deserts and steppes more tightly.

Although the caravan route – crossing the Canal at al-Qantara – clearly went into decline, in the interior of the Arabian Peninsula the Bedouin did not stop playing a central role. The pilgrim caravan had traditionally been an important source of income and occasionally, if negotiations between Ottomans and Bedouin were not successful, a target for Bedouin, but, according to the French Consul in Suez, the situation deteriorated in the first years of the twentieth century and most of the pilgrims from Algeria began to travel by sea.[61] Still, even in the age of the steamship, the last stretch between Jidda and Mecca required resorting to caravan mobility, which did not always prove easy, as problems such as shortages of camels could keep pilgrims of different origins on the shores of the Red Sea for many days.[62]

If the governmental penetration of desert regions surrounding the Canal, particularly the Sinai, proved at times difficult, and sometimes met outright resistance, this was thus even more apparent further 'east of Suez'. Here, the ambivalent relationship of different political entities, such as the British Empire, the Ottoman Empire and Egypt, as well as their problems of governance and experiments with classification, organisation and information transfer were particularly obvious. The Ottoman provincial government of the Hijaz, especially, had a long history of tense relationships with specific Bedouin tribes.[63] In 1892, for example, highlighting once again the vulnerability of the new means of communication, groups of armed Bedouin approached Jidda and cut the telegraphic cables that connected the city with Mecca and Egypt. As a result the Ottoman garrison in Jidda had to be reinforced.[64] It was not only the Ottoman government that found it challenging to secure its presence. European consular services also met with frequent opposition – in 1895, for

---

[60] Cromer, *Rapport de Lord Cromer*, p. 33.
[61] ANOM, GGA 16H/88: Consul Altemer Suez à Consul Meyrier Port Said, Suez, 5 January 1908.
[62] TNA, FO 423/15: Réponse de la direction des services sanitaires et d'hygiène publique en date du 20 Mars courant, sur le voyage à la Mecque de la grande caravane Égyptienne; ANOM, GGA 16H/83: Consul de France à Djeddah à M. Jonnart, gouverneur général de l'Algérie, Jidda, 16 February 1910.
[63] Burton, *Sir Richard Burton's Travels in Arabia and Africa*, p. 41, for instance, described an attack by the 'Utayba, 'the bravest and most lawless of the brigand tribes of the Moslem's Holy Land'.
[64] Schmidt, *Through the Legation Window*, p. 157.

instance, the chancellor of the French Jidda Consulate was attacked by Bedouin.[65]

The complications that the Egyptian pilgrim caravan encountered between Jidda and the holy towns of Mecca and Medina in the 1880s, 1890s and 1900s are instructive in regard to the difficulty that the Egyptian government and western powers had in bringing desert mobility under their control and allow us to cast our eyes briefly on the Arabian Peninsula east of Suez. These complications point to the often antagonistic relationships between caravan and Bedouin mobilities and to the complex inter-imperial situation connecting the Ottoman and British Empires.

During the annual pilgrimage, the protection of the caravan became a challenge when, after the British occupation, the liability for the pilgrim caravan's organisation shifted from the Ottoman Empire to Egypt.[66] Positions in the complex structure of the caravan were highly sought after, as the often very elaborate applications and petitions in the Egyptian archives attest.[67] At the same time, the Egyptian government attempted to save money on the journey, for instance when it came to the protection fees paid to Bedouin roaming the desert between Jidda and Mecca to guarantee safe passage to the holy places.[68] As a result, burglaries outside of Jidda and complaints from the Egyptian pilgrims who demanded additional securities were common. In 1900, for instance, the *Egyptian Gazette* reported that the road to Medina was impassable because of Bedouin violence.[69] In 1908 the payment of large sums to the Bedouin did not stop them opening gunfire on the caravan obliging it to return to Medina, ask the governor for assistance and make their way again after 28 days via a different route.[70]

As a result the Egyptian government and the colonial powers experimented with a range of measures to solve such conflicts, ranging from the classification of desert tribes and the acquisition of reliable information on

[65] Quai d'Orsay, Affaires diverses politiques 1815–1896, Tome IV, Egypte 24: Dr Axélos au ministre des Affaires étrangères, Rhodes, 21 October 1895. See also Freitag, 'Handelsmetropole und Pilgerstation', 73.

[66] See DWQ, Majlis al-Wuzarā', Niẓārat al-Dākhiliyya 18/ﻭ, 0075–007523.

[67] See DWQ, ʿĀbdīn 546 and 547. Besides choosing the leaders and guardians of the caravan, the Khedive distributed a number of annual bursaries for the journey.

[68] DWQ, Majlis al-Wuzarā', Niẓārat al-Dākhiliyya 18/ﻭ, 0075–007531.

[69] 'Notes from Mecca', *Egyptian Gazette*, 6 March 1900.

[70] DWQ, Majlis al-Wuzarā', Niẓārat al-Dākhiliyya 18/ﻭ, 0075–007563 for 1908, particularly Ministère de l'Intérieur, Rapport sur le pèlerinage, Cairo, 14 May 1908. For problems in 1904, DWQ, Majlis al-Wuzarā', Niẓārat al-Dākhiliyya 18/ﻭ, 0075–007553.

them, to the more centralised organisation and protection of the caravan. The former reminds us of the scientific and classifying approach sketched out in the first section of this chapter and shows how such classification was employed for political means. It was a matter of intense debate as to which tribes could be trusted and which ones were untrustworthy. The exact assessment of the Hijaz region's human geography was closely linked to reflections about the best route for the caravan to follow.[71] This led to the experimentation with rather complicated trajectories, including ships, the new Hijaz railway and different camel rides in between illustrating the not always smooth combination of 'old' and 'new' mobilities, rather than the outright replacement of traditional desert mobility with modern facilities.[72]

A further strategy was centralised organisation in order to make the journey easier to supervise, encouraging all Egyptian pilgrims to join the official caravan and to avoid individual travel.[73] In this context, the budget of the caravan for security issues, such as telegrams, information from the secret service and of course payments to the Bedouin, was a matter of annual debate, as well as the number of soldiers and other staff escorting the caravan between Jidda and Mecca.[74] In addition, the Egyptian government also had to allow British troops to participate in the guarding of the caravan.[75]

Despite this involvement of European powers in the organisation of their subjects' journeys to the holy cities, the frequent attacks of Bedouin on the pilgrim caravan clearly marked the limits of European as well as Egyptian and Ottoman influence east of Suez. The following section moves once again to the closer proximity of the Canal, in order to show that on the ground, such controls were impossible to effectuate without resorting to the assistance and collaboration of desert dwellers. This need

[71] See ANOM, GGA, 16H/83: French Consul Jidda, 'Rapport trimestriel sur la situation politique du Hedjaz', 4 April 1909.

[72] DWQ, Majlis al-Wuzarā', Niẓārat al-Dākhiliyya 18/ﺡ, 0075–007563: Ibrahim Bey Moustapha to Ibrahim Pacha Naguib, 7 June 1908.

[73] DWQ, Majlis al-Wuzarā', Niẓārat al-Dākhiliyya 18/ﺡ, 0075–007560: Ministre de l'Intérieur Moustapha Fahmy à Son Excellence le Ministre des Finances, Cairo, 5 December 1904.

[74] DWQ, Majlis al-Wuzarā', Niẓārat al-Dākhiliyya 18/ﺡ, 0075–007556: Ministre de l'Intérieur Moustapha Fahmy ministre des Finances, Cairo, 5 December 1904; ibid., 0075–007556: Comité des finances, notes au Conseil des ministres, December 1904; ibid., 0075–007559: Secrétaire financier, ministère de la Guerre, 21 January 1905; ibid., 0075–007560: Comité des finances, note au Conseil des Ministres, Cairo, 27 December 1905; ibid., 0075–007575: Ministère de l'Interieur, Bureau de traduction, no date.

[75] See Villiers-Stuart, *Egypt after the War*, pp. 221 ff; Cromer, *Rapport de Cromer*, p. 101.

to collaborate and adopt strategies that were otherwise deemed traditional points to the fact that, once it came to its practical application, the doctrine of the civilising mission was not as straightforward as envisaged by its proponents.

Acceleration with the help of desert mobilities

If the intended acceleration and deceleration of certain movements could not always be controlled and if the civilising mission could not proceed as smoothly as many expected, the reliance on the techniques and skills of those easily moving in deserts and steppes presented a further complication to the neat model of 'traditional' and 'modern' mobilities in the descriptions analysed at the beginning of the chapter. As will become clear in the following, not only the construction of the Canal, but also its later functioning, depended on the same desert mobilities that were deemed backward in other contexts. If caravans and Bedouin were on the one hand hampered, on the other they were necessary to build, expand and patrol the Canal. In order to cope with the desert environment, European governments and companies, as well as individual travellers, necessarily had to rely on skills that only Bedouin could provide. The very acceleration that the Canal was meant to bring thus relied to a significant extent on those mobilities it decelerated.

Camels versus steam

First and foremost, travellers were dependent on Bedouin as guides and cameleers if they wanted to venture into the desert, just as it was before the opening of Canal. Dealing with the assistance of Bedouin was no simple affair and – as the case of the Egyptian caravan proceeding to Mecca showed – presupposed some knowledge of their tribal configurations, a fact that several travellers made plain, in an article published by the *North American Review* in 1856, after their journey through the Sinai. They noted that every tribe had the exclusive right to protect travellers in its own district with the Arabs of al-Tur, 'by far the most tractable sons of the desert', conducting those journeying from Cairo to Suez, or on to Mount Sinai and Aqaba. In order to travel on from Aqaba to Petra, one had to be escorted by the Alouin, 'the most fierce and extortionate of the Bedouin Arabs'.[76]

---

[76] 'Three new routes to India', *North American Review* 172 (1856), p. 149.

It was not only individuals who had to make use of the Bedouin's skills and familiarity with the territory as well as the sturdiness of camels to proceed through the desert. Even before the building work of the Suez Canal had begun, the shipping companies had already relied on camels and caravans transporting coal from the Mediterranean to the Red Sea for the steamer line between Suez and Bombay. When the construction of the Canal was initiated, the contrast between desert life and industrial life became most obvious. Many of the forced labourers digging the Canal were *fellahin* from Upper Egypt, and were not recruited from the nomadic population of the region. Still camels and camel drivers were essential for the provisioning of the building sites. Water, food, building materials and disassembled dredgers made their way through the arid regions on the reliable backs of camels following Bedouin routes. Once the dredgers were in place, the mechanisation of the building site released many workers from their exhausting work, but camel caravans continued to be the supply lifeline of one of the largest global infrastructure projects of the day.

The plate and the photographs (Figures 14–16) illustrate how even steam engines had to be transported to the building site with the help of camels. This reliance on camels was not at all a question of time and technological advancement. In the 1880s, when *Excelsior* was first performed, the

Cliché de l'Illustration.

Transport dans le désert d'une machine locomobile.

Figure 14 'Transport of a Locomotive in the Desert'. *La construction du canal de Suez, 1859–1869,* bound volume of lithographs.

Figure 15 'Building Site Bracalis, Fresh Water Canal', photograph by
Hippolyte Arnoux.

situation had not changed very much, as Figure 16, depicting the extension
works of the Canal, shows. The mechanisation of the Canal work might
have served to solve the problem of forced labour, yet it did not provide an
answer to the ambiguous relationship between steam and desert mobility
when it came to constructing, deepening and widening or maintaining
the Canal.

Employing indigenous forms of organisation

The reliance on local expertise went beyond the simple employment of
camels in the desert. The British occupation as well as the Suez Canal
Company also had to draw on indigenous patterns of organisation.
Whereas Canal workers guarded the Canal itself, the parallel fresh water
canal was protected by members of the tribes of the regions of Sharqiyya
and Qalyubiyya, even if the division of responsibilities did not always work

Figure 16 'Extending the Canal in the 1880s', photograph by Hippolyte Arnoux, *Photographe de l'union des mers: Le Canal de Suez vers 1880* (Paris: Centre Historique des Archives Nationales, 1996).

out. In 1885, the governor of the Canal District complained that, despite the precise numbers of guards demanded by the Egyptian Ministry of the Interior, at no given time had the quantity of men provided by the tribes reached the amount assigned to the specific posts.[77] Yet this was not the only case of reliance on indigenous forms of organisation, as the following examples will illustrate.

At times it was proposed to revert to tribal organisation altogether. In 1889, the Committee of Directors of the Suez Canal Company debated how to deal with cases of theft and unruliness on the shores of the Canal.[78] One suggested remedy to the problem was the return to older forms of local administration that granted the previously disempowered sheikhs a considerable amount of independence. By doing so, the sheikhs would be

[77] DWQ, Majlis al-Wuzarā', Qanāt al-Suways 5: Ministre de l'Intérieur signé Abdulkader, Note au Conseil des ministres le 7 Zulkehde 302 (August 1885).
[78] ANMT, 1995060/1478: 'Le brigandage dans le canal', *Le phare de Port-Saïd et du canal de Suez*, 3 December 1889, p. 1.

held responsible for security in their respective territories, a high official of the company proposed to Ferdinand de Lesseps in January 1890, arguing that the old structures of local governance on the sides of the Canal had been dismantled too rapidly after 1882.[79] Even if there is no evidence to show whether this proposition was further discussed or even enacted, it does show that tribal organisation could not only be seen as 'backwards', but on the contrary as a solution to very modern constellations.

The question of governance over the tribes was also phrased even more explicitly as a critique of the British regime of occupation. An article in a local newspaper listed all the attacks by groups of Bedouin in the year 1889, concluding that the British administration was utterly incapable of assuring Egypt's security. It claimed that the British had done everything to advertise in Europe that their presence in Egypt was crucial for the country's well-being, but that they had failed to deliver on the ground; on the contrary, together with the 'victors of Tel el-Kebir', theft and robbery had made inroads in Egypt. The author argued that, before the British occupation, Egypt was as safe as any civilised region in Europe. Now everything had fallen into chaos, precisely because the British behaved as they had done in India and had downgraded the local administrators. The article called for the reinstatement of the local *mudirs* who, by being degraded, had been humiliated by British policemen in the eyes of the local population. Soon, in the author's view, robbery and crime would then stop being as menacing.[80]

Such a reliance on 'native' strategies and skills did not only figure in the idea of returning limited political power to the sheikhs around the Canal. In the case of the pilgrim caravan, where the strategic allocation of protection money was crucial to fend off Bedouin tribes, Bedouin were at the same time employed as indispensable guards. And as seen above in the context of the 1882 occupation, the collaboration of desert tribes was perceived as a valuable asset. If in the sources referred to at the beginning of this chapter, the uncontrollability of the desert was often emphasised, it therefore also proved necessary to use their strategies to take control of desert territories. Beyond the simple employment of camels, the experimentation with indigenous forms of organisation points to the contradiction of the civilising mission as well as to an alternative narrative of globalisation, which integrated traditional elements.

---

[79] ANMT, 1995060/1478: Agent supérieur à F. de Lesseps, Cairo, 7 January 1890.
[80] ANMT, 1995060/1478: 'Gendarmes et brigands', Cairo, 3 January 1890, name of newspaper not legible.

The Camel Corps

Cooperation was hence indispensable to transform the desert into a governable space. The Camel Corps provides an example combining the use of camels with the reliance on traditional allegiances and forms of organisation. From 1896 onwards, a Camel Corps section of the Coastguard Administration was employed to oversee the deserts around the Canal and to prevent the smuggling of salt (on which there was a state monopoly), tobacco and hashish. The Camel Corps was also bound to ward off the illicit landing of pilgrims on the Red Sea coast and, not always successfully, to patrol Egypt's borders.[81]

Of course camel cavalry was not unique to Egypt and had been employed for instance by the French in the Sahara as part of the Army of Africa, operating in Algeria, and by the Ottoman Army in Syria. Yet the driving forces behind the Egyptian Camel Corps, which in 1904 established its Red Sea headquarters in the Victoria Barracks built before the opening of the Suez Canal, were particularly international. It was a joint effort of British, Italian, German, French and Egyptian initiative, pointing to new forms of international organisation beyond the international conferences mentioned in earlier chapters.

The Corps was headed by André von Dumreicher, a descendant of a German-Danish family that had formed part of Alexandria's European community since the late eighteenth century.[82] Dumreicher commanded about 500 cameleers whose task it was to secure a border of more than 4,000 kilometres in length. Often, a section of these camel riders were delegated to do police work or enforce *cordons sanitaires* when fears of epidemics circulated.[83] If the Nile Valley had by then been brought under quite close administration, according to Dumreicher's portrayal, the deserts, comprising 96 per cent of Egyptian territory, had been in part untouched by the government until the Camel Corps was charged with its surveillance. It was thus 'not a question of seizing a few camel-loads of smuggled salt but the Government's prestige itself was at stake', as Dumreicher put it.[84]

---

[81] See Owen, *Power and Politics in the Making of the Modern Middle East*, p. 10.

[82] von Dumreicher, *Fahrten, Pfadfinder und Beduinen in den Wüsten Ägyptens*, esp. pp. 1–3, 170–1. See also Lackany, *Quelques célèbres Allemands en Egypte*, pp. 8–12.

[83] On the use of Bedouin to enforce *cordons sanitaires*: DWQ, Majlis al-Wuzarā', Niẓārat al-Dākhiliyya 18/ﺏ, 0075–007551: Note au Comité des finances, Cairo, 16 December 1903.

[84] von Dumreicher, *Fahrten, Pfadfinder und Beduinen in den Wüsten Ägyptens*, p. 139.

Similarly to the ethnographer Ernst Klippel, Dumreicher had great sympathy for the Bedouin and admired their impressive abilities of being able to track footprints and other traces in the desert, combining, like Klippel, the romantic and the scientific view of the Bedouin. Despite the fact that it was his duty to enforce it, he also criticised government policies such as the salt monopoly and illustrated how cumbersome the introduction of new legal systems was for the Bedouin way of life.[85] While the Camel Corps used the strategies of the desert dwellers to track illicit mobility, Dumreicher was at the same time proud to point out that they were actually perfecting these techniques and strategies, as they could fit out depots at strategic points from where the refreshed patrols on the 'best riding camels of the world' could take up the chase of the 'thirsty and hard-pressed smuggler caravans'.[86] With its combination of European resources and belief in progress, international backing and organisation and the reliance on desert skills, the example of the Camel Corps ties together many elements emphasised in this chapter.

As the closer analysis of different moments in the regulation and resistance of desert mobilities of the 1880s, 1890s and 1900s shows, the interaction between the Canal system and the desert was much more complex than the European depictions highlighted at the beginning of the chapter insinuated. For one, the political, infrastructural, classifica-tory and bureaucratic interventions were depicted as regulations of apparently uncontrolled mobilities. At the same time the role of the Bedouin in times of crisis was unforeseeable; they could either become allies or trigger conflicts, as the events around 1882 show. What is more, the western powers could not even begin to undertake their endeavours without reliance on 'native' skills. If the mobilities of the desert were thus hampered by the Canal, they also came to be employed in new spheres of activity, adding a whole new facet both to the question of mobility and its control in the Canal Zone and to the more global question of imperial penetration and resistance. Bedouin and caravans were thus seen by many European observers on the one hand as remnants of a bygone age and on the other they not only made their presence felt but were necessary for the Canal undertaking in the broader sense. In spite of the examples of the practical reliance on Bedouin skills in order to bring the region surrounding the Canal under closer governmental control, they still serve particularly well to show how the distinction, and what is more

---

[85] Ibid., p. 180; see also *Le spectateur*, 2 May 1931, printed in von Dumreicher, *Le tourisme dans les deserts d'Égypte*, p. 143.

[86] von Dumreicher, *Fahrten, Pfadfinder und Beduinen in den Wüsten Ägyptens*, p. 167.

acceleration and deceleration, of different mobilities was to be effectuated. If other categories such as race, class, gender, nationality and religion played a role in the process of 'channelling mobilities', the example of 'desert mobilities' and the expressions and images to characterise them, introduced at the beginning of the chapter, show particularly clearly how mobility itself was frequently at the centre of the argument.

5   Dhows and slave trading in the Red Sea

It was not only the deserts on either side of the Canal that were perceived as frontiers of civilisation, as wild and savage, timeless and unchanging; the traditional ships that ploughed through the Suez Canal and the Red Sea triggered similar associations on the part of the steamship passengers. With the Suez Canal and the previously dreaded Red Sea developing into arteries of world traffic, there were pre-existing forms of maritime transport that were not integrated into the imperial circulatory system. The Red Sea now carried two forms of mobility that were in the view of western contemporaries as sharply distinguished as the desert and the Canal, namely the western steamers and the traditional trading, fishing and pearl-diving boats.

Like the Bedouin tribes on the shores, these traditional ships posed challenges to western powers in terms of governance and control. It was the fight against the slave trade, that centrepiece of the western civilising mission, that brought the tension between the different attitudes towards traditional shipping most clearly to the fore.[1] By the late nineteenth century, the abolition of slavery and the slave trade had developed into a part of British national identity and foreign policy.[2] Yet there were also explicitly international efforts to limit the slave trade in the region. As will come to light in the course of this chapter, the measures taken in the name of freedom and civilisation put new constraints on the mobilities of the Red Sea. Furthermore, the status of the Suez Canal and the Red Sea as a boundary between Africa and Asia might have become particularly visible in specific locations, such as at al-Qantara with its caravan ferry. But it was also highlighted by phenomena like the illicit movement of people between the Arabian and African coasts of the

---

[1] On the connection of abolition and the civilising mission, see Osterhammel, *Sklaverei und die Zivilisation des Westens*.

[2] See Davis, *The Problem of Slavery in the Age of Revolution*, pp. 343–468; Swaminathan, *Debating the Slave Trade*, pp. 171–217.

Red Sea. As in the case of the desert mobilities on the shores of the Canal and further east of Suez, the relationship between the different modes of movement veered between moral disapproval, governmental penetration, resistance and cooperation.

The pattern of acceleration and deceleration can thus be clearly traced when looking at the increasing obstructions of dhow mobility due to economic reasons, imperial entanglements and international agreements. At the same time, it will be shown that the implementation of these new regulations could only be effected by resorting to local skills for the acquisition of information or the conduct of checks on the shores of the Red Sea. The deceleration of a specific kind of mobility was thus complemented with the reference to other categories justifying tighter controls, such as gender, race and religion. What will emerge clearly in this and the following chapter is how Islam developed into a focal point of the imperial powers' worries concerning the limits of the civilising mission, the danger of conflict or revolt in the colonies and the fear of contagion and epidemic disease. Yet the strategies of various empires of how to deal with these worries differed quite substantially. Despite such differences the empires had to cooperate, for instance when it came to combating slavery and the slave trade. Hence the example of the slave trade shows particularly well how the 'rules of globalisation' were shaped by the entanglement of different empires and international agreements and how they were therefore often in conflict with the political preferences of a single empire.

As in the preceding chapter, this chapter moves east of Suez into the Red Sea in order to explore the themes of imperial competition and the channelling of mobility, meaning the control, exclusion and streamlining of mobility. This chapter hinges on the international conference against the slave trade in Brussels (1889–90), but occasionally looks at the decades before and after this date. It first tries to understand the impact of the Canal on the traditional shipping in the region; then it throws light on attempts to tightly control certain ships in the Red Sea as they became associated with the slave trade between the African and Asian coasts; finally it shows, in parallel to the preceding chapter, how these increasing controls were coupled with a reliance on skills that only the otherwise derided 'natives' could provide and that were often described as 'backwards' or 'belonging to a bygone age'. Highlighting the specific case of the collision of different forms of shipping in the Suez Canal and 'east of Suez' in the Red Sea makes it possible to use the theme of mobility in order to gain insights into the intricacies of different reactions that the civilising mission engendered.

Dhow shipping and slave trading east of Suez

Before we can enter the debates on slavery and slave trading in the Red Sea, in terms both of the discourses developing in Europe and of the actual problem encountered in situ, we have to pause a moment and glance at the panorama of shipping that the Suez Canal and the Red Sea accommodated on their waters. Even if the Suez Canal was mainly populated by large steamers and small steam-driven pilot boats, it was also used by other crafts providing a variety of services reminding us of the scenario that Isabel Burton described in the passage quoted in the last chapter. The Red Sea, one of the homes of the dhow, the traditional ship of the eastern shores, obviously continued to be used by a number of ships different from the western type sent out by the large European shipping companies.

Ships on the Red Sea and on the Canal

Before the introduction of steamships, mainly dhows were able to cruise the Red Sea, renowned and feared for its dangerous and difficult climatic conditions, reefs and currents. 'Dhow' was an umbrella term used in the West for about 80 Arabic names identifying different types of sailing boats that were widespread not only in the Red Sea but also in the Arabian Gulf and the Indian Ocean. These varied widely in form and size, from small one-mast shipping boats to large transporters with three masts. The common denominator was a diagonal stern that gave them their typical shape. Common types included the small *felucca* used in Egypt, the rather heavy two- or three-sail *baghla* and the even larger *sanbūk*, one of the biggest ships navigating the Red Sea before the age of steam.[3]

Like the caravans, whose proficiency in traversing the desert had once been widely admired, the skills of the dhows and their navigators were devalued in the West when steamships came to be perceived as the superior form of navigation. What is more, the dhows (and caravans) seemed to belong to another era. Francis Frith, one of the early photographers travelling the Middle East, recorded Suez during his trip in 1860 (Figure 17). The town itself barely caught his interest. Rather

---

[3] Most comprehensive works on the dhow focus on a particular region or community, see Gilbert, *Dhows and the Colonial Economy of Zanzibar*; Agius, *Seafaring in the Arabian Gulf and Oman*, for the different names of boats see p. 13; Krajewski, *Kautschuk, Quarantäne, Krieg*; Sheriff, *Dhow Culture of the Indian Ocean*.

Figure 17 'Suez', photograph by Francis Frith, *Cairo, Sinai, Jerusalem, and the Pyramids of Egypt: A Series of Sixty Photographic Views* (London: J. S. Virtue. 1860), pl. 28.

he focused his lens on some dhows on the Red Sea shores and paired them evocatively with camels in the foreground.

In the comment adjoining the photograph, reference was made to the dhow boats' glorious past:

Such boats have, for ages, perhaps since the days of the Phoenicians, been the carriers of the Red Sea. In the best days of Arab commerce such boats ventured to the Golden Chersonese, the seas of China and Japan, and the Spice Islands, and brought thence those marvellous tales, of which the best known is the story of Es-Sindibád of the Sea.[4]

The opening of the Suez Canal added a whole new traffic volume to the Red Sea region, while traditional dhows kept frequenting its shores for petty trade and fishing. Yet, unlike the prediction of Frith, who had expected Suez to develop considerably once the Canal was completed,

---

[4] Frith, *Cairo, Sinai, Jerusalem, and the Pyramids of Egypt*, no page number. See also Nickel, *Francis Frith in Egypt and Palestine*; Frith, *Francis Frith's Egypt and the Holy Land*.

the town did not expand at all. In fact, the indigenous community, and especially the fishermen on their dhows, suffered considerably, highlighting the deceleration that the Canal could bring for some. West, the British Consul, explained in a report of 1881 that the hardship was a result of both the essential 'character of the native', who only worked to satisfy his immediate needs, and the heavy taxation system in place, which did not create an incentive to earn money. The report went on to describe the fishing community of Suez in more detail. Egyptian fishermen were taxed highly according to the size of their vessels. At the same time Europeans and European companies operated large cargo boats and steam launches on which no tax was levied. The Greeks, Italians and Maltese were, as a result of the capitulations, also exempt from taxation. In effect, only they were able to earn their living through fishing. The report concluded: 'Hence the native ever labours under a disadvantage but that is the rule of the land.'[5]

Despite the competition from modern boats, some local ships continued to frequent not only the Red Sea but the Canal too. Navigating next to the big steamers and tugboats employed by the Canal Company, they catered for the Canal towns and adjacent settlements. Using either the fresh water canal or the Suez Canal itself, they joined together with the small bumboats to sell their goods to passing steamers and their passengers.[6] Apart from that, western travellers seldom had contact with the dhows, with a few exceptions, such as the adventurous Andrew Carnegie who left his steamer and sailed on a dhow to Suez to catch a train for Cairo.[7] Most others contented themselves with curiously observing these (in their eyes) antiquated vehicles or with buying photographs featuring their distinctive sails alongside the large steamers (Figure 18).

Captains and Suez Canal pilots largely disliked the smaller barks on the Canal as they complicated their tasks.[8] Still the local ships also received some protectionist treatment. The Suez Canal Company agreed, in a convention with Prime Minister Nubar Pasha, to collect lower fees from small vessels navigating the Canal between Port Said and Ismailia, especially when they were empty or carried cargoes of local produce destined

---

[5] TNA, FO 78/3334, sheet 138: Report on the Trade, Commerce and Navigation at Suez for the Year 1880.
[6] On 'bumboats', see Burton, *A. E. I. Arabia Egypt India*, p. 70; Marshall, *Passage East*, p. 64.
[7] Carnegie, *Round the World*, p. 263.   [8] See Parfond, *Pilotes de Suez*, p. 133.

Kantara . Kilomètre 44.

Navire passant devant la gare.

Figure 18 'Al-Qantara Kilometre 44: Steamship Passing in Front of the Station', photograph by Hippolyte Arnoux.

for consumption in Port Said, Ismailia or Lower Egypt.[9] Occasional problems caused by the local boats, such as accidentally destroyed lanterns that fishermen broke when hunting for cormorants, attracted the anger of the Company officials.[10] Just like the images juxtaposing steamships and dhow boats, on an administrative level such minor incidents not only illustrate the different *users* of the Canal, but also its different *uses*.

[9] DWQ, Majlis al-Wuzarā', Qanāt al-Suways 5, 0075–017017: Conventions des 13 et 18 décembre 1884.
[10] ANMT, 1995060/1478: Chef du service du transit à de Sérionne, agent supérieur de la Compagnie, 15 April 1901.

Debates on slavery and slave trade 'east of Suez'

Whereas the small boats on the Suez Canal were perceived at worst to be annoying and obstructive, or quaint relics of earlier times, the reputation of the dhows on the Red Sea was more ominous, as they were frequently associated with the morally loaded issue of the slave trade. The abolition movement in the Atlantic had gained strength over the course of the nineteenth century; the Thirteenth Amendment of 1865 officially ending slavery in the USA was passed during the construction of the Suez Canal and reverberated in the campaigns against the *corvée*. After these successes in the Atlantic realm, the slave trade 'east of Suez' increasingly became a target of abolitionists. Contrary to the 'industrialised' slave trade in the west, here it was associated with the dhows, which were seen as particularly evasive and difficult to control. Here slavery and the slave trade were less explicitly disconnected than in earlier British discourses; on the contrary, they were often not separated at all in the Red Sea realm.

In this context, 'east of Suez' came to be interpreted as marking the frontier of civilisation. Despite the fact that the Red Sea had clearly changed since the Frith expedition of 1860, and had turned from a challenge to any navigator into the artery of global transportation, the dramatist Eugène Brieux, travelling to India and Indochina, pointed to the slowness of the Canal passage itself and exclaimed:

But how the civilised world is rapidly gone! Five days by ship since Marseilles, at constant speed, it is true, but not much faster than a bicycle, one day at walking speed on the Canal, and here we are in a sea where life and human activities are only manifest in the wake of the large steamers. It is an enormous highway where there are only passers-by: it is bordered by two deserts and if we were shipwrecked, we would not be saved in touching the earth.[11]

Brieux made clear that he saw the passage through the Suez Canal as a passage between the 'civilised world' and its counterpart. He painted a picture of a Red Sea peopled only by large steamers and merely referred to the deserts on its shores as dangerous and possibly deadly space.[12]

Like Brieux many Europeans expressed an interest in debating the state of civilisation in the Middle East in a typically orientalist manner. In this context the abolition of the slave trade and of slavery more generally became a central concern. After the official abolition of slavery, first in the British Empire and later in the USA, these states – despite or because of their long involvement in the trade – quickly established themselves as defenders of humanity and took on the charge of protecting poor souls in Africa from

---

[11] Brieux, *Voyage aux Indes et en Indo-Chine*, pp. 8–9.   [12] Ibid., pp. 9–10.

being sold into captivity.[13] In the ballet, *Excelsior*, Manzotti had clearly linked the Suez Canal to the abolition of slavery. The Suez Canal thus became once again a frontier of civilisation, this time dividing a world that had rid itself of the stain of slavery and a world that was still buying and selling human beings. Accordingly, west and east of Suez came to stand for a world apparently freed from slavery and the slave trade and one that was not.[14]

What is more, many connected slavery directly with Islam. Étienne-Félix Berlioux, geography teacher at the Lycée Impérial in Lyon and later university professor in the same city, drew a direct line from what he called a war of a new kind, i.e. the fight for the abolition of the slave trade in the Islamic world, to the opening of the Suez Canal, which had attracted the broader European public's attention to matters concerning the 'Orient':

The twenty thousand spades turning the earth whose sound woke the desert, the whistles of the steam engines, the noise of the dredgers come to rest and gradually fade out; a fresher current mixes itself with the Red Sea tides, weighed down with salt: a long line of vessels from all countries, all nations has already opened a parade that will last forever. Here comes honest commerce, occidental civilisation, here comes freedom. Freedom has to begin by shattering the chains of slaves, and the slave trade has to cease forever. Conquering nature, separating the continents, reuniting the seas, and fertilising the desert, this is a great undertaking. But the greatest achievement will be to return civilisation and liberty to these countries of barbarism and servitude.[15]

He characterised Islam as a religion that inevitably brought with it fatalism and slavery and efficiently summarised the problems of combating the slave trade: first he blamed Egyptian officials for shielding it; then he cited the sheer size of the territories of Egypt and Sudan; and finally he mentioned the difficult supervision of the Red Sea, which formed the 'great market' and the 'great warehouse' of black slaves. So far, the lonely and desolate conditions in the Red Sea had been ideal for the slavers, providing them with countless hiding places.[16] However, Berlioux was sure that this would change as soon as the Canal opened. He linked this hope figuratively to the mixing of the fresh waters of the Mediterranean with those of the Red Sea, weighed down with too much salt.[17]

---

[13] Osterhammel, 'Aufstieg und Fall der neuzeitlichen Sklaverei', pp. 349, 368; see also Bayly, *Birth of the Modern World 1780–1914*, pp. 402–10: 'Slavery's Indian Summer'.

[14] For the various Islamic discourses on slavery and abolition, see Clarence-Smith, *Islam and the Abolition of Slavery*; for the different forms of slavery in the Ottoman context, see Toledano, *Slavery and Abolition in the Ottoman Middle East*, see also Toledano, *The Ottoman Slave Trade and its Suppression* on the process of abolition, on international involvement and on the different conventions.

[15] Berlioux, *La traite orientale*, pp. v, ix–x. See also Binger, *Esclavage*.   [16] Ibid., p. 215.

[17] Ibid., p. 215.

For Berlioux, the task of the Canal would thus only be completed once it had flooded Egypt with civilisation and had freed it from all servitude. Despite using analogies from nature, such as that of the fresher western waters versus the saltier eastern ones, in the course of his argument, Berlioux made it clear that for him the division of humanity into two parts (one mobile, one stagnant) was determined not by climatic conditions or race alone, but most importantly by religion. Here, the Suez Canal was positioned most clearly as a boundary between two worlds – one of Christianity, freedom and civilisation and the other of Islam, slavery and backwardness:

These words of freedom, words that condemn the tyranny of rulers and the blind servitude of their subjects, that condemn slavery, they have been said towards Mecca, towards this Isthmus which we are piercing, they have been said with the ten commandments, about the oriental and occidental world; this is the boundary between the two worlds, two ideas, the battle field where the fight between light and darkness, life and death, servitude and liberty has to be fought. The first blow against servitude should be the destruction of slavery.[18]

He went on to defend the civilising mission and the responsibility of Europeans towards Africans as a part – albeit somehow defective – of the human family.[19]

Resounding some of the motifs introduced by Manzotti, Berlioux was not the only one to connect the abolition of slavery with civilisation, even if his formulations give a particularly outspoken example of the rhetoric of the civilising mission. The slave trade thus came to be a justification of colonialism, since many Europeans agreed that the best way to stamp it out was via the exercising of western control.[20] What is more, it was increasingly perceived as a clash of religions. Islam was stigmatised as condoning slavery and therefore being less civilised; consequently Mecca came to be perceived as the centre not only of Islam but also of the region's slave trade.[21]

There were divergent voices of course such as the well-known Dutch traveller to Mecca, Christiaan Snouck Hurgronje. He described slavery in Arabia as a phenomenon that had to be distinguished from western slavery and that had, in some cases, a civilising effect. He interpreted the institution of Islamic slavery as a paternal relationship and as much more benevolent than its western counterpart. When he observed an Arab who beat his slave, he concluded that it was wrong to adopt 'Uncle Tom impressions' to the slave owner as he would punish his own son just as severely and concluded that '[t]he traveller has witnessed no scene of slave life, but an example of

---

[18] Ibid., p. 215.   [19] Ibid., p. 228.
[20] See Cooper, 'Conditions Analogous to Slavery', esp. p. 115.
[21] See, for example, the explorer Lejean, 'La Traite des esclaves en Égypte et en Turquie', 912.

the Arab "pedagogy", which is the same for slaves and offspring and is entirely out of agreement with modern ideas'.[22]

Snouck Hurgronje condemned the hypocrisy of the western civilising mission and its 'anti-slavery fraud', which served goals that were far from humanitarian and benevolent. The involvement of European states in Africa, he claimed, was causing much more misery and suffering than the slave trade of Muslims in these regions. The European representatives in Africa were often 'broken individuals' serving the jealous politics of a European power. True Christians were therefore always embarrassed when they saw on the one hand the 'half-naked negro representing our culture with top hat and brandy bottle' and on the other the 'quiet industrious black Muhammedan'. Snouck Hurgronje consequently criticised the European colonisation of Africa, which came in the guise of the abolition of slavery, but in fact resulted in the exploitation and mistreatment of the African population and concluded that the Africans had in fact neither called for European colonisers nor for Arab slave traders.[23]

Still, Snouck Hurgronje's position remained singular among European travellers and commentators from different origins. Most fell in line with Berlioux, praised the western civilising mission and abhorred occurrences of slave trading in the African-Arabian context. Often reference was made to the missionary activities of Muslims in Africa and to the Qur'an, which apparently did not outlaw the possession of slaves. Already in 1872, an author in the *Anti-Slavery Reporter*, a journal founded in 1825 by a Scottish anti-slavery campaigner, stated that:

slave merchants ... are generally missionaries for the extension of the Mohammedan religion, and they do what they can for the propagation of Islam in these interior districts of East Africa, and I must say, with great sorrow, that they have succeeded so wonderfully in their mission that tribe after tribe has become subject to the false religion of Mohamed and thus a road for the slave merchant is being prepared from the Red Sea to the interior of Africa.[24]

In these visions, the Canal thus figured as the frontier of civilisation in the most literal sense, separating the zone from which the slave trade had already been banned from the zone where this endeavour was still pending. It remains to be seen to what extent these forceful and confident statements translated into action and, if they did, what kind of action was envisaged.

---

[22] Snouck Hurgronje, *Mekka in the Latter Part of the 19th Century*, p. 21. See also Chafik Bey, *L'esclavage au point de vue Musulman*.

[23] Snouck Hurgronje, *Mekka in the Latter Part of the 19th Century*, pp. 22, 24–5.

[24] *Anti-Slavery Reporter*, 1 July 1872, quoted in Muhammad Ali, *The British, the Slave Trade and Slavery in the Sudan*, p. 72.

Slavery and slave trading in the Red Sea

The debates and opinions outlined above might insinuate that there was a large amount of slave trading on a daily basis in the Red Sea documenting the poignant attitudes that Europeans developed towards the phenomenon. This European perspective, however, does not provide us with a clear picture of the situation on the ground, or rather, in the Red Sea. The numbers of actual or alleged slaves traded between the shores of the Red Sea are impossible to assess.[25] Furthermore it is difficult to get access to the experiences of the slaves themselves.[26] Despite unreliable quantifications, many agreed that the trade with human beings persisted after the opening of the Canal. In the instructions dispatched to the British slave patroller McKillop, Khedive Isma'il stated that some people had even gone so far as to evaluate the number of slaves transported between Africa and Arabia at 30,000 per year, which was, in the eyes of Isma'il, 'of course strongly exaggerated'.[27] As for the prices, according to another slave patroller, they apparently ranged generally from 100 to 150 dollars for young women, 200 to 300 for Abyssinian girls and 50 to 100 dollars for boys, while men were 'of less value'.[28] The sources hence call attention to the uncertainty connected with the actual amount of trading, an uncertainty that would increase as attempts to clamp down the traffic between Africa and Arabia intensified.

One target of this clampdown was not the dhows but the steamers of European or Ottoman steam shipping companies. Before 1869, specific shipping lines had already come to be associated with the slave trade, for example the Egyptian Azizie Company sailing between Alexandria and Constantinople.[29] The opening of the Suez Canal – assessed so positively in Berlioux' account – proved however to be a double-edged sword for those who came to control Red Sea mobilities in the name of combating the slave trade. On the one hand, in the 1870s, the Royal Navy and the Bombay Marine were able to increase their searches, but on the other, the growing numbers of ships and passengers generated more and more opportunities to disguise the traffic.[30] Of course it was particularly annoying for patrollers and officials if Britons were involved in the smuggling of slaves through the Canal. The *Sheriff Khessan*, for instance, was an Ottoman

---

[25] For an overview, see Collins, 'The African Slave Trade'.
[26] See Troutt Powell, 'Will that Subaltern Ever Speak?'
[27] TNA, FO 881/3082: Mr Vivian to the Earl of Derby, Cairo, 13 January 1877, Inclosure: Instructions addressed to McKillop Pasha by Ismail.
[28] TNA, FO 881/3342: Letter Sir Admiral R. McDonald with return of vessels captured in 1876. Red Sea & Persian Gulf, 23 June 1877.
[29] TNA, FO 141/69: Foreign Office to G. E. Stanley Esq., 15 July 1869.
[30] Burdett (ed.), *Slave Trade into Arabia*, vol. 1, p. ix.

vessel, but its commander was British. Foreign Secretary Lord Granville had to make clear that British subjects would be punished no matter what the nationality of the ship itself.[31] Its commander stated in a letter to the consul of Suez that he carried several slaves and that 'each + every steamer from the Yemen for Constantinople has always a number on board'.[32]

Even if the Canal and the steamships using it became the sites of occasional controls, as we will see in some more detail in the last section of this chapter featuring the connection between the Mecca pilgrimage and the slave trade, the main theatre of efforts to fight the trade was located 'east of Suez' and targeted traditional dhows. We thus once again have to adjust our zoom and focus. The increasing European presence in the Red Sea that came with the sheer volume of Canal traffic resulted in manifold debates and questions of authority and responsibility as well as of interference with mobility, for instance, when fugitive slaves swam from pearling dhows towards British ships. Such individual cases became connected with larger inter-imperial and international concerns and considerations, as the following section will show.

Imperial and international interventions

As Britain aimed to increase its influence in Egypt, and western empires more generally tried to solidify their stake in the regions bordering the Red Sea and Indian Ocean, the fight against the slave trade became a political issue of the first order. At the same time the measures taken against it were far from undisputed and conjured up a phase of experimentation and of negotiation of competences and liabilities. Furthermore the fight against the slave trade triggered secondary problems, such as the intricate question of responsibility for undertaking checks on boats in open waters. In this section, imperial and international responses to the slave trade in the Red Sea will be reviewed in turn.

Inter-imperial conflicts

In the last decades of the nineteenth century, the control measures in the Red Sea were marked by experiments with the acquisition of trustworthy information, checks and controls. They were dominated by imperial

---

[31] TNA, MT 9/71: Correspondence rel to practice of conveying slaves in British vessels to Constantinople for sale, with a statement of Capt Cumming of the Sheriff Khessan rel to traffic in Slaves in the Red Sea 1873, Foreign Office to the Secretary of the Board of Trade, no date.

[32] TNA, MT 9/71: Captain Cumming to Consul at Suez, 16 September 1872.

powers referring to their political but also civilisational role in controlling mobility on the Red Sea. At the same time, these measures brought inter-imperial problems and conflicts to the fore, involving at least three empires: the British, the French and the Ottoman. Control measures were headed by British patrolling agencies. Rather than interfering in the practice of slavery in the interior of the African continent or the Arabian Peninsula, the British, as the driving force of the anti-slave trade movement in the region, clamped down on the slave boats while in transit. As a result of their established efforts against the slave trade since the 1820s and their strong position within the international balance of power, they had more authority than others to stop vessels and search them.[33]

In Egypt itself the British launched various attempts to gain control over the slave trade, even before they actually occupied the country. A first convention of 1877 laid out procedures for dealing with liber-ated slaves that could not be sent back home. In an act of reciprocity it gave the Egyptian authorities a free hand to stop and search British steamers that might be involved in the trade. However there was a caveat: ships sailing under the British flag had to be sent to the nearest British authority for trial; also, vessels belonging to the large steam-ship companies remained exempt from all enquiries.[34] A further step towards increasing British influence was the creation of an Egyptian Office of the Slave Trade Abolition Service, naturally placed under British control.

After the occupation of 1882, the British presence in Egypt became even more tangible in the combating of slavery and the slave trade as Britain conceived it as its responsibility to completely rid the country of slavery. In the late 1880s, Britain increased its efforts to fight the slave trade again, mainly through reinforcing Royal Navy patrols.[35] Nevertheless, in order to ease cooperation with the local elites and consolidate their influence, the British granted at the same time certain concessions regarding the holding of domestic slaves in Egypt proper.[36] This distinction between the trading and the holding of slaves provides a telling example of the balancing act which marked colonial rule in many contexts. On the one hand European

---

[33] Burdett (ed.), *Slave Trade into Arabia*, vol. 1, p. v.

[34] See TNA, FO 881/3082: Mr Vivian to Earl of Derby, Cairo, 13 January 1877. For the 'Convention between the British and Egyptian Governments for the Suppression of the Slave Trade' of 4 August 1877 and further agreements, A. L. P. Burdett (ed.), *Slave Trade into Arabia*, vol. 3, pp. 213 ff.

[35] See sources in Burdett (ed.), *Slave Trade into Arabia*, vol. 4.

[36] Quai d'Orsay, Affaires diverses politiques 1815–1896, Tome IV, Egypte 21: M. Cogordan, agent et consul général de France en Egypte à M. Hanotaux, ministre des Affaires étrangères, Cairo, 28 September 1894.

principles were introduced as central to the legitimisation of colonial enter-
prises at home and abroad; at the same time concessions towards these
principles were always necessary for the local stabilisation of colonial rule.
'East of Suez' more radical methods were employed than in Egypt itself.
The most drastic measure against the slave trade was a blockade of the Red
Sea, which simultaneously was part of the early actions against the Mahdist
movement which was fighting against British-Egyptian colonial rule in
Sudan.[37] Even if the war only entered into full force after 1883 (lasting
until the Battle of Omdurman in 1898, where troops had arrived via
Dongola as cited in the quote at the beginning of Chapter 3), the anti-
colonial movement, led by the self-declared Mahdi Muhammad Ahmad,
started to gain force after General Gordon's demission in 1879. The blockade of 1885–86 illustrates the entanglement of several specific political
missions and activities in the name of ending the slave trade.[38] Reactions
included critical voices resounding reactions to earlier and in fact later
blockades. Some argued that the Sudanese population was hit much too
hard as it was dependent on the import of Arab grain across the Red Sea. The
sheikhs on both sides of the Red Sea particularly condemned the blockade as
being too extreme a measure. Consul Cameron at Port Said on the contrary
was very much in favour of it and telegraphed to Baring that the contraband
trade in grain was merely a means of paying for slaves and that the blockade
had already raised the price of slaves and should therefore be maintained.[39]
    The *cordon* on the coasts of Sudan did not remain the only naval
blockade in the name of combating the trafficking of slaves. In 1888
Great Britain and Germany imposed a similar measure on the territorial
waters of Zanzibar and Pemba.[40] However, there were also internal critics
of such initiatives, such as Edmund Robert Fremantle, the British
commander-in-chief of the East Indies Station. The East Indies Station
was the Royal Navy fleet responsible for the entire Indian Ocean, the
Persian Gulf and the Red Sea, with bases in Colombo, Trincomali,
Bombay, Basra and Aden. As alluded to in Fremantle's comment,
although the number of liberated slaves diminished in the region of the
East Indies Station from 814 in 1888, to 240 in 1889, it was far from clear

---

[37] See Troutt Powell, *A Different Shade of Colonialism.*
[38] TNA, ADM 116/72: Red Sea Slave Trade – Blockade of Ports 1885–1886.
[39] TNA, ADM 116/72: Telegram Consul Cameron to Sir E. Baring, Suakin, 19 April 1886.
    See also Burdett (ed.), *Slave Trade into Arabia*, vol. 4, pp. 159–69: Consul Cameron to Sir
    E. Baring, Suakin, 19 April 1886.
[40] Burdett (ed.), *Slave Trade into Arabia*, vol. 4, p. 292: Declaration of Blockade. Signed by
    the British Rear-Admiral Commander-in-Chief East Indies Station E. R. Fremantle and
    the German Rear-Admiral Commanding Flying Squadron Deinhard, Zanzibar, 29
    November 1888.

whether this was to be attributed to the successful reduction of slavery or, on the contrary, to the more successful mantling of it. Even if slavery was reduced, it was dubious whether this was a result of the blockade at all. Furthermore the sea blockade was very labour-intensive. Fremantle described the 'very strict and hard service' of the blockaders who were constantly underway and were boarding 1,200 to 1,300 dhows per month.

In his opinion, however, the section of the coast that was actually blockaded was already free from slaving and therefore the blockade had 'absolutely no effect' on the suppression of the slave trade.[41] Fremantle was convinced that the reduction of the trade was internal to Arab politics and due to the fact that most Arabs who held important positions in the region regarded the slave trade as 'doomed'. Somewhat paradoxically he still argued for maintaining the efforts as a measure of symbolic politics, so to speak, 'until the slave trade is finally stamped out'.[42]

French officials were apprehensive about the common cause of British and German cooperation, which the blockade and its joint patrols symbolised for them.[43] More generally, the British fight against slavery was suspected of being a pretext for colonialism rather than a benevolent action. Even if officials rarely voiced their opinion in a very open manner regarding these assumptions, individual commentators such as Jules Sakakini, French citizen and member of the London Society for the Abolition of the Slave Trade, was able to write in a letter to the French Minister of Foreign Affairs, that even if the British government had perhaps achieved something in the fight against the slave trade, it had always acted in the interests of Britain rather than in the interests of humanity.[44] British officials in turn watched French involvement in Africa with suspicion and believed that their ulterior objectives could only be 'Empire in Africa, and the power in case of war to obstruct England's communications with India'.[45] As in other fields, the

---

[41] Burdett (ed.), *Slave Trade into Arabia*, vol. 4, p. 421: Rear-Admiral Sir E. Fremantle to Admiralty, *Boadicea* at Bombay, 18 March 1890.

[42] Burdett (ed.), *Slave Trade into Arabia*, vol. 4, p. 422: Report Africa (East Coast) and Arabia, E. R.Fremantle, 1889.

[43] See, for instance, Burdett (ed.), *Slave Trade into Arabia*, vol. 4, pp. 294–5, Currie to Foreign Office, 19 November 1888.

[44] Quai d'Orsay, Affaires diverses politiques 1815–1896, Tome IV, Egypte 6: Jules Sakakini, citoyen français, membre actif de la société cosmopolite de Londres pour l'abolition de l'Esclavage à Monsieur Barthélemy St Hilaire, ministre des Affaires étrangères, Alexandria, 31 October 1881.

[45] TNA, FO 541/24 (see also FO 881/4619 for the same documents): Report on the Suppression of the Slave Trade in the North-East of Africa, the Soudan, and the Coast Provinces of Egypt in the Red Sea and Gulf of Aden, Considered from a Political and Commercial Point of View, G. Malcolm, Villa Ekdale, Freiburg in Baden, 8 November 1881.

interference in the name of combating the slave trade was thus both a welcome pretext to intervene in African and Arab territories (and waters) as well as a matter of imperial suspicion and competition.

The imperial competition between Britain and France crystallised in their refusal to grant each other authority to visit ships under their respective flags, and thus the aim to avoid the deceleration of one's own mobility. However, as mentioned above, most inspections targeted dhow boats. Still, there were problems with dhows misusing European and particularly French flags. In 1880, one of Fremantle's predecessors as commander-in-chief of the East Indies Station, William Gore Jones, went so far as to state that the French flag's protection represented the 'first and foremost' reason for persistence of the slave trade on the east coast of Africa which would otherwise quickly be eradicated. The French, however, refused to have their ships, or any ship carrying the French flag, searched by British patrols.

Connected with the arguments outlined above, Jones also took care to blame Islam more generally and the Ottoman Empire in particular. He distinguished the slave trade from the coolie system run by the British and referred to the Arabs' 'innate propensity to slave dealing' making the 'large and constant flow of slaves from the Egyptian to the Arabian coast' a purely Muslim affair (even if it was one hiding under a French facade) and calling for a convention with the Ottoman Empire in order to facilitate the inspection of the fast-sailing dhows travelling at night.[46] Thus, according to many British patrollers, the French Empire was just one obstacle to successful British controls in the Red Sea. More generally the Ottoman Empire was equally necessary as a partner to facilitate searches in the Red Sea region. In 1880 a convention between Great Britain and the Ottoman Empire was signed to facilitate the searches. Its enforcement was, however, not always guaranteed.[47] Still, the Ottoman Empire thus also played a decisive role in the creation of a system of comprehensive surveillance and its limits.

Despite these inter-imperial impediments to the tighter controls desired by the British, the microlevel reveals incidences of slavers being stopped and searched. Their cases provide some, even if limited insight into this particular kind of mobility. Take for example the case of a dhow captured by the Ottoman gunboat, *Sitt el-Bahar*, in 1884 near al-Luhayya in North

---

[46] TNA, FO 881/4337: Rear-Admiral Wm. Gore Jones to the Secretary to the Admiralty, Euryalus at Trincomalee, 24 September 1880.

[47] See Burdett (ed.), *Slave Trade into Arabia*, vol. 3, pp. 489–93: Convention between Her Majesty the Queen of Great Britain and Ireland and His Majesty the Sultan for the Suppression of the African Slave Trade, signed at Constantinople, 25 January 1880.

Yemen. According to an informant to the British Consul in Jidda, Jago, 52 slaves had been landed and the captain and crew of the dhow as well as five slave-dealers were imprisoned with the captain still having managed to secure four slaves for himself.[48] Jago was also informed that, even if fewer slaves were sold on the market in Mecca in 1884, 16 dhows were still reported to have landed 600 to 700 young Abyssinian and Nubian slaves close to Jidda for sale in the interior of the Arabian Peninsula. Providing snippets of the slave trade realities, Jago's report provides a valuable source as it illustrates the extent to which western political agents were dependent on second-hand news. Also, they could only modestly influence the political arena in this region; Jago, for instance, tended to receive only 'evasive' answers from the Ottoman governor in charge.[49]

Consequently problems in the choice and implementation of interventions run by one or several European powers were the order of the day. First, the inter-imperial conflicts between Britain and France, but also between Britain and the Ottoman Empire, complicated the issue. As mentioned above, from 1877 onwards a British-Egyptian convention and from 1880 a British-Ottoman convention were, at least nominally, in place, but no such agreements existed with France, for instance.[50] It was also difficult for western powers to get to grips with local structures, particularly in the Hijaz. In addition, the success of implemented measures was not easy to assess because the British had very limited access to information. In the context of the Red Sea mobility, it was not even clear who counted as a slave in the first place. For many contemporaries all these problems clearly hinted at the need for an international convention. As a continuation of the Berlin conference of 1884, and triggered by reports pointing to the persistence of slavery in the 'Congo Free State', in 1889 the conference of Brussels was organised to come to a solution concerning these problems.[51] The following section provides a close reading of the conference's declaration.

---

[48] *Correspondence with British Representatives and Agents Abroad, and Reports from Naval Officers and the Treasury, relative to the Slave Trade: 1884–85* (British Parliamentary Papers 1884–85, vol. LXXIII), No. 58: Acting Consul Razzack to Earl Granville, Jidda, 7 August 1884, and Inclosure: Letter received from Hodeidah.

[49] Ibid., No. 60: Consul Jago to Earl Granville, Jidda, 18 November 1884, Inclosure 1: Consul Jago to Osman Pasha, Jidda, November 8, 1884, and Inclosure 2: Osman Pasha to Consul Jago, Mecca, 17 November 1884.

[50] TNA, FO 541/24 (see also FO 881/4619 for the same documents): Report on the Suppression of the Slave Trade in the North-East of Africa, the Soudan, and the Coast Provinces of Egypt in the Red Sea and Gulf of Aden, Considered from a Political and Commercial Point of View, G. Malcolm, Villa Ekdale, Freiburg in Baden, 8 November 1881.

[51] See Miers, *Britain and the Ending of the Slave Trade* esp. pp. 236–91.

The international arena and the conference of Brussels

In the 1880s, the difficulty of coordinating inspections, the overlap of different spheres of sovereignty and the variety of agreements in place, led to attempts for international cooperation and culminated in the organisation of an international conference against slavery and the slave trade in Brussels (1889–90). The governments of Belgium and Great Britain invited representatives of all the powers who had participated at the Berlin conference of 1884, as well as delegates from Belgium's 'Congo Free State', to discuss how to put an end to the slave trade. With the abolition of the slave trade the stated theme of the meeting, it also formed a proxy to talk about other matters concerning Africa and its colonial future, such as the consumption of alcohol, arms trading, disputes of territories, import duties, the role of missionaries and so forth. Regarding the slave trade as such, the problematic points revolved around the right to search other vessels and in how far warships should be involved in the matter.[52]

The proceedings of the Brussels conference shared an exuberant rhetoric with the 1888 Suez Canal conference and in fact with many other international conferences. At the first meeting, Belgian statesmen as the hosts took the lead and were careful to avoid the theme of the accusations related to the Congo. Prince de Chimay addressed the delegates 'in the name of the brotherhood of nations and in that of civilization for the attainment of one of the noble aims that can animate humanity' and the president of the meeting, Baron Lambermont, greeted them with the following remark: 'Gentlemen you represent civilization in her most essential points – generosity, enlightenment, organized force.' In line with the general outlook of the conference and reflecting the voices heard at the chapter's beginning, slave trade was presented as the counterpoint of civilisation. Baron Lambermont referred to the slave trade as a 'wound, still open' that 'bleeds more copiously than before' with 300,000 to 400,000 humans traded yearly.[53]

Some pointed to the battles that had already been won. The British diplomat, Lord Vivian, lauded the efforts of Great Britain in abolishing the slave trade by referring to the impact of the 1841 quintuple treaty between England, France, Russia, Prussia and Austria in the aftermath of which slavery had stopped in 'all countries professing the Christian religion'. Focusing on the maritime slave markets, he noted that the

---

[52] *General Act of the Brussels Conference 1889–90; with annexed declaration* (British Parliamentary Papers 1890, vol. L).
[53] Ibid., pp. 2–4, 7.

Mediterranean had been freed from the slave trade for many years now, with the exception of those clandestinely conveyed as servants or passengers from Egypt, Tripoli and Morocco to the ports of the Eastern Mediterranean. However, in the Red Sea the slave trade was still rampant due to the 'climatic drawbacks, the shortness of the passage from shore to shore, the facilities which the configuration of the coast-lines gives to native craft engaged in the Trade and the abuse by slave-traders of the protection of European flags' all of which largely neutralised British efforts. Therefore, Lord Vivian concluded, the conference should concentrate on the Red Sea, the Persian Gulf and the African coast down to Madagascar – all located 'east of Suez'.[54]

The proceedings of the conference highlight the geographic configuration of the 'frontier of civilisation' and the process of channelling mobilities, which consisted most importantly in the distinction between different mobilities and the stigmatisation and deceleration of some of them. In the proceedings the Suez Canal emerged once again as a boundary between a world where slavery had been eradicated and one where this mission still had to be fulfilled. What is more, the proceedings, and particularly the declaration of the Brussels conference cemented the distinction between legitimate and illegitimate mobility, or more or less tightly controlled mobility, as a close analysis of the declaration's text can show.

The declaration attempted to regulate seafaring in the Red Sea much more closely. This effort was intimately connected with the mobility of dhows and other traditional forms of shipping, but also with the categories of religion and of race, laying down that no 'negro' seaman could be employed without prior consultation regarding the voluntariness of his engagement. These consultations were the duty of either the power of the flag under which the ship was sailing, or, alternatively, of the local authority. Furthermore the number of seamen had to be in proportion with the boat and its tonnage. The declaration also suggested that for the sake of tracking an eventual substitution of the seamen by slaves, seamen should be provided 'with a distinct mark' – without clarifying what kind of mark was envisaged.[55]

Regarding black passengers, the rules were even stricter. The captain had to declare them with their name, sex and height. Children should only be admitted when accompanied by a relative. Before departure, the passengers in question were called over, interrogated again, and then given or refused visas by the respective authorities. If no passenger was on board,

---

[54] Ibid., pp. 8–9.   [55] Ibid., pp. 180–1.

this had equally to appear on the ship's passenger rolls, which were to be checked at every port of call. Some concessions were, however, granted to these rather strict regulations. Very small fishing boats were exempt from some of the regulations: boats that were only partially decked and had a crew of 10 men or less, were exclusively used for fishing within the territorial waters, or employed in the coastal trade between the different ports of one power, and never left the coast further than five miles. These boats needed a licence, renewable every year, which also had to be communicated to the International Information Office.[56]

The declaration also offered a definition of 'native vessels', characterising them as ships that had the 'outward appearance of a native build or rigging' with the captain as well as the majority of the crew coming from a country bordering the coast of the Indian Ocean, the Red Sea or the Persian Gulf. These ships should only be granted a flag of one of the signatory powers if they were closely supervised and if the outfitters or owners were subjects or protected persons of the ship's flag, if they owned real estate in a district of authority and if they could prove their good reputation. The authorisation was subject to annual renewal and could be suspended or withdrawn at any time. Other standardisation measures included the obligation to inlay the ship's name and its tonnage on the stern and to print the port of registration on the sails.[57]

Besides the guidelines regarding particular travellers or seamen and the identification of ships, the declaration also contained specifications regarding the provision of infrastructure on land. Even if the main area of intervention was the sea, certain African regions were obliged to 'provide for the sanitary service and to grant hospitality and help to explorers and to all who take part in Africa in the work of repressing the Slave Trade'.[58] Another infrastructure-related section dealt with the question of how to return liberated slaves. Roads, railways and telegraphic lines should be constructed, if at all possible – alternatively an adequate living situation had to be found on the spot.[59] The declaration furthermore envisaged military posts being established at points notorious for slave trading, closely inspecting caravans upon their arrival on the coast (that is, on the border between Africa and Arabia), which would prevent the trade of persons brought from the African interior to the coast, but also 'the formation and departure landwards of the bands of slave hunters and dealers'.[60]

In addition to these local control points, an international information office should be created in Zanzibar that would collect all the licences for

---

[56] Ibid., p. 181.   [57] Ibid., p. 180.   [58] Ibid., p. 175.   [59] Ibid., p. 175.
[60] Ibid., p. 178.

flags, the list of crews and the registers of black passengers. This central-
ising institution highlights the vital role attributed to information already
encountered in earlier chapters. The institution would furthermore
assemble a European-language database of 'native ships' and keep dupli-
cates of registration documents. As a complement to this land-based
supervision, every ship of war was given the right to control vessels of
less than 500 tons (thus excluding the European large steamers) within a
zone extending between the coast of the Indian Ocean, Persian Gulf and
Red Sea from Beluchistan (today part of Pakistan) to Cape Tangalane in
Mozambique and down to Madagascar. In turn they were obliged to
report every such inspection to their own government and to the
International Information Office.[61]

Thus the declaration of the Brussels conference, which came in the
guise of the liberation of slaves, concurrently tightened the control of the
indigenous population's mobility. It added to the channelling of mobility
by distinguishing between different mobilities and experimenting with
control measures that reinforced these distinctions. The declaration
went as far as to state that 'on the African coast and on the adjacent islands
no negro passengers shall be shipped on board a native vessel except in
localities where there is a resident authority belonging to one of the
signatory powers'.[62] In the name of freedom and civilisation, and in an
age of largely passport-free travel, a rather extensive arsenal of measures
was outlined to register and to track certain travellers. In fact, also in the
eyes of some delegates and their governments, the declaration went too
far. In effect, France signed with exceptions only and the Netherlands
withdrew entirely.

The Brussels conference thus brought two themes most clearly to the
fore that are at the centre of processes of globalisation in the last decades
of the nineteenth century: the tension between free (and increasingly
rapid) movement and the clamp-down of other forms of mobility, which
were stigmatised, criminalised, classified and submitted to bureaucratic
control procedures; and the coexistence of imperial conflict and competition coupled with the need for international solutions and cooperation. Conferences such as the one in Brussels in 1889/90 provided both
an arena for such inter-imperial rivalry and a stage for the exuberant
rhetoric of the civilising mission and worldwide peace. Simultaneously
the realisation of the practical solutions established in the conference's
declaration were not always easy to bring about, as the following sections show.

[61] Ibid., p. 179.   [62] Ibid., p. 181.

Relying on local skills

With the declaration of the Brussels conference listing many measures of control, it is worth looking at their implementation more closely. In parallel to the ambivalent relationship between western political agencies and Bedouin skills in the Red Sea, local personnel, for instance as translators, and dhows as patrolling ships were necessary to effectuate control measures. While at the same time derided as outdated, indigenous forms of political organisation were crucial to make the desert controllable. Of course these were strategies that were already employed before the declaration of the Brussels conference, as the following analysis will show, yet they were reinforced in the years following 1890.

Acquiring information

As in the case of Dumreicher's Camel Corps, the reliance on indigenous skills was vitally important in order to make the control schemes work. In the decades before the Brussels conference, this had already been a field of experimentation and of official concern. One major obstacle was language – pointing again to the importance of middlemen in the everyday organisation of the European penetration of the Middle East. As virtually none of the officers responsible for the raids spoke Arabic, trustworthy translators had to accompany the Red Sea patrols. There were cases in which dhows that were 'actually engaged in legitimate traffic and with proper papers' were detained and sent to Suakin, as no one could read their Arabic-language documents. As a consequence the governor of Suakin directed all dhows to carry a pass in English, but as Egyptian officials did not follow the same strategy, the problem remained.

In 1877 a departmental committee consisting of representatives of the British Admiralty, the Treasury and the Foreign Office had already been appointed to give estimations of the costs of 'native interpreters' on the ships employed to fight the slave trade in the Red Sea.[63] The committee recommended that the staff of interpreters should consist of one first-class interpreter able to speak, read and write English as well as Swahili or Arabic, and 12 third-class interpreters 'with a fair colloquial knowledge of English and Swahili, and with sufficient colloquial Arabic to be

---

[63] TNA, FO 881/3369: Africa & Egypt Report Departmental Committee (Admiralty, Treasury, and F. O.). Cost of Native Interpreters on board HM Ships. Slave Trade on East Coast of Africa and the Red Sea (Messrs W. H. Wylde, R. Bell and J. W. Cole), 3 November 1877.
[64] Ibid.

understood'.[64] For the Gulf of Aden and the Red Sea they recommended two patrol ships equipped with two second-class interpreters and four third-class interpreters financed by the British Empire.[65]

The next difficulty was finding suitable and trustworthy interpreters. Captain Malcolm suggested the Christian schools in Syria or the American Mission in Cairo as institutions in which one might recruit. Maltese who spoke Arabic could also be engaged but he warned against the employment of men from Cairo, Suez, Port Said and Alexandria: 'They are glib talkers, but they translate most imperfectly, and can neither read nor write Arabic trustworthily, and are sure to deceive and accept bribes.' In order to secure their reliability and to make collaboration with Europeans more attractive, the translators had to be paid decently and to have a share in the prize money in instances of captured slavers.[66]

Besides formal translations, it was necessary to gain specific information from locals regarding the routes and hiding places of slave traders.[67] The collection of such information, however, posed fundamental challenges, because British patrollers and their middlemen found it difficult to find locals who were willing to collaborate, as Stanley Bosanquet, captain of the *Diamond*, explained:

> At Jeddah I set my Somali interpreter to learn what he could in the bazar, but he was at once denounced as my spy, and warned that the consequences of even talking about such matters might be serious to him, he being known as belonging to the 'Wild Swan' and this on the day after our arrival at Jiddah [sic].[68]

This scene points to the problem of acquiring trustworthy information at the local level, which was crucial in order to make the international agreements and declarations operational. This represented a persistent problem before and after the passing of the Brussels conference. It can thus be tied back to the difficult rulemaking processes of globalisation and to the limits of channelling mobility.

---

[64] Ibid.   [65] Ibid.
[66] TNA, FO 541/24 (see also FO 881/4619 for the same documents): Report on the Suppression of the Slave Trade in the North-East of Africa, the Soudan, and the Coast Provinces of Egypt in the Red Sea and Gulf of Aden, Considered from a Political and Commercial Point of View, G. Malcolm, Villa Ekdale, Freiburg in Baden, 8 November 1881.
[67] TNA, FO 881/4584: Reports Commander Morice Bey, near Massowah, 9 March 1877, 18 March 1877.
[68] TNA, FO 881/3522: Notes on Slave Trade in Red Sea, 9 February 1878. Memorandum by Commander-in-Chief *Diamond* G. Stanley Bosanquet.

Relying on dhows

In addition to the acquisition of reliable and speedy information and of trustworthy translations, the ships used for the patrols themselves needed to fulfil certain conditions. Due to the demanding navigation on the Red Sea, with its strong currents and scanty charts, Bosanquet suggested that in order to blockade the Red Sea coast effectively, a 'special class of fast-sailing small craft' had to be used with a larger steam cutter assisting when the weather permitted.[69] Beyond this, those involved in the process, such as Commander-in-Chief Jones, referred to the fact that different ships with indigenous crews were necessary in order to make the enterprise a success.[70] Captain George Malcolm, who served for seven months as director-general for the suppression of the slave trade in the Gulfs of Suez, Aden and the Red Sea in 1880/81, already suggested, in his report of 1881, that, despite the victory of steam, small sailing ships would be most suitable to capture the fast-moving slavers who navigated in the reefs. Additionally the Arabian shores were to be lined with tenders as 'no slaves will be embarked, neither will any sambook, baghla, sai'yah or katera [different types of dhows] venture out until the master ("nahoda") sees that the coast is clear'.[71] The return to technologies deemed 'old' or 'traditional' were thus essential in order to make the controls a success.

In yet another report, Malcolm pointed to the difficulty of identifying slave transporters in the first place. He suspected that many boats transited slaves only occasionally and then returned to their ordinary daily occupations, such as trading, fishing and pearl diving. Sometimes they could be identified as they carried more water than needed for their crew and passengers. Again Malcolm referred to the fact that the boats used for the slave trade were much faster than British steam cruisers. Their agility made it possible for them to wait for the shore to be clear and to then cross the Red Sea over the course of one night. Malcolm therefore argued for a fleet of one steamer and 15 dhows from which a 600-man-strong team would watch the coast from Suez to Cape Guardafui. Very much in parallel with Dumreicher's coastal guard, these men would not only keep the slave trade in check, but also all other evasions of customs and sanitary laws. If it stood united, as it had done against piracy,

---

[69] Ibid.
[70] TNA, FO 881/4337: Rear-Admiral Wm. Gore Jones to the Secretary to the Admiralty, Euryalus at Trincomalee, 24 September 1880.
[71] TNA, FO 541/21: Captain Malcolm to the Earl of Northbrook, Villa Ekdale, Freiburg in Baden, 12 October 1881.

Malcolm believed, the 'civilised world' could strike the 'death blow' to the slave trade by 1890 or 1900 at the latest – a very optimistic guess.[72] Other arguments for the use of dhows were of a more practical nature. The smoke of the steamers was too visible from far away and a depot of coal was always needed in close proximity, limiting the operable radius of the controls. The 'naked eye of the native' on the routine examinations of the horizon in the morning could apparently spot the mastheads of the ships from much further away than Europeans, giving the Navy boats only a very small chance of seizing a slave-trading dhow.[73]

In the decades following the Brussels conference dhow patrols were used more and more frequently. At the same time, the effectiveness of dhows and native officers was disputed as it was not at all clear that 'armed dhows having natives on board' would act in the way they claimed 'for native sympathies are entirely on the side of the slavers'. As in the case of translations and information acquisition, cooperation thus remained a risky undertaking on the part of the Europeans. Despite the 1880 convention between Britain and the Ottoman Empire, Ottoman ships could still not be searched, G. Davey concluded in 1898, and therefore 'the time is hardly yet ripe for the institution of any maritime police force in these waters'.[74] Despite the use of local translating skills and traditional forms of shipping in order to effectuate controls efficiently, there was thus a large discrepancy between the framework provided by the declaration of Brussels and its implementation in the Red Sea.

Controlling individuals: race, gender and religion

Some of the techniques necessary for the execution of checks had been established earlier, such as the reliance on local skills, and were adapted in the 1890s and 1900s. Others, including expanded rights to monitor and detain ships and individuals, had to be tested and adjusted to the local conditions. In this case, questions of acceleration and deceleration shifted from the emphasis on different means of mobility, with the specific targeting of dhows and local boats, to the categorisation of individual travellers on the move along the lines of race, gender or religion.

[72] TNA, FO 881/3829: Egypt: Report Slave Trade in Gulfs of Suez, Aden, and Red Sea (Capt. G. Malcolm), 22 July 1878.
[73] TNA, ADM 116/72: *HMS Falcon*, Suakim to Commander-in-Chief, Mediterranean, 2 November 1885.
[74] TNA, FO 78/5327: Consul Davey to R. N. O'Conor, Constantinople, Jidda, 25 October 1898.

Alongside the reliance on local skills and knowledge and in line with the Brussels declaration, registration and individual controls became key measures in controlling the movement of apparent slaves and slavers in the Red Sea. The alleged *trading* of slaves on dhows between the African and Arabian coasts was not the only problem that was to be dealt with through registration. Another issue was the *transportation* of slaves (bought, for instance in Mecca) – more and more often on board steamships – to the home countries of the pilgrims. The sometimes experimental introduction of new bureaucratic measures to register travellers, to instigate checks based on racial parameters, in line with certain aspects of the 1890 declaration, and to centralise this information to make it available where necessary, connects with broader issues regarding the bureaucratisation of space and the channelling of mobility.

Identification of slaves in Suez

In this context, Suez emerged as the control point, where slaves should be identified. The distinction between voluntary travellers and slaves was far from easy. Before the Brussels conference, extensive checks in Suez had already been introduced in order to stop the transfer of slaves bought at Mecca. These checks were organised along racial lines and targeted particularly unmarried women. They shall be illustrated by looking at one particular instance of reinforced controls in the Canal Zone in the mid-1880s.

Colonel Schaefer, head of the Egyptian Slavery Department since 1883, and Captain Crawford, commandant of the Suez police, conducted extensive checks in Suez and reported with satisfaction in 1886 to the authorities – perhaps slightly overstating the success of their scheme – that 'no single coloured person has been allowed to be passed without our getting satisfactory explanations about her position'. In order to identify their targets, Schaefer and Crawford's matrix was designed along the categories of race, gender and religion, focusing particularly on pilgrims returning from Mecca. With the total number of manumitted slaves given as 2,075 in 1885 and 2,628 in 1886,[75] in this period 119 persons were brought to the police office, of whom 78 turned out to be married women with their husbands, freed slaves who had undertaken the journey on their own initiative or servants accompanying their masters. 41 admitted that they had been purchased at Jidda. Of those 41 some carried papers of manumission while others did not possess such documentation. Only

---

[75] Correspondence Respecting Slavery in Egypt (British Parliamentary Papers 1887, vol. XCII), p. 7: Sir E. Baring to the Marquis of Salisbury, Cairo, 12 February 1887.

those without papers of manumission were directed to the Slave Home where they were taken care of. Others had been manumitted by their masters before the Qadi of Mecca, but were still equipped with manumission papers at Suez as they were frequently not aware that their masters had freed them in Mecca.[76]

Schaefer pointed out that this procedure of manumission actually went against the contemporary rules, as normally only those who themselves applied should be manumitted. He not only lobbied for the rules to be changed but also sent out preliminary guidelines for a procedure in which all slaves and their owners would be questioned at the office to distinguish slaves from voluntary travellers. If they had come with their masters and were leaving with them, no further action was to be taken. The police at Suez were furthermore requested to keep a list of 'all negresses or Abyssinians' entering the town. Further inspections were to be held aboard all ships bound for Turkey or any other country 'in order not to give trouble to pilgrims whose wives or families might be taken for slaves'. If the inspection in Suez proved impossible a telegram should be sent to Port Said in order to inspect the ship in question there. Every child under 12 and those slaves without 'freedom papers' were to be sent to Cairo either to be placed as servants in families or be returned to where they came from.[77]

Schaefer's proposal was received with considerable attention and triggered reactions in Egypt but also further away in Jidda. The British Consul in Jidda, Jago, quoted earlier, stated that as a result of the tight controls in the Canal Zone, pilgrims on their return from Mecca intending to take slaves with them were taking out manumission papers in Jidda (and in 40 cases in the last year had them legalised by Jago) in order to 'escape molestation at Port Said'.[78]

In Egypt, the Khedive agreed to register all slaves or servants leaving Egypt with the pilgrims and not to allow any to enter the country without the production of registered certificates.[79] Yet there were obvious shortcomings that hampered the implementation of such a radical plan. Baring was hopeful that this measure would prove successful for those landing in

[76] Ibid., p. 3: Lieutenant-Colonel Schaefer to Sir E. Baring, Cairo, 16 December 1886.
[77] Ibid., pp. 3–4: Lieutenant-Colonel Schaefer to Captain Crawford, commandant, Suez, 25 October 1886.
[78] Burdett (ed.), *Slave Trade into Arabia*, vol. 4, p. 253: Consul Jago to Marquis of Salisbury, Jidda, 4 April 1887; Tucker, *Women in Nineteenth-Century Egypt*, p. 174.
[79] Correspondence Respecting Slavery in Egypt (British Parliamentary Papers 1887, vol. XCII), p. 2: Conversation between Baring and Khedive; ibid., p. 6: Extract from the *Journal officiel*, 5 February 1887 – Circulaire approuvée par le Conseil des ministres, présidé par Son Altesse le Khédive, dans sa séance du mercredi, 26 janvier, 1887, et adressée aux moudirs et gouverneurs.

Egypt, if not always for those returning from Mecca and simply passing the Canal without disembarking in Egypt. In these cases, the implementation affected not only British and Egyptian steamers, but also those of other nationalities. Even if Schaefer's scheme thus could not be implemented in an all-encompassing manner, it illuminates the fact that mobility was categorised not only according to modes of conveyance and function of travel, but also according to categories such as race, gender or religion. If the limited implementation pointed for contemporaries to the necessity for an international agreement regarding these and similar searches, the declaration of the Brussels conference only brought a limited solution as the following section, returning from steamships to dhows, will show.

Controlling land and sea

Even after the 1890 declaration had been passed, there were conflicts between ships of different nationalities. For the time being, the problem of the misuse of French flags, mentioned above, was not solved. As France had not signed Article 32 of the Brussels convention granting the right to control ships, which the French delegates saw as an infringement on their country's sovereignty on the high seas, it was still very popular to be a dhow under French protection. There were different measures that dhow owners resorted to in order to receive French protection, such as buying land in the French colony of Djibouti and then registering their boats there.[80]

Despite these deficiencies, the British government, as one of the driving forces behind the Brussels declaration, took good care to implement it as fully as possible. In December 1895, a second convention between Britain and Egypt was signed in which Egypt formally laid down its commitment to combat the trade more forcefully. In effect Egypt granted British cruisers the right to 'visit, search, and if need be, detain any Egyptian vessel under 500 tons which shall be found engaged in the Slave Trade, as well as any Egyptian vessel of the same tonnage which shall be justly suspected of being intended for that trade', again targeting mainly dhows and indigenous shipping. The convention also expanded the definition of who counted as a slave, including 'white, negro or Abyssinian slaves destined for sale'.[81]

---

[80] Burdett (ed.), *Slave Trade into Arabia*, vol. 4, pp. 701–7: Commander and Senior Naval Officer Persian Gulf Division, *HMS Sphinx* to Admiral R. Kennedy, commander-in-chief, Basra, 1 January 1893.

[81] Convention between Great Britain and Egypt for the Suppression of Slavery and the Slave Trade, signed at Cairo, 21 November 1895 (British Parliamentary Papers 1896, vol. XCVII).

If the British focused their controls on the sea, other actors stressed the intricate relation between land and sea when it came to the slave trade. As a reaction to the expanded British powers to control the waters of the Red Sea, Khedive Abbas II tried to prove his power to exert political power inland and issued a proclamation to the sheikhs and tribesmen in the mountains along the Red Sea coast. The threatening gesture of the proclamation is worth quoting in full as it makes clear that the issue turned out, for the Khedive, to be about the reach of the state into inhospitable terrain far away from the political and economic centre of Egypt on the Nile:

It has come to the knowledge of His Highness the Khedive's Government that for some years past you have been encouraging the traffic of slaves through your countries to the Sea Coast where also you harbour the slave dealers from the Hegaz. This slave traffic is not only against the law of your country but against your religious law the more so as you commit this wickedness in peace and not war time. You think that on account of the distance from the River that you are safe from the arms of the law and can therefore abuse it without compunction, this is a great mistake, and the Slavery Department are here to-day to show you that His Highness's laws can be enforced even in the mountains across the desert.[82]

European powers launched similar attempts to counter British claims to power, by introducing their own strict measures of controls, often with the clear aim of expanding their areas of influence. In 1906, in order to structure the responsibilities of the 'signatory powers' more clearly, the Italians issued a memorandum, which was transmitted from Edward Grey to Lord Cromer, suggesting that every power would be responsible for the supervision of the Arabian coast opposite its African possession.[83] International and inter-imperial quarrels connected with political claims about controlling the coasts and hinterlands thus remained the norm.

Practically, the inspection of ships on the Red Sea remained a difficult undertaking. The case of two dhows found in 1902 on the Red Sea without papers but flying the Egyptian flag can serve to illustrate these difficulties and the sketchy information we can gain from the sources regarding the experiences of slaves and seamen on board these ships. The crew of the first dhow stated that they had come out for pearl fishing, but a young black boy on board claimed to be a slave and asked for protection. The second dhow carried excessive quantities of water and

[82] TNA, FO 78/5327: Proclamation to the Sheikhs & tribesmen of the Bisharin & Ababda Arabs & all Sub-tribal dwellers in the mountains along the Red Sea Coast, no date.

[83] Burdett (ed.), *Slave Trade into Arabia*, vol. 5, pp. 144–5: Sir Edward Grey to Earl of Cromer, F.O., 21 June 1906, Inclosure: Memorandum communicated by the Italian Embassy, 7 June 1906.

was therefore deemed suspicious. On their way to Suez the convoy got into bad weather and the dhows were completely destroyed. In the ensuing law case, Evelyn Baring backed Commander Gaunt, as the two dhows did not carry the papers required by the Brussels convention. However, the Department for the Repression of the Slave Trade concluded that the claims against the two boats could not be upheld before the martial court. The case of the dhow carrying the boy on board did make it before the courts in the end. It was subsequently abandoned, as the boy's evidence was much less specific than the statement he had originally made to Commander Gaunt.[84]

Gaunt was not the only commander who had trouble proving that a dhow, which did not fulfil some of the conditions set out by the 1890 convention, such as carrying the necessary paperwork, was actually trading with slaves. The reports of the patrols often contained cases such as that of a Turkish dhow captured without a passenger list in February 1902 'which despite breaching regulations, were not necessarily slave traders' or the Egyptian dhow, *Sultan*, that broke several regulations 'carrying seven negroes without permission' and had no permit to fly the Egyptian flag.[85] The checks that these ships had to undergo fleshes out what is meant by the channelling of mobility as it was effected in the Red Sea, and in this case the discrimination between the movement of steamers and dhows. At the same time, the difficulty to operationalise the 1890 agreement gives us an insight into the limits of internationalism once it came to implementation.

These limits of internationalism also entered the legal realm. Despite the existing conventions, many issues were settled on the grounds of bilateral agreements, such as a compromise of October 1904 between Great Britain and France resolving the dispute over the use of French flags by dhows from Masqat on the other side of the Arabian Peninsula for which the Permanent Court of Arbitration at The Hague had to get involved. The compromise stated that it was the right of each state to decide who could fly its flag, as long as three conditions were met: the owners or the possessors of the ship had to be either subjects or protected persons of the power whose flag they wanted to fly; they had to prove possession of real estate or other financial securities as well as a good reputation in that

[84] Burdett (ed.), *Slave Trade into Arabia*, vol. 5, pp. 36–8: E. F. A. Gaunt, Commander and Senior Naval Officer to Sir John Fisher, commander-in-chief, Mediterranean, *HMS Scout* at Port Said, 25 February 1902; ibid., pp. 42–4: Lord Cromer to Commander Gaunt, Cairo, 19 March 1902, forwarding Memorandum by Mr Machell, adviser to the Egyptian Ministry of the Interior.

[85] See Burdett (ed.), *Slave Trade into Arabia*, vol. 5, pp. 30–2: Commander Gaunt to Admiral Sir John A. Fisher, commander-in-chief, Mediterranean, *HMS Scout* at Massowah, 9 February 1902; ibid., pp. 34–5: E. F. A. Gaunt to Sir John A. Fisher, Report of detention of Egyptian dhow "Sultan", *HMS Scout* at Suez, 22 February 1902.

country; and they had to prove that they had never been involved in the slave trade. The court case concluded that the aim of the Brussels conference as a whole, and particularly of the disputed Article 32, was 'to admit to navigation in the seas infested by slave trade only those native vessels which are under the surveillance of the Signatory Powers'.[86] This case (and its definition of protection) provides a fitting illustration of the complicated issue of belonging in the Middle Eastern and Ottoman Empire context in and beyond the Red Sea, but also of the increasingly tight controls of non-European mobilities, which became obvious in connection with the paperwork dhows needed to provide.

Many problems thus remained after the turn of the century. Despite the aim of creating more transparency and clearer regulations, in 1900 an increase in the trade was reported which was explained by the famine raging in Central Africa as well as British and German East Africa, which 'had led the natives to offer themselves, with their wives and children, to the slave-dealers for sale, choosing the conditions of slavery rather than destitution and consequent death'. Yet the checks had also been increased and thus despite the conditions 'favourable to slave-dealing', the import of slaves into Turkey was not as much on the increase as it was in the Persian Gulf, pointing to the eastward movement of the civilising mission against the slave trade.[87] This progress was illustrated by debates just some months later, as to whether parts of the British patrolling fleet should relocate to the Mediterranean as the slave trade in the Red Sea had been more or less been brought under control.[88] The connection with the Mecca pilgrimage and its slave market, however, proved to be an enduring problem.[89]

Even if the implementation of the identification methods was at times problematic, the newly introduced controls of Red Sea shipping are an example of increasing constraints on certain kinds of mobility in the name of freedom or civilisation which were imbedded in broader global discourses on (anti-)slavery and religion. The controls sometimes were successful in freeing slaves, yet the sources also bring to light that far from all traditional boats carried slaves and that it was sometimes not at all

---

[86] Burdett (ed.), *Slave Trade into Arabia*, vol. 5, pp. 137–42: Permanent Court of Arbitration at The Hague, Award of the Tribunal of Arbitration constituted in virtue of the Compromise signed at London on 13 October 1904, between Great Britain and France.

[87] Burdett (ed.), *Slave Trade into Arabia*, vol. 5, pp. 3–4: Mr. Cornish to Sir A. Hardinge, Zanzibar, 24 February 1900.

[88] Burdett (ed.), *Slave Trade into Arabia*, vol. 5, pp. 5–6: Admiralty to the Under-Secretary of State, Foreign Office, 30 May 1900.

[89] OIOC, IOR L/PS/11/30: File 3459/1912 Hejaz. Murder of three Indians near Medina. Alleged attempt to revive the slave traffic on the pilgrim route. 19 July–18 September 1912.

evident for the western patrols who was to be identified as a slave in the first place. They fit well into the acceleration-deceleration paradigm outlined in earlier chapters, with Red Sea blockades as the most radical measure of deceleration. What is more, the practicalities of the controls of dhows in the Red Sea highlight the entanglement and conflict of different empires. They also point to areas where the binary of 'traditional' and 'modern', which many contemporaries easily employed, were difficult to uphold as the reliance on local equipment and middlemen proved essential. Hence they illustrate the intricacies of penetration, resistance and cooperation.

In this context the Canal and the Red Sea became – besides their function as an imperial connector – also spaces of delimitation and border control, separating Arabia and Africa, as well as being a moveable frontier of civilisation. This was most visible with the caravan route cut in two by the Canal. But the case of the slave trade is equally telling: most of the checks aimed at eradicating the trade occurred precisely during the transition between Africa and Arabia. Clearly, not only caravans and Bedouin, but also dhows were on the one hand threatened by more industrialised forms of conveyance (leading to the dwindling of opportunities in Suez, for instance) and sometimes – as in the case of slave trading – even criminalised.

Both the discourse on slavery and the slave trade 'east of Suez' and the practical controls of the Red Sea shipping shed light on the targeting of a specific mode of movement but also on the connection of mobility controls with categories such as race, gender or religion. Increasingly, and reinforced by the declaration of Brussels, checks on movement became racialised. They also targeted women travelling on their own or without a clearly identifiable marriage status. What is more, the perceived clash of civilisation and non-civilisation was attributed by many western commentators to Islam. This role will emerge even more sharply when looking in the next chapter at another specific form of mobility, the Muslim pilgrimage to Mecca.

6   Mecca pilgrims under imperial surveillance

The two forms of mobility surveyed in the preceding chapters – traversing the desert by camel and navigating traditional sailing boats – were fashioned by western travellers as counterparts to their own voyage on steamers and on the new waterway. At the same time the pilgrimage to Mecca (hajj) was also often perceived as a traditional or even 'archaic' movement associated with a religious fervour unsuited to modern times. Even if (as seen in Chapter 4) segments of the journey still had to be undertaken overland with the help of camels, large parts of the journey to Mecca were increasingly made on steamers. This 'modernisation of the hajj' created new practical problems of commercialisation, competition and surveillance. It also fostered fears of contagion, not only of disease, but also of political ideas – thus adding a new facet to the history of globalisation: faraway movements of travellers shuttling between Africa and Asia or within Asia could have political and sanitary repercussions in Europe. In order to counter these fears, as well as to avoid the possible costs of repatriation and subsistence of pilgrims, the last decade of the nineteenth century and the first decade of the twentieth witnessed the bureaucratisation of the hajj, which pointed to the limits of free movement in the imperial context but also engendered different forms of resistance and evasion.

This bureaucratisation can be elucidated by using the example of North African and particularly Algerian pilgrims under French rule who almost without exception travelled through the Canal. The chapter draws on French colonial archives, supplemented by British and Egyptian sources, which explains its emphasis on logistics and official procedures. Yet it connects these logistic and bureaucratic explorations with the larger fears and preoccupations that colonial powers connected with the pilgrimage, as it found reflection for instance in the reports of government inspectors accompanying the pilgrims on their journey. Always coming back to the Suez Canal, the chapter occasionally turns to the pilgrimage 'east of Suez', which increasingly worried colonial rulers and, more generally, Europeans. They were concerned by the idea that disease and political upheavals could spill over into the Mediterranean, as the opening of the Suez Canal had reduced the distance between Europe and the Muslim congregational sites of Mecca and Medina, which had now, as it were, shifted closer to Europe. After sketching the transformation of the hajj after the opening of the Canal and the British occupation of Egypt, as well as the main agents involved in organising, regulating and observing the pilgrimage, the focus will be more specifically on the concerns that western imperial powers came to associate with the pilgrims' mobility. As a reaction, and as a means of organising this mass event, regulations were developed around 1900 that give us clear insights into the workings of empires. For the long-distance control of mobile colonial subjects, different treatments of mobility were envisaged, such as forced movement (relocation and repatriation) or non-movement (with the frequent prohibition of pilgrimage), connecting clearly with the theme of acceleration and deceleration explored in earlier chapters. More specifically, this differentiation points to the conceptual broadening of mobility as a political tool in which acceleration was coupled with deceleration and standstill, but also to the limits of such political initiatives.

Transformations

In the late nineteenth and early twentieth centuries, the pilgrimage to Mecca was transformed. During this period new techniques of transport and new tools of supervision and control were introduced. While the organisation of the hajj had long been an important source of political legitimacy of the sultan of the Ottoman Empire and the presence of Ottomans near the holy sites, the transformation consisted in the exploration of new routes, the involvement of new companies and ships and in the increasing supervision of the journey, in particular by European colonial powers who, at least for certain trajectories, became the main agents involved in organising, regulating and observing the pilgrimage. In the following section, these three elements will be assessed in turn.

New routes

For centuries the pilgrimage to Mecca was a complicated and expensive undertaking, especially for those Muslims living far from the Hijaz. In the second half of the nineteenth century, however, it became a much more accessible mass phenomenon not least because of the development of steam navigation and the opening of the Suez Canal, with an estimated 3 million people undertaking the journey between 1879 and

1938.[1] Pilgrims from Syria, Egypt and Northern Africa began to abandon the tried and tested caravans and started to travel by ship, often through the Suez Canal. Indian pilgrims had followed maritime routes for a long time, of course, but steamer lines had now replaced traditional boats making the journey shorter and cheaper. The decline of the pilgrim caravans meant that the city of Jidda saw an enormous increase in steamships heading for its harbour.[2] Many of the growing number of pilgrims passed through the Suez Canal.[3] In the eyes of ʿUrabi, therefore, the Canal was not only the British route to India, but had also become the key to Mecca and Medina.[4] For the Muslims of the Mediterranean, in turn, the passage through the Canal also gained a special value as a *rite de passage*. In striking parallel to the changing dress codes of colonial travellers described in Chapter 1, the pilgrims shaved their heads and put on the prescribed attire for the visit to the holy cities following the Canal transit.[5] Consequently, despite the fact that fewer pilgrims were crossing Egypt by caravan, for many it remained 'the hyphen connecting their country to the destination of their pilgrimage'.[6] There were not only unprecedented numbers of religious travellers passing through Egypt on ships, but more and more Egyptians were undertaking the voyage themselves.[7]

However, the increase in the number of pilgrims passing through the Suez Canal did not automatically boost the local economy. Formerly the services necessary for the conveyance of pilgrims had been the main source of livelihood of the inhabitants of Suez. Now that the steamship companies had taken over its organisation, many pilgrims did not even pause at Suez at all.[8] In 1880 an unusually significant number of pilgrims had once again embarked at Suez, because the feast of sacrifice fell on a Friday: according to the statistics provided by the Consul of Suez in his annual report, 35,262 pilgrims took their passage from Suez, a considerable 14,372 more than in 1879, the majority of them being Egyptians, followed by Turks and North Africans, with over 8,000 pilgrims respectively, Javanese and Malays, with

---

[1] See McKeown, 'Global Migration', 162–3.
[2] See Freitag, 'Handelsmetropole und Pilgerstation', 68; see also Ewald, 'Crossers of the Sea', 78.
[3] See for instance ANOM, GGA 16H/83: M. Altemer, consul de France à Suez à Stephen Pichon, ministre des Affaires étrangères, Suez, 8 February 1909.
[4] See 'Arabi's Appeal to Gladstone', in Carter and Harlow, *Archives of Empire*, pp. 707–8.
[5] See for instance ANOM, GGA 16H/86: Rapport du commissaire du gouvernement à bord du navire à pèlerins l'Olbia de la compagnie Cyprien Fabre pendant le pèlerinage de la Mecque en 1902.
[6] Boniteau Bey, 'Le pèlerinage à la Mecque et les campements quarantenaires'.
[7] See Cromer, *Rapport de Lord Cromer*, p. 101.
[8] TNA, FO 78/2288: Consul West to the Secretary of State for Foreign Affairs, Suez, 13 September 1873.

just under 8,000, alongside 3,801 Syrians. Still the Consul concluded, 'the greatest number of Pilgrims now passes through the Canal which reduces the means of subsistence of the Natives of Suez, who have from time immemorial looked to the passage of Pilgrims as a means of earning their livelihood'.[9] Of the steadily increasing proportion of seafaring pilgrims, the Suez Canal thus saw a large part.[10] Suez itself, however, was left behind.

Companies and steamships

Besides all of its religious connotations, the hajj had also always represented a business opportunity. However, the stakes changed with the advance of steam in the late nineteenth and early twentieth centuries. Certain steamship companies successfully secured their share and, with government backing, established quasi-monopolistic positions for sections of the pilgrim traffic. This repartitioning of the shares highlights once again the role of private companies in shaping the specific features of globalisation around 1900 which has been explored in Chapter 3.

In 1875, the British government was concerned about the intervention of Egyptian officials in the Red Sea pilgrim traffic with the aim of securing it for the Khedival Steam Navigation Company (also: Khedivial Steamship Company). The Secretary of State for Foreign Affairs thus instructed Consul West at Suez to pay close attention to any interference by the Egyptian authorities in the transportation of Egyptian pilgrims to Mecca in favour of this company, which was harming the interests of British shipping in the Red Sea.[11] A similar allegation arose again in later years. Evelyn Baring, however, dismissed it in his report of 1906, stating that the Khedival Steam Navigation Company did not have a monopoly, and instead was simply the only one to submit itself to the increasingly tight regulations in place in Egypt.[12] The Egyptian government equally justified the preferential treatment of the company, as it was the only one that could guarantee the return of the large numbers of pilgrims without delay. Unlike its competitors, the Khedival Steam Navigation Company provided enough ships at the harbour of Yanbuʿ in time for the pilgrims' arrival from Medina, to avoid situations such as that of 1889 when about 1,000 Egyptian pilgrims and 1,500 Moroccans had waited there for a long time under dire conditions and without

[9] TNA, FO 78/3334, sheets 130–1: Report on the Trade, Commerce and Navigation at Suez for the Year 1880.
[10] See Miller, 'Pilgrims' Progress', 209.
[11] TNA, FO 78/2409: Draft Foreign Office to Consul West, London, 21 May 1875.
[12] Cromer, *Rapport de Lord Cromer*, p. 101.

sufficient water.[13] Other reports backed these opinions and called to attention earlier times, when the Egyptian pilgrims had been obliged to travel on board ships of Russian companies or *sanbūks* (large dhows) of the *Compagnie Maksoussah*. Since then, the deployment of *sanbūks* had become marginal as they could not cope with the sheer amount of pilgrims and provided less security than the steamers.

Many companies, such as *Norddeutscher Lloyd*, P&O and *Messageries Maritimes* did not want to take pilgrims aboard in the first place, especially for the homeward journey from Mecca as they would then face much stricter quarantine regulations and other controls.[14] The quarantine enactments point once again to the entanglement of different domains, such as the political and the commercial realms, as well as imperial and international levels of decision-making. As the new imperial and international regulations came to impose longer waiting times and stricter controls, many steamships consequently passed Jidda in a northerly direction without taking any pilgrims on board. As a result the Egyptian government had to agree with most of the demands of the Khedival Steam Navigation Company, since it otherwise risked the possibility that pilgrims might be left behind in Jidda.[15]

Many Europeans, especially those involved in the shipping business, did however not share the Khedive's and Baring's attitude that the factual monopoly of the Khedival Steam Navigation Company was serving the pilgrims' best interests. M. Anslijn, the Dutch Agent and Consul General in Egypt, told Consul Miéville in May 1883 that it would be preferable to have a European company undertaking the service between Qamaran and Jidda at a fixed price.[16] But in fact, quasi-monopolies were held by certain European businesses too. The pilgrims from French North Africa frequently travelled on ships of the company *Cyprien Fabre* from Marseilles founded in 1881.[17] Most of the southeast-Asian pilgrims were travelling on ships belonging to a consortium including *Holts* and *Rotterdamsche Lloyd*. In the last decades of the nineteenth century and in connection with the success of steam navigation, the pilgrimage thus became an 'imperial

---

[13] DWQ, Majlis al-Wuzarā', Niẓārat al-Dākhiliyya 18/ـ, 0075–007573: 'Adam iltizām al-hujāj al-miṣriyyin bi-l-safar fi bawākhir al-sharika al-khidīwiyya.

[14] DWQ, Majlis al-Wuzarā', Niẓārat al-Dākhiliyya 18/ـ, 0075–007576: Note Ministère de l'Intérieur, no date.

[15] DWQ, Majlis al-Wuzarā', Niẓārat al-Dākhiliyya 18/ـ, 0075–007578: Annexe au N° 5, Assemblée générale, no date.

[16] TNA, FO 423/13: Consul Miéville to Consul Cookson, Alexandria, 25 May 1883.

[17] CCIMP, HdC 157: Compagnie Cyprien Fabre 1881–1919.

trade' in which the Egyptian Khedival Steam Navigation Company actually represented the exception.[18]

The attempt to turn the hajj into an imperial trade did not always prove successful however, as the Thomas Cook Company's endeavour to participate in the organisation of the annual pilgrimage illustrates. In 1884 the British-Indian government commissioned the tourist agency to offer state-subsidised package tours from India to Mecca. The *Calcutta Gazette* reported how the government of India had time and again worried about the 'discomforts and sufferings' experienced by pilgrims during the journey. However, it had not wanted to intervene in religious affairs. In 1884, Cook offered to organise the pilgrims' transit between India and Mecca. The British-Indian officials concluded that the 'extensive experience gained by Messrs. Cook and Son in connection with the requirements of schemes of a similar character' – up to that point, the firm had specialised in tourism and had occasionally organised troop transports – and their success in such schemes demonstrated that the firm was qualified to 'assist the Government' in the standardisation of the pilgrim journeys between India and the Arabian Peninsula, which would be useful for the colonial government and convenient to the pilgrims.[19] Thomas Cook thus proposed an all-inclusive trip to Mecca and Medina and promised to comply with all regulations. Yet the enterprise was not successful. As the arrangements proved more expensive than planned, and as fewer pilgrims actually used the services, every year the scheme depended on large subsidies on the part of the British government in India and was heavily criticised, carrying increasingly fewer pilgrims, only being finally abandoned in 1894.[20]

Disregarding their limited success in India, Thomas Cook and Son attempted to branch out into North Africa, writing to the governor general of Algeria in April 1890 and presenting their services. However, the governor general replied that Algerians had to use only French companies.[21] Despite this preferential treatment of French companies, the young diplomat, Paul Lépissier, later French Consul in Baghdad and then Bangkok, complained in his report on the pilgrimage of 1910 that

---

[18] Miller, 'Pilgrims' Progress', 201–2.

[19] ANOM, GGA 16H/84: Supplement to the *Calcutta Gazette*, 10 February 1886 – Conveyance of pilgrims between India and Mecca by Messrs. Thomas Cook and Son.

[20] *Papers relating to the Arrangements made with Messrs. Cook & Son for the Conduct of the Pilgrim Traffic to and from the Red Sea during the Years 1884–1895* (Calcutta: Office of the Superintendent of the Government Printing, India, 1896).

[21] ANOM, GGA 16H/85: Thomas Cook Company au gouverneur général de l'Algérie, 20 March 1890; ibid.: Le gouverneur général de l'Algérie au représentant de la Compagnie Thomas Cook & Son, Algiers, April 1890 (no exact date).

the profits reaped from the business were meagre, hinting at the difficulty of controlling the pilgrims' embarkation as some ships, particularly of Russian origin, were in the hands of 'veritable pirates' doing anything to secure their share in the traffic.[22]

Notwithstanding frequent disputes regarding monopolies, concessions, routes and rewards, it was clear that in the last decades of the nineteenth century the pilgrim traffic had changed its major mode of conveyance, even if other, now marginalised, forms of transportation necessarily remained part of the pilgrim experience. As seen in Chapter 4, many pilgrims had to rely on a combination of means of transport and switched from ships to camels in Jidda or Yanbu'. The 'modernisation' of pilgrim mobility was thus not true for the whole trajectory and it was not true for all pilgrims. A pilgrim from Congo, for instance, who presented himself at the French consulate at Jidda in the early 1900s showed his passport containing stamps of all the French military posts he had passed by foot in the preceding years – of a group of 40 pilgrims leaving Congo, he was the only one to arrive.[23] Even pilgrims from North Africa often spent many years on the hajj, which remained an extremely expensive undertaking for most of them.

Also, regardless of the faster and increasingly standardised times and costs of travel, the conditions on the pilgrim ships were often less than salubrious. The near foundering of an entire ship which would have led to the death of almost a thousand pilgrims, as in the case of the steamer *Jeddah*, immortalised in Joseph Conrad's *Lord Jim*, was perhaps a singular event, but pilgrims often complained about their treatment.[24] Many untrustworthy operators attempted to multiply their gain to the disadvantage of their passengers. Regularly, old ships were used that were no longer deemed fit for the transportation of Europeans. Additionally the large amounts of baggage and food that the pilgrims carried – meals were seldom included in the fare – posed a challenge to the order and

---

[22] ANOM, GGA 16H/86: Le pèlerinage de 1910, le mouvement islamique et le comité, le mouvement arabe, le grand cherif et le Khedive, signed Paul Lépissier, Jidda, 25 January 1911 p. 2.

[23] Ibid., pp. 6–7; see also ANOM, GGA 16H/86: Rapport du commissaire du gouvernement à bord du navire à pèlerins l'*Olbia* de la compagnie Cyprien Fabre pendant le pèlerinage de la Mecque en 1902 for other Congolese pilgrims; for Algerian pilgrims who had walked all the way to the Red Sea, see CADN, Commission interministérielle des affaires musulmanes, vol. 1, Procès-verbaux des séances de la commission, Novembre 1911–Juillet 1914, 27 January 1912.

[24] See 'An Appalling Disaster: A Steam-Ship founders at Sea, and over 900 Persons Perish', *New York Times*, 11 August 1880. Joseph Conrad transforms the *Jeddah* into the *Patna* 'eaten up with rust worse than a condemned water tank' (*Lord Jim*, p. 17). See also Moore, 'Newspaper Accounts of the Jeddah Affair'. For complaints on ships, see, for instance, OIOC, IOR R/20/A/1497: The First Assistant Resident, Aden, 31 May 1910: complaints of pilgrims on board the *SS Islami*.

cleanliness of the decks. In 1880, the *Administration sanitaire de l'Empire Ottoman* had already circulated a message stating that the conditions on the steamers used for the conveyance of pilgrims were often abominable, with the exception perhaps of British ships regulated more tightly through the Passenger Vessels Act of 1803 and other following legislation intended to improve hygiene and provisions on board the ships. Unsurprisingly the sanitary administration of the Ottoman Empire thus continued to call for stricter and more uniform regulations.[25] Yet the difficulty to implement such regulations indicates the power of the shipping companies in charge on the one hand and the complicated trans-imperial nature of the hajj and its control on the other.

Observing the pilgrimage

Whenever pilgrims travelled on ships other than those reserved for their category of travellers only, their co-passengers observed them with astonishment and, sometimes, compassion. Isabel Burton described the 800 pilgrims who boarded her ship at Jidda during her journey in 1879 in detail; their hardships and diseases made her reflect on her own privileged situation.[26] The 'modernisation' of the pilgrimage thus suddenly could catapult the hajj into the trajectories of western travellers.

Besides these personal impressions, there were numerous official reports on the conditions of the pilgrims. As a sign of the closer governmental supervision and in connection with political and sanitary concerns connected to the pilgrimage, between the 1880s and the 1900s, official inspectors accompanied the pilgrims from French North Africa and noted their number, but also the sanitary conditions and special occurrences on board what were most often ships recycled after years or decades of European service. These inspectors carried a double function, checking on the one hand the adherence to certain minimum standards, on the other serving as rapporteurs and thus as instances of political control. Only very few of the inspectors filed positive reports, such as Brurache, government inspector of the 1902 pilgrimage on the steamer *Savoie*, who pointed to the recycling of ships which had been used in other contexts before. He stated that the ship he inspected had formerly served to transport 1,200 Italian emigrants to Argentina, yet now it was certified to carry 924 pilgrims only in order to assure the pilgrims comfort as well as good

[25] ANOM, GGA 16H/84: Administration sanitaire de l'Empire Ottoman, Circulaire aux agents de la santé, Constantinople, 28 April 1880.

[26] Burton, *A. E. I. Arabia Egypt India*, pp. 84, 94–106.

hygiene conditions, enabling the pilgrims for instance to practice the ritual ablutions when approaching the holy sites.[27]

Such positive statements remained the exception. The inspector accompanying the *Olbia* in 1902 – a ship dating from 1874, which had first been used in Britain and then bought by *Cyprien Fabre* for the purpose of transporting pilgrims– reported that the passengers had complained constantly about the medical services and the treatment of their luggage, which led him to compare the pilgrim transport to the slave trade. He cynically stated that transporting pilgrims was even more lucrative than trading sheep, since lost sheep could represent a ground for compensation, whereas dead pilgrims were simply immersed in the sea without further consequences. He also accused the companies of making false promises in their brochures and criticised the monopoly exerted by the association of the French companies *Caillol, St Pierre, Cyprien Fabre* and *Transports Maritimes.*[28]

Other assessments of the same year were not very positive either, for example the report of the inspector on the ship *Le Villequier*, again formerly in British use and then discarded. The inspector expressed his scepticism concerning the civilising mission: 'These poor pilgrims! All is their enemy: the heavens, the earth and the humans – both civilised and barbaric.' In his opinion cargo boats should not have been employed as pilgrim boats at all, but instead only such ships as had been put to the test in other mass transports, such as the conveyance of emigrants or troops.[29]

The depictions of the inspectors also provide us with glimpses of the pilgrims' Canal passage. Not only for colonial travellers and tourists, but also for pilgrims, the passage through the Canal was a significant moment during their journey. Inspector Gillotte accompanying the pilgrims from Bône to Jidda in 1905 included numerous photographs of the pilgrims and their situation on board, such as the one shown above, but also of the Canal and Port Said, in his report. He furthermore described particularly vividly the change of mood and behaviour that the pilgrims showed upon arrival in the Red Sea, even if he did not explicitly call it a *rite de passage*.

The well-being of the pilgrims was only one and, arguably, not the main concern of the French imperial agents' increasingly close supervision.

---

[27] ANOM, GGA 16H/86: Rapport présenté au gouverneur général de l'Algérie par M. Brurache administrateur commissaire du gouvernement pour le pèlerinage à la Mecque en 1902.

[28] ANOM, GGA 16H/86: Rapport du commissaire du gouvernement à bord du navire à pèlerins l'Olbia de la compagnie Cyprien Fabre pendant le pèlerinage de la Mecque en 1902.

[29] ANOM, GGA 16H/86: Confidentiel. Pèlerinage de la Mecque de 1902. Rapport du commissaire du gouvernement à bord du *Villequier*.

Figure 19 'Pilgrims on Board the *América*', photograph in the report of M. Gillotte, Administrateur de la Commune mixte d'Aïn-Témouchent, on the pilgrimage to Mecca in 1905.

Fears of contagion, both medical and political, often discussed under the heading of pan-Islam, came to be increasingly connected with the trip to Mecca and the return journey through the Canal to the sphere of the Mediterranean. What is more, the possible costs that the political authorities could encounter if the pilgrims could not pay for their return home was a matter of concern. At the same time, the different empires' relationship to Islam was marked by the apprehension of antagonising their Muslim populations which were perceived as increasingly globally interconnected. As a consequence of these concerns, which will be developed in some detail below, new measures of identification and supervision were introduced, once again often in an experimental and sometimes hesitant manner and frequently not entirely successfully.

Empire and religion: European concerns

The system of surveillance monitoring the hajj was triggered by various concerns related to contamination and invasion, which will be assessed in the following.[30] On the one hand, infectious diseases, such as cholera, which had haunted European cities since the 1830s, as well as new medical knowledge regarding disease causation, had sensitised Europeans to the spread of epidemics. Such epidemics were increasingly linked to the pilgrimage. On the other hand, it was not only infectious bacteria that had to be kept from diffusing through the Suez Canal, but also political ideas, such as 'pan-Islam', a catchall phrase referring to any common political project that could unite Muslims and lead them to revolt against colonial rule.[31] Finally, colonial governments worried about the dependency on governmental relief by those subjects venturing on the religious voyage.

Imperial attitudes towards Islam

Besides giving an insight into the techniques employed to control mobility and their more or less successful implementation in places such as the Suez Canal, the European empires' regulatory efforts concerning the pilgrimage raises questions regarding the relationship of empire and religion, more specifically Islam, but also regarding the boundaries of the colonial state's intervention more generally. The example furthermore sheds light on disagreements between the metropole, often opting for tighter controls, and the local colonial governments and agencies.

The treatment of the pilgrimage also illuminates the differing approaches adopted by the British and French Empires towards their Muslim subjects as well as inter-imperial observation and competition. The regulation of the hajj, representing a central example of the treatment of religion in the context of empire, was thus a matter of constant inter-imperial comparison. Also the relationship between western powers, particularly the French governmental agents, the (state-sponsored) companies transporting the pilgrims, and the *sharīf* of Mecca remained precarious and continually had to be negotiated.[32] Every new regulative measure implemented by imperial governments or agents furthermore carried the danger of upsetting not only the *sharīf* but also the Muslim population in the colonies.

---

[30] On the relationship between empire and religion more generally and Islam and colonialism more specifically, see Low, 'Empire and the Hajj'; Slight, 'British Imperial Rule and the Hajj'.

[31] On pan-Islam, see Landau, *The Politics of Pan-Islam*; for a more extensive discussion of British reactions see Özcan, *Pan-Islamism*.

[32] See ANOM, GGA 16H/85: Copie d'une lettre adressée au ministre des Affaires étrangères par le consul de France à Djeddah, Jidda, 14 January 1892 ; ANOM, AFFPOL (ministère des Colonies), Maroc 967: Ministre des Affaires étrangères au ministre des Colonies, Paris, 14 January 1908.

Particularly after the experience of the Indian Uprising of 1857–58, the British, or at least the colonial administrators on the ground, were often careful to avoid antagonising Muslim populations in India. The French administration in Algeria was often less concerned with such matters, at least to begin with. A further difference was the French state-centred approach, which often involved more bureaucracy, the introduction of new fees and stricter regulations, and was contrasted with the reliance on private initiatives in the British case, as the young French diplomat Paul Lépissier pointed out.[33]

It is useful to dwell on the report by Lépissier as it lends some insight into imperial perceptions of the pilgrimage. The European intervention – whether funded publicly or privately – was, according to Lépissier, still crucially necessary, as the pilgrims were susceptible to dangerous influences, such as religious foundations in Mecca providing food and shelter, and perhaps also dangerous ideas and thoughts. This potential corruption was particularly perilous, he argued, as the pilgrims consisted not of the rich or intellectual classes of the population, but of the 'ignorant and fanatical masses ... whose stupidity is immeasurable'. They were thus, according to Lépissier, susceptible to becoming overly excited by the voyage and by the number of Muslims they encountered in Mecca.[34]

The hajj and its regulation thus came to be symptomatic of the imperial differences, difficulties and conflicts that could be faced in other contexts as well. The British reverted at times to the strategy of 'outsourcing', as in the case of the (in the long run unsuccessful) attempt to commission Thomas Cook's company, but also of the Muslim 'protectors of pilgrims' employed in Indian harbours or benevolent societies financing the relief of Muslim pilgrims in need. France remained true to its state-centred approach. In 1911, a *Commission interministérielle des affaires musulmanes* was convened to review the modalities of their policies towards Muslims with representatives of the main governmental agencies and of all the colonies with Muslim inhabitants.[35] The French and British attitudes and strategies towards their Muslim populations thus differed considerably, yet they also changed over time with the years before the First World War heralding a more sensitive policy towards Islam in the French Imperial context in relation to compulsory military service of Muslim populations.[36]

---

[33] ANOM, GGA 16H/86: Le préfet du département d'Oran à M. le gouverneur general à Alger, Oran, 21 March 1906; ANOM, GGA 16H/86: Le pèlerinage de 1910, le mouvement islamique et le comité, le mouvement arabe, le grand cherif et le Khedive, signed Paul Lépissier, Jidda, 25 January 1911, p. 13.
[34] Ibid., p. 8.   [35] See Le Pautremat, *La politique musulmane de la France au XXe siècle.*
[36] Ageron, *Histoire de l'Algérie contemporaine*, pp. 168–82.

In the discussions of the *Commission interministérielle*, some claimed that France had to maintain its stringent attitude, as anything else would be interpreted as a sign of weakness; others argued, as the commandant de Saint-Exupéry did in April 1913, that 'it was particularly necessary for France to be more tolerant; our method of government has a bad reputation among the Muslims'.[37] Still, in line with the worries outlined earlier, one of the main concerns of the *Commission* was pan-Islam and one of its recommendations was the implementation of stricter measures of identification. On the one hand all Muslim travellers were meant to ideally possess a passport with a photograph instead of the identity cards or the passports with their generic personal description – a measure that was deemed still less insulting than the Berthillon method, involving physical and facial measurements and widely used for the classification of criminals. On the other hand the consuls sent to Jidda had to possess or acquire the skill of identifying people ethnically.[38] Measures of identification were thus constantly reconceptualised at meetings in Europe and subsequently adopted and changed in the different colonial contexts.

Contagion: disease and political ideas

The increasing colonial involvement in the pilgrimage and its growing bureaucratisation highlighted both the disciplining of religion more generally and the connection of such control measures with prophylaxes not only against epidemics but also against possible political upheavals. The fear of contagious diseases was one of the prime reasons for the growing concern over the pilgrimage. The Suez Canal was thus not only perceived as a frontier of civilisation separating western mobility from its 'eastern' counterparts, but simultaneously as a sanitary boundary between a modern Europe, where epidemics belonged, in theory, to the past, and disease-ridden areas of the world, such as Mecca and Medina, or India.[39]

The return of epidemic diseases to Europe in the second half of the nineteenth century agitated most European governments. The resurrected threat of contagious disease was particularly connected with cholera, but also with the plague.[40] However, from the 1880s onwards, with Louis Pasteur's and Robert Koch's advances in the scientific exploration

---

[37] CADN, Commission interministérielle des affaires musulmanes, vol. 1, May 1911–January 1916: Séance du 10 avril 1913.
[38] CADN, Commission interministérielle des affaires musulmanes, vol. 1, May 1911–January 1916: Séance du 3 mai 1912.
[39] See Harrison, 'Quarantine, Pilgrimage, and Colonial Trade'.
[40] See, for instance, Echenberg, *Plague Ports*.

of bacteriology, the concept of contagion was revolutionised.[41] As a result the transmission of diseases became more directly connected with the immediate contact between healthy and infected people or material. In an age of accelerating mobility, this very mobility therefore received a dangerous new side-effect.

As will be explored in further detail in Chapter 7, contagion was obviously a phenomenon that did not stop at the boundaries of nations and one that necessitated internationally coordinated action.[42] During the international sanitary conferences, debating cholera, but also plague and yellow fever, the Mecca pilgrimage was a recurrent item on the agenda. The conferences of 1866 and 1894 particularly made the topic their central concern. Pilgrims on their way to Mecca came to be seen as disease carriers par excellence. They were believed to bring plague or cholera from India to the Hijaz where they infected their fellow Muslims who then travelled through the Suez Canal on to North Africa, to the Levant, or to Russia carrying the germs to formerly disease-free regions.

The idea of contagion transcended the medical realm and entered the world of politics, as imperial governments, particularly the French, began to worry not only about transmittable diseases migrating via Mecca, but also about the dispersal of subversive ideas that were exchanged at the biggest meeting place of Muslims on the globe. Pan-Islam and connected anti-imperial activities moved to the forefront of many imperial agents. These fears could be connected to specific persons carrying the political ideas from one place to another, or to specific political events in one region, which would lead to a politically heated climate among the pilgrims meeting in Mecca. As a reaction to the uprisings of 'Urabi in Egypt and the Mahdi in the Sudan, the French took special steps to supervise the hajj in 1882, 1883 and 1884. In the eyes of the French imperial agents, the multi-ethnic composition of the pilgrims also carried the potential risk of unrest caused by political issues originating outside the Middle East. In 1900 the French government worried that the Chinese Boxer Rebellion could spill over and trigger anti-European upheaval in Islamic circles from Mecca to North Africa.[43]

In connection with broader political movements and developments, individuals came under suspicion as well. The global biography of one Brahim Aouat is particularly telling. Aouat came under the guarded eyes

---

[41] On fears of contagion in a more abstract sense, see Otis, *Membranes*; Bashford and Hooker (eds.), *Contagion*.
[42] See Huber, 'The Unification of the Globe by Disease?'
[43] ANOM, Affaires politiques (Ministère des colonies) (Maroc) 967: Ministère des Colonies, Service des affaires musulmanes, Paris, 3 July 1900.

of the French authorities in 1886 as a potential political agent of the *sanūsiyya*, a Sufi order active since the early nineteenth century that connected religious and political engagement and fought, for instance, against Italian colonial rule in Libya. The French diplomatic representative at Tunis collected intelligence proving that Aouat had commanded a caravan between Yanbu' and Medina for a considerable amount of time and that he had been interned in Constantinople. From there he had fled and taken refuge in Tunis, which had once been the home of his family. At the time of the French investigation he was leaving for Yemen where his family was in hiding among nomadic tribes. Aouat's story is definitely an example of far-reaching networks. The French official was finally convinced, however, that he had no political mission, but simply wanted to escape from Turkish imprisonment, which he had suffered for four years, and therefore recommended him to his colleague at Port Said so that he could pass without further hindrance.[44]

Around the turn of the century, the western fear of political activism was dissociated from specific individuals and became more general. Using a contemporary bacteriological analogy, French officials worried that the 'germ of the dream of pan-Islam' would be inculcated in their colonial subjects and that the missionaries of the *sharīf* of Mecca were sowing their propaganda particularly among pilgrims of regions that were already difficult for colonial powers to control.[45] The danger was directly related to the multi-ethnic composition of the pilgrimage, which observers (in direct counterpart to descriptions of the multi-ethnic Port Said) found so striking. During the pilgrimage, Jidda particularly was filled with an extremely varied crowd where, according to one French governmental inspector on board the *Cyprien Fabre* ship *Olbia*, all Muslim peoples – he listed Turks, Egyptians, Arabs, Russian subjects, Kalmaks, inhabitants of Bukhara in Uzbekistan, Circassians, Senegalese, Central Africans, Afghans, Indians, Javanese, Malayans, Persans, Tibetans and Chinese – were represented.[46]

As seen in connection with the events in China of 1900, this perception of Jidda, as a global locality where Muslims from all over the world met, carried a seed of danger in relation to colonial rule. The inspector on board the *Olbia*, Vauthier, thus went on to reflect on the danger of the

---

[44] CADN, Port Said 16: Résidence générale de la République française au consul de France à Port-Saïd, Tunis, 20 June 1886.

[45] ANOM, Affaires politiques (Ministère des colonies), Maroc 967: Ministère des Colonies, Service des affaires musulmanes, Paris, 3 July 1900.

[46] ANOM, GGA 16H/86: Rapport du commissaire du gouvernement à bord du navire à pèlerins l'*Olbia* de la compagnie Cyprien Fabre pendant le pèlerinage de la Mecque en 1902.

spread of political ideas, stating that the officials had often considered suppressing the pilgrimages, as a 'show of three or four hundred thousand pilgrims gathered from almost every point of the globe' could leave the ordinary pilgrim with an exaggerated idea of the force of Islam. This heated milieu, fanaticised by prayers and endured suffering, was to him most obviously a breeding ground of pan-Islamic ideas.[47]

Not all inspectors came to the same conclusion, however. Others in fact argued that the experience of the hajj could act as a deterrent to pan-Islamic ideas. Whereas Vauthier had claimed that the mere agglomeration of Muslims would spread revolt, another inspector on board the *Villequier* became convinced of the contrary, namely that the hajj highlighted the differences between their habits, languages and manners. He saw the fear of pan-Islam as a western creation: 'the idea of pan-Islam, as it is understood among us, would leave them quite perplexed if one were to try to explain it to them'. The Algerians, for example, he argued, hated the Bedouin of the Hijaz, despised the Bukharians and reproved the Turks and Asians.[48] In 1910 Paul Lépissier argued that the pilgrimage was in fact counterproductive to pan-Islam, as the crude religious practices, the systematic plundering of the pilgrims and the lack of comfort and security that those venturing on the journey to Mecca encountered left them with a rather bad impression. According to him the pilgrimage was thus much less of a threat to European influence than usually thought.[49] Furthermore, so was the opinion of some government officials, pan-Islam could also be inculcated into the Algerians at home without travelling to Mecca at all: there were recurrent worries regarding the manipulation of Algerians through sects, such as the abovementioned *sanūsiyya* who apparently sent envoys to North Africa to spread discontent.[50]

While some voices urged calm (obviously not without expressing their depreciation of the pilgrimage and Islam as such), they should be read as a reaction to the widespread discourse of the medical and political twin-danger of contagion connected with the annual meeting in Mecca. The fears of political contagion in Mecca were sustained by the mysterious impenetrability of the gathering for Europeans and remained en vogue

---

[47] Ibid.
[48] ANOM, GGA 16H/86: Confidentiel. Pèlerinage de la Mecque de 1902, Rapport du commissaire du gouvernement à bord du *Villequier*.
[49] ANOM GGA 16H/86: Le pèlerinage de 1910, le mouvement islamique et le comité, le mouvement arabe, le grand cherif et le Khedive, signed Paul Lépissier, Jidda, 25 January 1911, p. 9.
[50] ANOM, GGA 16H/84: Le gouverneur général de l'Algérie, Circulaire aux 3 préfets et aux 3 généraux, Algiers, 23 November 1898.

during the first decade of the twentieth century, drawing on spatial as well as medical concepts and metaphors.

Economic concerns and permanent emigration

A further apprehension of imperial powers connected to the pilgrimage was that pilgrims would overstretch their budgets during their journeys to Mecca and would either depend on governmental relief or be incapable of supporting their families at home. This concern pointed to the more general problem of who had to pay for colonial subjects running into difficulties – financial or otherwise – far away from home. This was obviously a problem not only encountered in connection with the Mecca pilgrims, but also fed into the increasing concern about indigent mobile subjects, as Chapter 8 will show in further detail. Yet in French Algeria, for instance, the Mecca pilgrims represented the largest single group of travellers and could thus be a very significant burden on the budget of the colonial state.

Most problematic were those who were not able to afford their return journey, as they could not be left drifting in the harbour towns of Jidda or Yanbuʿ. French government officials, who did not hesitate to intervene in religious matters, explained to their Muslim subjects that it was opposed to their religious duties to undertake the hajj without the possession of sufficient resources to sustain both oneself during the journey and the dependent family members that were left behind. The Egyptian government was also concerned about pilgrims who could not pay for their journey and issued a pamphlet, stating that according to religious rules only those who could afford it should travel to Mecca.[51]

Still there were many poor people who undertook the voyage despite such warnings. In both harbour cities serving the hajj, Yanbuʿ and Jidda, officials complained (potentially with the ulterior motive of depicting the Muslim *umma* as disloyal and fragmented) that pilgrims would literally die of hunger and thirst if the European consulates did not come to their assistance.[52] The premonition that mobile colonial subjects could become a burden on the colonial budget was thus a further reason for controlling the journey tightly if not always successfully as the following section will show.

[51] DWQ, Majlis al-Wuzarāʾ, Niẓārat al-Dākhiliyya 18/ب, 0075–007534.
[52] See ANOM, GGA 16H/84: Consul de France à Djeddah à M. Goblet, ministre des Affaires étrangères, Yanbuʿ, 27 September 1888.

Even if these pilgrims would not turn to the officials for relief, the fear of the hajj leading to permanent emigration rather than circular movement, was repeatedly voiced in the Algerian context.[53] Fears of imperial governments relating to the hajj could thus go beyond contagious return flows and include demographic outward flows. Such unwanted emigration was a further side-effect of mobility that needed to be channelled and controlled.

Regulating pilgrim mobility and the limits of regulation

These four concerns – the spread of disease, the communication of political ideas, the costs for the repatriation and subsistence of pilgrims and the possible permanent emigration of colonial subjects – led to the increasing involvement of western imperial powers with the pilgrimage, even if this involvement was not pursued with the same intensity by different empires as mentioned above. The British in India were reluctant to interfere in the religious practices of those under their rule, particularly after the experience of the Indian Uprising where Indian Muslims had formed a significant part of those revolting against British rule. Also, they were dependent on the collaboration with Muslims who were, for instance, staffing the Indian army. The French in Algeria often followed a much more interventionist course around the turn of the century. In both cases, however, pilgrim mobility was subject to newly installed controls in the 1890s and early 1900s. If the passage became cheaper (despite many cases of fraud and pilgrims complaining that the various fees they had to pay were too high), the regulations in terms of passports, visa prescriptions and sanitary controls certainly became more stringent as the century drew to a close. Some measures defined prerequisites that the pilgrims had to fulfil in order to be allowed to move. Others included active intervention, either moving persons forcibly or hindering their travel.

Defining preconditions for pilgrim mobility

In the 1880s the modes of dealing with the problems or fears outlined above were far from uniform. Still, the pilgrimage was more and more closely monitored. Besides the monopolisation of travel companies mentioned in the first section of this chapter, methods such as the notification or registration of pilgrims, individual permissions and compulsory visas, often coupled with the proof of sufficient funds and obligatory papers of

---

[53] See Ageron, 'L'émigration des musulmans algériens'.

identification, were introduced. Step by step the bureaucratic apparatus that dealt with the pilgrim traffic was inflated.

Some measures targeted the equipment of the pilgrim ships. In the context of the British Empire, 'native passenger ships' had been subject to specific treatment since the passing of an act of Parliament in 1876. The Pilgrim Ships' Act of 1895 went further and specified the sanitary conditions and staffing, the space allocated per person and so forth, on vessels transporting Mecca pilgrims. In the Egyptian context, the goal of better coordinating the pilgrimage included the attempt to transport all pilgrims to Suez together in special trains.[54] The Ottoman Empire in turn issued a brochure entitled *Règlement applicable aux navires faisant le transport des pèlerins*, specifying the duty of every ship to notify the authorities 24 hours before leaving, to carry certain papers, to strictly keep a passenger list and to adhere to specific health and food standards.

Additionally, every ship was to deposit 15,000 francs and be inspected regarding the maximum number of passengers that could possibly be transported safely, with the space per pilgrim fixed at 2 m^2 and 1.8 m in height, reminding us of the economisation of space encountered in connection with the lascars. The general Ottoman prescriptions also defined who was to count as a pilgrim at all: 'pilgrims of superior classes' did not fall under these regulations and were to be treated as passengers.[55] These measures also enabled the more or less accurate registration of all pilgrims on their way to Mecca, with detailed numbers even being published in the *Egyptian Gazette*.[56]

Other initiatives focused on individual pilgrims rather than on the companies and ships that provided their transportation. The incentive to oblige all Algerian pilgrims to use French shipping lines – although allegedly introduced out of concern for the well-being of the pilgrims – was a first measure in tracking this mobile group more easily; other initiatives came to complement it in the following years.[57] The door to stricter regulations was again opened by the Ottoman Empire. As early as 1880, it issued orders requiring passports from all passengers and pilgrims arriving in Jidda, whether Turkish or foreign subjects, and announced that those who came lacking such documents would be turned away from the ports of the Hijaz.[58]

---

[54] Cromer, *Rapport de Lord Cromer*, p. 101.
[55] ANOM, GGA 16H/84: Règlement applicable aux navires faisant le transport des pèlerins, Constantinople, 1880.
[56] See 'The pilgrimage', *Egyptian Gazette*, 21 February 1900.
[57] See ANOM, GGA 16H/84: Le gouverneur général de l'Algérie aux préfets et généraux d'Alger, d'Oran, de Constantine, Algiers, 10 March 1888.
[58] ANOM, GGA 16H/84: Supplement to the *Calcutta Gazette*, 10 February 1886, Conveyance of pilgrims between India and Mecca by Messrs. Thomas Cook and Son.

Officials of the British and French Empires at first claimed to simply fulfil the Ottoman stipulations. But soon they formulated more explicit regulations themselves regarding the journey to the holy cities. Some rules were specifically aimed at avoiding the economic dependency and destitution of pilgrims once en route. Shortly after the Ottoman rules came into force, the French Consul at Jidda called for the introduction of an obligatory proof of possessing sufficient funds to be able to return to one's own country, a measure that was already in place for Tunisian pilgrims. Also, if a pilgrim was running into financial troubles for other reasons, only those who could prove their identity and their ability to return the full amount later were to be helped.[59]

In the Franco-Algerian context, directives targeting the political connections of pilgrims soon supplemented these regulations. In 1885 the pilgrims had to prove the possession of sufficient pecuniary means, but also the absence of any past incidences that would render their contact with Egyptian and Sudanese pilgrims 'dangerous to our rule'; otherwise they would be refused permission to travel for several years.[60] This regulation resounded the fears connected with pan-Islam described earlier, but reflected more specifically the worry that the movements in Egypt and Sudan, connected with the figures of 'Urabi and the Mahdi, could radiate beyond those territories and transform into a more explicitly anti-European and anti-colonial uprising.

The specific situation of Algeria, after the uprisings led by al-Muqrani in the early 1870s and the introduction of the *Code de l'indigénat* of 1875, as part of France proper, yet with a distinction existing between French citizens (able to move freely) and colonial subjects (submitted to much tighter regulations), found expression in the attempt to control the religious mobility of the *indigènes* much more closely. Hence in the late 1880s the Algerian government became more explicit about mobility restrictions. In a circular of 1888 to the prefects of Algiers, Oran and Constantine, the governor general gave directions relating to the granting of permission to travel to Mecca to 'indigenous' Algerians. The authorisation was to be considered as a favour granted by the government and only to be accorded to those with a good reputation and who were 'free from all fanatism'; it would be refused to those who, because

---

[59] ANOM, GGA 16H/84: Consul de France à Djeddah à M. Goblet, ministre des Affaires étrangères, Yanbu', 27 September 1888. The *résident général de Tunis* adopted the measure on 16 November 1886.

[60] ANOM, GGA 16H/84: Dépêche télégraphique, gouverneur général de l'Algérie au préfet de Constantine, Algiers, 12 August 1885; Division de Constantine, Section des affaires indigènes au gouverneur général, Constantine, 5 August 1885.

of their past misdemeanours, could be suspected of having interests other than fulfilling their religious duties.[61]

As the bureaucratic system to enforce these regulations grew in size, the regulations were standardised in the following years. In 1892, every Algerian pilgrim had to prove the possession of 1,000 francs and only received a passport (which had to contain the name, age and address of the carrier) if they could present a return ticket. Travel was limited to French ships equipped with a steam steriliser and a medical practitioner designated by the government. The only companies licensed to carry pilgrims were *Cyprien Fabre*, the *Société Maritime Algérienne*, *M. M. Agello* and *Brunache*.[62] These regulations not only represented the privileging of French shipping interests, but also the attempt to reduce the number of penniless pilgrims floating near the holy cities or in one of the harbour towns on the way back.

The inter-imperial convergence concerning the rules and regulations outlined above was a result of inter-imperial monitoring and coordination. The rules in place in the British colonies were to a certain extent coordinated with those in force in the French colonies, for example regarding the education of medical officers on board.[63] In parallel to the British Pilgrim Ships' Act and the Ottoman *Règlement applicable aux navires faisant le transport des pèlerins*, a *Règlement sur le pèlerinage de la Mecque* was issued in 1895 for Algerian pilgrims, containing largely the same elements as the British measures. Besides the duty to prove sufficient funds for the return journey, prospective pilgrims also had to demonstrate that they were able to pay their taxes and sustain their families left behind in Algeria. Additionally they had to provide a guarantor who stayed in their community and was willing to take over all charges in case they could not do so. The *Règlement* also contained guidelines as to what the pilgrims could bring with them. Weapons to fend off Bedouin attacks, for example, were only allowed if they had already been in the pilgrim's possession before the journey.

As in other cases encountered earlier, intermediaries played a crucial role in connecting the administrative apparatus with the individual pilgrims or rather in making the mass of pilgrims administratively manageable. The Algerian pilgrims were divided into groups of 20 based on their regions of origin with a head for every group designated by the officials or by the

---

[61] ANOM, GGA 16H/84: Le gouverneur général de l'Algérie aux préfets et généraux, d'Oran, de Constantine, Algiers, 10 March 1888.

[62] ANOM, GGA 16H/84: Le gouverneur général de l'Algérie aux 3 généraux, 3 préfets, Algiers, 9 April 1892.

[63] See *General Instructions for Pilgrims to the Hedjaz and a Manual for the Guidance of Officers and Others Concerned in the Red Sea Pilgrim Traffic* (Calcutta, 1911 and 1922).

group itself. This sheikh or *kabīr* had to be able to read French and Arabic and to notify the French Consul in Jidda about all incidents during the pilgrimage or, alternatively, on their return to the French authorities in Algeria. These intermediaries were also in charge of distributing food and more generally acting as middlemen between the pilgrims and the authorities.[64] In parallel to the organisation of coal heavers or seamen or of controlling the Red Sea shipping and desert mobilities more closely, intermediaries were thus central in enforcing the controls drafted in international or imperial settings.

Some of these measures in place in France were not adopted in the British colonial context, however, reflecting the tensions between the Indian government in Britain and the local officials: whereas the former advised that a regulation that obliged pilgrims to deposit sufficient funds for their return journey was useful, the local authorities often opted for minimal interference. If there was a certain amount of inter-imperial convergence, the example of the bureaucratisation of pilgrim mobility shows that there were different attitudes concerning interferences with the cultural practices of the colonised population that paralleled developments in other policy areas and that these attitudes were shaped by administrative cultures and past experiences. The example also illustrates not only the divergences between empires but also the conflicts within empires, most often between political actors in the metropole and in the colonies.

Yet besides the imperial administrations of Britain, France and the Ottoman Empire, there were other actors. It was thus not only the European empires attempting to strengthen their grip on their Muslim populations who made such a bureaucratic effort. In line with the French and British empires, and under the aegis of the British occupational power, the Egyptian government issued very similar rules specifying obligatory passports, proof of funding and mandatory deposits of 100 Egyptian pounds per pilgrim. Simultaneously they confirmed the privileged role of the Khedival Steam Navigation Company as the one and only company that the state could recognise as a pilgrim transporter, since it was at that moment the only one to accept the tight rules the government had issued allegedly with the sole aim of granting the pilgrims the best conditions possible for their journey.[65] In return the

---

[64] ANOM, GGA 16H/85: Bulletin officiel du gouvernement général de l'Algérie, Année 1895, n° 1381, Pèlerinage de la Mecque – Règlements. See also CADN, Port Said 123: Gouvernement général de l'Algérie, Règlement de la pèlerinage de la Mecque (Algiers: Imprimerie orientale, 1895).

[65] DWQ, Majlis al-Wuzarā᾽, Niẓārat al-Dākhiliyya 18/ﻭ, 0075–007576: Note ministère de l'Intérieur, no date. See also ibid., 0075–007578: Annexe au n° 5, Assemblée générale, no date.

Ottoman Empire tightened its regulations in 1909–10, leading to African pilgrims who arrived in the Hijaz after a very long journey being refused entry, as some of them did not possess the relevant paperwork.[66]

Contrary to the rhetoric of the Egyptian government of acting in the best interest of the pilgrims, as the imperial and national regulations for individual pilgrims became more and more stringent (and increasingly uniform), the rules for the shipping companies were loosened in several respects, pointing to the forces of economic globalisation around 1900. Once again, this becomes clear when entering into the intricacies of global logistics. For Indian pilgrims, in the season 1905–06 the number of port-holes was no longer fixed at one porthole per 2 metres, but it was left to the shipping companies to decide as long as their density was 'sufficient to allow of a proper degree of lighting and ventilation'. Also the space required per pilgrim was further reduced, highlighting once again the economic interests behind this mass transportation.[67] The bureaucratisation of the hajj thus points both to the complicated interaction and competition between different state actors and attitudes and to the private interests of the companies involved, as the attempt to transport as many pilgrims as possible on one single ship makes clear.

Prohibiting the pilgrims' movement

Besides increasingly strict regulations from different bodies that attached specific conditions to journeys into the Hijaz, the imperial powers of Britain and France, as well as the Ottoman Empire, at times also attempted to hamper pilgrims' mobility altogether. Prospective pilgrims were either repatriated (if necessary against their will) or were hindered in their movement through temporary quarantine or prohibition of the entire pilgrimage. The growing involvement of western powers in Muslim core regions thus left its unmistakable stamp on the organisation of the annual pilgrimage which became visible for instance in the employment of British soldiers in guarding the Egyptian caravan.[68] This section comes back from the general level of the imperial surveillance of the hajj to the Canal Zone itself, where many

---

[66] OIOC, IOR R/20/A/2379, sheet 161: Administration sanitaire de l'Empire Ottoman: Dispositions speciales applicables aux pèlerinage du Hedjaz de 1909–1910, Année de l'Hegire 1327 (Simla: Printed at the Government Monotype Press, 1909); ibid., sheet 169: Marling to British Resident, Aden, Constantinople, 16 November 1909.

[67] OIOC, IOR R/20/A/2379, sheets 37–9: J. C. Fergusson Esq., Under-secretary to the Government of India to the Secretary to the Government of Bombay, General Department, Home Department.

[68] See Villiers-Stuart, *Egypt after the War*, p. 221.

of these controls were to be enacted. In the following, one specific type of control – sanitary control – will be singled out, looking in some detail at the pilgrims' lazaretto at al-Tur close to Suez. In this manner, quarantine stations more generally will emerge as symptomatic global spaces of acceleration and deceleration, a theme that will receive even closer attention in Chapter 7. Then, other attempts on the part of the political authorities to prescribe forced immobility to the Mecca pilgrims will be reviewed.

One of the aims of the bureaucratic regulations attached to the pilgrimage was the singling out of this form of mobility as specific and clearly bounded. The close interweaving of the pilgrimage and other traffic in the Canal Zone could appear problematic. This was particularly an issue, as seen above, when cases of contagious disease appeared in the Hijaz. Epidemics had struck the region before the opening of the Canal – for example when cholera broke out in 1866 – and the period following the Canal's opening was not free from such intrusions either. In 1878, the cholera appeared in Mecca.[69] During the 1882 pilgrimage even a few cases of plague were identified. The medical doctor Abdur Razzack expressed the fundamental fears connected with such apparitions when he wrote about the 'ghastly spectre of cholera [that lies] hidden somewhere amongst the pilgrims, like the woes of the human race in Pandora's box'.[70] Such statements make clear how the pilgrims were identified as disease carriers par excellence.

To disentangle the different mobilities, and to keep cholera and plague out of Europe, a system of quarantines was implemented. Pilgrim ships had to spend a certain amount of time in the quarantine station, al-Tur, in the Gulf of Suez (or at one of the other Red Sea stations, such as Qamaran) before they were allowed to enter the Canal; or, if coming from the Mediterranean, they were held in Cyprus.[71] Of course the quarantine was also a business, leading Maurice Boniteau to comment that, for al-Tur, the annual pilgrimage was its 'tourist season'.[72] Upon arrival the ships were divided into three categories, 'sound', 'suspect' and 'infected', and the duration of their quarantine was established accordingly. Furthermore the length of stay in al-Tur depended on potential outbreaks of disease as well as on international negotiations. The 1905–06 regulations introduced stricter passport controls and centralised the payment of quarantine fees as a lump sum on the part of the shipping companies or the captain. Still the

---

[69] See TNA, FO 78/2863: British Consulate, Suez, to Foreign Office, 4 January 1878.
[70] TNA, FO 881/4762: Dr Abdur Razzack, Report on the 'Haj', 1882.
[71] TNA, FO 78/2409: HM Consulate Port Said to Earl of Derby, 19 November 1875. In 1878, for example, ten days of quarantine were compulsory, see TNA, FO 28/2863: British Consulate Suez, 4 January 1878.
[72] Boniteau Bey, 'Le pèlerinage à la Mecque et les campements quarantenaires', p. 663.

length of quarantine was reduced from 15 to 12 days for the first patient and from 12 to 10 in the case of subsequent patients. Those ships that had not paid their fees in full were subjected to further quarantine and dues as a penal measure irrespective of sanitary necessity.[73]

The concept of quarantine as such and the institutions in place were criticised from many sides. For the shipowners, quarantines were problematic as the pilgrim ships often ran on a tight schedule between Jidda and Suez.[74] Occasionally ships were not allowed to disembark their passengers as the quarantine station was overcrowded and so the ships were ordered to stay in close proximity to al-Tur, serving as floating quarantine stations. In 1878 the *St Osyth* was unable to land the pilgrims it had on board and was due to return to Jidda to transport more remaining pilgrims. The commanders complained that it was very difficult to find vessels to take the pilgrims under these circumstances and the whole transfer of pilgrims would become impossible if ships on their way to return to Jidda were kept in port for an indefinite period of time 'for the sole purpose of using them as Lazaretti'.[75] This measure was also criticised as being counterproductive, since prolonged stays on crowded ships would contribute to the bad health condition of the pilgrims rather than help it.

The British Consul at Suez, West, who visited the scene, suggested as a counterproposal the encampment of the pilgrims in the desert. He implied that the strict quarantine regulations might be an Egyptian revenge of some sort for the decline of business in Suez and a measure to 'inhibit foreign vessels from interfering with a trade which before the opening of the Canal was almost exclusively in the hands of the Khedive', as there could be 'no sanitary reason' to keep them on the unhealthy ships.[76] On a more fundamental level these cases of overcrowding in the quarantine stations illustrate to what extent the mass transportation of pilgrims had become not only a political issue and a commercial enterprise but also a logistical challenge.

Even when the pilgrims were admitted into the quarantine station of al-Tur, there were many complaints regarding its bad resources and the treatment of pilgrims, which was particularly disagreeable for women, as

---

[73] OIOC, IOR R/20/A/2379, sheet 37: J. C. Fergusson Esq., Under-Secretary to the Government of India to the Secretary to the Government of Bombay, General Department, Home Department (Sanitary); sheet 67: India Office London, 4 October 1906.

[74] TNA, FO 78/2863: Consul West to Secretary of State for Foreign Affairs, Foreign Office, 25 January 1878.

[75] TNA, FO 78/2863: Consul West, Suez to Secretary of State for Foreign Affairs, Suez, 1 February 1878.

[76] Ibid.

their privacy was not always respected.[77] Furthermore, the food was too expensive and of low quality, the facilities were overcrowded and there were not enough trains to transport the Egyptian pilgrims between al-Tur and Suez after their confinement had ended.[78] Pilgrims also complained about the unclean and brackish drinking water and the insufficient number of tents.[79] Most painful for the pilgrims was the 'exorbitant' sum that every pilgrim had to deposit before departure for this purpose, a measure that also hurt the rich as they usually travelled with a considerable entourage.[80]

At times the discontent flared up and turned into open revolt. Such moments of rebellion were particularly critical within the bounded space of the quarantine station. In 1893, the *Conseil sanitaire* informed the prime minister of Egypt, Riaz Pasha, that more than 12,000 pilgrims were in the camp of al-Tur and five other ships were about to arrive. The director of the camp had telegraphed that the pilgrims were on the verge of starting a rebellion. He feared lack of water, insufficient personnel and military guards among other grave shortcomings. In a subsequent letter, the board stated that the director of al-Tur had maintained the prohibition regarding the disembarkation of further pilgrims into the camp, as the camp could not hold more than 11,000 pilgrims. It asked the Egyptian government to send troops as quickly as possible in order to avoid disorders on board and in the station.[81] Such incidences illustrate the difficulty of effectively channelling and tightly controlling the mass mobility of the pilgrims.

Quarantine was not the only measure used to keep pilgrims from moving freely, just as fear of contagious diseases was not the only worry associated with the pilgrimage. The most radical obstruction to movement was the complete prohibition of travel, a measure often justified on medical grounds that was most frequently, but not exclusively, used by the French government in Algeria. In 1897, the International Sanitary Conference in Venice received the news from the British delegation that the British government

[77] See Huber, 'Unification of the Globe by Disease?', 469.
[78] DWQ, *ʿĀbdīn* 547, 0069–011257: Taqrīr tafṣīlī ʿan khaṭ sayr al-maḥmal al-sharīf.
[79] DWQ, Majlis al-Wuzarā', Niẓārat al-Dākhiliyya 2/4, 0075–001344: Traduction d'une lettre de la Sublime Porte en date du 18 Charval 1308.
[80] DWQ, Majlis al-Wuzarā', Niẓārat al-Dākhiliyya 2/4, 0075–001352: Traduction d'une lettre adressée au président du Conseil des ministres par Son Excellence le président du Conseil législatif, 22 December 1902.
[81] DWQ, Majlis al-Wuzarā', Niẓārat al-Dākhiliyya 18/ـ, 0075–007537: Conseil sanitaire maritime et quarantenaire d'Egypte. Communication faite à la présidence du Conseil par le directeur du campement de Tor, al-Tur, 25 July 1893.

had decided to prohibit the pilgrimage from India to Mecca during that season. Every delegation expressed the opinion of its respective government and the conference finally voted that the powers that ruled over Muslim populations would limit the pilgrimage of that year as much as possible. Yet an article in the newspaper *Le Temps* noted: 'This is a grave measure, particularly at a moment when Muslim fanaticism finds itself over-excited by plague and hunger.'[82]

In that year, imperial worries were mainly focused on the plague. In 1898 the pilgrimage was banned again on similar grounds.[83] In 1899 Algerian pilgrims were still held back because of plague cases in the Levant. In 1900 the French authorities highlighted the plague and cholera in Arabia and the plague in India and were highly concerned that the respective governments did not react. A medical journal reported that 9,000 potentially infected pilgrims had already passed through the Canal.[84] In that year France withdrew permission to travel to Mecca at the last moment.

In years of disease outbreaks the Egyptian government opted for a reduced pilgrimage, shying away from a complete ban. In 1898 the Egyptian minister of the interior reacted to the demands of the Ottoman sanitary administration and ordered all Egyptians to return to Egypt as soon as possible. Egypt thus sent a small caravan that accompanied the *mahmal* and suggested that all Egyptians postponed their journey until the following year.[85]

The question as to whether the religious journey was to be permitted, or not, often led to discord between those responsible in Algiers and the central administration in Paris. After the cases of plague in 1900, there were extensive debates as to whether the pilgrimage should be allowed in 1902. The Algerian government argued that care should be taken not to upset the Muslim population; the officials in Paris clearly opted in favour of prohibition.[86] This measure was deemed necessary because Indians

---

[82] CAMT, 1995060/1422: Agence Havas, Informations, 22 February 1897; 'Les décisions de la conférence sanitaire internationale', *Le Temps*, 1 April 1897.

[83] CADN, Port Said 125: Ministère des Affaires étrangères à M. Daumas, consul de France à Port-Saïd (Mesures prises en France et en Algérie contre la peste), Paris, 3 February 1897.

[84] ANOM, GGA 16H/87: 'Hygiene internationale. La peste en Arabie et le pèlerinage aux lieux-saints en 1900', *Semaine médicale*, 14 February 1900.

[85] DWQ, Majlis al-Wuzarā', Niẓārat al-Dākhiliyya 18/ﻭ, 0075–007543: Présidence du Conseil des ministres au ministère de l'interieur, 2 April 1898; ibid., 0075–007544: Ministère de L'Intérieur, Note au Conseil des ministres, Cairo, 10 May 1898.

[86] ANOM, GGA, 16H/87: Ministère des affaires étrangères au gouverneur général de l'Algérie, Paris, 9 February 1900.

could travel freely to Mecca despite the fact that several regions of the subcontinent had seen outbreaks of the plague. Additionally cholera had apparently broken out in Egypt. In 1903 the British allowed the Indian pilgrimage, but it was recommended that pilgrims postponed it to the following year. They could only leave from Bombay or Chittagong and had to undergo medical observation beforehand.[87]

Debates as to whether to call off the pilgrimage were founded on sanitary as well as on political grounds, but additionally assessed the pilgrimage as a factor of potential economic destabilisation. Even if the pilgrimage of Algerian Muslims was permitted in 1907, the prefect of Oran argued that it would have been better to ban the pilgrimage that year due to the 'pan-Islamic tendencies' in the Levant, in Egypt and more generally in the Muslim world, because of the Algerian internal state of affairs and the material condition of many pilgrims. According to the prefect, they often sold their animals or their land in order to afford the pilgrimage and consequently came back to miserable lives. This was particularly virulent in years of bad harvests, like that of 1907, where the 'natives' were meant to be discouraged from leaving the country at all.[88] Also, in later years, reference was made to the precarious situation of the pilgrims and the fact that they should be hindered from travelling.[89]

The treatment of the pilgrimage thus brought the paternalistic strand of colonialism to the fore, in this case at the cost of free movement. This played a part when defining strict parameters that pilgrims had to satisfy before being allowed to undertake their journey. It also figured when the political authorities decided to prohibit the pilgrimage together. The prohibitions could be justified on sanitary, political or financial grounds. As the following section will show, such prohibitions did not stop all pilgrims from travelling however, rather there were many different types of transgression and evasions.

Evading controls

The British Pilgrim Ships' Act and the French *Règlement* of the early 1890s, mentioned above, marked the beginning of growing international

---

[87] ANOM, GGA, 16H/84: M. Homery, gérant du consulat général de France à Calcutta à M. Delcassé, ministre des affaires étrangères, Calcutta, 10 October 1903.

[88] ANOM, GGA, 16H/88: Préfet du département d'Oran au gouverneur général de l'Algérie, Oran, 7 January 1907.

[89] See ANOM, GGA, 16H/89: Préfet du département de Constantine au gouverneur général (Direction des affaires indigènes), Constantine, 28 August 1912; CADN, Port Said 123: Ministre des Affaires étrangères à M. Meyrier, consul de France à Port-Said, Paris, 30 October 1911.

and imperial standardisation in the regulation of the pilgrimage. However, the translation into action of these attempts to manage pilgrim mobility efficiently proved rather problematic. Even if numerous bureaucrats were defending the rationalisation of individual and collective controls time and again, there were countless holes in the newly created systems and numerous travellers transgressing the tightly knit identification measures. The strict mobility regulations introduced in various imperial contexts led to experimentation with different strategies to circumvent them. The most significant of these strategies was concerned with the forging, losing or incorrect usage of identity papers. Other more straightforward cases of fraud consisted in the application of bribes. The bureaucratisation of the pilgrimage around 1900 thus brought both rulemaking and rulebreaking most clearly to the fore. In what follows, evasions of different kinds and clandestine departures will serve to illustrate the limits of the channelling of pilgrim mobility.

Not only individual cases of fraud, but sometimes mistakes on the part of officials undermined the new bureaucratic system and led to a large number of casualties. This was the case with a ship carrying Javanese pilgrims, which arrived in Jidda in January 1902. Even though the steamer's papers mentioned cholera cases in the Dutch colonies in Java, about 10 pilgrims had died en route and during observation at the quarantine station at Qamaran further victims had passed away, the doctor responsible let the passengers depart for Jidda and from there on to Mecca after just five days of observation. When the authorities realised the mistake, they decided against informing the pilgrims. By mid-April, around 16,000 pilgrims had apparently died because of the outbreak of disease that could be traced back to this error.[90]

Evasions of controls on an individual level were of course more frequent than a whole ship slipping through the security measures. In years in which the pilgrimage was permitted, there were numerous ways around sanitary and other controls. Mirza Mohammed Hosayn Farahani, a Persian pilgrim travelling through the Canal in 1885 on his return from Mecca, described how the controls could be avoided with the help of a little bit of bribe money.[91] In 1901 the *Foria*, travelling from Philippeville (now Skikda), was inspected in Port Said. The French Consul found 502 pilgrims on board yet the ship was only authorised to carry 424. The captain, who was aware of the larger number, declared that, while the embarkation had taken place under police surveillance during the day, the additional passengers had

---

[90] ANOM, GGA, 16H/86: Pèlerinage de la Mecque de 1902. Rapport du commissaire du gouvernement à bord du *Villequier*, pp. 14–15.

[91] Farahani, *A Shi'ite Pilgrimage to Mecca*, p. 171.

boarded the ship clandestinely during the night. The Consul did not push the issue much further and just made a note on the health certificate and the passenger list, because any delay could have caused the ship to miss its slot for the Canal.[92] Some forms of rulebreaking were thus tolerated on the part of the captains and consul in order to avoid the risk of a slowdown, which could turn out to be very costly.

Particularly in years when French officials called off the hajj, pilgrims explored alternative ways of getting to Mecca, a fact that government agents were well aware of. According to the minister of the interior, the sanitary services reported that the official prohibition would not hinder the clandestine departure of a number of pilgrims who, on their return journey, would not undergo any special surveillance. In this case, the prohibition of the pilgrimage in fact enhanced the danger of contagion rather than diminished it.[93] The French Consul at Suez reported how some pilgrims that were determined to fulfil their religious duty apparently evaded the controls. They crossed the border from Algeria to Tripolitania and got hold of Turkish passes to the Hijaz. When they returned, they reclaimed their Algerian affiliation in order to be repatriated free of charge.[94] An alternative strategy was to take out a passport for a different destination, Malta or Tripolitania for instance, and to travel clandestinely from there. Papers could thus be used not only to channel mobility in a way that was suitable to empires and the emerging international mobility regime, but also to transgress regulations and to twist the bureaucratic apparatus. The making of such rules thus went hand in hand with the breaking of them.

In addition to the use of the wrong papers, there were many other practices of circumventing controls by forging, losing or duplicating documents of identification. One problem was the coexistence of various pieces of identification for a single person, such as passports and identity cards. Another was related to the visas the consuls had to issue.[95] Many pilgrims did not come for a visa to the consulate or alternatively did not collect their passport after having handed it in. Instead, Jidda developed into a thriving black-market for tickets of all sorts. People who had missed their journey back home or had lost their tickets simply bought the return

---

[92] CADN, Port Said 123: Consulat de France à Port-Said, Procès-verbal, Pèlerinage à la Mecque, Infraction constaté à bord du *Foria*, 16 March 1901.

[93] ANOM, GGA, 16H/88: Ministre de l'Intérieur au gouverneur général de l'Algérie, Paris, 27 September 1906.

[94] ANOM, GGA, 16H/88: Le ministre des Affaires étrangères au gouverneur général de l'Algérie, 11 January 1908.

[95] See, for instance, ANOM, GGA 16H/83: Altemer, consul de France à Suez, à Stephen Pichon, ministre des Affaires étrangères, 8 February 1909.

tickets of pilgrims who had died on the journey.[96] Other illegal measures included returning as a destitute under a false name and then reclaiming the deposit put down before the departure under the real name.[97] Despite all attempts to control the departures tightly, there were thus always many more pilgrims en route than the number of travel permissions granted beforehand.[98]

As a response to these evasions, the governments experimented with different forms of documents in order to make them forgery-proof. Increasingly, passports included, in the French-Algerian context, if not a photograph, at least information on the height, the colour of hair, eyes and skin, the shape of eyebrows, nose, mouth, chin and face and any special features. Also the new design of passports introduced in the early 1900s made them more difficult to reproduce.[99]

The obsession with paperwork was even cause for derision and went to the heart of conflicts over citizenship status in Algeria. The Algerian newspaper L'Akhbar mocked the regulations in an article of September 1891.[100] Some of the accompanying officials also criticised the identification procedures. Gillotte, administrator of the town of Aïn-Témouchent, argued that the visa procedures at the French consulate in Jidda were futile because they represented a lot of work for the consul, but at the same time, the passes and visa were not even checked by the Ottoman officials in the Hijaz who apparently had better things to do during the pilgrimage than to ascertain the identity of the Muslims travelling.[101] There were thus always problems not only with the standards on the pilgrim ships but also with the purpose and applicability of the, theoretically, increasingly wide-reaching measures of identification.

As a matter of fact, the controls were often circumvented altogether. In years in which the pilgrimage was prohibited, many pilgrims illicitly undertook their journeys. The prohibitions were again connected with the economic factors related to the hajj, as seen in 1889, when the shipping company Crispo, the local agent of Cyprien Fabre, had prepared for the pilgrimage and had already begun to sell tickets. When the permission to undertake the hajj was withdrawn, the company complained about serious losses because of this 'belated prohibition' and stated that, just

---

[96] See ANOM, GGA 16H/86: Rapport du commissaire du gouvernement à bord du navire à pèlerins l'Olbia de la compagnie Cyprien Fabre pendant le pèlerinage de la Mecque en 1902.
[97] Egyptian Gazette, 9 January 1900.
[98] See ANOM, GGA 16H/86: Rapport de M. Gillotte, administrateur de la commune mixte d'Aïn-Témouchent sur le pèlerinage de la Mecque en 1905; ANOM, GGA 16H/87: Consulat de France à Port-Said, Procès-verbal, Pèlerinage de la Mecque, Amiral Jacobsen.
[99] Compare passes of 1872 and 1906: ANOM, GGA 16H/83 and ANOM, GGA 16H/88.
[100] ANOM, GGA 16H/85: L'Akhbar, 19 September 1891.
[101] ANOM, GGA 16H/86: Rapport de M. Gillotte, administrateur de la commune mixte d'Aïn-Témouchent sur le pèlerinage de la Mecque en 1905.

as every year, there would be a considerable number of pilgrims leaving clandestinely from neighbouring ports anyway.[102] There were always persons who did not fulfil the identification requirements and had not received individual permission to travel. Others did not have sufficient funds to return to their home countries but still made their way to Mecca. In short: the newly introduced controls could not prevent costly repatriations.[103] The *Liste des Indigènes partis pour La Mecque le 10 Juillet, sans permission* illustrates that even those who illicitly started their journeys were meticulously registered.

In the context of repatriations of such clandestinely departed pilgrims, Port Said came to occupy a central position. The French Consul in Port Said argued for extensive checks at his port, because, as he saw it, it would be best to identify those who did not fulfil the requirements *before* their passage through the Canal, as long as they were still in the more easily supervised Mediterranean realm, and arrange for their repatriation from there.[104] In this case, the repatriation expenses had to be reimbursed – even if certain shipowners agreed (or were ordered) to take the pilgrims free of charge, there were still the costs for food and supplementary fees that were levied at borders and other points of passage.[105]

This meant that the repatriations were expensive for the Algerian government, averaging about 75 francs per person. However, the destitute pilgrims had to be returned and could not be left without any means of subsistence in the Hijaz or in the Canal towns. Consequently, other, and supposedly better, solutions were trialled to retrieve the money from the Algerian pilgrims themselves. These trials were not often successful because, according to the French governor general in Algeria, the pilgrims took care to hide their identity by indicating a false point of departure. He concluded that more thorough controls had to be implemented in Algeria that would take effect before the pilgrims had left in order to reduce the expenses for the colony's budget.[106] If these controls in

---

[102] ANOM, GGA 16H/85: Compagnie française de navigation à vapeur Cyprien Fabre au gouverneur général d'Algérie, Alger, Marseilles, 1889 (no date).

[103] See, for instance, ANOM, GGA, 16H/87: Ministère des affaires étrangères au gouverneur général de l'Algérie, Paris, 5 June 1901; ANOM, GGA, 16H/88: Le préfet du département d'Alger au gouverneur général, Algiers, 14 August 1906: pèlerinage de la Mecque, 74 pèlerins débarqués à Alger le 11 août.

[104] See ANOM, GGA, 16H/87: Consul Port Said, à Son Excellence M. Delcassé, ministre des Affaires étrangères de la République française, Port Said, 21 March 1901.

[105] See for instance ANOM, GGA, 16H/87: Ed. Fockenberghe (Consignations, Affrêtements, Armements, Commission-Trasit, Assureurs Maritimes) au préfet d'Alger, Dunkirk, 2 October 1901.

[106] ANOM, GGA, 16H/88: Gouverneur général de l'Algérie à Monsieur ... Divisions Alger, Oran, Constantine, Territoires Biskra, Laghouat, Algiers, 27 May 1907.

Algeria were not successful, officials were charged with noting all clandestine departures so that travellers who did not comply with the regulations could be stopped as early as possible. They were also supposed to inform the governor as to whether the pilgrims came from a trustworthy family able to act as a guarantor in the case of any outstanding fees.

In 1907 the French Minister of Foreign Affairs instructed the consulates of Port Said and Suez more clearly concerning the repatriations. The Algerian government had asked the Ministry of Foreign Affairs not to allow any repatriation funded by the Algerian budget without clarification of the state of destitution, the origin and the nationality of the person in question. It therefore demanded the surname, first name and address of the destitute Algerians by telegram before agreeing to pay for their return.[107] Yet, despite the very detailed briefings to the consuls, the question of what would happen to the destitute pilgrims in cases in which Algerian officials refused repatriation remained unanswered. Also, even with reinforced controls, the departure of a particular person from Algeria often only became known after the return of the pilgrims. To tightly supervise the mobility of colonial subjects thus proved a most complicated endeavour. The evasions on different levels – the forging or misuse of papers, clandestine departures and repatriations, and the ambivalent interference of empires with their Muslim subjects – point to the experimental status of processes of rulemaking as well as rulebreaking. They furthermore show exemplarily the inter-imperial relationships shifting between mere observation, comparison, imitation or dissociation.

In the decades surveyed in this chapter, the journey of the hajj, which more and more frequently carried pilgrims through the Canal, was subject to growing imperial involvement, regulation and commercialisation. The chapter brings out the specific features of global localities that complement those already encountered, specifically the harbour town of Jidda, which carried very different characteristics from Port Said, and the quarantine station at al-Tur. What is more, the imperial dealings with religion give the 'frontier of civilisation' a further meaning which complements the topoi of the desert and the slave trade. The various scales under investigation, ranging from the Red Sea and the Arabian Peninsula to the specific location of the Canal, show how and where different measures of distinction, differentiation, bureaucratisation and regulation in relation to different mobilities were tested.

Yet, as became obvious in the context of the bureaucratisation of desert space or of the controls of Red Sea shipping, even if confidentially phrased

---

[107] CADN, Port Said 123: Ministre des Affaires étrangères au consul de France à Port Said, Paris, 7 October 1907.

in the language of the civilising mission, these measures were always only partially successful. The necessity of being able to identify pilgrims globally went hand in hand with a good deal of experimentation involving different restrictions, bans and identification documents. Furthermore the reorganisation of the pilgrimage along imperially and internationally standardised lines gives insights into the global organisation of mass transportations, which found its most telling illustration in the reuse of steamers in the waters of the Red Sea that were not deemed fit for European traffic. This recycling process points to the fact that, at least in part, the pilgrimage to Mecca was a European business. Beyond this, it was most clearly a European concern as well. The fact that Europeans were worrying so much about movements from a non-European point of departure to a non-European destination not only brings the colonial realities of the day to the fore but also highlights the implications of globalisation around 1900, marked by the perception of a shrinking global space answered by the more rigid distinction between different mobilities.

Part III

Checkpoint: tracking microbes and tracing travellers 1890s–1914

7 Contagious mobility and the filtering of disease

In 1940 the French sociologist, geographer and political scientist André Siegfried expanded on the thoughts of Joseph Arthur de Gobineau and iterated the metaphor of Suez as the border between Europe and Asia. Yet he went beyond this familiar trope by referring to the Suez Canal as Europe's sanitary boundary and as a bulwark against the intrusion of unwanted elements, identifying a new line of defence by recalibrating the scale of globally active dangerous migrants to the dimension of microbes:

> When one arrives at Suez, writes Gobineau, the domain of the strange and peculiar is no longer far distant; it is right here that the Asian atmosphere begins. Asia is the continent of mystery, but also of contamination; it is a hearth of dirt and corruption. The occident has to defend itself incessantly against this contagion, which, in the form of the great epidemic diseases, will spread quickly all over Europe unless surveillance is constant and the guards are perfectly organised.[1]

Three factors of this 'European bulwark' are particularly noteworthy and will lead us through this chapter: the development of new institutions and new scientific methods and techniques (accompanying a growing belief in science); spatial arrangements such as the passage in quarantine, lazarettos and *cordons sanitaires*, which established the Canal's central position in the surveillance system referred to by Siegfried; and the division of travellers into distinct groups that received differential treatment.

The turn of the century witnessed a growing urge among empires to collect information about travellers. One major concern was to identify disease carriers, another to identify individuals on the move, which will form the main theme of Chapter 8. The standardisation of mobility and the increasing necessity to 'know about' mobile subjects also raised the question of how far (geographically speaking) a state or an empire was responsible for its citizens and subjects. Disease as a global issue par excellence serves very well to clarify further the argument regarding acceleration and deceleration. From certain areas that were traditionally

---

[1] Siegfried, *Suez, Panama*, p. 126.

labelled as disease-ridden, the emphasis was shifted to specific groups and categories. In this chapter, the three analytic threads outlined in the introduction – acceleration and deceleration, rulemaking and rulebreaking and the classification and categorisation of mobilities – are thus woven together.

As seen in the preceding chapter, pilgrims were often held responsible for wider-ranging problems. In the specific case of the pilgrimage to Mecca, but also in other contexts, the region of the Suez Canal had a particular role as a sluice gate permitting individuals, but also potentially dangerous ideas and microbes, to be filtered and identified. In line with Siegfried's perception, the Suez Canal after 1900 became not only a space of increasingly standardised transition, but also an area where – in contrast to the wide-open oceans and seas – it was possible to install specific inspection arrangements. In the narrow waterway, one could not only passively watch ships pass by, but also actively interfere with them. Apart from being a point of connection and comparison between different mobilities, the Canal came to function as a filter or semi-permeable membrane, simultaneously serving to keep traffic flowing and controlled. Already in the 1870s and in connection with the danger that cholera epidemics posed to Europe, the Suez Canal became not only a symbol for the growing interconnectedness but also a point which had to be controlled to keep Europe free from the cholera. The question of how to make this global crossroads secure while keeping the 'lifeline of Empire' open to commercially and politically significant modes of travel was essential. The case of the Mecca pilgrims thus highlights the new speed of mass movement, which created the perception that control was crucially needed but not easily achieved.

Some of these issues became apparent immediately after the opening of the Canal, and there were earlier outbreaks of disease, yet this chapter highlights the increasing bureaucratic standardisation in dealing with such outbreaks from 1890 onwards. To explain the gradual transition towards more regulated travel, it will occasionally return to the 1880s, when advances took place in the field of bacteriology and vaccination. The 1880s were a time of conflicts in scientific, military and political arenas; regulations and checks became more rigid and more coordinated from 1890 to 1914. The Canal thus developed into a boundary, not only in a metaphorical sense, but also very practically in terms of rule enforcements and controls. The chapter first assesses the political instruments developed to tackle the issue of contagion, then turns to spatial arrangements and finally looks at scientific and bureaucratic measures aimed mainly at the distinction between dangerous disease carriers and unsuspicious travellers.

Political instruments

From the very beginnings of the construction work, disease and its prevention had played a part in the Canal Zone.[2] In 1865, a cholera epidemic violently struck Ismailia; among others, de Lesseps' own grandson died of the disease. After the Canal's opening, the Canal Zone witnessed a variety of outbreaks, for instance in the years following 1882 and around 1893, when 46 people in Ismailia died of cholera in one day alone.[3] In these years, as seen in Chapter 6, large numbers of victims were claimed in Jidda and Mecca, but also in the Canal area itself.[4]

Yet contagious diseases were problems of a global order that transcended the narrowness of the Canal. The cholera epidemics of the second half of the nineteenth century particularly scared western officials and were resented as the 'return of the plague' with all its medieval connotations. In contrast to medieval times, however, modern means of communication and transportation carried not only passengers and goods, but also germs and bacteria much faster than ever before.

Both the local and the global threats of disease outbreaks required political action. States and other actors in charge of the smooth operation of infrastructures were not always responsible for knowing about the identity and status of individual travellers, but it was often essential to be informed about their state of health. The need to acquire information and take action against the propagation of contagious diseases required experimentation with different political instruments on a global scale, such as international conferences or councils. In the next section, the necessities and limitations of internationalism will be assessed by looking at two levels: first the international sanitary conferences and then the Egyptian *Conseil sanitaire maritime et quarantenaire*.

International conferences

From 1851 onwards a number of international sanitary conferences highlighted many of the issues relating to international meetings figuring in earlier chapters. These conferences were convened in the wake of the

---

[2] See Montel, *Le chantier du canal de Suez*, pp. 206–12: 'Un chantier médicalement surveillé'; see also Aubert-Roche, *Rapport sur l'état sanitaire des travailleurs et des établissements du canal maritime de l'isthme de Suez*.
[3] See ANMT, 1995060/1421: Épidémie de 1883.
[4] See, for instance, Schmidt, *Through the Legation Window*, pp. 159–60 for descriptions of the 1893 epidemic in Mecca. For earlier concerns, see TNA, FO 78/2188: British Consulate Suez to Her Majesty's Secretary of State for Foreign Affairs, Foreign Office, Suez, 15 September 1871, 2 November 1871, 15 December 1871; TNA, FO 78/2233: Consulate to Foreign Office, Suez, 6 January 1872, 9 September 1872.

cholera epidemics in Europe and in order to conjoin the efforts of politics and science in the field of disease prevention.[5] The 1885 conference in Rome proved unsuccessful (as did the Suez Canal conference of the same year) and only highlighted the antagonism between Britain and the other European nations.[6] The 1890s and 1900s, however, saw a political and scientific rapprochement with the conferences of Venice (1892 and 1897), Dresden (1893) and Paris (1894, 1903 and 1912) continuing the process of standardisation and internationalisation in disease prophylaxis.[7] The 1907 convention of the conference of Rome prescribed the creation of an international office of hygiene in Paris to collect and distribute information regarding outbreaks of diseases.[8] It was not only the organisation and rhetoric of the meetings, therefore, that showed similarities to other internationalist endeavours of the late nineteenth and early twentieth centuries, there were also thematic parallels: just as in the Brussels conference on slavery, for instance, the bundling and transmission of information was presented as a central strategy at the sanitary conferences. Also, as was the case during other such meetings, the language of cooperation hid underlying antagonisms, for which the new internationalism in fact provided a stage.

The proceedings of the international sanitary conferences emphasise that contagion was perceived to be a truly global problem. Against the background of the European cholera epidemics, the dual nature of the new rapidity of transportation had become evident: on the one hand beneficial for commerce and colonialism, on the other hand representing a threat. Many contemporaries agreed that the only solution to the problem was global cooperation (or at least the cooperation of the 'Western world') and that the propagation of disease thus had to be debated and resolved internationally. What was more, the delegates at the conferences struggled with defining which agents would realise the controls under discussion, be they international committees, consuls, or the Egyptian authorities. A further 'international' topic was of course the degree to which global traffic could be hampered by disease prevention. A possible way out was provided by the proposal of certain 'modern' and 'scientific' tools to fight disease without slowing down communication, such as checks run by medical officers with a standardised education, vaccinations, or disinfection with the aid of various chemicals or sterilisers.

---

[5] Huber, 'The Unification of the Globe by Disease?'; Harrison, 'Disease, Diplomacy and International Commerce'.

[6] See, for example, ANMT, 1995060/1422: *Morning Post*, 12 June 1885.

[7] See ANMT, 1995060/1422.

[8] ANMT, 1995060/1121: Arrangement international signé à Rome le 9 décembre 1907 pour la création, à Paris, d'un office international d'hygiène publique (Paris: Imprimerie nationale, 1938).

Yet besides the discussion of practical and scientific matters, the international sanitary conferences served to define the scope of common action, which, according to Adrien Proust, delegate at the international sanitary conference 1892 in Venice, had to crystallise in specific locations. He reacted to British intransigence to quarantine issues with reference to the Suez Canal:

The English argument: 'Everyone is master in his own house' would be irrefutable if the ships did not pass through the Canal, which is a common gate to England and to the other European nations. Here the question is not only national; it is international.[9]

According to Proust and many of his contemporaries, the Canal thus brought advantages, but also uncontrollable dangers and therefore necessitated a new form of global responsibility, where different nation states and empires as well as science and politics had to pull together. Besides international conferences held far away from the Canal, trustworthy local bodies of governance had to be installed to enact the recommendations.

The Conseil sanitaire maritime et quarantenaire d'Egypte

The entanglement of politics and science proved to be full of conflicts once measures were implemented, and the internationalisation of disease prevention was not easy to accomplish. The implementation of rules and stipulations issued for instance by the international sanitary conferences points to the problems that the application of these rules could pose on the ground.

In the 1870s the Ottoman Empire strengthened its passport and quarantine regulations leading to discontent among western states and particularly in Britain. Captains complained when their ships were held back and the passengers suffered from the bad sanitary conditions in the quarantine camps. These complaints were often formulated on scientific grounds arguing that quarantine was generally useless. Ferdinand de Lesseps strongly expressed his dislike of quarantines and particularly of their execution in Egypt:

I have been witness during my recent stay in Egypt of so many acts that were arbitrary, useless and ruinous for commerce undertaken by a sanitary administration acting without responsibility and without fixed rules, that I have been pressed since my return among you to attract your attention so that you can enlighten the government and public opinion.[10]

---

[9] Protocoles et procès-verbaux de la conférence sanitaire internationale de Venise inaugurée le 5 janvier 1892 (Rome, 1892), p. 116: n° 4, Séance du 9 janvier 1892.
[10] 'Les quarantaines. Académie des sciences, Séance du lundi 20 mars 1882, Note de Ferdinand de Lesseps sur les quarantaines imposes à Suez aux provenances maritimes de l'Extrême-Orient', Le Canal de Suez: Bulletin décadaire, 12 May 1882.

There were other influential critics of Egyptian sanitary politics. Soon after 1882, Evelyn Baring argued that in fact only scientists should discuss matters of disease. But, since Europe (meaning continental Europe) held 'a deep rooted belief' in the efficacy of quarantine, Baring thought that Egypt had the right to do what it deemed necessary.[11] However, as time progressed, he grew increasingly critical of the local organisation of the quarantine system and of the Egyptian Board of Health, 1881 reconstituted as *Conseil sanitaire maritime et quarantenaire d'Egypte*, in particular. In line with the statements made at the international sanitary conferences, mentioned above, there was a developing consensus among Europeans that the sanitary organisation of Egypt had to be brought under international control as Egypt occupied a central position in any global system of prophylaxis.

The *Conseil sanitaire maritime et quarantenaire* had its origins at the 1866 sanitary conference in Constantinople.[12] Its main concern was the protection of Egyptian territory from the introduction of contagious disease. As well as the management of the lazarettos and quarantine institutions and the collection and transmission of information regarding disease outbreaks, the *Conseil sanitaire maritime et quarantenaire* was in charge of the sanitary police guarding the Egyptian coastline of the Mediterranean and the Red Sea as well as the borders in the desert.[13]

Following the ongoing protests of European powers regarding the institution's inefficiency, the *Conseil sanitaire* was reorganised in 1881, this time along international lines, with its composition reflecting the increasing European influence in Egypt.[14] The regulations of 1881 were reformed several times. In 1891 the number of Egyptian members was reduced from 17 to three, justified by the fact that it was an international institution after all. In exchange, the Egyptian government was offered the funds necessary to finance the construction of lazarettos and to amend the state deficit. Simultaneously the total number of members was reduced from 23 to 17, representing all the powers that had a self-defined interest in the Mediterranean and the 'Orient', that is Germany, Austria-Hungary, Belgium, Britain, Denmark, Spain, France,

---

[11] TNA, PRO 30/29/295: Sir E. Baring to Earl Granville, Cairo, 5 November 1883.
[12] DWQ, Majlis al-Wuzarā', Niẓārat al-Dākhiliyya 2/4, 0075–001334: Ṣūrat Amr ʿālī mubīn bihi waẓāʾif majlis al-ṣaḥa al-baḥriyya wa-l-kwarantīnāt; see also ibid., 0077–0013336: Extrait de la convention internationale faite à Paris le 3 février 1852 et publiée le 15 Juin 1853. Dispositions particulières relatives à l'Orient et à l'Egypte.
[13] TNA, PRO 30/29/295: Règlement général de police sanitaire maritime et quarantenaire, esp. p. 86.
[14] TNA, PRO 30/29/295: Extracts from Report to the Egyptian Maritime and Quarantine Board of Health, 6 June 1881; Decree Méhémet Tewfik, 3 January 1881.

Greece, the Netherlands, Italy, Portugal, Russia, Sweden and Turkey as well as two Egyptian delegates with voting powers.[15] Since its very beginnings there were discussions regarding the truly international character of the enterprise. In an article of September 1882 the journalist Étienne Fabre, known for his critical stance towards Britain, accused the delegates of following their national interest rather than the international good and coupled this observation with a general critique of internationalism. In the case of disease protection this defect of internationalism was however particularly problematic as it was crucial to prescribe tight measures in order to 'stop the progression of the diseases which rule in the Orient and which ships or caravans can transport into Europe'.[16] In a familiar rhetoric, according to Fabre, Europe had to unite to build up its bulwarks at its margins.

During the 1882 cholera epidemic, the Canal Company still defended harsher measures of control against the reclamations of ships and against the protests of several chambers of commerce, even though the British and Ferdinand de Lesseps were opposed to stricter controls in the Canal Zone. While de Lesseps argued that a simple observation of 24 hours would be more than sufficient, the *Conseil sanitaire* decided that for ships coming from Bombay or Aden, there would be seven days of quarantine for infected ships, which would be isolated at al-Tur. All others would be held according to a fixed timetable (six days for those having spent eight days on sea, five for nine days and so forth – 13 long days on sea reduced the length of observation to a mere 24 hours, as Ferdinand de Lesseps had wished) at the quarantine station of Moses' Wells.[17] These prescriptions were more than a simple local nuisance as they led to global delays and were thus resented on a worldwide level.

In 1883 the *Conseil sanitaire* considered Bombay contaminated. Cases of cholera had appeared in Egypt that year and many debates ensued as to whether the mobility of Egyptians should be restricted. The British, however, criticised the fact that ships, after having travelled from Bombay to Egypt, were still considered infected despite the long trajectory that lay behind them. In this context the *Conseil sanitaire* became a

---

[15] DWQ, Majlis al-Wuzarā', Niẓārat al-Dākhiliyya 2/4, 0075–001340: Contentieux de l'état. Présidence du conseil des ministres et ministère de l'Intérieur A. S. E. Riaz Pacha, ministre de l'Intérieur et président du Conseil des ministres, Cairo, 14 February 1891; ibid., 0075–001341: Ministère des Affaires étrangères à Son Excellence Riaz Pacha, président du Conseil des ministres, Cairo, 25 January 1891.

[16] ANMT, 1995060/1046: Étienne Fabre, 'L'Europe en Egypte', *Le télégraphe*, 3 September 1882.

[17] ANMT, 1995060/1046: Étienne Fabre, 'La question des quarantaines', *Le télégraphe*, 7 September 1882.

counter-imperial institution that – sometimes successfully – proved its stamina against the British occupation in Egypt.

Just like the management of pilgrim mobility, the containment of infectious disease brought the salient issues of globalisation around 1900 – for instance that action in one area of the world could have repercussions in another far away region – most clearly to the fore. What is more, the sanitary policies in Egypt showed to what extent the international regulation of transportation had become part of a global power struggle. The answer to this struggle was the experimentation with novel political institutions and instruments – in name international, though mostly reflecting the power balance of the time. The scientific explanations of disease also shifted, calling for different measures in order to fight it, mainly centring around space, science and classification, as will be seen as this chapter progresses.

Spatial arrangements

As seen in earlier chapters, the Suez Canal proved particularly complicated on the level of political authorities. It concurrently provided a precise location in which Europeans had to act in order to be safe. As a delegate of the 1894 international sanitary conference put it:

> It is not in Europe, in fact, that we have to wait for the arrival of the cholera to combat it. It is far away, on the routes that it usually follows, where it is important to endeavour to block its passage. The Suez Canal is a defile at the exit of which an immense radiance stretches across the whole Mediterranean Basin due to the considerable maritime relations.[18]

At the sanitary conferences, Egypt, or more precisely the Suez Canal, thus emerged as a central position for Europe to put up its guards against disease, as Siegfried and others argued as well.[19] This identification of specific geographical locations points to the emergence of new sluice gates where global controls could be effectuated.

Clearly, sanitary measures and political interests were closely intertwined in the Canal Zone. This was true both in organisational matters, such as in the attempts to create new institutions that were to be solid enough to provide for Europe's security, but also in practical terms. The character of the Suez Canal as a magnet, drawing people in from all directions, also mattered in terms of disease propagation. As seen in Chapter 1, its central position was often phrased in medical imagery, as

---

[18] *Conférence sanitaire internationale de Paris* (Paris, 1894), p. 29: Protocole n° 1, Séance du 7 février 1894.

[19] See also Boniteau, 'Le pèlerinage à la Mecque et les campements quarantenaires', 660.

a waist, a windpipe, or an artery, showing that specific cultural connotations came with the new spatial configurations. In this manner, the location came to be seen both as a weak point and an interstice, filtering microbes in the networks of world transportation. This idea was put into operation through spatial configurations that featured the Canal as an anti-contact zone as well as through special scientific technologies and tools of bureaucratic control reviewed later in this chapter. In the next section, different spatial arrangements such as the Canal as a zone of non-contact, the functions of the lazaretto and the identification of specific origins of disease will be reviewed in turn.

The canal as anti-contact zone

To the Australian physician Dr Mackenzie, the Suez Canal did not radiate modernity and civilisation, but represented a dangerous path to infection:

> Dreary desert as far as the eye can see on either side and the canal itself muddy and abominably offensive to the sense of smell. Visions of Enteric fever amongst the souls under my care would keep rising in my mind & made me impatient with our slow progress.[20]

At the sanitary conferences and beyond, debates raged as to how to make the passage through this dangerous space safe enough without hindering smooth traffic. The compromise of how to keep the Canal open yet controllable took the name of 'voluntary quarantine' or 'passage in quarantine' and was connected with the more militarised *cordon sanitaire* guarding the Canal.

The concept of 'passage in quarantine' emerged both out of lofty debates at the conferences and practical experimentation and stood for the avoidance of all contact between steamer and shore. It functioned both ways, with the concern sometimes being about diseases being introduced into Egypt and sometimes about diseases already in Egypt that the passing ships dreaded to contract.[21] The 'passage in quarantine' had previously been tested for pilgrim ships in 1875.[22] Likewise the regulations enacted in reaction to the cholera epidemics of 1883 prohibited every communication

---

[20] Account of a voyage to Australia by Dr Mackenzie, quoted in Pearson, *The Indian Ocean*, pp. 238–9.

[21] Among many other ships passing in quarantine, see CAOM, GGA 16H/86: Rapport du commissaire du gouvernement à bord du navire à pèlerins l'Olbia de la compagnie Cyprien Fabre pendant le pèlerinage à la Mecque en 1902. See also TNA, FO 2/232: Consul Cameron, Port Said, 10 October 1879; Reymond, *Le port de Port-Said*, p. 97.

[22] See, for instance, ANMT, 1995060/4904: Règlement pour le transit des pèlerins de provenance brute ou suspecte, 3 September 1875; CADN, Le Caire 283: Dossier général canal de Suez: Transit en quarantaine.

between the crews of the ships coming from contaminated harbours and the population of Egypt. However, in order to pass through the Suez Canal, ships had to take a pilot on board, which clearly represented a contact between the shore and the ship; therefore the regulation was first either equivalent to a prohibition of using the Canal at all or – if pilots were no longer employed – the increase of the risk of accidents.[23]

Yet the system soon became more elaborate, with the creation of a whole bureaucratic apparatus for the guarantee of non-contact. In reaction to the 1880s' conflicts around quarantine regulations, expressed at the international sanitary conferences, the British negotiated a deal in 1891: British ships from any origin destined for a port in the United Kingdom should be allowed to pass the Canal unhindered under three conditions – all ships, including war vessels, had to undergo medical checks and questioning at Suez; the commander had to give his word that the information provided was correct; and every infected or suspect ship would pass through the Canal with two sanitary guards on board, who made sure that there was no contact between the ship and people or entities on the shores of the Canal. It could not stop anywhere in the Mediterranean and all the ports on the way would be informed via telegraph at cost to the ship. Every country was free to decide on the punishments in the event that a vessel stopped (except in cases of emergency of course). Non-British ships could either opt for regular quarantine or follow these directives.[24] Also, as the director of the *Conseil sanitaire*, Walter Frederick Miéville informed the shipping agents, this measure would necessitate an augmentation of the passage fees per ship. After some reflection the shipping agents accepted the higher tax in order to avoid delays at either end of the Canal.[25]

Yet it was not enough to make the Canal a non-contact zone on paper, the system also had to be put into practice, revealing the intricate practical implications of the regulations debated at international conferences and other meetings. The Canal Company reacted by increasing the team of pilots. Every pilot who had spent time on a contaminated or suspect ship had to undergo individual quarantine for one, two, or seven days.[26]

---

[23] Caird Library, P&O/17/1&3: Suez Canal Quarantine Restriction. Memorandum.

[24] TNA, FO 93/11/60: Protocol. Alexandria Board of Health. Quarantine, Suez Canal (not to be published), London, 29 July 1891.

[25] CADN, Le Caire 283: Worms, Josse & Co au Comte C. Lepeletier d'Aunay, Agent politique et consul général de France, Le Caire, Suez, 12 February 1887.

[26] ANMT, 1995060/4904: Rapport sur l'organisation du transit des navires en quarantaine volontaire, Ismailia, 14 June 1899; ANMT, 1995060/4906: Compagnie universelle du canal maritime de Suez, Commission des finances, Séance du 3 janvier 1882, Extrait du procès-verbal, N 632: Quarantaines, établissement de chalands lazaret, augmentation de l'effectif des pilotes.

If the Egyptian territory was deemed disease-ridden, the pilots travelled on a boat in front of the steamer. The Canal traffic could thus be upheld, but the solution was problematic for the Canal towns and particularly for Port Said, as the town lost its income if the ships were not stopping at its harbour. The maintenance of the Canal towns with food and water also proved to be complicated, because the newly built towns did not have any agriculture attached to them and depended on the import of vegetables and the like from Damiette and other places.[27]

As the 'passage in quarantine' was put into practice, more elaborate procedures were introduced. Ships traversing the Canal and claiming this status flew yellow flags and were marked by yellow lights at night. They had to take two guards on board to ensure the absence of any kind of contact between land and ship. Those able to prove uninterrupted passage in quarantine were finally suspended from the usual 24-hour-long observation, as their isolated passage through the Canal was counted as equivalent.[28] This, however, required absolute segregation, which meant that no person could have any contact with the shore, but also any waste or dead bodies, for instance, had to be stopped at all costs from exiting the microcosm of the ship.[29] A certain Mr Hooker, writing in the *Egyptian Gazette*, therefore turned his attention

to the necessity for meticulous surveillance regarding the steamers transporting pilgrims when they are at anchor at night in the Lake Timsah in order to prevent that dirt and filth from being thrown overboard, as the current of the lake would push them on the shore near inhabited villages.[30]

In addition to the guards accompanying the ships through the Canal, the shores were watched in order to avoid illicit passages across the Canal itself. In 1890 the *Conseil sanitaire* established three sanitary posts along the waterway and asked the Egyptian minister of the interior to establish seven other posts in order to allow the exercising of efficient surveillance of the Asian bank.[31] Opposite every one of the sanitary stations, military posts were established, each composed of eight men on dromedaries (once again pointing to the entanglement of desert mobilities and the steamers), to prevent the illicit crossing of pilgrims from the Arabian

---

[27] ANMT, 1995060/1046: Étienne Fabre, 'Le choléra en Égypte', 29 June 1883.
[28] TNA, PRO 30/29/295: Règlement pour le transit par le canal de Suez.
[29] See Quai d'Orsay, Correspondance politique, Egypte 40: Règlement de navigation dans le canal maritime de Suez, janvier 1911; see also TNA, FO 78/3011: Consul West to Secretary of State for Foreign Affairs, 4 September 1879.
[30] ANMT, 1995060/1421: *Egyptian Gazette*, 5 September 1890.
[31] ANMT, 1995060/1421: *Egyptian Gazette*, 18 August 1890.

side to Africa.[32] The 'passage in quarantine' was thus turned into a *cordon sanitaire*.

With this *cordon sanitaire* in place the Canal passage was further militarised. Pilgrim ships could only navigate throughout the day and necessary stopovers at night were limited to Lake Timsah near Ismailia. During transit the ships were subject to double surveillance, one on board by the officers and sanitary guards and a second on the shores of the Canal. Armed soldiers accompanied their whole trajectory on a Canal Company boat. They were ordered to shoot every pilgrim trying to jump from the ship. In parallel two soldiers on camels followed the ship on shore. Thus secured from inside and outside, the pilgrim ships traversed the Canal in groups of two or three. While in harbour, taking provisions or disembarking crewmembers was strictly prohibited; the only people who could disembark at Port Said were the sanitary officers and the pilots who went straight into quarantine on land.[33] Similarly strict *cordons sanitaires* were enforced in 1891 and 1893. This spatial configuration of the strictly guarded separation between the ship and the shore made the phrase of the Canal as non-contact zone – used as heading for this section – most clearly palpable.

Of course there were exceptions to this non-contact and it was never entirely enforceable, not least due to the necessity of implementing checks and controls introduced in earlier chapters. As seen above, one complication was the pilots who still had to come on board to ensure a safe passage without delays or accidents. Another was how to count and identify the pilgrims under these conditions, if the ship should pass without any contact with harbour or shore. In 1897 a mixed solution was chosen: officials had the right to go on board and check the pilgrims, but at the same time the ships had to transit the Canal in quarantine.[34] Such procedures turned the area into a complicated semi-permeable membrane rather than a zone of complete separation.

Yet problems of complete non-contact could also be a matter of overlapping authorities. As the century drew to a close, in 1898, the Egyptian minister of the interior, Moustapha Fehmy, gave instructions for 'active surveillance' in order to hinder *sanbūks* and other small boats from illicitly

---

[32] ANMT, 1995060/4907: Compagnie universelle du canal maritime de Suez, chef du service de transit et de navigation à M. Ferdinand de Lesseps, Ismailia, 25 August 1890 and further documents.

[33] ANMT, 1995060/4907: Dispositions prises par le Conseil sanitaire maritime et quarantenaire dans sa séance du 26 août 1890; ibid.: L'ingénieur en chef de la Compagnie au président, 24 August 1890.

[34] ANMT, 1995060/4907: Mesures à appliquer aux navires à pèlerins transitant le canal maritime en état de quarantaine, approuvées par le Conseil dans sa séance du 23 juin 1897.

transporting pilgrims across the Canal and to prevent any attempt by individual pilgrims or groups trying to swim across the Canal. Fehmy asked the Suez Canal Company to give orders that everyone wanting to enter Egypt should be turned away and identified to the authorities.[35] The company replied that it was prepared to comply with the request, but that its agents did not have sufficient authority to rebuke anyone without it leading to significant resistance or open fights.[36] In 1899 military forces were again guarding the Canal coasts, first commencing on the coasts of the Red Sea and then on the Canal banks themselves. On the Arabian side, police posts would hinder pilgrims from moving any further before having accomplished the quarantine requirements. Furthermore a number of cruisers were positioned at strategic points.[37]

This militarisation of the Canal Zone in the name of identifying travellers and stopping microbes points to a new function of the Canal as a sluice gate between diseased and disease-free zones of the globe. It also illustrates the limits of such controls and the problems of making them fully enforceable. Furthermore it points to the importance of passing without delay and the fear of slowdowns. An additional element in this control system became effective when either complete non-contact was not possible or for those who still had to board suspect ships, such as pilots and guards. Then lazarettos and quarantine stations had to be used which will be submitted to a closer analysis in the next section.

The micro-level: lazarettos and quarantine stations

Besides the elaborate anti-contact system established to avoid the global delays normally connected to sanitary surveillance, old-fashioned quarantine stations were still in place.[38] Such establishments catered, for instance, for pilots and guards who went into quarantine after duty on potentially infected ships. In what follows, lazarettos and quarantine stations shall be assessed as global microcosms shedding light not only on measures of global regulation but also problems and improvisation emerging in relation to such measures.

---

[35] ANMT, 1995060/1425: Moustapha Fehmy, ministre de l'intérieur, à l'agent supérieur, Cairo, 14 April 1893.
[36] ANMT, 1995060/1425: Charles de Sérionne au ministre de l'Intérieur, Ismailia, 18 April 1893.
[37] ANMT, 1995060/4907: 'La défense sanitaire', Le phare de Port-Saïd et du canal de Suez, 15 April 1899.
[38] On the development of quarantines in the Mediterranean more generally, see Panzac, Quarantaines et Lazarets.

A closer analysis of the practice of quarantine illustrates that very different institutions were in place in or near the Canal Zone. For pilots and guards who had entered suspect ships, the Canal Company possessed several 'floating lazarettos'.[39] Before the 1890s, four such barges had already been put into service with the significant investment of 484,000 francs.[40] However, the convention of the 1897 Venice conference gave the green light to passage in quarantine and reformed their general guidelines, replacing the former stays in lazarettos in favour of disinfection and observation en route. When Egypt was defending itself against an external disease, the steam steriliser on a pontoon was used for the disembarking pilots; if Egypt was infected and the clients of the Canal wanted to protect their ships they took on pilots and guards after prior isolation on the barges, which served as quarantine stations.[41] Yet the aim of the Canal Company was to build proper lazarettos in the Canal towns too, more precisely two 'isolation pavilions' in Port Said and Port Tawfiq. In 1899 the company planned to construct a lazaretto paid for by the *Conseil* and within it a separation to isolate pilots at the cost of the company. After some haggling between both parties, mainly involving the financing of the project, it was finally built at some distance from Port Said. Still, in the case of outbreaks of diseases within the Canal towns themselves, improvised isolation stations had to be put up that required a choice of location pointing to social and ethnic hierarchies within the urban layout of the Canal towns.

Some sanitary institutions also aimed at checking groups of travellers before they could even reach the Suez Canal. The quarantine station for pilgrims at al-Tur, mentioned in Chapter 6, was complemented by a newer station at Moses' Wells, constructed in 1894 close to Suez, which was created to serve non-pilgrim travellers.[42] The biblical connotation of the name echoed earlier references to the Red Sea region as origin of

---

[39] ANMT, 1995060/4906: Compagnie universelle du canal maritime de Suez, Comité de direction, Séance du 15 septembre 1893, Proposition (Remplacement de chalands lazarets par des constructions à terre); see also Caird Library, P&O/17/1&3: Suez Canal Quarantine Restriction. Memorandum (1888), mentioning the 'Canal Company's floating hospital'.

[40] ANMT, 1995060/4906: Comité de direction, Séance du 15 septembre 1898, Remplacement de chalands lazarets par des constructions à terre.

[41] ANMT, 1995060/4906: Projet de lazaret et de maisons d'isolement pour pilotes et gardes autorisés, 1899; ibid.: Compagnie universelle du canal maritime de Suez, Comité de direction, Séance du 10 août 1899, Extrait du procès-verbal.

[42] ANMT, 1995060/1422: Avis officiel. Conseil sanitaire maritime et quarantenaire d'Égypte, Cahier des charges pour la mise au concours de la construction des établissements à créer à la station sanitaire des sources de Moïse, prés de Suez (Égypte) (Supplément au *Journal official*, 1 January 1894). See also DWQ, Majlis al-Wuzarā', Niẓārat al-Dākhiliyya 2/4, 0075–001347: Ministère des Affaires étrangères, Note pour le Conseil des ministres, 31 May 1893.

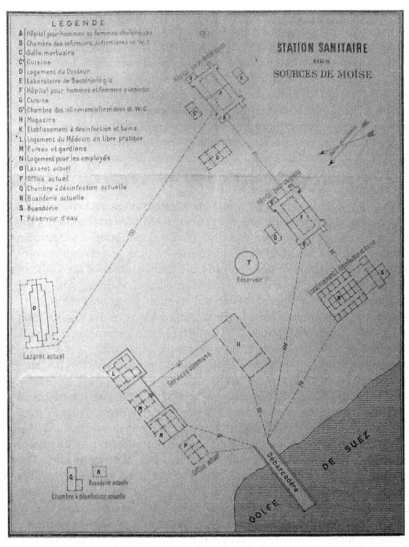

Figure 20 Map of the Quarantine Station at Moses' Wells, *Supplément au Journal officiel*, 1 January 1894.

Judaism and Christianity. Yet other elements visible on the map of the station (Figure 20) point to the emphasis on up-to-date science, such as the bacteriological laboratory or the focus on sterilisation and disinfection. The spatial arrangement and the exact notation of the distances between different elements of the quarantine status indicate the focus on isolation and segregation, not only in relationship to the outside world but also between different groups and functions within the camp. The three stages on the right side, disinfection, lazaretto for suspects and lazaretto for cholera stricken, point to this separation, which obviously had always been a guiding principle of lazarettos. At the same time, the clear indication of the functional sequence for those entering the lazaretto from the sea, almost reminds us of such sequences in factories. The architecture of the lazaretto was furthermore explicitly location-independent and could be replicated at any coastline around the globe. Yet there was one feature that clearly indicated its location in the desert: the lazaretto at Moses' Wells did not need an outside limitation, as the desert was deemed a sufficient shield against escape.

The financing of stations such as Moses' Wells, their security and the fight against uprisings could all pose problems. As seen in Chapter 6, the pilgrims' lazaretto at al-Tur and the quarantine station at Qamaran proved difficult to guard, with the lazarettos not only experiencing complaints, but outright rebellion. In 1884 the management of the Gabbari lazaretto in Alexandria also reported incidents of violence within the institution. Miéville triggered a proposal to grant the guards the right to shoot every inmate crossing the barriers, considering this the best solution for avoiding similar situations.[43] The camps also became increasingly militarised and needed more and more armed personnel – yet at times the Egyptian army had difficulties even providing the guards for the camp at al-Tur.[44]

As the complaint of the Egyptian army makes clear, the international institutions were not always guarded by international personnel, nor were they financed internationally. The closer scrutiny of those interned also obviously engendered higher costs. The question of who had to pay for this defence system against disease came up time and time again. The Egyptian administration, for one, did not deem it justifiable to fully finance the quarantine station at al-Tur, as most inmates were from other countries. In 1891, 11,950 persons had been interned at al-Tur, of which 5,389 were Egyptians. In 1893, the ratio was 31,000 to 6,692. Despite the justification of Egyptian complaints, the costs of international disease bulwarks were not easy to repartition internationally.[45]

---

[43] DWQ, Majlis al-Wuzarā', Niẓārat al-Dākhiliyya 2/4, 0075–001337: Ministère de l'intérieur à Nubar Pacha, président du Conseil des ministres, Cairo, 7 October 1884.
[44] DWQ, Majlis al-Wuzarā', Niẓārat al-Dākhiliyya 2/4, 0075–001339: Note pour le Conseil des ministres, August 1886.
[45] DWQ, Majlis al-Wuzarā', Niẓārat al-Dākhiliyya 2/4, 0075–001346: Le Conseil sanitaire maritime et quarantenaire et le gouvernement égyptien, n.d.

The costs of the *cordon sanitaire*, too, were resented as being exorbitant. In 1896 the Egyptian Financial Committee awarded a loan of 3,000 Egyptian pounds for quarantine measures.[46] At the same time the Suez Canal Company demanded reimbursements, because they paid for the boat that accompanied the pilgrim ships during the passage through the Canal.[47] The attempt to introduce 'isolation on the move' rather than permanent quarantine stations thus also led to frequent debates regarding funding on the one hand and the power of coercion and the role of the military on the other.

The closer look at the spatial layout and organisation of the quarantine stations of Moses' Wells and al-Tur highlight a number of central themes, such as the question of internationalism, the problems of finance and control, the emphasis on science and 'progress'. A further theme, as seen in the comparison between al-Tur and Moses' Wells, was of course the differentiation of such institutions regarding class, professional function and ethnic origin. But before entering this debate we will stay with the theme of space and disease, looking at the identification of specific regions as regions of disease origin.

Defining regions of disease origination

In addition to the lazarettos and the passage in quarantine, a spatial configuration that came to play an important role in distinguishing between dangerous and risk-free travellers was the concept of disease origin. According to the preconception shared by many, Europe had overcome epidemic disease since the Middle Ages, but there were still disease-ridden areas haunted by epidemics, particularly in the 'Orient'. The plague especially was depicted as an 'oriental disease' long before the opening of the Canal; and cholera was also described either as an Indian disease or as originating in Mecca and Medina.[48] In the context of the danger radiating from potential epidemics, it mattered that those places that were perceived as their cradle had moved significantly closer to Europe through the global shortcut at Suez. In this section, two of such

---

[46] DWQ, Majlis al-Wuzarā', Niẓārat al-Dākhiliyya 2/4, 0075–001365: Comité des finances, Note au Conseil des ministres, Cairo, 22 February 1896.

[47] DWQ, Majlis al-Wuzarā', Niẓārat al-Dākhiliyya 2/4, 0075–001346: Affaires étrangères, Note pour le Conseil des ministres, Cairo, 31 May 1893.

[48] See, for example, de Beauregard, *Notice historique*; de Castro, *Cholera in Egitto nel 1883*; Tambacopoulo, *De la peste*; di Wolmar, *Abhandlung über die Pest*.

concepts of disease origin east of Suez will be explored, first looking at India and then at Mecca and Medina.

Outbreaks of cholera and plague were diagnosed at different locations around the world, but the international sanitary conferences had established a consensus that cholera originated from India.[49] Consequently the *Conseil sanitaire maritime et quarantenaire d'Egypte* opted for a strict handling of ships coming from that region.[50] Yet some voices, often those with a strong interest in rapid traffic between Europe and Asia, argued against treating Bombay as permanently cholera-contaminated. Complaints regarding the restrictions accompanying the definition of India as the origin of disease came from individuals and corporations alike, who feared that the measures would lead to a considerable loss for British shipping firms and to complications with colonial management. The Viscount Enfield, Under-Secretary of State for India, argued that if the present views of the sanitary boards were acted upon, India would be in 'perpetual quarantine' generating an 'almost intolerable' obstruction to communication between the United Kingdom and its South-Asian possessions.[51] To him it was crucial to make the distinction between epidemic and sporadic cholera in India. Only if an epidemic prevailed should the Indian ports be considered infected as there were irregular cases of contagious diseases in European harbours as well:

> It appears to his Lordship as useless and irrational to place in quarantine at Suez a perfectly healthy ship arriving from Bombay because there are a few sporadic cases of cholera among the 750,000 inhabitants of that city, as it would be to place in quarantine at Antwerp healthy arrivals from the Thames because London is hardly ever totally free from small-pox or scarlet fever.[52]

With Enfield promoting a differentiation of the severity of Indian diseases, other British defendants of unobstructed traffic argued that the epidemics originated not in India at all, but in Mecca and Medina, illustrating the extent to which 'scientific knowledge' was in fact political and a matter of debate. Miéville from the *Conseil sanitaire* questioned the 'ascertained fact'

---

[49] See TNA, FO 423/14: Minutes of Proceedings of the Maritime and Quarantine Sanitary Board, 5 June 1883 – cholera in Saigon; CADN, Port Said 125: Ministère des Affaires étrangères à M. le consul de France, Paris, 22 November 1900 – before that date, Smyrna, Beirut, Aden, Port Said, Adelaide, Sydney, Tamataye, New Caledonia and Paraguay had been treated as being contaminated by the plague.

[50] CADN, Port Said 48: Conseil sanitaire, maritime et quarantenaire d'Egypte. Séance du 1er février 1887.

[51] TNA, PRO 30/29/295: Earl Granville to Earl of Dufferin, London, 5 January 1882.

[52] TNA, PRO 30/29/295: Viscount Enfield to Mr Lister, 22 December 1881; see also ANMT, 1995060/1046: Étienne Fabre, 'Une Commission internationale en Egypte', 31 May 1883.

that cholera was imported to the Hijaz by Indian pilgrims and not engendered by the dire sanitary condition of the holy places themselves.[53] Richard Burton had already voiced the idea that disease originated at the holy sites of Islam in reaction to the feast of sacrifice and the thousands of animals slaughtered on this occasion when he stated: 'The revolting scene, aided by a shade temperature of 120° Fahr., has more than once caused a desolating pestilence at Meccah. The cholera of 1865 has been traced back to it; in fine, the safety of Europe demands the reformation of this filthy slaughter-house.'[54]

In a report of 1882 the Indian medical officer Abdur Razzack, stationed in Jidda, drew a similar connection between the cholera and the sacrificing of animals at Muna near Mecca. The decaying animal bodies in combination with the exhaustion and fatigue of the pilgrims after their journey worried him especially. He also alleged that cholera had its point of origin among the lower classes and thus added a social explanation to the spatial one. Razzack (writing just a year before Robert Koch's expedition to Egypt and his subsequent isolation of the Vibrio cholerae) did not believe that cholera had migrated from India, due to the fact that the journey was too long. Rather, he argued, it was endemic in Muna, where it was sustained by the bad quality of air, water and the harsh climatic conditions. Yet, he admitted, due to the limited medical knowledge of the causation of the disease, the true origin of the cholera was difficult to assess.

Abdur Razzack's opinions were still very much phrased in the language of 'miasmata' and the belief in the spontaneous outbreak of disease.[55] This belief was shared by more illustrious persons, such as Ferdinand de Lesseps. Lesseps stated in 1882 that the cholera was not originating in India but could emerge anywhere, completely spontaneously.[56] Even after Koch's findings of 1883, the bacteriological consensus took a long time to establish itself and could coexist with other explanations of disease causation.

Bureaucratic and scientific instruments

The spatial distinction of persons deemed healthy and diseased became most obvious in the militarised passage of ships through the Canal and in the bounded space of the lazaretto, where groups were – at least theoretically – strictly separated according to the date of their arrival and

---

[53] TNA, FO 423/14: Consul Miéville to Consul Cookson, Alexandria, 5 June 1883.
[54] Burton, *Sir Richard Burton's Travels in Arabia and Africa*, p. 55.
[55] TNA, FO 881/4762: Dr Abdur Razzack, Report on the 'Haj', 1882.
[56] 'Les quarantaines. Académie des sciences, Séance du lundi 20 mars 1882, Note de Ferdinand de Lesseps sur les quarantaines imposées à Suez aux provenances maritimes de l'Extrême-Orient'. *Le canal de Suez: Bulletin décadaire*, 12 May 1882.

their contact with infectious disease. Yet the categorisation went beyond these different forms of isolation and connects with the argument regarding the distinction of different categories of mobility, running through this book. Travellers were classified regarding the risk they carried in terms of disease propagation, with specific bureaucratic and scientific methods being employed to deal with them without slowing down the traffic through the Canal. In this last section, bureaucratic procedures, scientific methods and, most importantly, the identification of dangerous disease-carriers, which related to the question of positively and negatively connoted travel running as one thread through this book, will be reviewed in turn.

Bureaucratic procedures

In addition to the militarised passage in quarantine, the Canal's cordoning off and the strict scrutiny of the quarantine stations, bureaucracy and new methods of prophylaxis were used to hinder microbes from breaking through the Canal. Such bureaucratic procedures were also a matter of timing as they could severely delay the passage through the Canal. As in other aspects, the crucial themes were the interaction of different empires and the rapid transmission and centralisation of information.

Among the bureaucratic measures tried and tested in the Canal Zone were certificates that attempted to make every ship traceable. In 1870 ships had to show a certificate from the last harbour they had visited in order to travel freely and to avoid lengthy observation.[57] In Port Said or Suez, every ship, whatever its origin, had to undergo medical checks such as inspections, interrogations, medical visits and enquiries. Ships had to provide the relevant visa or special patents and were always deemed suspicious as soon as they carried pilgrims 'or other similar masses'.[58] Since its opening, the Canal thus became a checkpoint for diseases, yet this task became more and more important as the century drew to a close.

Consequently, one of the main administrative tasks of the consul at Port Said was to issue bills of health for British ships. In the late 1890s, the British Consul wanted to get rid of this procedure, claiming that he issued about 800 bills of health per year and that the cessation of the measure would significantly reduce his workload.[59] When the regulations were loosened, however, the abolition of compulsory bills of health caused a loss of income from consular fees. The changing bureaucratic procedures

---

[57] ANMT, 1995060/1028: 'Avis à la navigation', *L'Egypte*, 4 June 1870.
[58] TNA, PRO 30/29/295: Règlement pour le transit par le canal de Suez.
[59] TNA, FO 78/3011: H. B. Consulate to the Chief Clerk FO, Port Said, 1 April 1879; TNA, FO 78/5036: Despatch Mr Cameron, Port Said, 5 July 1899.

were also sometimes perceived to be very confusing, with the shipmasters unaware of the current procedures and the consuls having to repeatedly explain them.[60] Alongside the more or less successful attempts to organise the bureaucratic requirements more efficiently, the rapid transmission of information regarding disease outbreaks came to play an increasingly prominent role both at the international conferences and in practice. If a suspect ship passed through the Canal in quarantine, telegrams informing the important harbours in the Mediterranean of the fact were compulsory. Information regarding the state of health of the entire isthmus was also widely circulated so that ships could take the necessary precautions and pass in quarantine in order to avoid delays in France.[61]

What is more, the educational requirements of medical staff became more and more standardised and obliged medical officers on ships and doctors in the lazarettos to produce certificates from European and American institutions of education. Beside these higher medical standards, specific prescriptions as to who was authorised to instigate notification and isolation were also introduced. Within Egypt, a decree of 1912 prescribed that only doctors, owners of a house or apartment, or school directors could declare the outbreak of a disease.[62]

All these attempts at standardisation point to the importance that was attributed to more efficient bureaucratic measures. Their central aim was the trustworthy acquisition of information regarding disease cases on board steamers passing through the Canal and then, most importantly, the centralisation and global diffusion of this information via new technologies. Still such procedures, obviously difficult to enact and prone to error, were only one side of the coin: the diffusion of information via telephone and telegraph was complemented with new scientific measures.

Scientific measures

The rapid transmission of information concerning outbreaks of disease via the newly laid telegraph lines and the increasing professionalisation of

---

[60] See, for instance, TNA, FO 78/5238: British Consulate to Marquess of Lansdowne, Port Said, 16 October 1902; TNA, FO 78/5238: British Consulate to Marquess of Lansdowne, 4 November 1902.

[61] See, for instance, ANMT, 1995060/1421: Telegram Summaripa au consul français Suez, 7 May 1898; see also DWQ, Majlis al-Wuzarā', Niẓārat al-Dākhiliyya 2/11/.

[62] DWQ, Majlis al-Wuzarā', Niẓārat al-Dākhiliyya 2/11/ب, 0075–002714: Ministère de l'Interieur, Note pour le Conseil des ministres, Cairo, 27 July 1892.

those involved in prophylactic processes were paralleled by other measures, which were perceived to be particularly up to date and in line with scientific progress. One was chemical disinfection, the other vaccination. Such procedures went further than those of sterilisation and segregation practised in lazarettos such as Moses' Wells. They connected with the newest scientific experiments of late nineteenth-century science and with the developing chemical industry as well as drawing on the expertise gained at the first mass vaccination schemes in Egypt and elsewhere.

Steam sterilisation was developed in the second half of the nineteenth century in connection with the introduction of pasteurisation. The often-revised regulations of the quarantine stations specified not only how humans should be disinfected, but also goods or letters that were seen as prone to transporting disease.[63] Even if their effectiveness was repeatedly questioned, the steam sterilisers became more and more sophisticated. By the 1890s every pilgrim ship had to carry at least one of these machines.[64]

At the same time steam sterilisation was increasingly complemented with chemical disinfection. In this context, and once again highlighting the Suez Canal as an experimental field, different chemicals and sterilisers were tested with varying degrees of success. Already at the 1866 international sanitary conference in Constantinople, the results of experiments with calcium chloride and ferrous sulphate had been discussed.[65] In 1896, the doctor Lathuroz-Viollet, sanitary and maritime physician on board the pilgrim ship *Gallia*, reported on the use of at least six different chemical substances in the disinfection incubators.[66] The large number of chemicals employed for disinfection illustrates the experimental stage, which, however, was often combined with a confident belief in the most up-to-date science.

In addition to the use of chemicals, vaccination increasingly gained ground around 1900.[67] The Institute Pasteur began to send anti-plague serum to the Suez Canal Company in the late 1890s to contribute to the work of the company's doctors, who in turn reported their experiences

---

[63] TNA, PRO 30/29/295: Mesures sanitaires applicables aux provenances de choléra dans les ports Egyptiens, Hardes et effets (sent 1882).
[64] See ANMT, 1995060/1418: Prospectus Geneste et Herrscher; TNA, FO 423/14: Minutes of Proceedings of the Maritime and Quarantine Sanitary Board, 5 June 1883; ANMT, 1995060/1420: Médicaments divers expediés ou essayés en Egypte.
[65] Procès-Verbaux de la conférence sanitaire internationale ouverte à Constantinople, N° 27, Séance du 20 août 1866.
[66] CAOM, 16H/86: Pèlerinage à La Mecque. Comptes-rendus des autorités accompagnantes. 1896–1939: Pèlerinage à la Mecque. Rapport de M. Lathuroz-Viollet, Médecin sanitaire maritime commissionné par le Gouverneor Général à bord du 'Gallia'.
[67] See Bashford, 'Foreign Bodies', pp. 39–60.

with it.[68] When cases of plague were reported in 1899–1900, Auguste-Louis-Albéric Prince d'Arenberg, the head of the Suez Canal Company, asked for more vaccine straight away.[69] The French administration attempted to equip all ships travelling to the Far East with anti-plague vaccine with the financial help of the *Société de bienfaisance* of Port Said.[70] And it was not only the Far East that represented a danger: the doctor Camboulio argued in 1901 that most of the rats in the Arab quarter of Port Said were infected with bubonic plague.[71] As Mecca and Medina were seen as particularly dangerous, the compulsory vaccination of pilgrims was considered. Yet not all coped well with the unfamiliar method of vaccination – a young officer for instance, to his embarrassment it seems, fainted when he was given the injection.[72] The experiments with vaccination were thus wide-scale, despite the fears connected with this invasive measure.

Both the search for the ideal method of disinfection and sterilisation and the testing of vaccination illustrate that not only was the Canal Zone to become a control point with a full scientific arsenal but it was also turned into a space of scientific experimentation. This also meant that there was a lot of debate regarding the efficiency of these measures. Securing the sluice gate of Suez against disease was thus not a straightforward procedure. It was complemented with the distinction between those travellers who were not likely at all to transmit disease and those identified as potential disease-carriers.

Classification of travellers

Even those who did not primarily link the causation of cholera to the localities of Mecca and Medina still deemed Muslim pilgrims to be particularly worrisome in terms of the spread of epidemics. At the same time, highlighting the difference between various mobilities and identifying

[68] ANMT, 1995060/1420: Peste – Sérum Antipesteux.
[69] ANMT, 1995060/1420: Arenberg à Docteur Roux à l'Institut Pasteur, Paris, 15 February 1900; see also ANMT, 1995060/1425: Épidémies de peste: télégrammes, rapports, correspondance, notamment de Cambouliou, Gauthier, Sérionne, plans, graphiques, procès-verbaux des conferences des chefs de service en Egypte et du comité de direction, articles de presse, 1899–1907.
[70] See CADN, Port Said 85: Le ministre de la Marine au consul de France à Port-Said, Paris, 11 July 1900.
[71] ANMT, 1005060/1425: Dr Cambouliu au l'agent supérieur, Port Said, 2 August 1901; see also TNA, MT 10/1024: Telegram from Sir N. O'Conor, Constantinople, 1 August 1906.
[72] Caird Library, JOD/103: Diary kept in *HMS Royal Arthur*, 1–15 November 1911, on a voyage from Portsmouth to Port Said (the first 26 pages of a Wireless Telegraph Signal logbook, 8 November 1911).

pilgrims, for example, as prime propagators of cholera and plague also served to keep other, more profitable forms of mobility free from constraints. This strategy connects with a major theme running through the book, targeting specific forms of mobility such as Bedouin and pilgrim, but also certain Canal workers and seamen, as potentially dangerous. Others by contrast were positively connoted and should be allowed to move as quickly as possible translating into more limited checks and controls.

The international sanitary conference of 1892 proposed separate quarantine stations for western travellers and pilgrims, which was realised with the functional division between al-Tur and Moses' Wells. At the 1894 conference in Paris, the delegates prescribed strict isolation for pilgrims, while quarantine in general was depicted as anachronistic. But other groups could also play the role of disease carriers: Étienne-Félix Berlioux, for instance, connected the pilgrimage but also the slave trade with the propagation of epidemics.[73] The singling out of specific travellers – Indians, pilgrims, slaves – thus formed an important element in international strategies applied to cope with potential sources of disease.

Identifying at-risk groups of travellers was not free from complications, however. The regulation of the pilgrim traffic was a nuisance to the shipping companies and colonial governments as it could possibly engender dangerous political implications of discontentment or even revolt against colonial rule. Other apparently disease-prone groups, such as seamen and pilots, occupied a central role in enabling and securing the mobility of western powers.[74] From the perspective of the colonial powers, their control was, if at all possible, to be kept to minimum, in order to avoid delays and slowdowns.

The case of seamen illustrates the struggle for efficient bureaucratic procedures to avoid slowdown. Medical checks and certificates were one reason that made the hiring and firing of seamen in Port Said a complicated affair.[75] As seen in Chapter 3, confirmation of the state of health of a sailor was essential when captains wanted to discharge seamen. These certificates had to be endorsed by a medical practitioner, but, as the British Consul, Cameron, complained, it was not at all evident which doctor had the authority to sign them. He argued that captains should be obliged to produce a certificate issued by the British hospital, which took care of all seamen under British protection. He described the provision of

---

[73] Berlioux, *La traite orientale*, p. 170.

[74] See TNA, PRO 30/29/295: Règlement général de police sanitaire maritime et quarantenaire (1882), article 41.

[75] For issues concerning medical certificates and checks of seamen, see for instance TNA, FO 78/4963; TNA, FO 78/5036; TNA, MT 23/78.

medical certificates as a source of constant annoyance to the consulate and called for clearer definitions regarding the choice of an unbiased and reliable medical practitioner.[76] At the same time as the consulates called for more standardised procedures concerning seamen, they also sought ways to oblige seamen to take out insurance. In order to finance the medical care of seamen, and to avoid sensitive questions of nationality and protection, the charge of an obligatory annual fee per employed seaman was considered and partly enacted.[77]

Time and time again tensions between private companies and international representatives emerged. These included debates regarding the handling of sick seamen if the ship wanted to pass in quarantine without any delay. Such debates were sometimes triggered by individual cases, as that of a Swedish seaman, L. Bengtson, who had been discharged while suffering from an injury in Suez and moved on to Port Said in 1902, where it was concealed that he was suspected of being infected with the plague. During the investigation, it came to light that other seamen, such as a Chinese boatswain in Moses' Wells, were under suspicion of suffering from bubonic plague without the consulate's knowledge. In a letter to the British Board of Trade the consul, hitting the nail right on the head, displayed these cases as the product of the tension between the 'two contending forces in the Canal, namely, an independent international Quarantine board which is growing stricter in its regulations, versus the ship owners, Masters and Agents who claim rapidity of transit'.[78]

Lord Cromer expressed his support of Consul Cameron's approach that no shipping agent should deal with a seaman from a British ship without the consul's knowledge and consent. He further stressed that, according to the Merchant Shipping Act of 1894, seamen had to be discharged by the consul whatever their disease.[79] The case of Bengtson highlights the hierarchies and tensions between the different agents and their opposed interests. It also illustrates the importance of an individual being traceable in the event of an outbreak of disease. Furthermore, issues concerning seamen were often truly global, as this case illustrates very well – it not only included a British ship and a Swedish seaman, but also the French Consul and *Conseil Sanitaire*.

---

[76] TNA, FO 78/5036: D. A. Cameron to Marquis of Salisbury, Port Said, 29 June 1899.
[77] TNA, FO 78/5165: FO Draft Consul Cameron, 20 July 1901. See also TNA, MT 9/708: Port Said Consul – Lady Strangford Hospital Port Said.
[78] TNA, MT 9/721: Cameron to the Assistant Secretary, Marine Department, Board of Trade, Port Said, 17 March 1902.
[79] TNA, MT 9/721: Cromer to Cameron, Cairo, 13 March 1902.

Due to the emphasis of the origin of a disease, non-European seamen were subjected to even more stringent regulations. Egyptian stokers had to undergo quarantine before boarding a ship – the only alternative being the provision of sterilisers and other instruments for disease prevention on board. In 1892 a circular of the *Conseil sanitaire* prescribed that all ships travelling between Port Said and the Far East had to disembark their Egyptian stokers at Suez and isolate them there if they wanted to transit the Canal in quarantine.[80] The British Consul recapitulated the regulations for the discharge of seamen in the Canal Zone according to which:

> no fireman (white or black) and no 'native' deckhand, can be discharged at Port Said from homeward bound ships. A seaman, engaged at Port Said for the run eastward to be discharged at Port Said, must be discharged at Suez for Port Said, and sent here by railway after disinfection at Moses' Wells.

The procedure of discharge was allowed to take place via telegram, in order to facilitate the task for the vice consul in Suez, and in order to avoid his having to travel from Suez to Port Tawfiq, the port on the other side of the Canal, each time a British ship was in harbour. This, however, did not relieve the vice consul from his tedious duty of reporting every single man left behind in quarantine.[81]

Another group that had to submit to particular precautions were the Canal workers. In the light of the intricate connection between the reputation of the Canal route and the question of quarantine and its avoidance, the Canal Company worried a great deal about illness and death among its employees and workers and it was repeatedly pointed out that the general state of health had to be bettered. A further concern was the possibility of outbreaks of malaria and the threat of contagion.[82] As an answer to these fears, the Suez Canal Company proposed standardised measures. During the 1896 cholera epidemic in Egypt, every worker returning from his holidays who had or might have traversed a contaminated town had to undergo five days of observation in Port Said, Ismailia, or Suez before returning to his position. During this time he could be employed in the secluded workshops, but not in the stations on the Canal's shores or in any

---

[80] TNA, MT 23/78: Egyptian Stokers. Special measures taken in regard to those on board ships in quarantine making the voyage between Port Said and the East and vice versa. See also TNA, MT 9/432: G. M. Gould to the Assistant Secretary, Marine Department Board of Trade, Port Said, 18 February 1892, regarding separate articles for Arab seamen at Port Said.

[81] TNA, MT 9/721: Consul Cameron to the assistant secretary, Marine Department, Board of Trade, Port Said, 9 May 1902.

[82] See, for instance, ANMT, 1995060/1421: Epidémies de choléra; ANMT, 1995060/1423. Epidémies: études, rapports, circulaires (1885–1911), déplacements d'employés ou d'ouvriers atteints de la fièvre (1885–1895).

other position with wider public contact. What is more, when on leave the workers were not permitted to travel in inner Egypt (except in very urgent cases) in order to keep the Canal Zone and Egypt proper as strictly separated as possible.[83]

Others were to be ushered through the Canal Zone as smoothly as possible. Troops were generally susceptible to disease outbreaks, yet, as mentioned in the context of the British troop action in 1882, it was crucial to the imperial powers' global strategies to avoid delays and detainment in order to stay true to the new speed of interventions. Usually the health among troops was much worse when they returned from their duties in Asia.[84] Sometimes there were serious outbreaks of disease on board troop ships, and in this case the authorities took particular care not to mix them with the pilgrims in the lazaretto. In order to avoid lengthy quarantine, troops were sometimes also disembarked and disinfected before they could continue their journey.[85] The British always tried to negotiate less stringent controls for their postal steamers and vessels of war, yet French officials who claimed in the 1880s that British troops had introduced cholera into Europe, opposed these measures.[86]

Besides the targeting of different professional groups, race and class played a decisive role. The simple distinction between Europeans, North Americans, and a few privileged Asian travellers on the one side, and everyone else on the other, which was so clearly represented in the steamers' architecture, was maintained concerning medical checks and during outbreaks of disease. The more privileged first- and second-class travellers scoffed at the sanitary controls that all other passengers had to undergo, with their indignant reactions highlighting their class-consciousness. Emily Lorimer, the wife of a colonel in the Indian Army, and later political agent in Bahrain, described the medical checks in Alexandria as an unreasonable demand and a farce, specifying that '[o]f course it is no farce with crew or 3rd Cl. Passengers'.[87] Ralph

---

[83] ANMT, 1995060/1421: Procès-verbal de la conférence tenue à Ismailia le 15 juillet 1896.

[84] See, for example, CCIMP, Messageries Maritimes 302, Laos (1897–1907): Ligne de Chine, Voyage no. 14, Laos, ligne de Chine, Rapport général, Marseilles, 30 June 1902.

[85] See, for instance, TNA, MT 23/203: Quarantine – Claim by authorities at Suez on account of disinfection of troops disembarked from a certain Indian Troop Service transport.

[86] See TNA, FO 423/15: Consul Cookson to Earl Granville, Alexandria, 27 March 1884; Dr Mackie to Consul Cookson, Alexandria, 4 April 1884; Quai d'Orsay, Affaires diverses politiques IV, Egypte 7, Sous-dossier précautions sanitaires à l'occasion de l'envoi des troupes anglaises de l'Inde en Egypte.

[87] OIOC, Mss Eur/F177/4: Emily Lorimer to her father, Athens, c/o Thos. Cook & Son, Bombay, 6 February 1911.

Strachey, another colonial traveller, also complained about the medical checks in a letter to his sister in 1892:

We shall get in to Port Said tonight, or rather tomorrow morning at the deadly hour of 3, when we have all got to turn out and parade on the deck to poke out our tongues to the Port Said medical inspector. Isn't it rot?[88]

When European passengers were obliged to undergo not only medical checks, but outright quarantine, they were outraged. P&O expressed their fury at placing all ships from Bombay under quarantine in the early 1880s (and thus before the routine passage in quarantine) since the result was to keep them for three days in the dreaded heat of the Red Sea. Furthermore Egypt was harming itself, as the passengers were losing at least a week of the time they had allotted for a visit to the country of the Pharaohs. P&O officials went on to state that '[i]t is really monstrous that a perfectly healthy ship, carrying a surgeon, and full of European passengers, should thus be obstructed by Regulations so antiquated as to be entirely out of harmony with the medical knowledge and experience of the present day'.[89]

Specific examples show the forms that this outrage could take. In 1884, the steam ship, *Mira*, carrying first-class passengers only, had suffered one case of cholera among the crew close to Colombo. Subsequently, it was not only obliged to undergo one day of quarantine in Colombo, but upon arrival at Suez was also ordered to return to al-Tur and remain in quarantine for seven days. The passengers were disembarked under protest. Revealing their class-based understanding of disease causation they went on to explain that:

the sailor who died had acquired the germ of his sickness by bad food and worse drink while on shore in Calcutta, and that there was absolutely no ground for submitting the ship to such treatment as that to which a vessel crowded with deck passengers whom dirt and disease had rendered a probable source of pestilence might properly be subjected.

The protests became even more intense after two of the passengers had inspected the very plain sheds reserved for them to sleep in. They univocally condemned the absurdity of forcing them off the ship while the crew remained on board. In the end all of them had to remain in quarantine and their criticisms went unheard as not one of the lazaretto's staff understood English anyway. They concluded in their report that after

---

[88] Women's Library, Philippa Strachey: Ralph Strachey to Philippa Strachey, *SS Sutlej*, 19 October 1892; see also Maspero, *Lettres d'Egypte*, p. 19, Boulaq, 8 December 1883, p. 44, Boulaq, 6 January 1884, p. 221 Boulaq, 24 April 1886, p. 252 Giza, 12 May 1900, p. 337, Cairo, 11 July 1904.

[89] TNA, FO 423/13: Mr Bethune (P&O) to Earl Granville, London, 23 May 1883.

their time in the quarantine station, they were vindicated in their original position that their 'lives and health, especially as regards the ladies and children, have been seriously, and, as we think, needlessly, imperilled'.[90]

If disease did break out on board, the differentiations between social classes became even more palpable. At the same time the hierarchical orderliness of the ship's social structure was in danger of being temporarily unhinged. When cases of plague were diagnosed on the *Laos* in 1901, the captain reported afterwards that one stoker, named Sablé-Assen, had been particularly helpful and assiduous towards his sick colleagues, acting as an auxiliary nurse, which was all the more noticeable as the other members of the crew and especially the Arabs had been upset when seeing the great difference between them and the passengers in the eyes of the sanitary service. In this case the European passengers had no reason to complain: while 18 Arabs were left behind in the lazaretto, all Europeans on board continued their journey unhindered.[91]

Increasingly, the hospital facilities and the ambulance in Port Said took care to provide specific services for European passengers, including the case of contagious diseases in which everyone was to be transported to the government hospital where, at least from 1911 onwards, Europeans would receive special treatment.[92] Upon calling an ambulance, the information demanded not only concerned the type of disease but also the class of the passenger.[93] More generally, the rapidity with which passengers were treated was improved. In 1908 a Marine Ambulance Service was introduced in Port Said, mainly created to transport patients from ships to the hospital 'with as little discomfort as possible' and with emergency ships arriving, at the latest, one hour after having been called by telephone. Highlighting once again the use of modern technologies, in the case of infectious diseases a phone call with the port-police office was necessary for further instructions.[94]

The handling of European passengers and their complaints illustrates the move from the mere localisation of disease and measures of segregation and separation to the identification of specific groups carrying diseases and of others being immune to it. This identification was combined

---

[90] TNA, PRO 30/29/295: 'The Pleasures of Quarantine', extract from the *Egyptian Gazette*, 20 May 1884.

[91] CCIMP, Messageries Maritimes 302, Laos (1897–1907): Commandant au directeur de l'exploitation Marseille, Laos, 28 July 1901; ibid., Laos à directeur de l'exploitation, 29 July 1901.

[92] CADN, Port Said 124: Gouvernorat du canal de Suez au consul de France à Port Said, 2 January 1911.

[93] CADN, Port Said 123: Governor Suez Canal, Ambulance Service Port Said, October 1914.

[94] ANMT, 1995060/1419: Marine Ambulance Service – Port Said.

with certain scientific and bureaucratic methods serving to avoid delays. Such practices also affected the associations connected to the Canal. In contrast to Dr Mackenzie, quoted above, for whom the Canal Zone was a germ-ridden area, the doctor W. J. Simpson thought that it was particularly safe as the

merchant ships passing the Suez Canal bringing tea, jute, wheat, and other Indian produce to the European markets have not upon them crowds of Hindus and Mussulmans, poor or rich, from infected districts, but a few better-class Europeans belonging either to the commercial, military, or official class.[95]

The theory that certain areas of the globe were particularly disease-ridden was thus slowly replaced by the firm conviction that certain groups of travellers were dangerous while others had almost a natural immunity to infections. Not astonishingly, most often these distinctions regulated speeds in a way that was in line with the interests of empires and companies.

The years under analysis here show a wide variety of different measures and a large amount of debate around questions of disease propagation and its prevention. But around 1910, something of an equilibrium was reached. In the decades preceding this date the envisioned strategies of how to turn the Suez Canal into a bulwark against disease, while simultaneously keeping it open for trade and traffic, were highly contingent on the changing perceptions of disease and contagion, yet also on political interests. They furthermore permeated many different levels – from the global of the international conferences to the microscopic of the newly identified *vibrio cholerae*. In this manner, other global localities, such as the quarantine station, came to play an important role. Here one could not only witness upheavals, but also the limits of the bacteriological revolution, which became particularly clear with geographic distinction and distinctions made between different groups remaining a central measure in the fight against disease. Furthermore, the lazarettos as well as the Canal as a whole became a space of scientific experimentation, with the introduction of sterilisation, disinfection, vaccination and the like, but also of bureaucratic experimentation, introducing complicated procedures of classification and non-contact as well as the standardised education of medical officers. The running of the lazarettos and the implementation of the 'passage in quarantine' point, furthermore, to the intricacies of the politics and of course the financing of internationalism. A large bureaucratic apparatus (both nationally and internationally organised) was needed in order to turn the Canal not only into a functioning connection, but also into a fully controllable sluice gate between Europe and Asia in Siegfried's

---

[95] Simpson, 'Maritime Quarantine and Sanitation in Relation to Cholera', 151.

sense. Yet this bureaucratic and scientific bulwark was not without problems as, for instance, the protests in lazarettos or, of course, the cases of disease outbreaks show. At the same time other problems still awaited their solution, such as the liabilities of paying for certain services and the identification of international or inter-imperial travellers, as well as the question of how far the responsibility of empires for their subjects reached once they were moving further away and at a faster rate. Yet, as we shall see in the next chapter, these problems emerged not only in the context of disease, but came as concomitant to the faster and more wide-reaching mobility of European citizens and colonial subjects.

8 Rights of passage and the identification of individuals

The problems relating to disease and contagion encountered in the previous chapter engendered numerous questions concerning the classification of those moving about in the region of the Suez Canal. In the case of a passenger contracting a disease on board – even if he or she did not raise suspicions concerning contagion – it was important to know the identity of that particular person in order to find out who was responsible for providing relief. To mention but one example: when Dina Abramovich, an Ottoman subject, fell ill on a French steamer and could not continue her journey, she was first escorted to the French consulate in Port Said by the captain of the ship on which she was travelling and then transferred to the Ottoman authorities once her identity had been ascertained.[1] Yet it was not only disease that could lead to demands of identification, as will become evident in the course of this chapter.

The history of documentation and identification practices has so far been studied mainly in national contexts.[2] More recently, these topics have also begun to be explored in imperial settings and more specifically in Egypt.[3] Contrary to those arguing that the passport system was 'born' during or after the First World War,[4] the material evaluated in this chapter shows that the period before the First World War was a phase of experimentation not only regarding disinfection measures and vaccination, but also in the field of identification documents and procedures. This phase of experimentation is crucial in order to understand the more unified system of identification, which emerged after the war. In this phase, measures were often piecemeal and differed from one case to another. Instead of travelling on a single

---

[1] CADN, Port Said 47: Consul to S. Exc. Mouheb-Pacha, gouverneur du canal de Suez, 28 May 1907.

[2] See, among others, Torpey, *The Invention of the Passport*; Caplan and Torpey (eds.), *Documenting Individual Identity*.

[3] For the Egyptian case, see Hanley, *Foreignness and Localness in Alexandria*. See also Mongia, 'Race, Nationality, Mobility'; Radhika Singha, 'Settle, Mobilize, Verify'.

[4] See Torpey, 'The Great War', p. 269.

passport, certain people carried several documents proving their allegiance to a state and other institutions, such as the company that employed them, thus leaving behind them a paper trail of records and passes.[5] Its complex international and extraterritorial situation, and its status as a transit station of all kinds of mobilities connected to imperial endeavours, meant that the Suez Canal serves well to illustrate the development of such an apparatus of identification. The larger question that the cases surveyed here often triggered was to what extent – in terms of both geographical distance and literal engagement – states, and especially political constructs as amorphous as empires, were responsible for their subjects. This question of responsibility largely explains why the more coercive treatment of certain mobile people, including repatriation and forced removal, became a political imperative. In this context, mobility was not so much differentiated with regard to its purpose or mode of movement, but also by categories such as class, gender, race and nationality.

Focusing on specific biographies of travellers, but of a different sort from those rather privileged travellers surveyed in Chapter 1, this last chapter moves destitute persons, stowaways, criminals and prostitutes into the centre. It investigates the growing standardisation of identification and control measures before 1914 and the reactions that this standardisation engendered. After a survey of the papers and identification practices in use in the Suez Canal Zone, the chapter draws attention to the different groups mentioned above, and to the tools used to gather information about and classify them. Besides providing us with a further exemplification of how mobility was channelled and controlled, the individual life-courses appearing in this chapter allow us to look at globalisation 'from below'. Yet, while in Chapter 1, ego-documents of privileged travellers form the central body of sources, the lives of less privileged travellers have to be teased out from the official archives. After a more general part on identification practices before the First World War, the emphasis is thus on specific biographies, whose trajectories show that the very mobility on which empires depended could also present a liability.

Identity on the move

Notions of identity and nationality – as the term suggests – are often analysed within the bounded space of the nation.[6] In an age of increasing

[5] Fisher, 'Official Responses to Foreign Travel', 962–3.
[6] See, for example, Brubaker, *Citizenship and Nationhood in France and Germany*; Fahrmeir, *Citizens and Aliens*; Dieter Gosewinkel, *Einbürgern und Ausschließen*; for an imperial perspective see Gammerl, *Untertanen, Staatsbürger und Andere*.

mobility, however, questions of nationality and belonging were negotiated not only at home, but also outside the nation in question. If an obstacle occurred in the limbo state between home and away, the identity of a traveller – and the ability to prove that identity – could assume crucial importance. Before the First World War, both the documentation and the categories employed were far from uniform, especially in the case of empires. The imperial expansion of the late nineteenth century meant that European empires were increasingly composed of many dependants of varying status. British citizenship, for instance, was complex.[7] There were British subjects (from Britain or a British colony, natural-born or naturalised) and British protected persons belonging to a protectorate, protected state, mandate or trust territory. In France, the terms were equally multi-layered.

In imperial contexts two responsibilities of the state were crucially connected to 'nationality', 'citizenship' or 'subjecthood': the state had to be able to identify and 'know about' its citizens or subjects, at least in certain situations; and states had certain minimal responsibilities to provide relief and assistance. Identity (or belonging to a political entity) mattered if anything unforeseen occurred and individual travellers had to be supported, identified, or punished. In these contexts it could also become important for the empires to control the mobility of their subjects, either by hindering them from moving or by forcibly removing them.

The population of Port Said was quite unusual as it consisted mainly of people directly connected to the business of mobility – suppliers, service personnel, seamen waiting for the next hire, consuls, merchants, prostitutes, barkeepers and so on. Many regarded Port Said as a temporary dwelling place, like the seasonal coal heavers, for example. They were complemented by those who spent a night or even just a few hours in Port Said, such as troops on the way to their colonial stations or to other overseas operations, shipping crews, colonial officers and tourists disembarking for some shopping and entertainment.[8] For our purposes, all these transients form part of Port Said's population on the move, which was recorded, identified and catered for by the consuls in the town. In the following, the question of papers and identification in the last decades before the First World War will be assessed in three ways, by looking first at who was in fact singled out in Port Said and had to provide identification, second at the question of identity in the Canal Zone and Egypt more generally, and

---

[7] See, for instance, McClelland and Rose, 'Citizenship and Empire'; Fahrmeir, *Citizens and Aliens*, esp. pp. 43–52 'Defining a British Subject 1800–1870'; Karatani, *Defining British Citizenship*; Berchtold, *Recht und Gerechtigkeit in der Konsulargerichtsbarkeit*, pp. 224–36.

[8] Dori, 'Esquisse Historique de Port-Said', 312.

finally at the specific uses (and misuses) of papers in a world where papers – at least for some – mattered more than conventionally acknowledged.

Passport-free travel in the belle époque

From its early days, the Suez Canal, as a place where ships had to register, had emerged as a place of information gathering. Yet as the following snapshots reveal, passport-free travel was a reality for many. The issue was complicated by the contradiction of the politics of free movement as practised in the British Empire and the tighter controls asked for by the Ottoman Empire, highlighting once again the intricacies of the Canal Zone as an international and inter-imperial zone.

The Suez Canal Company's guidelines regarding the passage, the *Règlement de navigation*, prescribed that a ship intending to proceed through the Canal had to provide the transit office with extensive information, ranging from the nationality and tonnage of the steamers to the number of passengers and crew.[9] The statistics of the Suez Canal Company meticulously divided passengers into categories of military personnel, civilians and 'specials', whereby the last category was specified as containing pilgrims, emigrants and deportees.[10]

Yet some individuals were singled out from this statistical encapsulation. Increasingly, as the British hold on Egypt solidified, the staging of the passage of administrators and royal visitors served to epitomise British domination abroad.[11] The local newspaper reported the passage of important persons and the Canal Company received notables with thoroughly prepared and standardised ceremonials. The Duke and Duchess of Connaught, Queen Victoria's seventh child and his wife, transiting the Canal in December 1902, were received at a ceremony where they were given medals of the Suez Canal Company that had been coined especially for them – a ceremony that the Duke and Duchess of Cornwall and York,

---

[9] See, for example, ANMT, 2000036/0201: Service du transit, récapitulation générale: registre (années 1905–1912); Quai d'Orsay, Correspondance politique et commerciale nouvelle série 1897–1918, Egypte 40: Règlement de navigation dans le canal maritime de Suez, January 1911.

[10] See, for instance, Assemblée générale des actionnaires, 54e Réunion – 2 juin 1908. Rapport présenté au nom du Conseil d'administration par le Prince Auguste d'Arenberg, président, p. 16: Mouvement des passagers dans le canal de Suez pendant les 30 dernières années (1878–1907).

[11] See Caird Library, HTN/230 Hamilton, Sir Louis Henry Keppel, Admiral, 1892–1957: Papers relating to *HMS Venus* at Dover, Torbay, and various other ships, including *HMS Vanguard* at Portsmouth, and King George V and Queen Mary at Port Said en route for India, November 1911; see also Pouchepadass, 'Itinerant Kings and Touring Officials', p. 251; Cohn, 'Representing Authority in Victorian India'.

the future King George V and Queen Mary, had equally enjoyed when passing through a year earlier.[12] According to the *New York Herald*, in October 1905, George and Mary, now the Prince and Princess of Wales, passed through Port Said for the second time on their way to India and only saluted from the bridge as the Princess was seasick. On their return, the British Consul, the governor of the Canal District and high officials of the Canal Company received them. A police corps saluted and many residents – Europeans and 'natives' as the newspapers pointed out – had come to witness the celebrations. The streets were decorated and flagged. For the third passage of George V in 1911–12 on his way to his coronation at the Delhi Durbar and back, an even larger effort was made, which found proportional reflection in the Canal Company's bills.[13]

Whereas these members of the royal family received a lot of attention, the well-to-do first- and second-class European passengers featuring in Chapter 1 – albeit often perceiving the passage as an individual moment of transition or *rite de passage* – otherwise proceeded without much official notice. The Canal Company did not worry about the status of such persons. In their case, identification had the sole purpose of calculating fees and documenting performance. The captains of the steamers had to provide passenger lists, but (in contrast to the pilgrims, for example) individuals did not have to supply documents of identification to a government official of whatever allegiance.[14] Thus, for many British and French travellers before the First World War, carrying a document when travelling to or through Egypt was not crucial. When Jules Verne's hero Phileas Fogg, on his journey between London and Bombay, arrived in Suez – in a chapter tellingly entitled 'Which once more demonstrates the uselessness of passports as aids to detectives' – he went to the British consulate to have his passport stamped. There, the consul asked him: 'You know that a visa is useless, and that no passport is required?' Phileas Fogg replied that he

---

[12] ANMT, 1995060/1746: Voyageurs recommandés: visites et traversées du canal par des personnalités, lettres de recommandation, 1864–1956, esp. Compagnie universelle du canal maritime de Suez, Comité de direction, Séance du 18 décembre 1902, Communication re réception de L. L. A. A. R. R. le Duc et la Duchesse de Connaught à Port Said; and ibid.: Compagnie universelle du canal maritime de Suez, Comité de direction, Séance du 11 avril 1901, communication re passage par le Canal le L. L. A. A. R. R. le Duc et la Duchesse de Cornouailles et d'York.

[13] ANMT 1995060/1747: Voyageurs recommandés: visite dans l'isthme: passage du canal de personnalités: correspondance, presse, photographies de navires 1905–1922, esp. Sous-dossier passage du Prince de Galles par le canal 1905; Sous-dossier Passage du Roi Georges V par le canal 1911–1912.

[14] See, for instance, Quai d'Orsay, Correspondance politique et commerciale nouvelle série 1897–1918, Egypte 40, Canal de Suez p. 96; Bundesarchiv, R/901/75677, Band 1, Schiffahrt Nr. 129: Compagnie universelle du canal maritime de Suez, Règlement de navigation, édition de janvier 1913.

was well aware of this fact, yet he wanted to prove his passage through Suez with the aid of an official visa.[15] While Phileas Fogg was, as always, well prepared, other travellers were surprised that they did not have to provide more extensive documentation. The German traveller August Vasel, for example, noted with amazement in his diary that one did not have to show one's passport at Port Said at all.[16]

The passport-free travelling of the *belle époque* was therefore a reality for some. In fact, British travellers were largely annoyed each time passport or quarantine regulations became stricter.[17] If travel guides advised tourists to bring passports, this was mainly to be on the safe side when it came to changing money and cashing cheques at the bank. Accordingly passports were rather needed for the stay itself than for the transit between two places. The late-nineteenth-century Baedeker for Egypt still advised carrying a passport, the editions of 1908 and 1914, however, stated that:

Passports are not absolutely necessary; and one's visiting-card practically serves all its functions in the interior. Banks, however, frequently require strangers to establish their identity by some such document; and the countenance and help of consuls also must depend upon the proof of nationality offered to them by the traveller.[18]

Class and status distinctions, on which the travel experience of the late nineteenth and early twentieth centuries to a large extent depended, consequently found expression in the division between those whose identity was routinely checked and those who could pass incognito. This was even more crucial in the Suez Canal Zone, which as a nominal part of the Ottoman Empire, fell under this Empire's regulations.

Keeping, losing and changing nationality

Foreign nationals dwelling in the Suez Canal Region more permanently had, in accordance with an Ottoman Order in Council of 1899, to register every year with their consul to maintain their nationality.[19] Anyone neglecting to do so lost his or her foreign status and by default became an Ottoman subject. It was thus the onus of the subject to retie himself to his state as represented through its mobile outpost, the consul. This implied that nationality was far from inalienable; rather the individual was responsible for maintaining it. Two biographical cases drawn from

---

[15] Verne, *Around the World in Eighty Days*, p. 28.
[16] Vasel, *Reisetagebücher und Briefe*, p. 63.   [17] Pemble, *The Mediterranean Passion*, p. 33.
[18] Baedeker, *Egypt and the Sudan: Handbook for Travellers* (1914), p. xv.
[19] See, for instance, TNA, FO 78/5238: Cameron to Marquess of Lansdowne, Foreign Office London, Port Said, 19 May 1902.

the archives will serve to highlight the complicated issue of nationality in Egypt in an age of migration, which at times was less a matter of personal identity than a possession of more or less value.

Sometimes a person either feared losing his or her nationality or consciously wanted to give it up. The odyssey of Hadjee Ali Akbar Namazee, who falls into the first category, represents a particularly complex story of migration and an illustration of the paperwork connected to it. In 1901 Namazee filed a petition at the British Foreign Office in London, stating that he had left Rangoon 50 years prior, had resided in Madras until 1869, where he had received a Madras passport, and thereafter had moved to Cairo. There he had registered – as prescribed – every year with the consul for 15 years. In 1885 he had moved on to Baghdad, then back to Madras. Upon his return to Cairo, Consul Raphael Borg refused to recognise him as a British subject although he claimed to have shown documentary evidence for every year of his residence. Namazee asked the Foreign Office for assistance, as he had been 'more than thirty years subject to English Government'. After some correspondence between London and Egypt, the British consulate in Cairo stated that neither the Ottoman nor the Persian authorities had protested against the British protection of Hadjee Ali Akbar Namazee. However, the question was still whether Hadjee Ali Akbar Namazee should be styled in the registration as 'Naturalised British Indian Subject', as he had gained this status in Madras, or as 'British protected person', as he had spent a large part of his life outside of British India.[20]

Others did not fight to keep their status but aimed at giving it up deliberately – for instance in the case of Paolo Rizzo, a 33-year-old native of Malta residing in Port Said. In 1902 Rizzo wanted to renounce his British nationality and to become an Austrian subject in order to be able to occupy a higher position in the Austrian Lloyd, which had employed him for the previous 25 years. Rizzo therefore asked 'although very reluctantly' to be allowed to give up his British nationality in order to become an Austrian subject. The British Consul at Port Said consulted the Foreign Office, as the procedure to be followed was somewhat unusual. First Rizzo had to stop registering with his consul. As a consequence he would lose his British nationality and become an Ottoman subject. In fact, the consul explained, he had to employ the threat of this loss of status every year to make 'certain poorer members of the Maltese community' register and pay the required fee. Rizzo then could in a second step, if the

---

[20] TNA, FO 78/5165: Petition el Haji Ali Akbar Namazee to Secretary of State for Foreign Affairs, Consulate Cairo to Marquess of Lansdowne, Foreign Office London, Cairo, 6 April 1901.

Austrian government agreed, transfer to Austrian nationality. The consul made clear that the renunciation of British citizenship was unconditional and could not be reassumed if there was any difficulty with his gaining Austrian citizenship.

Even though the outcome of Rizzo's case is not documented, it highlights the fact that, in a colonial and extraterritorial context, identity and nationality could sometimes be understood less as a part of individual identity than as a tool of economic utility or even as a currency – Rizzo had to ponder whether it was more profitable to keep his British nationality, which was certainly the most valuable nationality of the time in terms of the liberties and privileges associated with it, or whether he should give it up in order to climb the career ladder within his company.[21]

Documents and papers

In Port Said and the Canal Zone, the distinction between suspicious and unsuspicious mobility was made palpable through the fact that some groups had to provide officials with information regarding their status and identity whereas others passed unhindered. Certain groups, like pilgrims and transiting troops, were actively supervised. Some professionals, such as seamen who, as seen earlier, often fell under specific regulations, also had to carry specific forms of documentation.[22] This led to the coexistence of a variety of passes, ranging, besides passports, from laissez-passers to workers' certificates and discharge books. The papers in circulation were thus highly diverse and different ports and shipping lines demanded different proofs of identity. They were, however, no less important: seamen who had misplaced their discharge books, for instance, could not sign onto another ship and therefore lost the basis of their livelihood.[23] It could thus matter crucially to have one's own documents, referring not only to official documents proving one's identity but also to papers issued by other agencies such as employers.

Since the possession of papers became increasingly central for some, the forging of papers began to escalate. This phenomenon has already been highlighted in connection with pilgrims travelling to Mecca, yet in the decades preceding the First World War, it developed into a more general trend. Besides the production of fake passes, it became a frequent

---

[21] TNA, FO 78/5238: D. A. Cameron to Marquess of Lansdowne, Foreign Office, London, Port Said, 19 May 1902; Draft FO to Consul Cameron, 31 May 1902; Letter FO to Consul Cameron, 16 July 1902; Draft FO to Consul Cameron, 26 September 1902.

[22] See, for instance, AFL, 1997/002/3600: Livre professionel du marin.

[23] See, for instance, TNA, FO 78/4461: Statement of William Murphy, stowaway; Statement of Charles Wellcome, stowaway.

offence to carry papers belonging to another person, which was again most often observed in the context of the more and more tightly regulated pilgrimage to Mecca. The French Consul at Jidda reported already in 1885 on how someone had presented himself with 'two authentic passes issued in Algiers' in order to receive a French passport. When asked to prove his identity through the testimony of an Algerian, who had to be a long-time resident of Jidda, he disappeared. The consul decided not to arrest the person in order not to alert his accomplices in Algeria, but kept the papers under pretext. Subsequently, he learned that the commerce of forged passports received on bearing false witness prospered on a large scale not only in Jidda but also in Egypt, mainly involving Algerians, Moroccans and Tripolitans.[24]

However, the forgery or absence of papers were not the only reasons that could make identification by means of papers impossible; it was equally problematic if too many documents existed. The name Emil Bringer, for instance, brought up several passports and diverse spellings and it was therefore impossible to allocate such papers correctly.[25] In the Suez Canal Region transliterations of Arabic names presented an additional hurdle to unambiguous identification. If matters of identification of people on the move were thus prevalent in the Canal Zone, they were not always clear-cut and often provided riddles to the consuls. At the same time the resolution of such riddles could be an urgent affair relating to large costs for individuals ending up in the Canal Zone, such as stowaways and destitute travellers.

The canal as terminus: repatriation of stowaways and destitute travellers

As described in Chapter 3, the Suez Canal was not only a place of passage, it was also a magnet, drawing in, alongside workers from the Mediterranean Basin, all kinds of people who had problems moving on. The consular files are teeming with cases of distressed persons or stowaways, highlighting the existence of a mobile 'underclass' venturing to the colonies in search of better opportunities.[26] Their journeys were, however, often interrupted at Port Said and frequently ended with them being sent back to their places of

---

[24] See CAOM, GGA 16H/83: Ministère des Affaires étrangères, Direction politique au gouverneur général de l'Algérie, Paris, 9 February 1886; M. Castalot de Bachoué, vice-consul de France à Djeddah, à M. de Freycinet, ministre des Affaires étrangères, Jidda, 22 January 1886.

[25] TNA, FO 78/4064: Consul Burrell to Marquis of Salisbury, Port Said, 24 April 1887.

[26] For a study of similar groups of people in India, see Fischer-Tiné, *Low and Licentious Europeans*.

departure. This particular kind of mobility tested the limits of state responsibility in practical and financial but also in juridical and political terms since in these cases the boundary between despair and criminal behaviour was particularly difficult to define. In this context, the political and economic imperatives for controlling people on the move in order to know about the colonial population and to minimise costs became clearly visible. As will become evident in the following, in the distinction between mobility that was tolerated or even encouraged and mobility that was suspicious, social, racial and gender hierarchies played a central role. Here, Port Said assumed the role of a 'dumping ground' or terminus for different kinds of problematic mobilities.[27]

Destitute and indigents: the costs of forced mobility

'Distressed seamen' and 'distressed subjects', according to the vocabulary of the day, were a common category in Port Said's consular proceedings and turned up so frequently that the British Consul even kept a 'Distressed Seamen's Account Book'.[28] The question why they should be repatriated, sometimes against their will, was both economic and political. The problem of who had to pay for them brought the global implications of empires into relief, highlighting the costs of mobility and the question where the limits of imperial responsibility could lie. Port Said as an inter-imperial hub looked at other port cities to learn how they dealt with such issues, but also experimented with its own forms of registration and bureaucracy. These strategies frequently did not prove successful in averting costs, as the following section will show.

Seamen often depended on assistance if they could not find employment in Port Said and thus had specific infrastructures dedicated to them. Both Rudyard Kipling and the American traveller, Harry A. Franck, took up the theme of seamen lingering in Port Said in their writings.[29] Franck, a student at the University of Michigan, had accepted a bet to travel around the world without taking any money with him at all after he had finished college. At Port Said he ended up stowing away because he could not find suitable employment as a white seaman. His description illustrates the extent to which Port Said, as a transit station, was also a terminus for all

---

[27] See Clancy-Smith, *Mediterraneans*, p. 89; Clancy-Smith, 'Marginality and Migration'.
[28] TNA, FO 78/3011: Consulate Port Said to the Chief Clerk Foreign Office, Port Said, 1 August 1879.
[29] Kipling, 'The Limitations of Pambé Serang'; Franck, *A Vagabond Journey Around the World*, pp. 237–50.

kinds of people without sufficient funds to move on.[30] Franck's destitute condition was of course part of his chosen adventure – 'real' seamen could face more serious problems and were dependent on the negotiation of minimal relief from the consulates or benevolent societies.

Sometimes the complications were, however, not related to the financing of subsistence and return, but to more practical questions regarding the costs of forced mobility. When 'lunatic seamen' or other unruly characters faced repatriation, many ships refused to take them on board.[31] The two local hospitals of Port Said could not cater for psychological problems and it was sometimes the case that British nationals reluctantly had to be transferred to the Cairo Asylum (which was deemed as not being suitable for Europeans), rather than being immediately sent home.[32] Only in rare and pressing cases did the Canal Company make an exception regarding fees: in January 1914 an official of the Suez Canal Company asked its director in Paris for advice regarding a letter of Messieurs Stapledon, agents of the shipping company Bucknall Steamship Lines. They demanded reimbursement for three shipwrecked persons that the steamer, *Kasenga*, had taken on board somewhere on the Indian Ocean. As the case was so special and clearly defined, it would not offer a precedent for other free passages and so the request was granted as an exception.[33]

Not only forced mobility, also forced immobility was expensive. There were debates as to how to reduce the expenses caused by distressed seamen or 'deserters and impostors'. A certain Mr Fry suggested, in a letter to the British Consul at Port Said, the so-called Genoa method, which implied forced immobility, that is the imprisonment of every seaman left behind through his own fault and without papers or discharge books. The consul replied that usually the Egyptian police apprehended and delivered destitute people to the consulates only after they had wandered about Port Said for some days. As their ship had usually left by then, it was impossible to verify their story except through unusual methods, such as the testing of a person who claimed to be from Zanzibar in Swahili. However, even then he thought that it was not justifiable to put them into the Egyptian prison, 'unless they could be brought in as rogues and vagabonds'.[34]

---

[30] Franck, *A Vagabond Journey Around the World*, pp. 237–40.
[31] TNA, FO 78/3957, sheets 98–107: Correspondence regarding a violent 'lunatic', William Daly, from Ireland.
[32] TNA, FO 78/5165: Cameron to Marquess of Lansdowne, Port Said, 14 December 1901.
[33] ANMT, 1995060/4993: Chef du service du transit à M. le directeur de la Compagnie universelle du canal maritime de Suez, Ismailia, 27 January 1914.
[34] TNA, BT 15/62: Geo. S. Fry to Consul General, Port Said, no date; British consulate general to the accountant general, Finance Department, Board of Trade, Port Said, 13 June 1912.

The problem that destitute travellers and particularly distressed seamen posed to the authorities was the flipside of increased global mobility and it highlighted the multiplicity of actors and agencies involved in dealing with imperial voyagers of this specific kind. Destitute travellers who could not afford to proceed with their journey often turned directly to their consulate for assistance. In 1871 the British Consul at Suez, West, was advised to use 'the greatest circonspection [sic] and economy in dealing with cases of relief to be afforded to distressed British Subjects abroad'.[35] Yet by 1906 Consul Cameron of Port Said demanded more authority when dealing with indigents due to the geographical position of Port Said, in order to process them 'promptly and cheaply' and only report at the end of the month, if at all necessary.[36]

In accordance with this limited authority, the consuls usually tried all other means before putting the money on their own bill. Sometimes those repatriated eventually reimbursed the money, as in the case of El Hadja Fatma bent Mohamed el Bejaoui, who returned the money spent on the repatriation of her husband by the *Société française de bienfaisance* of Port Said.[37] This society, that had branches in many localities around the globe, was the major benevolent organisation catering for French citizens or imperial subjects abroad. It very often took over the consular responsibilities of providing relief and in turn received money for those shipped home or catered for in Port Said.

Yet most often the official bodies did not receive any reimbursement of the individuals in question. The 23-year-old Francis Carroll from North Wales, for instance, who wished to return from Australia to Britain in 1893 only managed to get as far as Port Said and contacted the British Consul as he lacked the means to complete his journey. The consul wrote to Carroll's father and brother to fund the return of their relative. However, Carroll's brother answered that the whole family was financially badly off and that Carroll's father had already paid for the passage to Australia so he would not be willing to finance the return journey of his son as well. While Carroll himself signed an undertaking to repay the disbursement made on his behalf, the consul did not receive any of the

---

[35] TNA, FO 78/2233: Consul West, Suez, 16 March 1872, referring to a circular dispatch of Viscount Enfield, dated 22 February 1872.
[36] OIOC, IOR L/PJ/6/777: File 3007 Consul Cameron to India Office, Port Said, 30 August 1906; see also OIOC, IOR L/PJ/6/772: File 2384 Judicial and Public Department. Repatriation of two destitute natives of India at Port Said.
[37] CADN, Port Said 16: Le résident général de la République française à Tunis à M. Laffont, consul de France à Port-Said, Tunis, 17 May 1903. See also CADN, Port Said 57, Comités, associations et sociétés de bienfaisance.

over four pounds that he had spent, and therefore had to appeal to the Foreign Office to settle his account.[38]

Just like the Foreign Office, the India Office was usually not eager to reimburse the consulates either. In 1887 the Duke of Edinburgh sent a 'distressed Native of India' from Jerusalem to Port Said at his own expense with the request that the man be conveyed on to Bombay. P&O waived the passage and the consulate paid for food and Canal dues only. The Foreign Office then aimed to reclaim the sum from the India Office, its officials, however, refused on principle to pay for the repatriation of 'natives' who found themselves in dire straits after having travelled 'of their own accord to other countries'. However, as this case was somewhat special, due to the involvement of the Duke of Edinburgh, they agreed to pay this time round.[39] The situation was slightly different for British residents of India however. In 1906 Cecil Hartley Clements of Hyderabad, who had left Karachi in February 1905 to study law at the Middle Temple in London and had his remittances cut off after one year of studies, made it to Port Said using the cheapest transport, but could not travel any further. As in precedent cases, he was to be sent to Bombay at the expense of Indian revenues and at the cheapest rate available.[40]

Other cases ignited the consul's suspicion straight away. In the case of a group of stranded Indians, the India Office informed the consul that they did not pay for their dependants simply being moved from one location abroad to another. Even before the consul could obtain further information, the group was suddenly able to depart for Marseilles, leaving the consul under the impression that they were not as poor as they had pretended.[41] Others were shifted around between different Mediterranean harbours, as was the case with two Punjabi brothers wanting to immigrate to the United States in 1908. The Port Said Consul reported to Viscount Morley that they had travelled via Naples to New York, but had not been allowed to land in the United States and had thus returned again via Naples to Alexandria, proceeded from there to Khartoum and – failing to find work – on to Port Sudan, where they obtained a free passage to Suez. The British Consul in Naples refused to

[38] TNA, FO 78/4521, sheet 239: Gould to Earl of Rosebery, Port Said, 22 December 1893.

[39] OIOC, IOR L/PJ/6/194: File 234 Foreign Office, 11 February 1887, subject: Claim for £1.18.0 on account of food + canal expenses of a native of India sent from Port Said to Bombay; India Office to the Under-secretary of State, Foreign Office, 12 March 1887.

[40] OIOC, IOR L/PJ/6/745: File 320 Judicial and Public Department, February 1906, subject: Requests sanction to repatriation of Mr. C. H. Clements, a distressed Indian pleader at Port Said.

[41] OIOC, IOR L/PJ/6/339: File 241 Public Department, 8 February 1893, subject: Alleged British Indian Subjects (4) destitute at Marseilles – as to relief and passage to Port Said.

take full responsibility and conveyed them to the next frontier only, 'which means sending them to a foreign port where they are an equal embarrassment to some other of His Majesty's Consuls'. He complained that as he had 'no control over the people who choose to ship from here to the United States, I am constantly liable to indigent British subjects being returned from thence as "undesirables"'.[42] These individual cases highlight the different instances of problematic mobility as well as the attempts to regulate them within different governing agencies.

Inter-imperial migration presented the British Consul with a further set of liabilities. Ashagar Ali, aged 25, was given six months leave from his employment in the Medical Department of Bahawalpur to find work in Port Sudan. As he failed to do so, he was brought to Suez begging to be sent back to India in order not to lose his job there.[43] In reaction to such cases, the British Consul at Port Said asked for controllable immigration procedures for poor Indians travelling to Egypt, by demanding, for example, a 10 pound deposit for every passport issued.[44] These intricacies of intra-imperial movement furthermore highlight the paradox, that empires depended on mobility but at the same time, mobility could become a liability. They furthermore point to the limits of control and channelling as such movements could hardly be prevented.

India was not the only colony with which such payments had to be negotiated. In 1889 Vice Consul Maling of Port Said sent an account to the Foreign Office of all the expenses incurred for Maltese prisoners and for hospital and burial expenses of indigent Maltese, adding that in the future he planned to apply directly to the Maltese government for recovery of such advances.[45] The costs for distressed British subjects, therefore, did not necessarily fall to the British government. Of the payments made by the consulate towards 'distressed subjects' in the last quarter of 1885, amounting to over 93 pounds, Malta had to account for about 26 pounds and the Board of Trade for about 2 pounds.[46] The French Consul also reclaimed money from different sources, such as the Tunisian

---

[42] OIOC, IOR L/PJ/6/867: File 1641/1908 subject: Destitute Indians – repatriation from Naples + Port Said: British Consulate General, Naples, 9 June 1908.

[43] OIOC, IOR L/PJ/6/903: File 4126, subject: Repatriation of distressed native of India named Asghar Ali: Consul General, Port Said, 22 October 1908.

[44] OIOC, IOR L/PJ/6/907: D. A. Cameron to the Right Honourable Viscount Morley, O. M.&C, India Office, London, Port Said, 21 November 1908.

[45] TNA, FO 78/4317: Burrell to Marquis of Salisbury, Foreign Office, Port Said, 5 May 1890.

[46] TNA, FO 78/4330: Schedule of payments made by Consul at Port Said during the quarter ended 31 December 1883; Account of hospital treatment for the undermentioned distressed British Subjects, during the year 1883.

government.[47] As these various cases illustrate, for the destitute travellers to get help from the consulate and for the consulates to reclaim their expenses was crucially bound to the destitute citizens proving their identity.[48]

As well as giving an insight into the interaction between different agencies of empire, these proceedings also offer glimpses of colonial biographies that are not usually in the limelight. Hannah Sheldrake, for instance, travelled to India in 1864 in order to get married. When she arrived she found that her intended husband had disappeared. She remained in India nevertheless and made a living through giving knitting lessons. Twenty-four years later, in 1888, she left India on a medical doctor's advice in order to live near Norwich, where her father had left her a cottage, although she was 'destitute and unable to obtain private assistance' to pay for the journey.[49] Another woman appearing in these files was a spinster too: Jane Snook, aged 55 and born in East Knoyle near Hindon. She was employed at the railway station of Ismailia for four months each year as ladies' attendant (a job she was anxious to keep) and had spent nearly 20 years in Egypt and claimed not to have any friends there who could help her financially. Wrongly identified, she was relieved for some time by the Austrian Consul who thought that she was married to an Austrian subject, but as this was proven not to be the case she had to be relieved by the British consulate.[50]

Some traces were lost soon after their appearance in Port Said. Bondi, an Indian from Punjab, spoke a dialect that, apart from two or three shopkeepers, no one in Port Said could understand. He had been taken up in Beirut and had been sent to a 'lunatic asylum', on the grounds that 'his mind was unhinged from the effects of starvation and fatigue' during his journey from Baghdad to Damascus. The British Consul in Syria let him go with a note that the consul at Port Said should get him to Jidda. However, the captain who was supposed to take him aboard refused at the last minute as Bondi was 'too unwell and troublesome'. After Bondi

---

[47] CADN, Port Said 16: Consul à M. Cambon, ministre plénipotentiaire, résident général à Tunis, Port Said, 18 August 1886; Consul à M. Lagarde, ministre plénipotentiaire, gouverneur de la côte des Somalis à Djibouti, Port Said, 23 September 1898.

[48] See, for instance, TNA, FO 78/4461: Statement of Jacques Holsten, a distressed British Subject.

[49] TNA, FO 78/4154: Statement as to Hannah Sheldrake a Distressed British Subject arrived at Port-Saïd on the 2nd October by an Austrian Steamer from Calcutta, signed Burrell, Consul Port Said, 19 November 1888. See also TNA, FO 4250: Burrell to the Marquis of Salisbury, Port Said, 31 December 1889, for the case of Joseph Tobin who had lived in India since the age of six.

[50] TNA, FO 78/4461: Statement Jane Snook, signed Vice Consul Maling, Port Said, 1 December 1892.

refused to board a ship travelling directly to India, the consul declined to have anything further to do with him. Bondi disappeared soon after and the consul was left with the task of reclaiming the money spent on 34 days of providing his subsistence.[51] This snippet of Bondi's biography points to the limits of the global channelling of mobility, ranging from the impossibility to understand his language at Port Said to his refusal to comply with forced removal and his eventual disappearance.

Learning from other port cities

The British consulate at Port Said was of course not the only institution facing problems of this kind – even though such cases were particularly numerous in this transit point. In fact the consulate and other Port Said institutions frequently looked at other port cities and how they dealt with figures such as Bondi and, most importantly, who paid for them there. Aden and Alexandria, for instance, had to deal with very similar issues too. In the case of other French consulates in Egypt, the treatment of impecunious French citizens varied from case to case and their decisions were mostly informed by economic utility. The French Consul at Cairo calculated whether it cost more to repatriate a person or to reimburse the *Société française de bienfaisance*, which was in charge of providing relief. It was important, he stated, that the consulates did go ahead with repatriations only after prior authorisation and only in cases where it seemed absolutely necessary.[52] The calculations of the French consulate also reveal that besides nationality or origin other categories such as gender also played a role. It was more expensive to repatriate a woman than a man, as the latter could be sent at the very cheapest rate, while women were supposed to enjoy somewhat better conditions.[53] Repatriation was thus a differentiated practice and its funding a highly political issue, as the French Consul feared that limited financial support for repatriations from Egypt would directly harm the reputation of France.[54]

---

[51] OIOC, IOR L/PJ/6721: File 1310 Judicial and Public Department, subject: Relief of a distressed native of India by the Consul at Port Said.

[52] CADN, Le Caire 441: Consul de France au Caire à M. le Vicomte Dejean, chargé d'affaires de France en Egypte, Cairo, 21 October 1908.

[53] The subtotal of the repatriation of a woman added up to 90 francs, while the men's rate was 55 francs; see CADN, Le Caire 441: Consul de France au Caire, à M. Geoffray, ministre de France en Egypte, Cairo, 3 February 1909.

[54] CADN, Le Caire 441: Consul de France au Caire à M. le Vicomte Dejean, chargé d'affaires de France en Egypte, Cairo, 21 October 1908.

Some towns opted for very strict countermeasures. The Aden Pilgrim and Pauper Regulation of 1887 was expanded in 1904 to prevent not only 'indigent natives of Asia and Africa' but also poor Europeans and Americans from landing in Aden.[55] The administration of Aden argued that such measures had now become necessary as every year they had to return penniless Europeans to their countries. Soon this British-Adenese regulation also found application in Port Said and Suez, providing a good illustration of how the towns learned from each other. The implementation of the strict regulation in Aden and elsewhere was not unambiguous, however, as the government of the British Somaliland protectorate, for instance, and also the British Consul at Port Said were not sure what to do with distressed British Indian subjects who were usually sent to the nearest British port, which was, in both cases, Aden. Furthermore, as a shipping company complained, it was impossible to know who was a 'pauper' if everyone had paid their fare. Despite these objections, the India Office stated in 1908 that the measure was vital 'owing to the special circumstances of Aden, which is primarily a fortress and ill-adapted for the purposes of persons in search of the means of earning a livelihood' and it was, according to the officials and just like in Port Said, almost impossible to find employment in Aden. In order to remedy the shortcomings they suggested that every passenger deposit a sum of money (150 rupees for Europeans and 50 rupees for natives) during the journey to cover their subsistence once they disembarked.[56]

However, this proposition engendered further problems of classification: persons in permanent paid employment, such as 'native firemen' or 'coolies', who were crucial to keeping the business of mobility going but were poorly paid and had no savings whatsoever, had to be exempted. The coaling station on the island of Perim challenged the regulation too as it would not be able to engage any 'coolies' through Aden if they had to be able to present a sum of 50 rupees on their return. But the Political Resident of Aden defended the measure since, according to him, it was of the highest importance that Aden's particular location 'which affords for dumping on it indigents and undesirables from other parts' was kept free of 'Somali and other immigrants in search of a job' who would not be able to sustain themselves.[57]

[55] OIOC, IOR L/PJ/6/907: File 4500 British consulate general to the Right Honourable Viscount Morley, Port Said, 21 November 1908; 'Aden Pilgrims and Paupers Regulation of 1904', also carried out in Port Said and Suez.

[56] OIOC, IOR R/20/A/2583 esp. sheet 69: India Office to Under-Secretary of State Foreign Office, 12 February 1908; ibid., sheet 144: Aden Residency, 29 September 1910.

[57] OIOC, IOR R/20/A/2583, sheet 145: H. F. Jacob, First Assisstant Resident, Aden, 19 December 1910; sheet 343: number of persons deported during the past three years at the expense of the Aden Settlement.

Besides such monetary guarantees, another procedure in the aim for tighter control was the registration of travellers. This procedure was increasingly employed in the first decade of the new century. In 1906, the Foreign Office issued a guideline expressing a desire 'to encourage as much as possible the practice of registration of British subjects at His Majesty's Consulates in foreign countries'.[58] There was a clear social bias in these measures. Permits to enter Sudan, for example, were only required of persons travelling third class and who were not government employees on government warrants or bona fide natives of that country.[59] Similarly the identification methods themselves were applied with social discrimination: in 1912, the government of India decided to leave the taking of a thumb impression to the judgment of the local authority in the case of 'educated British subjects'. While the bureaucratic apparatus employed to track travellers was thus extended, it was very much concerned with tracking *certain* travellers, not all. The analysis of destitute travellers thus provides both insights into the social history of globalisation and the regulation and channelling of global mobilities, which was above all structured by social categories but also by race and gender. The case of Aden also illustrates the problems of this differentiation of the freedom to move according to social categories in a place where the cheap labour of poor and mobile workers was essential.

Stowaways and 'vagabonds'

Port Said frequently became the last stop for travellers unable to afford their onward journey or seamen failing to be hired by the passing steamers. Yet it was also a 'dumping place', to use the drastic phrase employed by the Political Agent of Aden with reference to his own town, as every year numerous stowaways were disembarked in Port Said. In the consulates' dealings, these stowaways sat somewhere between destitution and criminal behaviour, since many of them were very young and consequently seldom convicted, but still required repatriation. Using the questionnaires that the stowaways had to answer when handed over to the consul as sources, we will attempt in the following to reconstruct a small part of their mobile lives.

The stowaways' experiences differed fundamentally from the romantic adventures of college graduate, Harry Franck, mentioned earlier. Most of them stowed away on ships leaving European ports, and not in Port Said itself, as Franck had. Instead they were extradited, once discovered during

[58] OIOC, IOR R/20/A/2422, sheet 1: Foreign Office, 9 March 1906.
[59] OIOC, IOR R/20/A/2422, sheet 219: Sudan Gazette. Permits to enter the Sudan.

the passage across the Mediterranean, to the consul at the first port of call – which often happened to be Port Said.[60] In the consulate the first objective was, as usual, identification, but as stowaways rarely carried papers, the officials had to rely on their personal statements to identify them as British, French, or other, nationals.[61]

What can we gather from the consuls' questions and the stowaways' replies, which of course only provide selective, situational and homogenised information? Often the stowaways were minors or young men from North England, Scotland or Wales (most frequently from Cardiff, Liverpool or Birkenhead) with westward-travelling stowaways forming the exception.[62] Younger stowaways generally referred to their parents as being poor, out of work, or invalids and certainly unable to support them or pay for their repatriation.[63] James Denning for instance, aged 14, a milkman's assistant, claimed that his father was an unemployed 'invalid, nearly blind and deaf' and therefore 'could not keep him'. The 14-year-old John Evans, to give another example, had worked as a butcher's boy but had lost his job and equally saw no other way of supporting himself.[64]

The accounts of how the stowaways had entered the ship and how they were treated upon discovery varied widely. Twelve-year-old John Melvin from Liverpool, for instance, said that he saw his friend boarding a steamer and just followed him. Fourteen-year-old John Rooney claimed that he had heard of others going on board and that after their discovery the captain made them do light work, like washing the decks or cleaning brass work. Yet the treatment on board was not always described in such a friendly manner, as the consul and the stowaways likewise complained about captains who simply left them behind. In a letter of November 1889, the British Consul at Port Said reported that five boys aged 13 to 16 had wanted to reach Calcutta for work while one of the boys, Elias Healy, aged 16, stowed away assuming the ship was bound for America 'where he has a rich aunt'. They had been cast ashore by the master of the steamer, *Governor*, from Liverpool, who had neglected to inform the consulate. According to the consul, this was not the first case in which

---

[60] Stowaways are an under-researched topic. See, for instance, Walters, 'Schiffahrtsindustrie', 70– 91. Walters, however, overstates the contrast between a world of free movement and the recent development of tighter controls, for example, for stowaways.

[61] See TNA, FO 78/3702; TNA, FO 78/4583; CADN, Port Said 103.

[62] TNA, FO 78/4317, sheet 233: Consul Burrell to Marquis of Salisbury, Port Said, 24 May 1890: Two stowaways from Singapore on the *SS Restitution*.

[63] See, for instance, TNA, FO 78/4317 sheet 245: Statement of Two Stowaways arrived at Port Said by *SS Waverley* on 16 July 1890, signed by Maling (acting consul), Port Said, 18 July 1890.

[64] TNA, FO 78/4250: Statement of two stowaway boys arrived at Port Said on 1 June 1889 by *SS Suffolk*.

'a British Ship Master abandons at an Oriental Port Stowaway boys' without reporting them.[65] Asked about their destinations only a few had left the ship at Port Said voluntarily, including the 18-year-old labourer, James McMahon, who upon arrival at Port Said had disembarked hoping to find temporary employment there yet could not find any.[66] Many stowaways replied that they were bound for Australia or for Indian cities like Calcutta, such as William Connor who wanted to go to the colonies believing that there was 'plenty of work'.[67] Occasionally a stowaway had planned to get to America but ended up on the wrong steamer.[68] While readily reporting their initial dream destinations to the consul, some at this point simply wanted to return home.[69]

At times older men stowed away too. The stories of unemployed seamen link Port Said not only with Britain and India but with all the big harbours around the world. Some had deserted their posts, such as Albert Florence from Aberdeen who had left the *Gladstone* in Bahia because he thought 'the ship was leaky'.[70] A few admitted that sailors had assisted them in hiding away or that they had planned their actions meticulously.[71] Others even claimed to be unintentional stowaways, like Francis Cunningham who apparently went on board a steamer to see friends, drank too much and fell asleep only to wake up once the ship was moving.[72]

Most of the stowaways were easily identified as belonging to a specific country, but in some cases their identity remained uncertain. This was the

---

[65] TNA, FO 78/4250: Burrell to Marquis of Salisbury, Port Said, 27 November 1889, Summary of Statements made by five Stowaway boys ex *SS Governor*, 24 November 1889.

[66] TNA, FO 78/4250: Statement of Wm Spilletts, a stowaway, arrived at Port Said on 14 October 1889, by *SS Beresford* and James McMahon and Hugh Rice Stowaways arrived at Port Said on 2 November 1889, by *SS Clan Murray*.

[67] TNA, FO 78/3702: Statement William Connor, attached to letter *SS Strathairly*, Port Said, 22 November 1884.

[68] TNA, FO 78/4317, sheets 248–9: Maling to the Marquis of Salisbury, Port Said, 3 September 1890 – two boys planning to go to Calcutta; TNA, FO 78/4394: Statements of two stowaways (James Brennan, 23, and William Morris, 17) hoping to get to New York, but ordered off the ship in Port Said; TNA, FO 78/4521: Statement of the stowaways John Morre, William Coughlin, John Barry and Cornelius Connolly (planning to get to Australia).

[69] See TNA, FO 78/4583: Statement of three stowaways Joseph Bennet, John Humphries and Thomas Murphy, landed from *SS Aston Hall* (wanting to return home).

[70] See TNA, FO 78/4583: Statements of James Joseph Smith and Albert Florence – stowaways landed from *SS Ariadne Alexander*, signed Maling, Port Said, 25 January 1894. See also TNA, FO 78/4461: Statement of Charles Wellcome Stowaway (born in South Africa, was discharged in Hong Kong in 1891 and lost all of his certificates of discharge); ibid.: Statement of the Stowaway William Furshaw, 37 years of age.

[71] See, for instance, TNA, FO 78/4461: Statement of three stowaways, Port Said, 22 February 1892.

[72] TNA, FO 78/4461: Statement of the stowaway Francis Cunningham, Port Said, 3 February 1892. See also TNA, FO 78/4583: Statement of William Curtin, distressed British subject landed from *SS Aymestry*.

case with one Doba Vugnullon, whom the agent of the *Messageries Maritimes* had accused of having stowed away on the steamer *Natal*: 'This individual is without papers and claims to have been born in Nankin (China) of unknown parents; he would thus be of Chinese nationality.' As he had been found on a French ship, the French Consul had to deal with him in the first instance and then passed the case over to the governor of the Canal District.[73]

The consul usually aimed to repatriate stowaways quickly and inexpensively, mostly trying to find a ship on which they could work their passage back. It was difficult, however, to negotiate moderate rates for returns from Port Said and sometimes he had to spend several days making enquiries paying for the subsistence of the stowaways in the meantime.[74] Only rarely were they tried before the consular courts. In 1884 the consul complained that it was impossible to detain under-age stowaways, because the British consulate did not have a separate prison, but used two small rooms in the Egyptian jail, which were shared with other European consulates and consequently were always full of Maltese and British seamen, Greeks and others, rendering a stay particularly dangerous for young boys. The British Consul thus arranged for them to stay in a boarding house.[75] While he was considerate in relation to the young boys, older men were more easily imprisoned.[76]

Time and again the consul tried to make it clear that the large number of stowaways at Port Said was an issue that should raise concern in Britain, as the sheer number disembarked at the port caused not only organisational difficulties on site but also created substantial costs 'at home', once again pointing to an often neglected facet of globalisation.[77] In some years the number of stowaways handed over by masters to the consul was indeed copious. In 1888 a single week brought 25 cases. The year 1890 also saw many cases of stowaways.[78] The 1891 files contain numerous reports, with 1892 showing a slight reduction.[79] In the first half of 1894, the consul invested more than 90 pounds in the subsistence and repatriation of

---

[73] CADN, Port Said 47: Consul de Suez à Mouhes Pacha, gouverneur du canal de Suez, Port Said, 20 January 1909.

[74] See, for instance, TNA, FO 78/4317: Consul Burrell to Marquis of Salisbury, Port Said, 24 February 1890.

[75] See TNA, FO 78/3702, sheets 161–4: Consul Burrell to Earl Granville, Port Said, 24 November 1884.

[76] See TNA, FO 78/4675, sheets 220–1: Acting Consul Maling to Marquis of Salisbury, Port Said, 27 November 1895.

[77] See TNA, FO 78/4154: Consul Burrell to Marquis of Salisbury, Port Said, 9 April 1888.

[78] See TNA, FO 78/4317.

[79] For 1891, see TNA, FO 78/4394; for 1892 TNA, FO 78/4461.

stowaways and destitute British subjects.[80] This enumeration gives evidence that the costs that this mobility could engender were significant. Yet the stowaways provide us with more than an illustration of the downside of increasing global and imperial mobility. However limited the sources, these biographies open up new interpretations of the visions of empire and globalisation that these individuals possessed and how they connected them with their own life courses.

As the stowaways' proceedings illustrate, their treatment was mainly negotiated between the consulate, the ministries in London and the shipping companies. Yet there were cases of 'vagabonding', which required the governor of the Canal District to get involved. The following paragraphs highlight how the European discourse on vagrancy, *vagabondage* or *Landstreicherei*, which was briefly touched upon in the introduction, was connected with individual cases turning up in Port Said. This discourse is particularly interesting, as the accusation brought forward was related directly to mobility and thus led to the hardening of the boundaries between different categories of mobility. What is more, the distinction of unwelcome travellers was once again made along the lines of categories such as nationality and ethnicity, but also gender and social background.

In the years before the First World War 'vagrants', 'vagabonds' and 'mendicants' were arrested in increasing numbers in Port Said as elsewhere.[81] In 1907, the governor of Port Said reported the case of a couple and their two daughters, 'itinerant street singers', who had arrived in Port Said without any funds and lived off begging. The local authorities had demanded urgent measures as 'scandalous scenes' on the street were upsetting Port Said's population. Against this background the consul thought it necessary to repatriate them as quickly as possible. This repatriation was depicted as both an expulsion and a humanitarian action, as the husband had amputated legs, the wife was eight months' pregnant and the children were only three and five years old respectively. The consul explained that there was no establishment in Port Said that could take care of such individuals and that they were 'hardened vagabonds' who did not even want to stay in the hotel room that the *Société de bienfaisance* had organised for them.[82]

There were numerous similar, if perhaps slightly less extreme, cases. Faced with involuntary repatriation, some reacted violently.[83] Others

---

[80] See TNA, FO 78/4583: FO 21 February 1894, 2 June 1894, 28 June 1894.
[81] See, for example, OIOC, IOR R/20/A/724.
[82] CADN, Port Said 260: Affaires étrangères, direction des consulats et des affaires commerciales, sous-direction des affaires de chancellerie au préfet des Bouches-du-Rhône à Marseille, 13 March 1907.
[83] CADN, Port Said 260: Le consul de France à Port-Said à M. Pichon, ministre des Affaires étrangères à Paris, Port Said, 10 June 1908.

already on their way to being repatriated (from Saigon or to Hong Kong, for example) missed their ships voluntarily in Port Said.[84] Yet even successful repatriations did not solve all problems, as the future of those sent home was often uncertain. Officials of the *Messageries Maritimes* complained particularly that many were simply let loose in Marseilles and never paid anything back to the company. They therefore demanded more thorough measures against those travelling without tickets even before they were arrested 'in flagrante delicto of vagabonding'.[85] But the Ministry of Justice still refused to take any more decisive action (or to reimburse the *Messageries Maritimes*, for that matter) referring to the rulings of a court case that showed that merely embarking clandestinely on a ship did not yet constitute an offence.[86]

Even if not chargeable in the courts, beyond their anecdotal quality, cases such as that of the family accused of vagabonding add an important aspect to the history of mobility and acceleration around 1900: mobility could – besides the costs it engendered and the questions of security that came with it – also relate to negative stereotypes which mirrored global concerns regarding mobile lifestyles referred to in the introduction. The debates in both the French and British colonial contexts regarding individuals that the French Consul at Port Said tellingly called 'people without permission or resources who are the scourge of our colonies', show that by 1913 the question of illicit mobility formed an important undercurrent to discussions about how to administer possessions abroad and showed the limits of the channelling of mobility.[87]

Networks of crime and prostitution

Most of the cases dealt with at Port Said's consulates involving dubious identification oscillated between the consul's duties of providing relief and organising repatriations on the one side and tracking down others who wanted to move on yet were to be arrested on the other. The numerous stowaways and penniless in Port Said illustrate that as

---

[84] See, for instance, François Mérianne to be repatriated from Saigon – CADN, Port Said 260: Le consul de France à Port Said au préfet de Bouche-du-Rhône, Marseille, Port Said, 3 May 1911; see also the case of Fernand Maxime Julien Roche, Compagnie des Messageries Maritimes à M. le consul général de France à Port Said, Port Said, 16 December 1912.

[85] CADN, Port Said 260: Messageries Maritimes à M. l'Agent, 27 December 1913.

[86] CADN, Port Said 260: Le ministre des Affaires étrangères à Léon Côte, consul de France à Port-Said, Paris, 1 October 1913.

[87] CADN, Port Said 260: Le consul de France à Port-Said à M. Pichon ministre des Affaires étrangères, Port-Said, 11 October 1913.

soon as someone encountered financial trouble abroad he or she often ended up in the grey zone between legality and illegality. Yet some incidents were clearly identified as crimes. Besides petty offences and fights, for which Port Said had become notorious (albeit sometimes in an inflated fashion), smuggling and prostitution came to play an important role.[88] As seen in Chapter 1, Port Said itself was famed as a seedbed for indecent behaviour. Yet this mattered not only in terms of a history of perception but also in terms of control practices. The global search for fugitive offenders and the town's pivotal position in networks of prostitution and white slavery will be highlighted in the following sections.

Fugitive offenders

Faster global mobility also meant that criminals could move around the globe with greater speed. Troublemakers and criminals were either threatened with forced immobility – imprisonment in Port Said – or forced mobility – the removal to another destination. Yet first they had to be arrested and identified, which could be problematic for instance, if different spellings of a single person's name circulated.

The case of Serafino Calleja – variously spelt Gallija, Galleja, Calleia, Kallerr, Kalleri, Callere, or Callero – a bumboat man 'well known at Port Said as of the lowest class of Maltese and a noted scoundrel' provides a telling illustration. The consul warned him in 1885 that in the case of any further offence he would be liable for deportation and expected this to have a notable effect on his behaviour.[89] In spite of this warning, he was arrested in 1887 for murdering a certain Popolo Pace (Paolo Pace, Paul Patche). Having subsequently escaped from custody, he was tracked down eight years later in Australia. Yet by then it was no longer possible to put him on trial, as too much time had elapsed to make bringing him back to Egypt worthwhile. Furthermore, the main witness of the case, Andrea Ferrugia (also by then a resident of Australia), would only attend if provided with a free round trip. Because of the considerable expense, Lord Salisbury was of the opinion that it was wiser to 'let the matter

---

[88] The most spectacular smuggling stories are perhaps provided by de Monfreid, *La Croisière du hachich*, transporting hashish from Greece to Suez. See also CADN, Le Caire 427, Dossier contrebande, sous-dossier affaires de hachiche; CADN, Port Said 48, Douanes égyptiennes.

[89] TNA, FO 78/3830: Letter of complaint, 13 November 1885; Letter of Burrell, no date.

drop'.[90] The example thus highlights not only the difficulty to ascertain identities but also the problems that global criminal cases could entail in terms of cost and different legal systems.

However, the Suez Canal Region was not only a place that criminals fled from, it also had a wider-reaching role in global networks of crime. Since the opening of the Canal, the towns at either end of it had become locations in which to await and arrest international fugitives. Jules Verne's *Around the World in Eighty Days* provides, once again, an illustration of the phenomenon, with the detective choosing this particular location to wait for Phileas Fogg.[91] The scene in Verne's novel was paralleled by non-fictional occasions of global searches and the display of 'wanted' posters that caught the passengers' eye upon arrival. The criminal activities that were tracked were multifarious. Sometimes they consisted of capital offences: a Swede who was sentenced to death in 1890 'for having exchanged intelligence with enemies of the French state and having supplied them with weapons and ammunition' in Indochina was searched for globally.[92] More frequent were cases of theft or fraud. A person who had stolen diamonds in Johannesburg or another that misappropriated money in Saigon were traced with warrants of apprehension posted in consulates around the globe, among them Port Said.[93] The obsessive gambler, Louis Marie Caignan (see Figure 21) had fled Hanoi after stealing 165,000 francs.

Sometimes the searches proved successful, as in 1901, when Consul Cameron reported that two British deserters had hidden on a United States Army transport and were arrested on the information of the captain in Port Said.[94] Yet actually arresting these fugitive offenders often proved difficult. One problem was, as in other contexts, the financing of transport.

---

[90] TNA, FO 78/4675, sheets 138–9: Draft, Foreign Office to Consul Gould, Port Said, London, 24 July 1895; sheets 179–81: Consul Gould to Marquis of Salisbury, Port Said, 28 June 1895; sheet 183–4: Chief Consular Court, Alexandria, Cookson to Consul Gould, Alexandria, 4 June 1895; sheet 185: Police Department, Inspector General's Office to the Principal Under-Secretary, Sydney, 5 April 1895; sheet 186: Jules P. Rochaix, detective, to inspector general of police, Sydney, 2 April 1895; sheets 187–9: statement Andrew Ferrugia.

[91] See Verne, *Around the World in Eighty Days*, pp. 32–7.

[92] CADN, Port Said 16: République française, Indochine française, Protectorat de l'Annam et du Tonkin, Cour criminelle du Tonkin, Hanoi, 2 August 1890.

[93] See, among others, CADN, Port Said 260: Telegram consul Port Said au ministre de France, Le Caire, Port Said, 22 June 1903; ibid., Consul général de France à M. Daumas, consul de France à Port Said, Cairo, 20 November 1894; ibid.: Altemer au ministre de France, Le Caire, Port Said, 22 June 1905; ibid.: Gouverneur général de l'Indochine à M. le consul de France à Port Said, Saigon, 26 June 1909; ibid.: Administration de la justice, tribunal de Saigon, Mandat d'arrêt (Riegler).

[94] TNA, FO 78/5165: British Consul Port Said to Marquess of Lansdowne, Port Said, 3 August 1901.

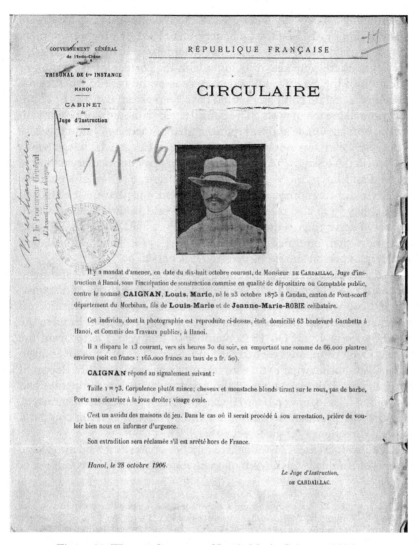

Figure 21 Warrant for arrest of Louis Marie Caignan, 1906.

Another developed around the cooperation, or lack thereof, between consuls and the governor of the Canal District who had to give the order to arrest a person.[95] Furthermore, extraterritorial legislation played a role when it came

---

[95] See, for example, CADN, Port Said 260: Consul au gouverneur du canal, Port Said, 6 November 1913.

to determining if a person could be taken into custody or not. In the case of the British Empire, the Fugitive Offenders Act of 1881 gave the consuls more leeway to arrest persons once certain preconditions were met.[96] However, there were also difficulties with the correct interpretation or application of the Fugitive Offenders Act, as in the case of whether the manager of a coaling company should have been arrested in 1891 in Suez on a 'criminal breach of trust'. The consul acted without prior permission from the Foreign Office and was reprimanded immediately, as in this case the Fugitive Offenders Act was not applicable in Egypt, which legally was not a British possession.[97] Another example of this intermediary nature of Port Said and Egypt more generally was the transportation of a prisoner from one place to another, as criminals did not only have to be tracked globally, they were also moved around the world to the places in which they would serve their sentences. At times Port Said or Suez were thus barely more than intermediary information relays in which information that a certain person should be arrested was passed on.[98]

These transports of prisoners could be difficult to effectuate and there were many cases of evasion.[99] They also led up to questions of responsibility and cooperation, as revealed in the case of Terence Arthur Forrest Garvin, an American citizen who had to be transported from India to the United States in 1893. On 18 September of that year a letter from the Thomas Cook Company reached the Under-secretary of State for India in Whitehall enquiring what to do with this prisoner, who was to be deported from Calcutta. However, none of the Atlantic steamship companies had been willing to take him on board because of his 'admitted bad character'. Yet, as he was an American citizen, the India Office in London could not give clear directions on how to act either.[100]

Such individual cases illustrate three functions tying Port Said into global networks of criminality: as a point of origin for criminals, such as Galleja; as

---

[96] 'A Bill intituled an Act to amend the Law with respect to Fugitive Offenders in Her Majesty's Dominions, and for other Purposes connected with the Trial of Offenders' (British Parliamentary Papers 1881, vol. V).

[97] OIOC: IOR R/20/A/724, sheets 225–47: Various letters and telegrams concerning the case (1891). Only after Egypt had been turned into a protectorate was the Fugitive Offenders' Act applicable, see 'A Bill to Enable the Fugitive Offenders Act, 1881, to be extended to Protected States' (British Parliamentary Papers 1914–16, vol. I).

[98] See, for instance, TNA, FO 78/2863: Telegram London to Consul West, Suez (1878). 'Forward following to Consul Beyts Jeddah: Release immediately British Indian Subject Rafiah Khan imprisoned by you for assault. Sigd R. A. Cross, F.O'.

[99] See CADN, Le Caire 277: Consul de France à Alexandrie à M. Poincaré, Président du Conseil Ministre des Affaires étrangères, 20 December 1912 A.s. du transport des prisonniers à bord des paquebots des *Messageries Maritimes*.

[100] OIOC, IOR L/PJ/6356: Thomas Cook & Son to the Under-Secretary of State for India, India Office, Whitehall, 18 September 1893.

a place where fugitives could be identified and extradited; and as a passage-way for the transfer of criminals between the scene of the crime and the locus of their process of punishment. Besides stowaways and vagabonds, the identification and transportation of criminals thus provides a further aspect to the 'rights of passage' and illustrates the forms that the channelling of mobility could take at this global sluice gate.

Prostitution and 'white slavery'

A further issue connected to questions of identification, which high-lights the nexus between forced and free movement and the increasing propensity to trace people globally and links it with questions of gender and the danger attached to women travelling alone, was pros-titution and 'white slavery'. Port Said had not only become infamous for its number of brothels and the sale of pornographic images, but it also came to be suspected as a nodal point in the transfer of prosti-tutes. Once again, international cooperation was presented here as the solution to problems of identification and control. In this section we will begin by looking at prostitution and 'white slavery' more generally, how it became tied to the location of Port Said and finally how once again international conferences were seen as the best instru-ment to tackle the issue.

During the late Victorian period, prostitution had become a thorn in the side of the middle classes in Britain and elsewhere. A large pamphlet-based literature developed referring to prostitution and more specifically to what came to be called 'white slavery', that is the trading of European girls to staff brothels in Egypt, Asia and other regions.[101] For some, such as Jules Lenoble, 'white slavery' was directly correlated with increased mobility and communication, as 'the multiplication of colonies, the devel-opment of commercial relations, the more and more intimate connection of peoples as a result of communication measures, in a word, the civilising process, are thus the active agents that have created and propagated white slavery'.[102]

In this context, Egypt, and more particularly Port Said, came to play a decisive role:

---

[101] See, for example, de Montépin, *La traite des blanches*; Borel, *The White Slavery of Europe*; Tacussel, *La traite des blanches*. See also Fischer-Tiné, '"White Women Degrading Themselves to the Lowest Depths"'; Jäger, 'International Police Co-operation'; Bristow, *Prostitution and Prejudice*; Levine, *Prostitution, Race and Politics*.

[102] Lenoble, *La traite des blanches*, p. 13.

Egypt often serves as first stop for the woman who has been intended for debauchery. Here she has her apprenticeship and, some time later, she is ripe to be exported to Bombay, Shanghai or other places . . . The main cities of Egypt are filled with men and women practising white slavery; they form very dangerous elements for public safety and set traps for all honest women and girls.[103]

The harbour town of Port Said thus became an important stop in the global networks of prostitution, where pimps transferred women and where prostitutes stayed periodically before moving on.

Some of those who took up the fight against 'white slavery' explicitly related Port Said's position to its variegated population. In a pamphlet aimed at young men, the female activist, W. N. Willis, described Port Said as the 'new Babylon' adding to the characterisations and analogies collected in Chapter 1. She stated:

That Port Said is a seething bed of infamy, a distributing ground for dreadful secret diseases and hidden plagues, is well known to men who have travelled . . . Its inhabitants are a cosmopolitan crowd; every nationality under the sun – except, perhaps, the Chinese – is liberally represented in that one small town.[104]

In another contribution that she published together with a certain Mrs Mackirdy, Willis' disgust of Port Said became even more explicit. Here she called Port Said, though small, the 'deadliest spot on earth' with its 'highly cosmopolitan population of Arabs, Turks, Roumanians, Afrikanders, Greeks, bloodthirsty islanders from the Aegean Sea, French, Germans, Poles, Egyptians, and Italians, with a slight sprinkling of English, intermixed in an unhealthy conglomerate of lazy lawlessness'.[105] For Willis and Mackirdy, what they called the cosmopolitanism of Port Said, and especially the mismatch between its size and the number of individuals that passed through it, was thus the root of its depravity.

Whereas the capitulations and consular protections were usually seen as a system highly beneficial to European states, nationality could also be used as an asset to escape prosecution. Once again, pointing to the variety of Port Said's population, Willis stated that the town's brothels were inevitably run by some 'coarse, bold, betrimmed Jezebel of Austrian, Russian, Greek, or French origin' who wanted to sell the services of her girls. However, according to Willis, the police could not take action against these brothel keepers since the capitulations allowed every European citizen to be judged by his or her consul only. She quoted a mistress of a Port Said brothel

---

[103] Kebedgy, 'La répression de la traite des blanches en Egypte', 29, quote from the 1906 congress on white slavery.
[104] Willis, *Anti-Christ in Egypt*, p. 139.
[105] Mackirdy and Willis, *The White Slave Market*, p. 44.

stating in broken English: 'De police nothing to me ... My consul my policeman and judge, too.'[106] Nationality could thus be employed as an argument to evade legal persecution.

If the police were, according to Willis, powerless in Port Said, then European campaigners had to fight against the problem. As in other domains surveyed earlier, a number of conferences were convened to deal with the issue on an international level. The decisive years of campaigning against 'white slavery' coincided with the beginning of the twentieth century and culminated in an International Convention for the suppression of white slave traffic signed in Paris in May 1910.[107] As in the case of the Brussels conference against the slave trade, and to a certain extent also the international sanitary and Suez Canal conferences, the conferences were partly concerned with communication and information. More concretely the measures entailed the establishment of offices for the rapid dispersal of information in frontier towns and seaports, a 'reciprocal exchange' of the lists of suspicious persons among these offices, and the creation of an international bureau in London, where the information would be collected.[108] Another suggestion concerned an international telegraphic code to enable faster action, in line with a standardised register of all cases on which information had been received including photographs, a system already in place in Germany.[109] As in the case of disease, modern technology and the rapid transmission and dispersal of information were seen as the best instruments to fight a problem perceived as a side effect to faster mobility more generally.

The major secondary aim of the international conference was networking, enabling contact between the various organisations acting in different

---

[106] Willis, *Anti-Christ in Egypt*, pp. 141, 148. See also Lenoble, *La traite des blanches*, p. 10; CADN, Port Said 120: Consul de France à Port-Said au gouverneur général du canal de Suez, Port Said, 4 February 1880.

[107] See Correspondence respecting the International Conference on the 'White Slave Traffic', held in Paris, July 1902 (British Parliamentary Papers 1905, vol. CIII); Correspondence respecting the international Conference on the 'White Slave Traffic', held in Paris, October 1906 (British Parliamentary Papers 1907, vol. C); Correspondence respecting the Fourth International Congress on the White Slave Traffic, held in Madrid, October 1910 (British Parliamentary Papers 1911, vol. LXIII); Correspondence respecting the International Conferences on Obscene Publications and the 'White Slave Traffic', held in Paris, April and May 1910 (British Parliamentary Papers 1912–1913, vol. LXVIII), International Convention for the Suppression of the White Slave Traffic, signed at Paris, 4 May 1910 (British Parliamentary Papers 1912–13, vol. CXXI).

[108] Correspondence respecting the International Conference on the White Slave Traffic, held in Paris, October 1906 (British Parliamentary Papers 1907, vol. C), p. 5.

[109] Correspondence respecting the International Conference on the White Slave Traffic, held in Paris, October 1906 (British Parliamentary Papers 1907, vol. C), p. 13.

regions of the world. There were expressions of support for the already existing societies and associations and thus a strengthening of non-state actors. Finally the debates touched on the issue of free movement lobbying for the strengthening of possibilities to stop someone on suspicion of trafficking from moving on. The campaigning participants time and again stressed the specific role of Egypt. The delegate of Alexandria stated, at the second session of the Paris congress for the suppression of white slavery in 1906, that 'if Europe provides the victims, it is Egypt that is the market' which is why all attention should be turned towards Egypt.[110] As in the case of epidemic disease, the answer to a global problem was thus both institutional internationalisation at the conferences and the localisation of the problem, this time not in India or at Mecca, but in Egypt.

During this process of internationalisation, William Alexander Coote, the secretary of the International Bureau for the Suppression of the White Slave Traffic in London, visited Egypt in 1905 to check on the progress made.[111] The implementation of the conventions of 1904 and 1910 involved the establishment of new institutions in Egypt, such as the *Ligue de prophylaxie sanitaire et contre la traite des blanches*, founded in Cairo in May 1909. In Port Said itself, the Port Said branch of the International Union for the Protection of Young Girls came to play an important role, as, according to its president, 'Port Said is, geographically, the point of convergence where the traffickers in human flesh send on their unhappy victims seeing the facility that the countries of the Far East offer for their exploitation'.[112] The association identified the harbour of Port Said as the place where one had to act before the girls entered Port Said itself. To replace controls on board or in the brothels, a surveillance bureau was installed next to the quays and just in front of the passport offices.[113] The localisation mentioned in the last paragraph thus went further than merely targeting Egypt as main theatre of white slavery. The layout of Port Said itself should be made useful to target the culprits.

However, to make these controls efficient, one not only needed international agreements and local branches of international associations

---

[110] Kebedgy, 'La répression de la traite des blanches en Égypte', p. 31.

[111] CADN, Le Caire 428, Dossier 1, Prostitution, Traite des blanches: Consul de France à Alexandrie à Son Excellence M. Delcassé, ministre des affaires étrangères à Paris, Alexandria, 27 March 1905.

[112] Women's Library, Ligue internationale pour la répression de la traite des blanches à Port-Said: Hadaya Bey (président de la Ligue internationale pour la répression de la traite des blanches à Port Saïd) à W. A. Coote, secrétaire de la Ligue internationale pour la répression de la traite des blanches, London, 10 September 1914.

[113] Women's Library, Ligue internationale pour la répression de la traite des blanches à Port-Said: Rapport de l'exercice mars–décembre 1914 et janvier–février 1915 (Port Said: Imp. L. Goldman, 1915).

implementing those agreements; national and imperial legislation also mattered – for example the British Empire's Fugitive Offenders' Act of 1881, mentioned earlier. Once the girls and women in question were identified, issues of expenditure and reimbursement arose regarding their repatriation. Campaigners opted for the easing of rules for arrest and repatriation, even if such a simplification was also accompanied with new problems of misuse and so forth.[114] Yet it was not so simple to integrate national and imperial legislation in this matter. The question who had the right to control, arrest, or repatriate – in cases when often many different nationalities and empires were involved – points to the problems and limits of the rules of globalisation as they have been developed in Chapter 3.

Obviously prostitution was not limited to Port Said, and increased controls, registrations and, if necessary, deportations were measures employed elsewhere too. The question of looking to role models provided by other harbour towns could be observed here as in other fields already depicted. As in the case of destitute travellers, it was Aden that took the lead in stricter regulations. Aden's government attempted to register all the city's prostitutes who were concentrated in the specific neighbourhood of Sheikh Othman.[115] It also made medical checks compulsory in order to try and come to grips with an epidemic of venereal disease raging in the area. Deportation, however, was a measure that some prostitutes actively lobbied against, even if they had to oppose petitions of inhabitants wanting them to leave.[116] In Aden, prostitution was also an issue that brought conflicts between the Arab and European populations to the fore. Neighbours of the Tawahi Division, where some European prostitutes from Italy and Germany had established themselves, complained that 'European men, such as soldiers, sailors, and Italians who have shops at Tawahi are in the habit of coming during the night ... sometimes these European men and the prostitutes are dancing together in the street before Public'.[117]

---

[114] TNA, T 1/11203: Suppression of the White Slave Trade: Arrangements for Repatriations of Victims. See also expenses for the repatriation of Ethel Florence Wyers from Beijing: TNA, T/11530.

[115] See OIOC, IOR R/20/A/1284: Lists of private prostitutes 1908–1912.

[116] OIOC, IOR R/20/A/2212: Office Note: block for prostitutes in Sheikh Othman; sheet 143: Medical Certificate of all European prostitutes on entering Aden; sheet 139: anonymous petition against the prostitutes (by a sufferer of 'Sefelice'), 11 November 1908 etc. See Howell, 'Sexuality, Sovereignty and Space'. In Gibraltar, similar measures were in place, p. 450: 'The power of expulsion was critical to the management of prostitution because disorderly women could be banished outright and venereally diseased women compelled to seek treatment.'

[117] OIOC, IOR R/20/A/2212, sheet 85: Report S. A. Khalifa, registration inspector; see also sheet 75: Annoyance caused to the public owing to the European prostitutes living in the Tawahi Bazaar 1905.

Although in pre-war Port Said no registration and deportation campaign against prostitutes was implemented on a similar scale to that in Aden, the entry of the Suez Canal became a place where men and women entangled in the networks of prostitution frequently were tracked and arrested, even if the searches did not always prove successful. One Joseph Vacher, for example, who had already been threatened with expulsion for reasons of 'special vagrancy' in Alexandria was suspected of staying in a Port Said hotel and practising 'white slavery', furnishing women for several brothels in Cairo, and was therefore imprisoned in 1907.[118] Likewise women had to be identified in Port Said, as in the case of Fernande Sauvan dite Riancourt née Albertella who was accompanied by her minor daughter and two men who lived off them.[119] Some of the searches' targets had several identities: Denis Vignoli was also known as 'Pépère' and as 'Vieux Denis' or 'le vieux Denis de Paris et d'Egypte' and used to live in Port Said, but his traces were lost somewhere in Malta.[120] This relates back to the multiplicity of names illustrated above – a most vivid image of the limits of both identification and the channelling of mobility more generally.

The assumption that the First World War and the inter-war period brought about a clampdown after a period of general freedom of movement needs qualification, especially if one takes into account the travelling population beyond those privileged travellers mentioned at the beginning of the chapter. As soon as travel procedures did not go according to plan, identity and its verification mattered a great deal. What is more, even if the openness of the *belle époque* rang true for some, it was highly dependent on the status of the individual traveller. For one, certain groups, such as socially disadvantaged, racially stigmatised or lone women, had to provide more extensive documentation than others. Also, those who were lacking funds, health, or sanity had to prove their identity to receive care and relief. Finally, incidences of crime required the identification of the respective parties involved, which sometimes started with the difficulty to agree on the spelling of a name. Identification was thus not so much about knowing a person's whereabouts per se, but was instead often linked to questions of financial or legal responsibility. Destitute passengers and stowaways highlighted the question of responsibility for nationals or colonial subjects on the move, which mostly came down to who should pay for any liabilities accrued by an individual turning up in

---

[118] CADN, Port Said 260: Consul général, chargé du Consulat de France à Alexandrie à M. Meyrier, consul de France, Port Said, Alexandria, 28 May 1907.

[119] CADN, Port Said 260: Consul général, chargé du Consulat de France à Alexandrie à M. Meyrier, consul de France, Port Said, Alexandria, 30 April 1907.

[120] CADN, Le Caire 428: Ministre des affaires étrangères à M. le ministre de France au Caire, Paris, 23 October 1913 and further correspondence.

the Suez Canal Zone. Besides cholera and plague, other concerns like prostitution and the global pursuit of criminals made the identification or detention of suspects at Port Said or Suez desirable.

In relation to the movement of stowaways and destitute travellers, different forms and functions of mobility which were often related to categories such as social class, race or gender, and the political aims connected to them came most clearly to the fore, touching on the one hand at the moral assessment of mobility as legitimate or illicit, on the other on the question of free movement and forced removal, or repatriation. The chokepoint of the Suez Canal thus became, in the truest sense of the word, a space of funnelling or channelling where free and forced, legitimate and illicit mobility were contrasted most sharply. Here, the nexus between identification and mobility – and between different modes of mobility, especially voluntary or forced movement, in the form of repatriation or deportation – became particularly palpable.

What is more, the focus on Port Said and the Canal Zone brings the problems and limits of identity and identification most clearly to the fore. This has been highlighted by the proliferation of forged passes leading to cases of multiple official identities. In case of the incorrect spelling of names, such multiple identities could also be created on the side of the officials. In dealing with these limits of political control and interference, officials in Port Said often looked abroad and tried to learn from other port cities, known for their harder line, such as Aden at the other end of the Red Sea.

The strikingly heterogeneous cases of persons stowing away, 'vagabonding', or ending up without funds thus kaleidoscopically connect the multifarious problems engendered by the identification and filtering of humans on the move. Furthermore they shed light on the variety of measures used to identify travellers and – together with the emergence of stricter laws and controls – on the increasingly narrow definition of what was deemed legitimate and illegitimate mobility. Finally they point to the costs of mobility engendered by subsistence and repatriations. On a more general level, the cases show that the official identity of a person was often in flux, which becomes most obvious when a multitude of names existed for one and the same person but also when nationality was treated as a currency as in the case of Paolo Rizzo. The global biographies at the centre of this chapter and the problems connected with mobility, which at the same time was so crucial for imperial and global enterprises, provide the part missing from the picture emerging through the descriptions analysed in Chapter 1. Highlighting both *rites de passage* and rights of passage, the book thus comes full circle with Port Said emerging not only as a point of passage but also as a terminus.

Conclusion: *rites de passage* and rights of passage in the Suez Canal Region and beyond

The analysis offered in the preceding chapters points to different – albeit overlapping – phases in the process of globalisation that crystallised around 1900 at the crossroads of the Suez Canal. An initial phase was concerned with the complicated institutionalisation of the new system of acceleration, bringing together different levels of decision-making, but also relying on different agents beyond the political realm, such as the various groups of workers concentrated in the Canal Zone. It furthermore witnessed the creation of a more and more standardised imagination of global space. This was followed by a second phase marked by the stigmatisation or bureaucratisation of *other* mobilities that did not fit into the frame of 'new' or 'modern' mobility. Increasingly, a sharp distinction was made between different mobilities. At the same time and somewhat paradoxically those types of mobility deemed modern and up to date had to rely on the skills connected to 'old' or 'traditional' forms of movement in many different ways. During a third phase in the early twentieth century, the main concerns related less to the distinction between different types of mobility than to the contradictions and dangers inherent in the very acceleration caused by the Suez Canal, steam navigation and other more rapid means of transport. These concerns became most visible in the fears associated with contagious disease and the handling of unruly mobilities, such as stowaways, destitute travellers and criminals who were a corollary to the faster circuits of movement.

These different elements of a history of acceleration and globalisation – complicated institutionalisation, distinctions drawn between different categories of mobility and (not always successful) bureaucratic regulation of its unavoidable and potentially dangerous side-effects – continued to matter after 1914 and were, of course, prevalent not only within the spatial confines of the Canal itself. This conclusion will therefore go beyond the example of the Suez Canal between 1869 and 1914 in three different ways, inserting its specific story into a larger temporal and spatial context. We will thus revisit the main dimensions in which the Suez Canal itself proved to be a good example of attempts to channel mobilities in an era of globalisation. First, going beyond the temporal confines of this investigation, the ruptures and continuities after 1914 will be put into perspective, throwing light on particular instances such as the Armenian refugee camp set up in the Canal Zone after the First World War, the transformation of the Canal into a major oil-carrying artery and the development of internationalism and international conferences after 1914. Then we will broaden the spatial scope and look at other global localities, such as Ellis Island, where similar mechanisms of exclusion were at work. In this larger setting, the concept of 'channelling' can finally be sharpened as a tool to analyse the ambivalence of globalisation and the intricacies of regulating movement around 1900. By highlighting the entanglements of different empires (in particular, the Ottoman, French and British) and the increasing importance of the 'international arena', a detailed investigation of the Suez Canal can advance not only (and most obviously) the history of migration and mobility, but global and transnational history more generally.

After 1914

The start of the First World War is often interpreted as a rupture and as the beginning of a new (and remarkably less global) era. Yet, in the microcosm of the Suez Canal, many conflicts and countermeasures that had shaped the new traffic artery before 1914 continued and intensified during the First World War and the inter-war years. While there were specific trends towards a reversal of globalisation after 1919, such as the growing Egyptianisation of port cities like Alexandria and Port Said (trends that would of course speed up after the Second World War),[1] this phase can also be interpreted as a continuation of the history of a globalisation long since in motion. There were, however, important shifts and changes, in terms of both new groups of people (and objects) using the Canal and new techniques employed to control certain mobilities more tightly.

In travel descriptions, the continuities were most striking. In the inter-war period, exactly the same images and analogies that Rudyard Kipling and other authors had established before the war were often employed. The theme of time travel and of the desert as an ancient space, for instance, came up time and time again.[2] Similarly, the personal transformation, the *rite de passage*, during the Canal transit was a recurring

---

[1] See, for instance, Garbati, *Nous et les Egyptiens*; Belli, *Remembrance of Nasserian Things Past*.

[2] It was even formulated in a film proposal – see ANMT, 2000036/0215: Projet de film Mme Barthas.

theme.[3] Interestingly enough, reflections on these continuities also emerged. The writer, painter and director, Jean Cocteau, for example, travelling in the 1930s, perceived himself as an epigone, a late-comer repeating what had been said and written about the Canal a thousand times.[4]

Many leisure tourists and colonial voyagers thus behaved in similar ways and reported their behaviours in the same familiar language. During and after the war, however, new mobilities emerged in the Canal Region. Sometimes what was new was the sheer volume of a specific type of mobility. During the First World War and as a reaction to the German-Turkish attack of 1915 fought back mainly by Indian and Australian troops, the militarisation of the Canal – and of Egypt more generally in its new status as a formal British protectorate – was naturally far greater than it had ever been.[5] Furthermore, the Canal now became the entry point for many serving in the eastern theatres of war. Yet there was also a new form of military movement that appeared in these waters when colonial soldiers went to fight in Europe, undertaking the voyage made by British and French colonial troops, encountered in Chapter 2, in reverse.[6] Like their European counterparts before them, they frequently commented on the Canal passage as the locale of a personal *rite de passage*, but also as the entrance to an embattled Europe. The Canal itself was described not as a road to peace and civilisation but as a highly guarded military sector.[7] Military lazarettos and camps added new and differently organised microcosms to the Canal Zone, complementing the smaller lazarettos of the pre-war period.

The Canal not only housed major hospital facilities catering for wounded soldiers from different war zones, but from 1915 on it was also the site of a refugee camp sheltering Armenians fleeing persecution and genocide in the Ottoman Empire. The camp added a new spatial config-uration to the Canal and is thus worth describing in some detail. Located near Port Fuad (opposite Port Said) and right next to the Shell Oil Company buildings, it was established by the Allied powers in 1915 and drew refugees from all over the Ottoman territories. They stayed in their temporary home in the Canal Zone for significant periods of time before being relocated to different destinations.

---

[3] See, for instance, Löwith, *Reisetagebuch 1936 und 1941*, pp. 19, 31–5; Nizan, *Aden Arabie*, pp. 80–1, 90–2.
[4] Cocteau, *Tour du monde en 80 jours*, pp. 65–6.
[5] Cf. Ruiz, 'Manly Spectacles and Imperial Soldiers in Wartime Egypt'.
[6] See among others Koller, 'The Recruitment of Colonial Troops in Africa and Asia'.
[7] See, for instance, Can and Durrwell, *Carnet de route d'un petit marsouin cochinchinois*, p. 17.

THE GRAPHIC, AUGUST 12, 1916

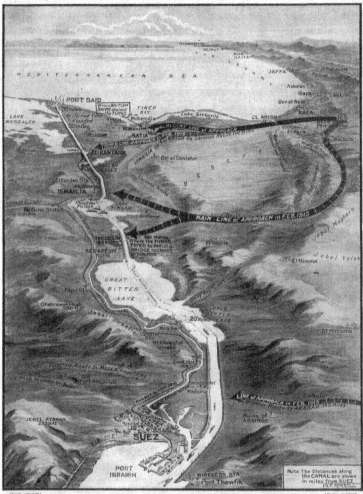

Figure 22 'Turkey in the Toils: Foiled at Suez. The Enemy's Disastrous Attack on the Canal', *The Graphic*, 12 August 1916.

In the immediate aftermath of the war, with famines raging in parts of the Ottoman Empire, an expedition of the American Committee for Relief in the Near East – an organisation also known simply as 'Near East Relief' which was set up with the principal aim of alleviating the suffering of the Armenian people and whose main supporter was the American ambassador to the Ottoman Empire, Henry Morgenthau – travelled to a number of cities, among them Port Said, to survey the situation and to provide photographic documentation for supporters of the humanitarian initiative in the United States.[8] The reports of the committee not only illustrate the religiously charged rhetoric that accompanied humanitarian action aimed at the relief of Christian groups who were discriminated against. The sheltering of refugees also highlighted new domains of international action: the creation of the legal categories of 'refugees' and 'minorities' deserving particular protection was intricately linked to the treaties of Versailles, Paris, Sèvres and Lausanne and more generally to the Wilsonian rhetoric prevalent after the war.

Apart from its humanitarian impetus, international concern also related to attempts to control the diffusion of large groups of people set in motion by the events of the war, mass killings and famines, as well as by the restructuring of territories along national lines. Furthermore

Figure 23 Armenian refugee camp in Port Fouad, opposite Port Said, next to the Shell Oil Company headquarters, no photographer, no date.

[8] For the general context, see Moranian, 'The Armenian Genocide and American Missionary Relief Efforts'.

Figure 24 Armenian Refugee Camp in Port Fouad, opposite Port Said, next to the Shell Oil Company Headquarters, no photographer, no date.

the Armenian refugee camp added a new facet to the Canal: if the sick and invalid soldiers stationed on the Canal's shores during the war had also been residents of the Canal Zone, sometimes for very long periods of time, refugees accommodated in direct proximity to the Canal and waiting for transfer to a safer location extended the limbo state which the Canal had come to symbolise for travellers since the 1870s to years before they were able to move on.

The camp itself, with its moveable tents, was a village caught between a temporary and a permanent existence and presented an altogether new mobile structure in the Canal Zone. Bedouin had, of course, used tents in the region for centuries, but the refugee camp was a very visible rupture with traditional desert mobility. The grid-like arrangement of mass-produced and uniform refugee tents presented a stark contrast to the highly personalised fabrics and the layouts shaped by tribal hierarchies that characterised nomadic encampments.

Beyond its topographic arrangement, the very location of the refugee camp next to the Shell Oil Company headquarters highlights a major shift in the use of the Canal after the First World War. Slowly, oil became the major global commodity transported via the Canal. The first oil tankers were conveyed through the Canal in the late 1890s, but the transportation of crude oil rapidly gained importance after the First World War and developed into an indicator of growing globalisation, which also represented an increasing dependency on certain commodities. Although passenger transportation shifted from the maritime highways to aeroplanes after the Second World War, thus leading to a wholly new set of infrastructural nodal points, the importance of global routes such as the Suez Canal did not diminish, as exemplified by concerns about the blockage of the Canal early in 2011.

While the camp illustrated international involvement in the region, the inter-war years obviously also saw the further institutionalisation of British colonial power in Egypt with, at the same time, continuities in the international organisation both of the Canal itself and of specific issues of mobility control. In the diplomatic realm, the international conferences of the 1920s reflected the intensification of developments that had begun at an earlier stage. Many new conventions built upon earlier internationalist projects, yet they were now often structured through the League of Nations. In 1922, for instance, all member countries of the League of Nations adhered to the 'white slavery convention' and committed themselves to tighter immigration and emigration controls regarding women travelling alone. They pledged to introduce regulations to protect women and children on emigrant ships, at ports of departure and arrival, as well as during the journey, and to put up warning notices in railway stations and in ports.

Yet, 'white slavery' was not the only issue pointing to continuities in the realm of international organisations and meetings. Regarding slave trading in the Red Sea, a new international convention 'with the object of securing the abolition of slavery and the slave trade' was signed by 37 states in 1926.[9] International conventions thus became wider-reaching and more standardised in the League of Nations setting, even if they had predecessors in the late nineteenth and early twentieth centuries. Yet some of the earlier, experimental international institutions were permanently abolished during the war, such as the Slave Trade Bureau in Brussels which had aimed to centrally collect all information regarding the slave trade and ceased operations in 1914.

Whereas the conferences still point to the continuities in the management of movement, on the ground, new techniques were employed and tested that transformed the practicalities of the fight against illicit mobilities. To combat the slave trade in the Red Sea, for instance, air controls and air raids were used for deterrence. From the late 1920s on,

---

[9] International Convention with the Object of Securing the Abolition of Slavery and the Slave Trade, signed at Geneva, 25 September 1926 (British Parliamentary Papers XXVI).

Royal Air Force planes replaced dhows in fighting the slave trade and –
an agreeable side-effect from the perspective of British commanders –
exerting tighter control in the region more generally.[10] On a smaller
scale, yet also representing the more standardised use of a 'modern'
technology, photographs were increasingly deployed to identify pilgrims, pointing yet again to experimentation with new measures and
techniques already prevalent in the field of identification around 1900.

The patterns put into practice between 1869 and 1914 – particularly
the themes of controlled acceleration and deceleration through the bureaucratisation of mobility controls and the distinction between different categories of travel – thus reverberated in many new guises beyond the temporal
limits of the present work. Even if new forms of movement were connected
with the Canal, such as refugee transports and oil tankers, and experiments
were made with new techniques of managing movement, they were clearly
linked to developments that had begun in the period surveyed in the main
corpus of this book.

Global intersections beyond the Suez Canal

Of course, it is worth going not only beyond the period under scrutiny in
this book but also beyond the Suez Canal as a space of intersection, in
order to clarify whether the Canal is unique in laying open the entanglements of imperial and internationalist decision-making characterising
globalisation around 1900, or whether the themes explored in this book
point to broader trends that could also be demonstrated in other localities
around the world. In this way, the analysis of global localities can be
expanded by some further examples.

At the beginning of this book, the reconceptualisation of global space
through technological developments and its resulting acceleration was
described. New infrastructures led to the development of concentrated
points of intersection, where different forms of mobility were interconnected in a particularly closely knit way. In such hubs, but also on board
ships and trains, passengers were grouped together in different classes
and separated from mobile workers, who enabled the transport of the
passengers in the first place; as seen in the example of the Suez Canal,
they were further divided into those who could pass unhindered and
those associated with the transmission of disease or political unrest.
Generally speaking, trains and ships, as well as railway stations and
harbours, were not only 'empires in miniature' as seen in Chapter 3,

---

[10] TNA, AIR 2/775: Prevention of the Slave Trade in the Red Sea – Enquiry re suitable
aircraft for use; see also Satia, 'The Defence of Inhumanity'.

but also became global microcosms of mobility pointing to hierarchies of mobility, attempts to channel and bureaucratise movements as well as to the limits of such attempts.

Mentioned in the introduction, the railway formed the central building block in the late nineteenth-century expansion of mobility. As points of departure and arrival, railway stations gave this development a symbolic form.[11] The author Théophile Gautier called them 'cathedrals of the new humanity'.[12] In striking contrast to earlier, rather functional buildings such as London's King's Cross station (construction 1851–52), the metaphorical use of this term gained literal form in railway stations such as St Pancras adjacent to King's Cross (1863–68) or Antwerp-Central (1895–1905), whose architecture borrowed explicitly from that of cathedrals. In colonial contexts, railway stations also formed central locations in newly built or redeveloped cities. The grand Victoria Terminus, now Chhatrapati Shivaji Terminus, in Mumbai, completed in 1888, exemplifies both the representative function of these buildings and the synthesis of different meanings in a particularly arresting way. In this case, it was not primarily elements of church architecture, which had become so prevalent in the style of the Victorian Gothic reaching its apogee in London's St Pancras station, but rather regional elements of Mughal architecture that were quoted.[13] Building styles of 'motherland' and colony were thus mixed in the very edifices where their populations met.

Yet, if railway stations celebrated acceleration through technological progress and the synthesis of different styles, their architecture also made the segregation of passengers into different 'classes' of mobility particularly palpable. Not only the trains themselves were organised according to different classes, with Indian trains being separated into as many as eight classes. Waiting halls were also divided according to different categories, all services were clearly kept apart and certain entrances reserved for specific travellers only. The separation between different forms of mobility thus took its most overt architectural form and became tangible in railway stations.

Just like railway stations, harbours were central intersections which also pointed to the division of different mobilities. The order and hierarchy of the ship stood in opposition to the lack of restraint encountered in the harbour, which had to be governed, regulated and policed by bureaucratic institutions. At the same time, buzzing harbours saw the development of exclusive spaces. Reserved for western travellers and established in a

---

[11] Still the best survey: Richards and MacKenzie, *The Railway Station*.
[12] Quoted in Dethier (ed.), *All Stations*, p. 6.
[13] See Metcalf, *An Imperial Vision*, pp. 92–4; Mackenzie, 'Points of Entry', 60–1.

standardised fashion almost everywhere around the globe, the premises of the British company Thomas Cook mentioned earlier could be seen as predecessors of today's VIP lounges. On the premises of this 'global player', where western passengers could collect mail and send telegrams, the connection to faraway Europe was stressed simultaneously providing protection against the location where they had landed – the port through which a uniformed employee of Thomas Cook ushered the arriving Europeans as quickly as possible. The spread of global brands that introduced international norms became most visible here, turning Port Said into just one nodal point in a global web, sharing, of course, many similarities with other such nodes.

While Thomas Cook offices provided privileged western passengers a safe space in the potentially unruly harbour setting, other 'ordering' institutions in harbours, such as – most iconically – Ellis Island, were paradigmatic for the border regimes developing in an era of faster mobility.[14] Seat of the immigration offices of New York from 1892 on and particularly concerned with regulating migration and preventing the import of contagious disease into the North American mainland, it shaped the immigration experience of millions. In the context of tighter entry controls from the 1880s on, immigrants were subjected to reading and writing tests, but also various health checks and questions regarding their political background. All in all, this procedure could take several days to complete. Slowly, immigration laws targeted more and more groups whose voyage to the United States was cut short at Ellis Island. Other immigrants tried to circumvent this threshold by accepting, for instance, an arranged marriage with someone already residing in the United States. Through these measures, Ellis Island signified the diversification, classification and registration of travellers. At the same time, control stations such as Ellis Island led to a slowing down of movement or, worse, its standstill or reversal, putting into question the concept of acceleration around 1900. Designed to hold 500,000 people, Ellis Island sometimes housed almost double that number and thus resembled a huge quarantine station with all the connected problems described in preceding chapters.

Of course there were spaces that showed even greater structural similarities to the Suez Canal than Ellis Island, which was, after all, an entrance rather than a passageway. Here, the Panama Canal, completed under the aegis of US military forces in 1914, immediately comes to mind. There are many parallels between the two large-scale building projects, not least the involvement of entrepreneur Ferdinand de Lesseps himself,

---

[14] See, for instance, Kraut, 'Proper Precautions', pp. 50–77; Cannato, *American Passage*.

who wanted to build on his successes at Suez by cutting the Isthmus of Panama as well, yet failed spectacularly. Another parallel is the sometimes difficult organisation of a large and international labour force or the attempt to replace workers with up-to-date technology.[15] Furthermore, both building sites had to fight against epidemic disease, although the perils of yellow fever proved even more difficult to overcome than the outbreak of cholera during the construction of the Suez Canal.[16] The sheer virulence of disease outbreaks and the number of fatalities during construction point to differences between the two building sites, as does the respective desert and jungle environments or the technological challenge of building huge locks in order to bridge the two seas.[17] There were, of course, also differences in the self-images that France, Great Britain and the US connected with their respective building projects during the periods of their creation.[18] What is more, the Suez Canal's central geographical position between the three continents of Europe, Asia and Africa was of course not replicated by the Panama Canal, while the Latin American position of the latter made for its own complications. This difference in location meant that, after its opening, the Panama Canal – even if perhaps the more spectacular building project – did not foster the variety of border metaphors or the array of different mobilities we encountered in the preceding chapters in relation to the Suez Canal.

Alongside newly constructed narrows, other places that funnelled mobility were located on natural narrows such as Tangier and Gibraltar. Often such narrows were equally perceived as unruly transitional places belonging to several worlds at once. This becomes particularly obvious in the case of Tangier – between 1923 and 1956 an international zone and famous for its extravagant literary life attracting a large number of European and American writers in the decades after the Second World War. Gibraltar on the other side of the Mediterranean boasted quite a different political setting with Britain forcefully asserting its hegemony over this strategic location. In the case of the port city of Aden, close to Bab al-Mandab, the point connecting the Red Sea and the Indian Ocean and mentioned on several occasions throughout this book, similar controls on seamen, prostitutes and coal heavers were exercised as in Port Said. As has been seen in various chapters, such comparisons were also explicitly drawn at the time when it came to experimentation with tighter controls.

---

[15] Greene, 'Spaniards on the Silver Roll' and *The Canal Builders*.
[16] Harrison, *Contagion*, pp. 130–8.
[17] Tenner, 'Digging Across Panama'; with an equally heroic impetus Parker, *Panama Fever*.
[18] See Missal, *Seaway to the Future*.

This potpourri of localities shows that the Suez Canal example touches upon more general worldwide trends and developments that can also be demonstrated elsewhere on the globe during different periods of globalisation. Yet the preceding examples also make clear that they all only share aspects with the Suez Canal, such as the unruliness of port towns, the iconic status of railway stations as symbols for the 'shrinking of the globe', the function of Ellis Island as a disease sluice gate, the international organisation of extraterritorial locations such as Tangier, the workers' organisation at Panama, or the strategic military concerns concentrated at Gibraltar. The juxtaposition of these different themes in one single location makes the Canal a particularly striking example for displaying a whole panorama of mobility in order to highlight the intricacies and paradoxes of globalisation.

Channelling mobilities

Seen from this larger-scale perspective – both temporally and spatially – the multifarious movements and meanderings traced throughout this book come together in six points of intersection resonating beyond the spatial junction of the Suez Canal:

(1) The Suez Canal is often mentioned in passing as one of the infrastructural *tours de force* that were indispensable to the 'great acceleration' of the late nineteenth century. Yet a closer analysis of the Canal Zone, and the flows of goods and people through it, shows that it is essential to speak of *mobilities* in the plural.[19] Even if various travel descriptions testify to a homogenisation of perceptions and metaphors, they cover the experiences of a specific (and privileged) group of travellers only. At the same time, the different modes of movement that converged in the single space of the Suez Canal – steamships, dhows and camels, to mention but a few – are obvious. Yet even on the steamship itself, there were distinct groups of travellers whose movements were structured by highly diverse motivations and destinations. Imperial infrastructure entailed more than just the repartitioning of troops and officials across the globe; it depended on a wealth of movements, as the survey of the labour circuits connected to the Canal system illustrates. This wealth of movements was categorised, however, with particularly salient distinctions between the experience of legal and illegal and voluntary and forced mobility. The period under survey saw all kinds of illicit

---

[19] See Huber, 'Multiple Mobilities'.

movements and, as a reaction to such incidents (when they came to light), forced mobility in the form of expulsion, deportation and repatriation. Even though many passengers tended to either ignore these various movements, or to shift them into the realm of the 'picturesque', it is crucial to differentiate between these mobilities, their experiences and implications, in order to get a more complete idea of what the changes during this period, due to faster means of transportation, actually entailed.

(2) None of the mobilities mentioned above remained untouched by the opening of the Canal. For all those channelled through the Canal, it was not only a geographical space of simultaneity but also a social space of encounter or mutual observation and, at times, of personal transformation. The global shortcut through Suez measurably abridged the journey between Europe and Asia, while the actual passage through the bottleneck was often perceived to be paradoxically slow. It is therefore useful to speak of simultaneous *accelerations and decelerations*. It was not only steam transportation that played a part in the accelerations – as the new and faster steamship mobility could at times be slowed down in spaces such as the Suez Canal, camels or dhows could prove more rapid and effective, when either the provision of food and material to the building sites, or the control of the bays of the Red Sea or of the desert on the Canal's shores, were at stake. In these cases western powers and the Suez Canal Company crucially depended on taking recourse to mobilities otherwise branded 'traditional', and therefore on cooperation with local agents. Decelerations, on the other hand, could go as far as preventing movement altogether. In the case of stowaways, for instance, the Suez Canal became a location of standstill and non-mobility. A device that accelerated movement could thus simultaneously disable movement in other ways.

(3) These accelerations and decelerations not only changed the perception of space and spatial configurations, they also carried political implications. The *tension between openness and control*, between a world of free and unhindered mobility and one marked by checks and containment, emerged as a central theme of the period. This tension figured particularly clearly in global hubs and chokepoints, such as the Suez Canal and its port cities. Many have described the time before the First World War as a phase of remarkable freedom of movement. Yet while rapidity of communication was crucial not only to colonial rule and imperial ventures but also to the commercial undertakings that accompanied them, some of its implications, such as the transmission of contagious diseases, the spread of political ideas and the flourishing of international circuits of crime, ran counter to all

positive associations. The passport-free travel of the *belle époque* rings true in terms of certain privileged travellers, yet as soon as more varied groups come into the picture, the map of borderless travel becomes more fragmented, with places such as the Suez Canal forming interstices or semi-permeable membranes through which mobility was filtered.

(4) In the travelogues of the period, the distinction between two facets of mobility – on the one hand a symbol of Western modernity, on the other being difficult to control or even a sign of backwardness (as in the case of Bedouin and pilgrims, for instance) – emerges time and time again. Yet the ambivalent stance towards acceleration, which was perceived as being both positive and risky, was reflected not only in travel descriptions of the time but also in *global rulemaking and rulebreaking*. The Suez Canal became a location for experimentation in the global management of mobility connected with increasing regulations and surveillance. This experimentation accounted for the proliferation of identification measures based on bureaucratic paperwork, including physical characterisations, photographs, passports, fingerprints and the singling-out of specific risk groups. The identificatory regulations were paralleled by the testing of various forms of scientific disease control, such as vaccination, disinfection, fumigation and isolation. The Suez Canal, as a space of experimentation in the realms of science, information management and identification, did not form a secluded and controllable laboratory, however, as it was exposed to a great many unpredictable influences. Not only was the application and creation of rules in the Suez Canal Zone marked by a high degree of improvisation, but as a space of transition it was necessarily and constantly being shaped by its openness and by the repercussions of external events. What is more, there was also experimentation with forms of resistance to the new bureaucratic control measures, for instance by playing with different identities or names. Standardisation was thus immediately followed by evasions of different sorts.

(5) The survey of this experimentation with the 'rules of globalisation' also sheds light on the *relationship between the global and the local* as well as *between the global and the individual* during an earlier phase of worldwide interconnectedness. It points to different spatial configurations and different geographies of the global, with the Canal functioning simultaneously as a magnet, a sluice gate and a semi-permeable membrane or boundary. The book brings to the fore different global localities one level below the Canal, such as the lazarettos, the harbour towns and the steamships. What is more,

it provides a wealth of global biographies of workers and stowaways and thus personalises processes that are often mentioned without reference to specific individuals or life stories. In this way, it can be shown that globalisation did not simply happen but was made by a wealth of agents, such as middlemen who were crucially necessary to bind together the global and the local. Highlighting the interplay between different levels of analysis, the book also points to different meanings of the global (and of globalisation more specifically) – whether related to ideas, perceptions, economics, work relations or something else. It does so in three ways. For one, the Canal was a place where different phenomena of a global scale were bundled together, where different global principles competed and where different meanings of the global coincided. These meanings oscillated between the universalist aspirations formulated in the context of the Canal's creation and imperial claims connected to the control of the Canal at times of war and peace, but also, for example, to the movement of pilgrims. Secondly, the survey of 'global localities' or 'global microcosms' offered on several occasions throughout the book points to different ways in which such a globality could play out locally. The study of a nodal point such as the Suez Canal, thirdly qualifies the simple opposition of the global and the local that is stressed in many works of globalisation studies and uncovers all the scales of rulemaking between the two, whether regional, imperial, inter-imperial or international. In each case it also points to the limits of such rulemaking because the interaction between these levels was far from unproblematic. One and the same rule often travelled down through many levels, frequently changing quite significantly on the way to implementation. The management of mobility thus appears as an activity that covered all echelons, from small-scale experimentation and cooperation with local actors, to international and inter-imperial negotiation.

(6) The Suez Canal was not only a place where imperial interests converged and were concentrated before their dispersal. The bottleneck of the Canal also funnelled and compressed different mobilities. Through the experimentation with different control measures, the Suez Canal emerged as a space of *channelling* in the truest sense of the word, making mobility controllable yet at the same time allowing it to run without any disruption or delay. However, even away from the space of the Canal, the period around 1900 appears as a phase that opened up and accelerated specific transits and trajectories, coupled with the attempt to control and clamp down on others. Globalisation between 1869 and 1914 was marked by an increasing propensity, not

always successful of course, to control certain individuals and groups while facilitating other movements necessary for colonial endeavours, commerce and war. A similar process can be detected at the level of perceptions and travel descriptions where the authors increasingly fit the other mobilities they encountered into preconceived images and expressions. Therefore, in connection with the time line suggested at the beginning of this conclusion, the period between 1869 and 1914 can be described as a period of standardisation not only of the new Canal system but also of the wider process of channelling global mobilities.

Bibliography

ARCHIVAL SOURCES

EGYPT

Cairo: Dār al-Wathā'iq al-Qawmiyya (Egyptian National Archives)
Majlis al-Wuzarā', Qanāt al-Suways
2, 5
Majlis al-Wuzarā', Niẓārat al-Dākhiliyya
2/4 Maṣlaḥat al-Ṣaḥa al-ʿUmūmiyya: al-Kwarantīnāt, 2/11/ⁱ Maṣlaḥat al-
Ṣaḥa al-ʿUmūmiyya wa-l-Awbiʾa: al-Ṭāʿūn, 2/11/ᴖ Maṣlaḥat al-Ṣaḥa al-
ʿUmūmiyya wa-l-Awbiʾa: al-Kūlīrā, 18/ ⁱal-Hajj wa'l-Maḥmal al-Sharīf,
18/ᴖ al-Hajj wa'l-Maḥmal al-Sharīf
Majlis al-Wuzarā', Niẓārat al-Harbiyya
8 ʿUrbān, 12 Jazīrat Sinā'
ʿĀbdīn
243 Qanāt al-Suways, 546 al-Tamāsāt al-Hajj, 547 al-Tamāsāt al-Hajj

FRANCE

Aix-en-Provence: Archives Nationales d'Outre-Mer
Gouvernement Général Algérie (GGA) 16H: Questions religieuses
83, 84, 85, 86, 87, 88, 89
Gouvernement Général Indochine (GGI)
14212, 14277
Affaires politiques (Ministère des Colonies) (Maroc)
967

Le Havre: Association French Lines
1997/002/3600 Livre professionel du marin
1997/002/4455 Rapports d'activité de l'agence des Messageries Maritimes de
Port Said
1997/002/4474 Rapports d'activité de l'agence des Messageries Maritimes de
Suez
1997/002/5032 Messageries Maritimes, *Au delà de Suez: Itinéraires et Tarifs Nos 1
à 33*, 1862 à 1882

Marseilles: Chambre de Commerce et d'Industrie Marseille-Provence
MR 4481: Navigation Maritime
Messageries Maritimes (Rapports de Voyages)
    241 Guadiana (1888–1907), 302 Laos (1897–1907), 362 Meï-Kong
    (1871–1876)
HdC: Histoire des Compagnies de Navigation
    157 Compagnie Cyprien Fabre 1881–1919

Nantes: Centre des Archives Diplomatiques de Nantes
Le Caire
    232, 277, 283, 284, 285, 427, 428, 441, 485
Port Said
    16, 17, 38, 47, 48, 57, 62, 82, 85, 103, 108, 120, 123, 124, 125, 155, 252, 260
Commission interministérielle des affaires musulmanes vol. 1, May 1911–Jan. 1916

Paris: Archives du Ministère des Affaires Etrangères Quai d'Orsay
Affaires Diverses Politiques 1815–1896, Tome IV, Egypte
    6, 7, 19, 20, 21, 24
Correspondance Politique et Commerciale Nouvelle Série 1897–1918, Egypte
    37, 38, 40, 110
Mémoires et Documents, Egypte
    15 (Canal de Suez 3), 16 (Canal de Suez 4), 17 (Canal de Suez 5)

Paris: Service Historique de la Défense, Château de Vincennes
Département de la Marine BB4 Campagnes
    1017, 1036, 1048, 1448, 1492

Roubaix: Archives Nationales du Monde du Travail
1995060: Compagnie universelle du canal maritime de Suez
    0159, 0941, 1026, 1027, 1028, 1031, 1046, 1121, 1418, 1419, 1420,
    1421, 1422, 1423, 1425, 1476, 1477, 1478, 1491, 1492, 1524, 1746,
    1747, 3601, 3602, 3603, 4904, 4906, 4907, 4993
2000038: Compagnie universelle du canal maritime de Suez
    0201, 0215, 0360

GERMANY

Berlin: Bundesarchiv
*R/901/75677: Auswärtiges Amt II Akten betreffend die Vermessung der Seeschiffe für
die Fahrt durch den Suezkanal*
    Band 1 Schiffahrt Nr. 129
R/901/77477: Auswärtiges Amt II Akten betreffend: den Suez-Kanal
    Band 42

Berlin: Geheimes Staatsarchiv Preußischer Kulturbesitz
I. HA Rep 89: Geheimes Zivilkabinett jüngere Periode
    13351

I. HA Rep 120: Ministerium für Handel und Gewerbe
A IX Nr. 23 Bd 12–16 Vermessung der Seeschiffe, 1873–1886

GREAT BRITAIN

Greenwich: Caird Library
P&O Archives
17/1&3, 50/4
HTN/230 Hamilton, Sir Louis Henry Keppel, Admiral, 1892–1957
JOD/103: Diary kept in HMS Royal Arthur, 1–15 Nov. 1911, on a voyage from
   Portsmouth to Port Said
MSS/85/007: Compagnie universelle du canal maritime de Suez. *Exploitation.*
   Règlement de Navigation. Annexe pour les Navires chargés de pétrol en vrac.
   Edition d'Avril 1907
MSS/88/012.3: Port Said, Patrol Duties, Journal kept by R. Sparrow from 1914
   to 1916

London: British Library, Oriental and India Office Collections

Mss: Manuscripts
Eur/F111 Curzon Collection
Eur/B235 Memoirs of Colonel Ross
Eur/C739 John Wilberforce Cassels
Eur/D604 Suez Canal Memoranda
Eur/F177 Emily Overend Lorimer Collection
Eur/F197 Younghusband Collection

IOR: India Office Records
L/MIL: India Office Military Department Records
   5/536, 7/5636, 17/4/563
L/PJ: Public and Judicial Department Records
   6/356, 6/194, 6/339, 6/382, 6/721, 6/772, 6/745, 6/777, 6/867, 6/903,
   6/907
L/PO/4/7: Unveiling of Indian War Memorial at Port Tewfik, Egypt
L/PS: Political and Secret Department
   11/30
R/20: Records of the British Administration in Aden
   A: 724, 1284, 1497, 2212, 2379, 2422, 2583
   E: 164

London: The National Archives
ADM 116: Admiralty: Record Office: Cases
   72
AIR 2: Air Ministry and Ministry of Defence: Registered Files
   775
BT 15: Board of Trade: Finance Department: Registered Files
   62

FO 2: *Foreign Office: Political and Other Departments: General Correspondence before 1906, Africa*
376
FO 2: *Foreign Office: Political and Other Departments: General Correspondence before 1906, Africa*
232
FO 78: *Foreign Office: General Correspondence before 1906, Ottoman Empire*
2188, 2233, 2288, 2409, 2509, 2632, 2639, 2863, 3011, 3334, 3462, 3467, 3586, 3702, 3830, 3831, 3957, 4064, 4154, 4250, 4317, 4330, 4394, 4461, 4521, 4583, 4675, 4963, 5036, 5165, 5238, 5308, 5327, 5372, 5436
FO 93: *Foreign Office and Foreign and Commonwealth Office: Protocols of Treaties*
11/60
FO 141: *Foreign Office and Foreign and Commonwealth Office: Embassy and Consulates, Egypt: General Correspondence*
69, 470, 571
FO 423: *Foreign Office: Confidential Print Suez Canal*
13, 14, 15
FO 541: *Foreign Office: Confidential Print Slave Trade*
24
FO 655: *Chief Clerk's Department and Passport Office: Collection of Passports 1802–1961*
596
FO 846: *Foreign Office: Consulate, Port Said, Egypt: Consular Court Records*
3, 4, 5
FO 881: *Foreign Office: Confidential Print (Numerical Series)*
3082, 3306, 3342, 3369, 3522, 3829, 4337, 4584, 4619, 4762
MT 9: *Board of Trade and Ministry of Transport and successors: Marine, Harbours and Wrecks*
71, 432, 708, 721
MT 10: *Board of Trade Harbour Department: Correspondence and Papers*
1024
MT 23: *Admiralty, Transport Department: Correspondence and Papers*
25, 26, 27, 41, 44, 45, 48, 52, 78, 153, 203, 232, 539
PRO: *Domestic Records of PRO*
30/29/295 Egypt: Quarantine Suez Canal, 1880–1884
T 1: *Treasure Board Papers and In-Letters*
1203
WO 95: *War Office: First World War and Army of Occupation War Diaries*
4360, 4417

London: Women's Library
Philippa Strachey
Eliza Tabor
Ligue Internationale pour la Répression de la Traite des Blanches à Port Said

UNITED STATES OF AMERICA

Cambridge MA: Fine Arts' Library Harvard
Harvard Semitic Museum Photographic Archives General,
    EgA I-VI, EgP XV
Harvard Film Studies Collection (HFSC), Middle East
    Box 1, 6
Near Eastern Relief Collection (NERC), Negatives and Prints II Palestine &
    Egypt.
Harvard Semitic Museum, HSM.83:005:005/AKP 128.13: La Construction
    du Canal de Suez, 1859–1869, Vues retrospectives (bound volume, Paris:
    Union Graphique, no year)
Photographs collected during the Royal Trip to India y E. G. H. HMS Serapis
    1875–6
Isaac Béhar, Souvenir de Port Said (booklet with postcards)

COLLECTIONS OF ARCHIVAL MATERIAL

A. L. P. Burdett (ed.), *The Slave Trade into Arabia 1820–1973* (Chippenham: The
Archives Editions, 2006), vols. 1–5

PRINTED SOURCES AND CONTEMPORARY
LITERATURE

OFFICIAL DOCUMENTS, CONFERENCE PROCEEDINGS AND SUEZ
CANAL COMPANY PUBLICATIONS (IN CHRONOLOGICAL ORDER)

Firmāns of 1854 and 1856, convention between the Egyptian government and the
    Suez Canal Company of 1866 in Boutros Boutros-Ghali and Youssef Chlala,
    Le canal de Suez 1854–1957 (Alexandria: Imprimerie al-Bassir, 1958),
    pp. 2–3, 4–7, 10–14.
Compagnie universelle du canal maritime de Suez, *Exploitation, transit des navires,*
    règlement de navigation etc. (1870).
Compagnie universelle du canal maritime de Suez, *Rapport à la commission*
    d'enquête sur la perception du droit de passage des navires traversant le canal
    (Paris, no date, probably 1871).
A Bill intituled an Act to amend the Law with respect to Fugitive Offenders in Her
    Majesty's Dominions, and for other Purposes connected with the Trial of
    Offenders (British Parliamentary Papers 1881, vol. V).
Archives diplomatiques: Recueil mensuel international de diplomatie et d'his-
    toire, Deuxième Série, Tome 14, Avril, Mai, Juin 1885 (Paris: Féchoz, 1885).
Correspondence with British Representatives and Agents Abroad, and Reports
    from Naval Officers and the Treasury, relative to the Slave Trade: 1884–85
    (British Parliamentary Papers 1884–85, vol. LXXIII).
Papers relating to the Arrangements made with Messrs. Cook & Son for the
    Conduct of the Pilgrim Traffic to and from the Red Sea. During the Years
    1884–1895 (Calcutta: Office of the Superintendent of the Government
    Printing, India, 1896).

Correspondence respecting Slavery in Egypt (British Parliamentary Papers 1887, vol. XCII).

Convention of 1888, in Boutros Boutros-Ghali and Youssef Chlala, *Le canal de Suez* 1854–1957 (Alexandria: Imprimerie al-Bassir, 1958), pp. 16–19.

General Act of the Brussels Conference 1889–90; with annexed declaration (British Parliamentary Papers 1890, vol. L).

Protocoles et procès-verbaux de la Conférence sanitaire internationale de Venise inaugurée le 5 janvier 1892 (Rome, 1892).

Conférence sanitaire internationale de Paris (Paris, 1894).

Convention between Great Britain and Egypt for the Suppression of Slavery and the Slave Trade, signed at Cairo, 21 November 1895 (British Parliamentary Papers 1896, vol. XCVII).

Compagnie universelle du canal maritime de Suez, *Assemblée générale des actionnaires, 46e Réunion 7 Juin 1900: Rapport présenté au nom du conseil d'administration par le Prince Auguste d'Arenberg* (Président) (Paris: Société anonyme de publications périodiques, P. Mouillot, 1900).

Correspondence respecting the International Conference on the 'White Slave Traffic', held in Paris, July 1902 (British Parliamentary Papers 1905, vol. CIII).

Compagnie universelle du canal maritime de Suez, *Accident du 'Chatham'*, September 1905.

Correspondence respecting the International Conference on the White Slave Traffic, held in Paris, October 1906 (British Parliamentary Papers 1907, vol. C).

Assemblée générale des actionnaires. 54e Réunion–2 Juin 1908. Rapport présenté au nom du conseil d'administration par le Prince Auguste d'Arenberg, Président.

Correspondence respecting the Fourth International Congress on the White Slave Traffic, held in Madrid, October 1910 (British Parliamentary Papers 1911, vol. LXIII).

Correspondence respecting the International Conferences on Obscene Publications and the 'White Slave Traffic', held in Paris, April and May 1910 (British Parliamentary Papers 1912–1913, vol. LXVIII).

International Convention for the Suppression of the White Slave Traffic, signed at Paris, 4 May 1910 (British Parliamentary Papers 1912–13, vol. CXXI).

General Instructions for Pilgrims to the Hedjaz and a Manual for the Guidance of Officers and Others Concerned in the Red Sea Pilgrim Traffic (Calcutta, 1911 and 1922).

A Bill to Enable the Fugitive Offenders' Act, 1881, to be Extended to Protected States (British Parliamentary Papers 1914–16, vol. I).

International Convention for the Suppression of the Traffic in Women and Children opened for Signature at Geneva from 30 September 1921, to 31 March 1922 (British Parliamentary Papers 1923, vol. XXIV).

International Convention with the Object of Securing the Abolition of Slavery and the Slave Trade, signed at Geneva, 25 September 1926 (British Parliamentary Papers, vol. XXVI).

Le canal maritime de Suez: Note, tableaux et planches (Ismailia, no year).

NEWSPAPER AND JOURNAL ARTICLES (IN CHRONOLOGICAL ORDER)

'Steam-Navigation to India', *The Times*, 13 August 1834, p. 5, col. E.

'Egypt', *Asiatic Journal and Monthly Register for British and Foreign India, China and Australasia*, vol. 15 (London: Parbury, Allen & Co, 1834).

'Three New Routes to India', *North American Review* 172 (1856).

The Illustrated London News 55/1567, 20 November 1869; 55/1570, 11 December 1869; 55/1571, 18 December 1869.

'Session 1869–70. Fourth Meeting 10th January 1870', *Proceedings of the Royal Geographical Society*, vol. XIV, no. 1, pp. 88–105.

'La communication electrique entre l'Inde et l'Europe', *Le canal de Suez: Journal maritime et commerciale*, 15 April 1870.

'Le consulat français à Port-Said', *Le canal de Suez: Journal maritime et commerciale*, 6 June 1870.

'Les États-Unis d'Amérique et le canal de Suez', *Le canal de Suez: Journal maritime et commerciale*, 10 March 1871.

'Commerce de la Cochinchine – Riz de Saïgon', *Le canal de Suez: Journal décadaire de la Compagnie universelle du canal maritime de Suez*, 24–26 August 1871.

'Le trafic du thé par le canal', *Le canal de Suez: Journal décadaire de la Compagnie universelle du canal maritime de Suez*, 24–26 August 1871.

'Les cotons de l'Inde et le canal de Suez', *Le canal de Suez: Journal décadaire de la Compagnie universelle du canal maritime de Suez*, 31 August 1871.

'La vapeur, la voile, et le canal de Suez', *Le canal de Suez: Journal maritime et commercial*, 14 September 1871.

'Le progrès dans les Indes', *Le canal de Suez: Journal maritime et commercial*, 21 September 1871.

'La civilisation au Japon', *Le canal de Suez: Journal maritime et commercial*, 26 September 1871.

'Le golfe Persique', *Le canal de Suez: Journal maritime et commercial*, 26 October 1871.

'Les derniers soupirs de la voile militaire', *Le canal de Suez: Journal maritime et commercial*, 7 December 1871.

'Séance du 2 février 1877', *Bulletin trimestriel de la Société khédiviale de géographie du Caire, Fascicule 4: Compte rendu des séances de la Société de la géographie.*

'An Appalling Disaster: A Steam-Ship Founders at Sea, and over 900 Persons Perish', *New York Times*, 11 August 1880.

'Les quarantaines. Académie des sciences, séance du lundi 20 mars 1882, Note de M. Ferdinand de Lesseps sur les quarantaines imposes à Suez aux provenances maritimes de l'Extrême-Orient', *Le canal de Suez: Bulletin décadaire*, 12 May 1889.

'Where Port Said's Stones Come From: The Ruin of Famagusta', *Egyptian Gazette*, 10 January 1900.

'The Pilgrimage', *Egyptian Gazette*, 21 February 1900.

'Notes from Mecca', *Egyptian Gazette*, 6 March 1900.

'The Wreck of the Chatham', *The Times*, 25 September 1905, p. 10.

'The Suez Canal: The Chatham Blown Up', *The Times*, 29 September 1905, p. 4.

'The Suez Canal: The Blowing Up of the Chatham', *The Times*, 30 September 1905, p. 5.

'1882: Souvenirs d'un Port-Saïdien', *Revue internationale d'Egypte* II/1 (September 1905).

PUBLISHED SOURCES AND CONTEMPORARY LITERATURE

Annuaire général de l'Indochine 1909 (Hanoi-Haiphong: Imprimerie d'Extrême-Orient, 1909).

Aubert-Roche, L., *Rapport sur l'état sanitaire des travailleurs et des établissements du canal maritime de l'isthme de Suez du 1er juin 1867 au 1er mai 1868* (Paris: Imprimerie centrale des chemins de fer, 1868).

Aubin, Eugène, *Les Anglais aux Indes et en Egypte* (Paris: Armand Colin et Cie, 1899).

Karl Baedeker, *Egypt and the Sudan: Handbook for Travellers* (Leipzig: Karl Baedeker, 1908).

Egypt and the Sudan: Handbook for Travellers (7th revised edn, Leipzig: Karl Baedeker Publisher, London: T Fisher, New York: Charles Scribner's Sons, 1914).

Egypt: Handbook for Travellers (Leipzig: Karl Baedeker, London: Dulau and Co., 1878).

Egypt: Handbook for Travellers (Leipzig: Karl Baedeker, 1898).

Egypt: Handbook for Travellers (5th revised edn, Leipzig: Karl Baedeker, New York: Charles Scribner's Sons, 1902).

Egypt: Handbook for Travellers. Part First: Lower Egypt, with the Fayûm and the Peninsula of Sinai (2nd edn, London: Dulau and Co., 1885).

Egypt: Handbook for Travellers, vol. 1: Lower Egypt and the Peninsula of Sinai (Leipzig: Karl Baedeker, 1895).

Baijnath, Lala, *England and India: Being Impressions of Persons and Things, English and Indian, and Brief Notes of Visits to France, Switzerland, Italy, and Ceylon* (Bombay: J. B. Karani, 1893).

Barrows, John Henry, *A World-Pilgrimage* (Chicago: A. C. McClurg & Company, 1897).

Beauregard, Réveillé de, *Notice historique et statistique sur l'epidémie du choléra en Egypte en 1865* (Marseilles: Typographie et Lithographie Cayer et Cie, 1878).

Berchère, N., *Le desert de Suez: Cinq mois dans l'isthme* (Paris: Collection Hetzel, 1863).

Berlioux, Étienne-Félix, *La traite orientale: Histoire des chasses à l'homme organisées en Afrique depuis quinze ans pour les marchés de l'Orient* (Paris: Librairie de Guillaumin et Cie, 1870).

Bernard, H. and Tissot, E., *Itinéraires pour l'isthme de Suez et les grandes villes d'Egypte: Navigation, chemins de fer, hôtels, monuments et lieux célèbres, calendrier, poids et mesures, vocabulaire français-égyptien, etc.* (Paris: Maisonneuve et Cie, Librairie-Editeurs, 1869).

Beylié (Général de), *Journal de voyage en Orient et en Extrême Orient* (Paris: Henri Charles-Lavauzelle, 1908).

Binger (Capitaine), *Esclavage: Islamisme et Christianisme* (Paris: Société d'éditions scientifiques, 1891).

Boniteau Bey, Maurice, 'Le pèlerinage à la Mecque et les campements quarantenaires', *Bulletin de la société khediviale de géographie* V/11 (Cairo: Imprimerie Nationale, 1901), pp. 647–67.

Bonnetain, Paul, *Au Tonkin* (Paris: Victor-Havard, 1885).

Borde, Paul, *L'isthme de Suez* (Paris: E. Lachaud, 1870).

Borel, T., *The White Slavery of Europe. With Supplement Relating to the Foreign Traffic in English, Scotch and Irish Girls* (London: Dyer Brothers, 1880).

Bourde, Paul, *De Paris au Tonkin* (Paris: Calmann Lévy, 1885).

Bourdon, Claude, 'Les "routes anciennes et les pistes" dans l'isthme de Suez (région entre la rive ouest du grand lac amer et Suez)', *Bulletin de l'Institut d'Egypte* Tome IX, Session 1926/27 (Le Caire: Imprimerie de l'Institut Français d'Archéologie Orientale, 1927), pp. 93–104.

Bousquet, Georges, *Le Japon de nos jours et les échelles de l'Extrême Orient* (Paris: Librairie Hachette et Cie, 1877).

Brieux, Eugène, *Voyage aux Indes et en Indo-Chine: Simple notes d'un touriste* (Paris: Librairie Ch. Delagrave, 1910).

Budde, E., *Erfahrungen eines Hadschi* (Leipzig: Fr. Wilh. Grunow, 1888).

Burton, Isabel, *A. E. I. Arabia Egypt India: A Narrative of Travel* (London/Belfast: William Mullan and Son, 1879).

Burton, Richard, *Sir Richard Burton's Travels in Arabia and Africa: Four Lectures from a Huntington Library Manuscript* (San Marino: Huntington Library, 1990).

Caddick, Helen, *Travel Diaries of Helen Caddick, 1889–1914, volume 1: Palestine & Egypt, 1889* (held by Birmingham Central Library, accessed on *Empire Online*, 11 February 2013).

Cameron, D. A., *Egypt in the Nineteenth Century or Mehemet Ali and His Successors until the British Occupation in 1882* (London: Smith, Elder & Co, 1898).

Can, François-Bertrand and Durrwell, George, *Carnet de route d'un petit marsouin cochinchinois: Impressions et souvenirs de la Grande Guerre* (Saigon: Imprimerie Albert Portail, 1916).

Capper, James Esq., *Observations on the Passage to India, Through Egypt. Also by Vienna through Constantinople to Aleppo, and from thence by Bagdad, and directly across the Great Desert, to Bassora. With Occasional Remarks on the Adjacent Countries, an Account of the Different Stages and Sketches of the Several Routes on Four Copper Plates* (London: Printed for W. Faden, Geographer to the King, Charing Cross, J. Robson, in New Bond Street, and R. Sewell, in Cornhill, 1785).

Carnegie, Andrew, *Round the World* (Garden City: Doubleday, Doran & Company, 1933).

Carré, Jean-Marie, *Promenades dans trois continents* (Paris: Éditions du Courrier Politique, Littéraire et Social, 1935).

Carruthers, Douglas, *The Desert Route in India being the Journal of Four Travellers by the Great Desert Caravan Route between Aleppo and Basra 1745–1751* (London: printed for the Hakluyt Society, 1929).

Castro, S. V. de, *Cholera in Egitto nel 1883: Sua Origine e Misure Igieniche e Quarantenarie con tavole grafiche* (Milan: Casa Editrice Dottor Francesco Vallardi, 1884).

Chafik Bey, Ahmed, *L'esclavage au point de vue Musulman. Communication faite à la Société khédiviale de Géographie dans ses séances des 26 novembre 1890 et 30 janvier 1891* (Cairo: Imprimerie Misr, 1938).

Chailley, Joseph, *Paul Bert au Tonkin* (Paris: G. Charpentier et Cie, 1887).

Chantre, Ernest, *Recherches anthropologiques dans l'Afrique Orientale* (Lyon: A. Rey & Cie, 1904).

Charmetant, Félix, *D'Alger à Zanzibar. Etudes et souvenirs d'Afrigue* (Paris: Librairie de la Société Bibliographique, 1882).

Chevalier, Michel, 'Exposition du système de la Méditerranée', in *Œuvres de Saint-Simon et d'Enfantin*, vol. 6 (Paris: E. Dentu, 1866), pp. 54–87.

Childers, James Saxon, *From Siam to Suez* (New York/London: D. Appleton and Company, 1932).

Choudry, Pearee Mohun, *British Experiences* (Calcutta: Shome, 1889).

Cocteau, Jean, *Tour du monde en 80 jours (Mon premier voyage)* (Paris: Gallimard, 1936).

Conrad, Joseph, 'Geography and Some Explorers', in Conrad, *Tales of Hearsay and Last Essays* (London: J. M. Dent and Sons Ltd, 1955), pp. 1–21.

Heart of Darkness (London: Everyman, 1995).

Lord Jim: A Tale (London: Penguin, 1994).

'Preface', in Richard Curle, *Into the East: Notes on Burma and Malaya* (London: Macmillan & Co, 1923), pp. ix–xxv.

Thomas Cook, *Programmes and Itineraries of Cook's Palestine Tours, with Extensions to Egypt and the Nile, Sinai, Petra, Moab, the Hauran, Turkey, Greece, and Italy for the Season of 1877–78* (London/New York: Thomas Cook & Son, 1877).

Thomas Cook & Son, *Egypt and the Nile*: Programme of Cook's Arrangements for Visiting Egypt, the Nile, Soudan etc. issued by Thos Cook & Son Managing Agents for Thos Cook & Son (Egypt) Ltd. 1900–1901.

India, Burma and Ceylon: Information for Travellers and Residents (London: Thomas Cook & Son, 1895).

Courtland Penfield, Frederic, *Wanderings East of Suez in Ceylon, India, China and Japan* (London: George Belle and Sons, 1907).

Couvidou, Dr H., *Voyage à travers l'isthme: Itinéraire du Canal de Suez* (Port Said: A. Mourès, 1875).

Cromer (Lord), *Rapport de Lord Cromer sur l'Egypte et le Soudan pour l'année 1906* (Traduction Française) (Le Caire: Imprimerie Nationale, 1907).

Dall, Charles Henry Appleton, *From Calcutta to London by the Suez Canal. Collections of letters by the Englishman's 'Roving Correspondent'* (Calcutta, The 'Englishman' Press, 1869).

Dedreux, Rudolf, *Der Suezkanal im internationalen Rechte unter Berücksichtigung seiner Vorgeschichte: Abhandlung zur Erlangung der Doktorwürde vorgelegt der Juristischen Fakultät der Rheinischen Friedrich-Wilhelms-Universität zu Bonn* (Tübingen: H. Laupp, 1913).

Deussen, Paul, *Erinnerungen an Indien* (Kiel/Leipzig: Lipsius & Tischer, 1904).

Dicey, Edward, 'Why Not Purchase the Suez Canal?' *Nineteenth Century* 14/78 (August 1883), reprinted in Carter and Harlow, *Archives of Empire*, vol. 1, pp. 638–55.

Dodu, Gaston, *Vers les terres nouvelles (explorateurs – explorations)* (Paris: Librairie Fernand Nathan, 1907).

Doss, N. L., *Reminiscences, English and Australian. Being an Account of a Visit to England, Australia, New Zealand, Tasmania, Ceylon etc.* (Calcutta: M. C. Bhowmick, 1893).

Dumreicher, André von, *Fahrten, Pfadfinder und Beduinen in den Wüsten Ägyptens* (Munich: Drei Masken Verlag, 1931) [English: *Trackers & Smugglers in the Deserts of Egypt* (London: Methuen, 1931)].

Le tourisme dans les déserts d'Égypte: rapport sur les possibilités du développement du tourisme de l'agriculture, de l'élevage du mouton et du chameau, et des recherches géologiques et archéologiques dans les déserts d'Egypte (Paris: La Rose, 1931).

Eckermann, Johann Peter, *Gespräche mit Goethe in den letzten Jahren seines Lebens*, ed. Christoph Michel (Frankfurt: Deutscher Klassiker Verlag, 1999).

d'Eichthal, Gustave, *Les deux mondes* (Leipzig: F. A. Brockhaus, 1837).

Enfantin, Prosper, 'Lettre d'Enfantin à Barrault, 8 août 1833', in *Œuvres de Saint-Simon et d'Enfantin*, vol. 4 (Paris: E. Dentu, 1866), pp. 55–60.

Ernst Ludwig, *Staatsbesuch im Indien der Maharajas: Tagebücher zur indischen Reise Großherzogs Ernst Ludwigs von Hessen und bei Rhein 1902/03*, ed. Eckhart G. Franz (Darmstadt/Marburg: Selbstverlag der Hessischen Historischen Kommission, 2003).

Farahani, Mirza Mohammed Hosayn (ed.), *A Shi'ite Pilgrimage to Mecca 1885–1886: The Safarnameh of Mirza Mohammed Hosayn Farahani*, ed. Hafez Farmayan and Daniel Elton (London: Saqi Books, 1990).

Fontane, Marius, *Voyage pittoresque à travers l'isthme de Suez* (Paris: P. Dupont, 1869).

Forster, E. M., *A Passage to India* (San Diego: Harvest/HBJ Book, 1984).

Franck, Harry A., *A Vagabond Journey Around the World: A Narrative of Personal Experience* (New York: Garden City Publishing Company, 1910).

French Sheldon, Mary, *Sultan to Sultan: Adventures among the Masai and other Tribes of East Africa* (London: Saxon & Co, 1892).

Friedrich Wilhelm, *Tagebuch meiner Reise nach dem Morgenlande 1869: Bericht des preußischen Kronprinzen Friedrich Wilhelm über seine Reise zur Einweihung des Suez-Kanals*, ed. Hans Rothfels (Frankfurt/Berlin: Propyläen Verlag, 1971).

Frith, Francis, *Cairo, Sinai, Jerusalem, and the Pyramids of Egypt: a series of sixty photographic views* (London: J.S. Virtue, 1860).

Francis Frith's Egypt and the Holy Land: The Pioneering Photographic Expeditions to the Middle East (Salisbury: Francis Frith Collection, 2005).

Garbati, Romolo, *Nous et les Égyptiens: Pour la défense des étrangers en Egypte* (Alexandrie: Procaccia, 1925).

Gennep, Arnold van, *Les rites de passage* (Paris: E. Nourry, 1909).

Herodotus, *Histories*, vol. ii, transl. A. D. Godley (Cambridge, MA: Harvard University Press, 1920).

Hobrecht, James, '... *Dschunken, Böte, Dampfer zogen hierhin, dorthin, das war nicht die kleine, – es war die weite, weite Welt, an deren Rand ich stand...': Die Briefe des Berliner Stadtbaurates James Hobrecht von seiner 'Dienst-Reise' nach Japan aus dem Jahr 1887* (Potsdam: Verlag für Berlin-Brandenburg, 2000).

Hull, Edmund C. P., *The European in India; or, Anglo-Indian's Vade-Mecum. A Handbook of Useful and Practical Information for Those Proceeding or Residing in the East Indies, Relating to Outfits, Routes, Times for Departure, Indian Climate and Seasons, Housekeeping, Servants, etc. etc.; Also an Account of Anglo-Indian Social Customs and Native Character. To which is Added a Medical Guide for Anglo-Indians: being a Compendium of Advice to Europeans in India, relating to the Preservation and Regulation of their Health. The Treatment of the More Prevalent, Sudden, and Dangerous Indian Diseases, for the Use of Those Beyond the Read of Medical Advice, and Others in Case of Emergency Until Medical Advice Can Arrive. To which is Added a Supplement on the Management of Children in India During Infancy and Childhood.* (London: Henry S. King & Co, 1874).

Humphreys, Rachel, *Travels East of Suez* (London: Heath, Cranton & Ouseley, 1915).

Hutton, James, *A Popular Account of the Thugs and Dacoits, the Hereditary Garotters and Gang-Robbers of India* (London: Wm. H. Allen and Co, 1857).

Jacobs, Carl Heinrich, *Die Schiffahrtsfreiheit im Suezkanal: Inaugural-Dissertation der juristischen Fakultät der Friedrich Alexanders-Universität in Erlangen* (Göttingen: E. A. Huth, 1912).

Kebedgy, Michel S., 'La repression de la traite des blanches en Egypte', *Extrait de la Revue du Droit international et de Législation comparée*, 2/XII (1910).

Kerr, S. Parnell, *From Charing Cross to Delhi* (London: T. Fisher Unwin, 1906).

Kessel, Joseph, *Marché d'esclaves* (Paris: Les Editions de France, 1933).

Kipling, Rudyard, *Life's Handicap: Being Stories of Mine Own People* (London: Macmillan & Co, 1964).

The Light that Failed (Harmondsworth: Penguin 1970 [1891]).

'The Limitations of Pambé Serang [1889]', in *Life's Handicap: Being Stories of Mine Own People* (London: Macmillan & Co, 1964), pp. 343–9.

'A Return to the East' in Kipling, *Letters of Travel (1892–1913)* (New York: Charles Scribner's Sons, 1970).

Rudyard Kipling's Verse, Inclusive Edition 1885–1918 (London: Hodder and Stoughton, 1922).

Klippel, Ernst, *Als Beduine zu den Teufelsanbetern* (Dresden: Verlag Deutsche Buchwerkstätten, 1925).

'Etudes sur le Folklore Bédouin de l'Egypte', *Extrait du Bulletin de la Société Khédiviale de Géographie* VII/10 (Cairo: Imprimerie Nationale, 1911).

Unter Drusen, Kurden und Teufelsanbetern (Berlin: Ullstein, 1926).

Wanderungen im Heiligen Lande: Ein Buch des Geschehens und Erlebens (Berlin: Hochweg-Verlag, 1927).

Kodak Catalogue (Rochester/London/Paris: Eastman Kodak Company, 1892).

Lamb Kenney, Charles, *The Gates of the East: Ten Chapters on the Isthmus of Suez Canal* (London: Ward and Lock, second edition 1857).

Lawrence, T. J., *Essays on Some Disputed Questions in Modern International Law* (Cambridge: Deighton, Bell and Co., 1885),

Leconte, C., *Promenade dans l'isthme de Suez* (Paris: Chaix, 1864).

Lejean, Guillaume, 'La Traite des esclaves en Égypte et en Turquie', *Revue des deux mondes* 88 (1870), 895–913.

Lenoble, Jules, *La traite des blanches et le congrès de Londres de 1899: Etude sur la protection de la jeune fille en France et à l'étranger* (Thèse pour le doctorat, Faculté de Droit de l'Université de Paris, 1900).

Lesage, Charles, *L'invasion anglaise en Egypte: L'achat des actions de Suez (novembre 1875)* (Paris: Librairie Plon, 1906).

Lewis, Oswald, *Because I've Not Been There Before* (London: Duckworth, 1929).

Löwith, Karl, *Reisetagebuch 1936 und 1941. Von Rom nach Sendai. Von Japan nach Amerika*, ed. Klaus Stichweh and Ulrich von Bülow (Marbach: Deutsche Schillergesellschaft, 2001).

Lynch, Thomas Kerr, *A Visit to the Suez Canal* (London: Day and Son Limited, 1866).

Macdonald, Robert, *The Great White Chief: A Story of Adventure in Unknown New Guinea* (London: Blackie & Son, 1908).

Mackinder, Halford J., 'The Geographical Pivot of History', *Geographical Journal* 23/4 (1904), 421–37.

Mackirdy, M. A. O. C. M. and Willis, W. N., *The White Slave Market* (London: Stanley Paul & Co, 1912).

Malabari, Behramji M., *The Indian Eye on English Life or Rambles of a Pilgrim Reformer* (Bombay: Apollo Printing Works, 1895).

Manzotti, Luigi, Marenço, Romualdo (music) and Stoltze, Adolf (text), *Excelsior: Dramatisches Ballet in 5 Acten* (Frankfurt am Main: Druck und Verlag von Gebrüder Knauer, 1891).

Martens, F., *Das Consularwesen und die Consularjurisdiction im Orient*, translated by H. Skerst (Berlin: Weidmannsche Buchhandlung, 1874).

Maspero, Gaston, *Lettres d'Egypte: correspondance avec Louise Maspero 1883–1914* (Paris: Editions du Seuil, 2003).

Mayhew, Henry, *London Labour and the London Poor: The Condition and Earnings of Those That Will Work, Cannot Work, and Will Not Work*, vol. 1 'The London Street-Folk' (New York: Harper & Brothers, 1851).

McMahon, William, *A Journey with the Sun Around the World* (Cleveland: The Catholic Universe Publishing Company, 1907).

Monfreid, Henry de, *La croisière du hachich* (Paris: Bernard Grasset, 1933).

Montépin, Xavier de, *La traite des blanches: confessions d'un bohème* (Paris: A. Degorce- Cadot, 1877).

Moussa, Ahmed, *Essay sur le canal de Suez: Droit et politique* (Paris: Jouve & Cie, 1935).

Mozoomdar, P. C., *Sketches of a Tour Round the World* (Calcutta: S. K. Lahiri & Co., 1884).

Mukharji, T. N., *A Visit to Europe* (Calcutta, 1889).

Murray, *A Handbook for Travellers in India and Ceylon including the Provinces of Bengal, Bombay, and Madras (The Panjab, North-West Provinces, Rajputana, Central Provinces, Mysore, etc.), the Native States of Assam* (London: John Murray, Calcutta: Thacker, Spink & Co, 1892).

A Handbook for Travellers in Lower and Upper Egypt (7th revised edn, London: John Murray, 1888).

A Handbook for Travellers in Lower and Upper Egypt (8th revised edn, London: John Murray, 1891).

Murray, G. W., *Sons of Ishmael: A Study of Egyptian Bedouin* (London: George Routledge and Sons, 1935).

Napoleon III, *Discours de son Altesse Impériale le Prince Napoléon. Banquet de l'isthme de Suez, 11 février 1864* (Paris: E. Dentu, 1864).

Nizan, Paul, *Aden Arabie* (Paris: François Maspero, 1961).

Nouvel abrégé de tous les voyages autour du monde, depuis Magellan jusqu'à d'Urville et Laplace (1519–1832) 2 tomes (Tours: A. de Mame et Cie, 1839).

Öthalom, Albert Ungard Edler von, *Der Suezkanal: Seine Geschichte, seine Bau-und Verkehrsverhältnisse und seine militärische Bedeutung* (Wien/Leipzig: A. Hartleben's Verlag, 1905).

Ovington, John, 'Ovington's Notes on the Red Sea Ports', in Sir William Foster (ed.), *The Red Sea and the Adjacent Countries at the Close of the Seventeenth Century as described by Joseph Pitts, William Daniel and Charles Jacques Poncet* (London: Printed for the Florence E. Hakluyt Society, 1949), pp. 173–81.

Palmer, E. H., *The Desert of the Exodus: Journeys On Foot in the Wilderness of the Forty Years' Wanderings. Undertaken in Connexion with the Ordnance Survey of Sinai and the Palestine Exploration Fund* (Cambridge: Deighton, Bell, and Co, 1871).

Paterson, Florence E., *Reminiscences of a Skipper's Wife* (London: James Blackwood & Co, 1907).

Peebles, J. M., *Around the World: Travels in Polynesia, China, India, Arabia, Egypt, Syria, and other 'Heathen' Countries* (Boston: Colby and Rich Publishers, 1875).

Piggot, Francis Taylor, *Exterritoriality: The Law Relating to Consular Jurisdiction and to Residence in Oriental Countries* (London: William Clowes & Sons, 1892).

Redwood, Ethel Boverton, *Wanderings and Wooings East of Suez* (London: John Long, 1913).

Richards, George Henry and Clarke, Andrew, *Report on the Maritime Canal Connecting the Mediterranean at Port Said with the Red Sea at Suez. Presented to both Houses of Parliament by Command of Her Majesty* (London: George Edward Eyre and William Spottiswoode, 1870).

Ritt, Olivier, *Histoire de l'isthme de Suez* (Paris: Librairie de L. Hachette et Cie, 1869).

Rodier, George, *L'Orient: Journal d'un peintre* (Paris: Victor-Havard, 1889).

Salem Bey, Mahmoud, 'Les voyageurs musulmans', *Bulletin de la société khédiviale de géographie* VI/8 (Le Caire: Imprimerie nationale, 1905), 417–34.

Salvator, Ludwig, *The Caravan Route between Egypt and Syria* (London: Chatto & Windus, 1881).

Schwally, Friedrich, *Beiträge zur Kenntnis des Lebens der mohammedanischen Städter, Fellachen und Beduinen im heutigen Ägypten* (Heidelberg: Carl Winter's Universitätsbuchhandlung, 1912).

Scott, James Harry, *The Law Affecting Foreigners in Egypt as the Result of the Capitulations. With an Account of their Origin and Development* (Edinburgh: William Green & Sons, 1907).

Seeley, John Robert, *The Expansion of England: Two Courses of Lectures* (Boston: Roberts Brothers, 1883).

Siegfried, André, *Suez, Panama et les routes maritimes mondiales* (Paris, 1940).

Simmel, Georg, 'Soziologie des Raumes (1903)', in Simmel, *Schriften zur Soziologie: Eine Auswahl* (Frankfurt am Main: Suhrkamp, 1986 [1983]), pp. 221–42.

Simpson, W. J., 'Maritime Quarantine and Sanitation in Relation to Cholera', *The Practitioner: A Journal of Therapeutic and Public Health* 48 (1892), 148–90.

Sinh Jee, Bhagvat, *Journal of a Visit to England in 1883* (Bombay: Education Society's Press, 1886).

Sleeman, W. H., *The Thuggs or Phansingars of India: comprising a History of the Rise and Progress of that Extraordinary Fraternity of Assassins; and a Description of the System which it Pursues, and of the Measures which have been Adopted by the Supreme Government of India for its Suppression* (Philadelphia: Carey & Hart, 1839).

Snouck Hurgronje, Christiaan, *Mekka in the Latter Part of the 19ᵗʰ Century: Daily Life, Customs and Learning. The Moslims of the East-Indian Archipelago*, translated by J. H. Monahan with an introduction by Jan Just Witkam (Leiden/Boston: Brill, 2007).

Stanley, Henry M., *How I Found Livingstone: Travels, Adventures and Discoveries in Central Africa Including an Account of Four Months' Residence with Dr. Livingstone* (New York: Scribner, Armstrong & Co, 1872).

My Early Travels and Adventures in America and Asia, vol. 2 (New York: Charles Scribner's Sons, 1895).

Stephan, Heinrich, *Das heutige Aegypten: Ein Abriss seiner physischen, politischen, wirtschaftlichen und Cultur-Zustände* (Leipzig: F. A. Brockhaus, 1872).

Tacussel, F., *La traite des blanches* (Paris: J. Bonhoure et Cie, 1877).

Tambacopoulo, D., *De la peste et particulièrement de l'épidémie de Zagazig en 1901* (Alexandrie: Imprimerie générale A Mourès et Cie, 1902).

Tarring, Charles James, *British Consular Jurisdiction in the East with Topical Indices of Cases on Appeal from and relating to Consular Courts and Consuls. Also a Collection of Statutes Concerning Consuls* (London: Stevens & Haynes, 1887).

Taylor, Alfred Dundas, *The India Directory. For the Guidance of Commanders of Steamers and Sailing Vessels compiled from the latest British official publications. Part the First from England to the East Indies by the Mediterranean and Suez Canal also by the Cape of Good Hope with interjacent Ports in Africa and the Brazil Coast of South America illustrated by charts of winds, currents, tides, passages and compavariation* (London: Smith Elder & Co, 1891).

Thackeray, William Makepeace, 'Notes of a Journey from Cornhill to Grand Cairo by Way of Lisbon, Athens, Constantinople, and Jerusalem, performed on steamers of the Peninsular and Oriental Company', in Thackeray, *A Legend of the Rhine, Notes of a Journey from Cornhill to Grand Cairo and The Book of Snobs*, ed. George Saintsbury (Oxford: Henry Frowde, 1908), pp. 81–255.

Thornton, Edward, *Illustrations of the History and Practices of the Thugs, and Notices of some of the Proceedings of the Government of India, for the Suppression of the Crime of Thuggee* (London: W.H.Allen and Co, 1837).

Tilt, Charles, *The Boat and the Caravan: A Family Tour Through Egypt and Syria* (London: David Bogue, 1847).

Treves, Frederick, *The Other Side of the Lantern: An Account of a Commonplace Tour Round the World* (New York: Funk & Wagnalls Company, 1913 [1905]).

Twain, Mark, *Following the Equator: A Journey Around the World* (London: Chatto & Windus, 1900).

Valentini, A. L., *Lascari-Bât: A Collection of Sentences used in the Daily Routine of Modern Passenger Steamers, where Lascars are Carried as the Deck Crew; also a Copious English-Lascari Vocabulary* (3rd edn, London: Miller & Sons, 1901).

Vasel, August, *Reisetagebücher und Briefe 1874–1893*, ed. O. Matuschek (Helmstedt: Appelhans Verlag, 2001).

Verne, Jules, *Around the World in Eighty Days* (New York: The Modern Library, 2004).

Vesey Fitzgerald, W. F., *Egypt, India, and the Colonies* (London: Wm. H. Allen & Co, 1870).

Villiers-Stuart, Henry, *Egypt after the War. Being the Narrative of a Tour of Inspection Including Experiences among the Natives with Descriptions of their Homes and Habits* (London: John Murray, 1883).

Voisin-Bey, François Philippe, *Le canal de Suez. Historique administratif et actes constitutifs de la compagnie des études et de la construction 1854 à 1869*, vol. 1 (Paris: Vve Ch. Dunod, 1902).

Weill, Raymond, *La presqu'île du Sinai: étude de géographie et d'histoire* (Paris: Librairie Honoré Champion, 1908).

Willis, W. N., *Anti-Christ in Egypt* (London: The Anglo-Eastern Publishing Co., 1914?).

Wolmar, Enrico di, *Abhandlung über die Pest, nach vierzehnjährigen eigenen Erfahrungen und Beobachtungen* (Berlin: Vossische Buchhandlung, 1897).

Yeghen, F., *Le canal de Suez et la réglementation internationale des canaux interocéaniques* (Thèse pour le doctorat soutenue devant la faculté de l'Université de Dijon le 23 Décembre 1927).

Young, John Russell, *Around the World with General Grant: A Narrative of the Visit of General U.S. Grant, Ex-President of the United States, to Various Countries in Europe, Asia, and Africa, 1877, 1878, 1879. To which are added certain conversations with General Grant on questions connected with American politics and history. With eight hundred illustrations*, vol. 1 (New York: Subscription Book Department, 1879).

SECONDARY LITERATURE

Abulafia, David, 'Mediterranean History as Global History', *History and Theory* 50 (2011), 220–8.

Adas, M., *Machines as the Measure of Men: Science, Technology, and Ideologies of Western Dominance* (Ithaca/London: Cornell University Press, 1989).

Ageron, Charles-Robert, *Histoire de l'Algérie contemporaine (1871–1954)*, vol. 2 (Paris: Presses universitaires de France, 1979).

'L'émigration des musulmans algériens et l'exode de Tlemcen (1830–1911)', *Annales* 22/5 (1967), 1047–66.

Agius, Dionisius A., *Seafaring in the Arabian Gulf and Oman: The People of the Dhow* (London/New York/Bahrain: Kegan Paul, 2005).

Aharoni, Reuven, *The Pasha's Bedouin: Tribes and State in the Egypt of Mehemet Ali, 1805–1848* (London/New York: Routledge, 2007).

Ahuja, Ravi, 'Opening up the Country: Patterns of Circulation and Politics of Communication in Early Colonial Orissa', *Studies in History* 20/1 (2004), 73–130.

'Die "Lenksamkeit" der "Lascars": Regulierungsszenarien eines transterritorialen Arbeitsmarkts in der ersten Hälfte des 20. Jahrhunderts', *Geschichte und Gesellschaft* 31 (2005), 323–353.

d'Allemagne, Henry-René, *Prosper Enfantin et les grandes entreprises du XIXe siècle: La colonisation d'Algérie: La création du réseau P.L.M.; Le percement de l'isthme de Suez; Le Crédit Intellectuel; Le 'Crédit Foncier'; Enfantin homme politique* (Paris: Librairie Gründ, 1935).

Alliance française Port Said, 'Port Said après l'Inauguration du Canal (1869–1900)', *Timsah* 44 (1997), 27–35.

Alloula, Malek, *The Colonial Harem* (Minneapolis: University of Minnesota Press, 1986).

Anderson, Matthew S., *The Eastern Question 1774–1923* (Basingstoke: Macmillan, 1991 [1966]).

Anstruther, Ian, *Dr. Livingstone I Presume?* (New York: E. P. Dutton & Co, 1957).

Arnoux, Hippolyte, *Photographe de l'union des mers. Le Canal de Suez vers 1880. Exhibition catalogue* (Paris: Centre historique des Archives Nationales, 1996).

Austen, Ralph A., *Trans-Saharan Africa in World History* (Oxford/New York: Oxford University Press, 2010).

Bade, Klaus, *Europa in Bewegung: Migration vom späten 18. Jahrhundert bis zur Gegenwart* (Munich: C. H. Beck, 2000).

Bagwell, Philip S., *The Transport Revolution from 1770* (London: B. T. Batsford, 1974).

Balachandran, G., 'Circulation through Seafaring: Indian Seamen 1896–1945', in Claude Markovits, Jacques Pouchepadass and Sanjay Subrahmanyam (eds.), *Society and Circulation: Mobile People and Itinerant Cultures in South Asia* (Delhi: Permanent Black, 2003), pp. 89–130.

Globalizing Labour? Indian Seafarers and World Shipping, c. 1870–1945 (Oxford University Press, 2012).

Baldwin, Peter, *Contagion and the State in Europe, 1830–1930* (Cambridge University Press, 1999).

Barak, On, *On Time, Technology and Temporality in Modern Egypt* (Berkeley: University of California Press, forthcoming).

Barakāt, 'Alī, *Taṭawwur al-milkiyya al-zirā'iyya fī miṣr wa athāruha 'ala al-ḥaraka al-siyāsiyya, 1813–1914* (Cairo: Dār al-thaqāfa al-jadīda, 1977).

Barrell, John, 'Death on the Nile: Fantasy and the Literature of Tourism, 1840–60', in Catherine Hall (ed.), *Cultures of Empire: Colonizers in Britain and the Empire in the Nineteenth and Twentieth Centuries* (New York: Routledge, 2000), pp. 187–206.

Barth, Boris and Osterhammel, Jürgen (eds.), *Zivilisierungsmissionen: Imperiale Weltverbesserung seit dem 18. Jahrhundert* (Konstanz: UVK Verlagsgesellschaft, 2005).

Bashford, Alison, 'Foreign Bodies: Vaccination, Contagion and Colonialism in the Nineteenth Century', in Alison Bashford and Claire Hooker (eds.), *Contagion: Historical and Cultural Studies* (London/New York: Routledge, 2001), pp. 39–60.

Imperial Hygiene: A Critical History of Colonialism, Nationalism and Public Health (Basingstoke: Palgrave Macmillan, 2004).

Bashford, Alison and Hooker, Claire (eds.), *Contagion: Historical and Cultural Studies* (London/New York: Routledge, 2001).

Bayly, C. A., *The Birth of the Modern World 1780–1914: Global Connections and Comparisons* (Oxford: Blackwell, 2004).

Beinin, Joel and Lockman, Zachary, *Workers on the Nile: Nationalism, Communism, Islam and the Egyptian Working Class, 1882–1954* (Princeton University Press, 1987).

Bell, Duncan S. A., 'Dissolving Distance: Technology, Space, and Empire in British Political Thought 1770–1900', *Journal of Modern History* 77/3 (2005), pp. 523–62.

The Idea of Greater Britain: Empire and the Future of World Order, 1860–1900 (Princeton University Press, 2007).

Belli, Mériam N., *Remembrance of Nasserian Things Past: A Social and Cultural History of the 1950s and 1960s in Egypt* (unpublished PhD dissertation, Georgetown University 2005).

Bentley, Jerry H. (ed.), *The Oxford Handbook of World History* (Oxford University Press, 2011).

Berchtold, Johannes, *Recht und Gerechtigkeit in der Konsulargerichtsbarkeit: Britische Exterritorialität im Osmanischen Reich 1825–1914* (Munich: Oldenbourg, 2009).

Berneron-Couvenhes, Marie-Françoise, 'Le personnel navigant les paquebots de la compagnie des Messageries Maritimes vers 1880–1900: composition et travail à bord', in Eric Barré and André Zysberg (eds.), *L'équipage, du navire antique aux marines d'aujourd'hui. Actes du colloque organisé sur l'île Tatihou du 13 au 15 mai 1999* (Ile Tatihou: Musée Maritime, 2001), pp. 201–9.

Black, Jeremy, *Maps and Politics* (London: Reaktion Books, 1997).

Blaise, Clark, *Time Lord: Sir Sandford Fleming and the Creation of Standard Time* (London: Weidenfeld & Nicolson, 2000).

Blake, Robert, *Disraeli* (London: Eyre & Spottiswoode, 1966).

Blyth, Robert, 'Aden, British India, and the Development of Steam Power in the Red Sea, 1825–1839', in David Killingray, Margarete Lincoln and Nigel Rigby (eds.), *Maritime Empires: British Maritime Trade in the Nineteenth Century* (Woodbridge: The Boydel Press, 2004), pp. 68–83.

Bois, Paul, *Le grand siècle des Messageries Maritimes* (Marseilles: Chambre de Commerce et de l'Industrie Marseille-Provence, 1992).

Bonin, Hubert, *History of the Suez Canal Company, 1858–2008: Between Controversy and Utility* (Geneva: Librairie Droz, 2010).

Suez: Du Canal à la Finance (1958–1987) (Paris: Economica, 1987).

Borscheid, Peter, *Das Tempo-Virus: Eine Kulturgeschichte der Beschleunigung* (Frankfurt/New York: Campus Verlag, 2004).

Bose, Sugata, *A Hundred Horizons: The Indian Ocean in the Age of Global Empire* (Cambridge MA/London: Harvard University Press, 2006).

Boutros-Ghali, Boutros and Chlala, Youssef, *Le Canal de Suez 1854–1957* (Alexandria: Imprimerie al-Bassir, 1958).

Brantlinger, Patrick, 'Victorians and Africans: The Genealogy of the Myth of the Dark Continent', *Critical Inquiry* 12/1 (1985), 166–203.

Braudel, Fernand, *The Mediterranean and the Mediterranean World in the Age of Philip II* (New York: Harper & Row Publishers, 1966).

Brendon, Piers, *Thomas Cook: 150 Years of Popular Tourism* (London: Secker&Warburg, 1991).

Brinton, Jasper Yeates, *The Mixed Courts of Egypt* (New Haven: Yale University Press, 1930).

Bristow, Edward J., *Prostitution and Prejudice: The Jewish Fight against White Slavery 1870–1939* (Oxford: Clarendon Press, 1982).

Brown, Nathan J., 'Who Abolished Corvée Labour in Egypt and Why?', *Past & Present* 144 (1994), 116–37.

Brubaker, Rogers, *Citizenship and Nationhood in France and Germany* (Cambridge MA/London: Harvard University Press, 1992).

Buettner, Elizabeth, *Empire Families: Britons and Late Imperial India* (Oxford University Press, 2004).

Bull, Deborah and Lorimer, Donald, *Up the Nile: A Photographic Excursion, Egypt 1839–1898* (New York: Clarkson N. Potter, 1979).

Burbank, Jane and Cooper, Frederick, *Empires in World History: Power and the Politics of Difference* (Princeton University Press, 2010).

Burton, Antoinette, *At the Heart of the Empire: Indians and the Colonial Encounter in Late-Victorian Britain* (Berkeley: University of California Press, 1998).

Busch, Hans, *Verdi's Aida: The History of an Opera in Letters and Documents* (Minneapolis: University of Minnesota Press, 1978).

Buzard, James, *The Beaten Track: European Tourism, Literature, and the Ways to Culture, 1800–1918* (Oxford/New York: Oxford University Press, 1993).

Campbell, Gwyn, *An Economic History of Imperial Madagascar, 1750–1895: The Rise and Fall of an Island Empire* (Cambridge University Press, 2005).

Cannato, Vincent J., *American Passage: The History of Ellis Island* (New York: Harper, 2009).

Caplan, Jane and Torpey, John C. (eds.), *Documenting Individual Identity* (Princeton University Press, 2001).

Carré, Jean-Marie, *Voyageurs et écrivains français en Egypte* (Le Caire: Institut français de l'archéologie orientale, 1956).

Carter, Marina and Bates, Crispin, 'Empire and Locality: A Global Dimension to the 1857 Indian Uprising', *Journal of Global History* 5 (2010), 51–73.

Carter, Mia and Harlow, Barbara (eds.), *Archives of Empire, vol. 1: From the East India Company to the Suez Canal* (Durham/London: Duke University Press, 2003).

Chalcraft, John, 'The Coal Heavers of Port Sa'id: State-Making and Worker Protest, 1869–1914', *International Labour and Working-Class History* 60 (2001), 110–24.

Chaudhuri, K. N., *Asia before Europe: Economy and Civilisation of the Indian Ocean from the Rise of Islam to 1750* (Cambridge University Press, 1990).
  Trade and Civilisation in the Indian Ocean: An Economic History from the Rise of Islam to 1750 (Cambridge University Press, 1985).
Christopher, Emma, Pybus, Cassandra and Rediker, Marcus (eds.), *Many Middle Passages: Forced Migration and the Making of the Modern World* (Berkeley: California University Press, 2007).
Church, Matthew, *The Jugular Vein of Empire: The Imperial Attachment to the Suez Canal from 1875 to 1956* (unpublished thesis, University of Louisville, 2004).
Clancy-Smith, Julia, 'Marginality and Migration: Europe's Social Outcasts in Pre-Colonial Tunisia, 1830–81', in Eugen Rogan (ed.), *Outside In: On the Margins of the Modern Middle East* (London: I. B. Tauris, 2002), pp. 149–82.
  Mediterraneans: North Africa and Europe in an Age of Migration, c. 1800–1900 (Berkeley: University of California Press, 2011).
Clancy-Smith, Julia and Gouda, Frances (eds.), *Domesticating the Empire: Race, Gender, and Family Life in French and Dutch Colonialism* (Charlottesville/London: University Press of Virginia, 1998).
Clarence-Smith, William Gervase, *Islam and the Abolition of Slavery* (London: Hurst and Company, 2006).
Cohen, Robin (ed.), *The Cambridge Survey of World Migration* (Cambridge University Press, 1995).
Cohn, Bernard, 'The Census, Social Structure and Objectification in South Asia', in Cohn, *An Anthropologist Among the Historians and Other Essays* (Delhi: Oxford University Press, 1987), pp. 224–53.
  'Representing Authority in Victorian India', in Eric Hobsbawm and Terence Ranger, *The Invention of Tradition* (Cambridge University Press, 1983), pp. 165–209.
Cole, Juan R. I., *Colonialism and Revolution in the Middle East: Social and Cultural Origins of Egypt's 'Urabi Movement* (Princeton University Press, 1993).
  'Of Crowds and Empires: Afro-Asian Riots and European Expansion, 1857–1882', *Comparative Studies in Society and History*, 31/1 (1989), 106–33.
Collier, Peter and Inkpen, Rob, 'The Royal Geographical Society and the Development of Surveying 1870–1914', *Journal of Historical Geography* 29/1 (2003), 93–108.
Collins, Robert O., 'The African Slave Trade to Asia and the Indian Ocean Islands', *African and Asian Studies* 5/3–4 (2006), 325–46.
Conrad, Sebastian, *Globalisierung und Nation im Deutschen Kaiserreich* (Munich: C. H. Beck, 2006).
Conrad, Sebastian and Sachsenmaier, Dominic (eds.), *Competing Visions of World Order: Global Moments and Movements, 1880–1930s* (New York/Basingstoke: Palgrave Macmillan, 2007).
Cooper, Frederick, *Colonialism in Question: Theory, Knowledge, History* (Berkeley: University of California Press, 2005).
  'Conditions Analogous to Slavery: Imperialism and Free Labour Ideology in Africa', in Frederick Cooper, Thomas C. Holt and Rebecca J. Scott, *Beyond Slavery: Explorations of Race, Labor, and Citizenship in Postemancipation*

Societies (Chapel Hill/London: University of North Carolina Press, 2000), pp. 107–49.

Cresswell, Tim, 'Introduction: Theorizing Place', in Ginette Verstraete and Tim Cresswell (eds.), *Mobilizing Place, Placing Mobility: The Politics of Representation in a Globalized World* (Amsterdam and New York: Rodopi, 2002), pp. 11–32.

Cronon, William, *Nature's Metropolis: Chicago and the Great West* (New York/ London: W. W. Norton, 1991).

Cvetkovski, Roland, *Modernisierung durch Beschleunigung: Raum und Mobilität im Zarenreich* (Frankfurt am Main: Campus, 2006).

Darwin, John, *After Tamerlane: The Global History of Empire since 1405* (London: Lane, 2007).

The Empire Project: The Rise and Fall of the British World-System, 1830–1970 (Cambridge University Press, 2009).

Davis, David B., *The Problem of Slavery in the Age of Revolution, 1770–1823* (Oxford/New York: Oxford University Press, 1999).

Dethier, Jean (ed.), *All Stations: Journey through 150 Years of Railway History* (London: Thames & Hudson, 1981).

Dewachter, Michel (ed.), *Ismailia et le Canal de Suez en 1900: Photographies anciennes, cartes postales de collection, aquarelles, documents et souvenirs divers* (Exposition-dossier Musée Champollion Figéac, 1994).

Dipper, Christoph und Schneider, Ute (eds.), *Kartenwelten: Der Raum und seine Repräsentation in der Neuzeit* (Darmstadt: Primus Verlag, 2006).

Dirks, Nicholas, *Castes of Mind: Colonialism and the Making of Modern India* (Princeton University Press, 2001).

Dori, L., 'Esquisse Historique de Port-Said', *Cahiers d'histoire égyptienne* VIII/4–5 (1956), 311–42.

Driver, Felix, *Geography Militant: Cultures of Exploration and Empire* (Oxford: Blackwell, 2001).

Dubois, Colette, 'The Red Sea Ports During the Revolution in Transportation 1800–1914', in Leila Tarazi Fawaz and Christopher A. Bayly (eds.), *Modernity and Culture: From the Mediterranean to the Indian Ocean* (New York: Columbia University Press, 2002), pp. 58–74.

Duff, R. E. B., *100 Years of the Suez Canal* (Brighton: Clifton Books, 1969).

Echenberg, Myron, *Plague Ports: The Global Urban Impact of Bubonic Plague, 1894–1901* (New York/London: New York University Press, 2007).

Eckert, Andreas, 'What is Global Labour History Good For', in Jürgen Kocka (ed.), *Work in a Modern Society: The German Historical Experience in Comparative Perspective* (Oxford: Berghahn, 2010), pp. 169–81.

Eickelmann, Dale F. and Piscatori, James, *Muslim Travellers: Pilgrimage, Migration and the Religious Imagination* (London: Routledge, 1990).

Engels, Jens Ivo and Obertreis, Julia (eds.), 'Infrastrukturen der Moderne: Einführung in ein junges Forschungsfeld', *Saeculum* 58/1 (2007).

Eschelbacher Lapidoth, Ruth, *The Red Sea and the Gulf of Aden* (The Hague: Martinus Nijhoff Publishers, 1982).

Euben, Roxanne L., *Journeys to the Other Shore: Muslim and Western Travelers in Search of Knowledge* (Princeton University Press, 2006).

Ewald, Janet J., 'Crossers of the Sea: Slaves, Freedmen and Other Migrants in the Northwestern Indian Ocean, c. 1750–1914', *American Historical Review* 105/1 (2000), 69–91.

Ewald, Janet J. and Clarence-Smith, William G., 'The Economic Role of the Hadhrami Diaspora in the Red Sea and Gulf of Aden 1820 to the 1930s', in Ulrike Freitag and William G. Clarence-Smith (eds.), *Hadhrami Traders, Scholars and Statesmen in the Indian Ocean, 1750–1960s* (Leiden/New York/ Cologne: Brill, 1997), pp. 281–96.

Fahrmeir, Andreas, *Citizens and Aliens: Foreigners and the Law in Britain and the German States 1789–1870* (New York: Berghahn Books, 2000).

Falah, Ghazi, *The Role of the British Administration in the Sedentarization of the Bedouin Tribes in Northern Palestine 1918–1948* (University of Durham, 1983).

Farnie, D. A., *East and West of Suez: The Suez Canal in History 1854–1956* (Oxford: Clarendon Press, 1969).

Faroqhi, Suraiya, 'Red Sea Trade and Communications as observed by Evliya Çelebi (1671–72)', *New Perspectives on Turkey* 5–6 (1991), 87–106.

Fawaz, Leila Tarazi and Bayly, Christopher A. (eds.), *Modernity and Culture: From the Mediterranean to the Indian Ocean* (New York: Columbia University Press, 2002).

Fink, L., *Sweatshops at Sea: Merchant Seamen in the World's First Globalized Industry from 1812 to the Present* (Chapel Hill: University of North Carolina Press, 2011).

Fischer-Tiné, Harald, *Low and Licentious Europeans: Race, Class and 'White Subalternity' in Colonial India* (Hyderabad: Orient Blackswan, 2009).

——'"White Women Degrading Themselves to the Lowest Depths": European Networks of Prostitution and Colonial Anxieties in British India and Ceylon ca. 1880–1914', *Indian Economic and Social History Review* 40/2 (2003), 163–90.

Fischer-Tiné, Harald and Gehrmann, Susanne (eds.), *Empires and Boundaries: Rethinking Race, Class, and Gender in Colonial Settings* (New York/London: Routledge, 2009).

Fischer-Tiné, Harald and Mann, Michael (eds.), *Colonialism as Civilizing Mission: Cultural Ideology in British India* (London: Anthem Press, 2004).

Fisher, John, 'Official Responses to Foreign Travel at the British Foreign and India Offices before 1914', *English Historical Review* 72/498 (2007), 937–64.

Fogel, Frédérique, *Une société savante entre deux mondes: La société khédiviale de géographie Le Caire (1875–1917)* (Mémoire de maitrise en ethnologie, Université de Paris X Nanterre, 1985).

Foulke, Robert D., 'Life in the Dying World of Sail, 1870–1910', *Journal of British Studies* 3/1 (1963), 105–36.

Franck, Irene M. and Brownstone, David M. (eds.), *To the Ends of the Earth: The Great Travel and Trade Routes of Human History* (New York: Hudson Group, 1984).

Freeman, Michael, *Railways and the Victorian Imagination* (New Haven/London: Yale University Press, 1999).

Freitag, Ulrike, 'Handelsmetropole und Pilgerstation: Djidda in spätosmanischer Zeit', *Comparativ* 17 (2007), 64–79.

Freitag, Ulrike and von Oppen, Achim (eds.), *Translocality: The Study of Globalising Processes from a Southern Perspective* (Leiden: Brill, 2010).

Gammerl, Benno, *Untertanen, Staatsbürger und Andere: Der Umgang mit ethnischer Heterogenität im Britischen Weltreich und im Habsburgerreich 1867–1918* (Göttingen: Vandenhoeck & Ruprecht, 2010).

Gardiner, Robert (ed.), *The Advent of Steam: The Merchant Steamship before 1900* (London: Conway Maritime Press, 1993).

Geppert, Alexander C. T., *Fleeting Cities: Imperial Expositions in fin-de-Siècle Europe* (Basingstoke: Palgrave Macmillan, 2010).

Geyer, Martin H., 'One Language for the World: The Metric System, International Coinage, Gold Standard, and the Rise of Internationalism', in Martin H. Geyer and Johannes Paulmann (eds.), *The Mechanics of Internationalism: Culture, Society, and Politics from the 1840s to the First World War* (Oxford University Press, 2001), pp. 55–92.

Geyer, Martin H. and Paulmann, Johannes (eds.), *The Mechanics of Internationalism: Culture, Society and Politics from the 1940s to the First World War* (Oxford University Press, 2001).

Ghosh, Biswanath, *British Policy towards the Pathans and the Pindaris in Central India, 1805–1818* (Calcutta: Punthi Pustak, 1966).

Gilbert, Erik, *Dhows and the Colonial Economy of Zanzibar* (Oxford: James Currey, 2004).

Gilmour, David, *Curzon* (London: John Murray, 1994).

Golia, Maria, *Photography and Egypt* (London: Reaktion Books, 2010).

Gordon, John Steele, *A Thread Across the Ocean: The Heroic Story of the Transatlantic Cable* (New York: Walker & Company, 2002).

Gosewinkel, Dieter, *Einbürgern und Ausschließen: Die Nationalisierung der Staatsangehörigkeit vom Deutschen Bund bis zur Bundesrepublik Deutschland* (Göttingen: Vandenhoeck & Ruprecht, 2001).

Graham, Gerald S., 'The Ascendancy of the Sailing Ship, 1850–85', *Economic History Review*, New Series 9/1 (1956), 74–88.

Greene, Julie, *The Canal Builders: Making America's Empire at the Panama Canal* (New York: Penguin, 2009).

'Spaniards on the Silver Roll: Labor Troubles and Liminality in the Panama Canal Zone, 1904–1914', *International Labor and Working-Class History* 66 (2004), 78–98.

Gregory, Derek, 'Scripting Egypt: Orientalism and the Cultures of Travel', in James Duncan and Derek Gregory (eds.), *Writes of Passage: Reading Travel Writing* (London and New York: Routledge, 1999), pp. 114–50.

Guldi, Jo, *Roads to Power: Britain Invents the Infrastructural State* (Cambridge MA/London: Harvard University Press, 2012).

Haddad, Emily A., 'Digging to India: Modernity, Imperialism and the Suez Canal', *Victorian Studies* 47/3 (2005), 363–96.

Hanley, Will, *Foreignness and Localness in Alexandria, 1880–1914* (unpublished PhD dissertation, Princeton University 2007).

Hansen, Bent and Tourk, Khairy, 'The Profitability of the Suez Canal as a Private Enterprise 1859–1956', *Journal of Economic History* 38/4 (1978), 938–58.

Harcourt, Freda, *Flagships of Imperialism: The P&O Company and the Politics of Empire from its Origins to 1867* (Manchester University Press, 2006).

'The High Road to India: The P&O Company and the Suez Canal, 1840–1874', *International Journal of Maritime History* 12/2 (2010), 19–72.

Harrington, Ralph, 'The Railway Journey and the Neuroses of Modernity', in Richard Wrigley and George Revill (eds.), *Pathologies of Travel* (Amsterdam/ Atlanta: Editions Rodopi, 2000), pp. 229–59.

Harrison, Mark, 'The British Army and the Problem of Venereal Disease in France and Egypt during the First World War', *Medical History* 39 (1995), 133–58.

Contagion: How Commerce Has Spread Disease (New Haven/London: Yale University Press, 2012).

'Disease, Diplomacy and International Commerce: The Origins of the International Sanitary Regulation in the Nineteenth Century', *Journal of Global History* 1 (2006), 197–217.

'Quarantine, Pilgrimage, and Colonial Trade: India 1866–1900', *Indian Economic and Social History Review* 29 (1992), 117–44.

Harvey, David, *The Condition of Postmodernity: An Enquiry into the Origins of Cultural Change* (Cambridge MA: Blackwell, 1990).

Headrick, D. R., *The Invisible Weapon: Telecommunications and International Politics, 1851–1945* (Oxford University Press, 1991).

The Tentacles of Progress: Technology Transfer in the Age of Imperialism (Oxford University Press, 1988).

The Tools of Empire: Technology and European Imperialism in the Nineteenth Century (Oxford University Press, 1981).

Ho, Engseng, *The Graves of Tarim: Genealogy and Mobility Across the Indian Ocean* (Berkeley: University of California Press, 2006).

Hochstadt, Steve, *Mobility and Modernity: Migration in Germany 1820–1989* (Ann Arbor: University of Michigan Press, 1999).

Hoerder, Dirk, *Cultures in Contact: World Migrations in the Second Millenium* (Durham/London: Duke University Press, 2002).

Homsy, Basile, *Les Capitulations et la protection des chrétiens au Proche-Orient aux 16., 17. et 18. siècles* (Paris: Paul Geuthner, 1956).

Hopkins, A. G. (ed.), *Global History: Interactions between the Universal and the Local* (Basingstoke: Palgrave Macmillan, 2006).

(ed.), *Globalization in World History* (London: Pimlico, 2002).

Horden, Peregrine and Purcell, Nicholas, *The Corrupting Sea: A Study of Mediterranean History* (Oxford: Blackwell, 2000).

Howarth, David and Howarth, Stephen, *The Story of the P&O: The Peninsular and Oriental Steam Navigation Company* (London: Weidenfeld & Nicolson, 1994 [1986]).

Howell, Philip, 'Sexuality, Sovereignty and Space: Law, Government and the Geography of Prostitution in Colonial Gibraltar', *Social History* 29/4 (2004), 444–64.

Huber, Valeska, 'Connecting Colonial Seas: The "International Colonisation" of Port Said and the Suez Canal during and after the First World War', *European Review of History – Revue européenne d'histoire* 19/1 (2012), 141–61.

'Highway of the British Empire? The Suez Canal Between Imperial Competition and Local Accommodation', in Jörn Leonhard and Ulrike von Hirschhausen (ed.), *Comparing Empires: Encounters and Transfers in the Long Nineteenth Century* (Göttingen: Vandenhoek & Ruprecht, 2011), pp. 37–59.

'Multiple Mobilities: Über den Umgang mit verschiedenen Mobilitätsformen um 1900', *Geschichte und Gesellschaft* 36 (2010), 317–41.

'The Unification of the Globe by Disease? The International Sanitary Conferences on Cholera, 1851–1894', *Historical Journal* 49/2 (2006), 453–76.

Hugill, Peter J., *Global Communications since 1844: Geopolitcs and Technology* (Baltimore/London: Johns Hopkins University Press, 1999).

Hunter, F. Robert, 'Tourism and Empire: The Thomas Cook & Son Enterprise on the Nile, 1868–1914', *Middle Eastern Studies* 40/2 (2004), 28–54.

Hyslop, Jonathan, 'Steamship Empire: Asian, African and British Sailors in the Merchant Marine, c. 1880–1945', *Journal of Asian & African Studies* 44/1 (2009), 49–67.

Jäger, Jens, 'International Police Co-operation and the Associations for the Fight against White Slavery', *Paedagogica Historica: International Journal of the History of Education* 38 (2002), 565–79.

Jalāl, Husayn and Mashhūr Aḥmad Mashhūr, *al-Ṣirāʿ al-dawlī ḥawla istighlāl qanāt al- Suways* (Alexandria: al-Haya al-Misriyya al-ʿāmma lil-kitāb, 1979).

Karabell, Zachary, *Parting the Desert: The Creation of the Suez Canal* (New York: Alfred A. Knopf, 2003).

Karatani, Rieko, *Defining British Citizenship: Empire, Commonwealth and Modern Britain* (London: Frank Cass, 2003).

Kaschuba, Wolfgang, *Die Überwindung der Distanz: Zeit und Raum in der europäischen Moderne* (Frankfurt am Main: Fischer, 2004).

Kennerley, Alston, 'Stoking the Boilers: Firemen and Trimmers in British Merchant Ships, 1850–1950', *International Journal of Maritime History* 20/1 (2008), 191–220.

Kern, Stephen, *The Culture of Time and Space 1880–1918* (Cambridge MA: Harvard University Press, 1983).

Kerr, Ian J., *Building the Railways of the Raj, 1850–1900* (Delhi/New York: Oxford University Press, 1995).

Köksal, Yonca, 'Coercion and Mediation: Centralization and Sedentarization of Tribes in the Ottoman Empire', *Middle Eastern Studies* 42/3 (2006), 469–91.

Koller, Christian, 'The Recruitment of Colonial Troops in Africa and Asia and their Deployment in Europe During the First World War', *Immigrants & Minorities* 26/1–2 (2008), 111–33.

Krajewski, Patrick, *Kautschuk, Quarantäne, Krieg: Dhauhandel in Ostafrika 1880–1914* (Berlin: Klaus Schwarz Verlag, 2006).

Kraut, Alan M., *Silent Travellers: Germs, Genes and the Immigrant Menace* (Baltimore: Johns Hopkins University Press, 1995).

Kreiser, Klaus, 'Public Monuments in Turkey and Egypt, 1840–1916', *Muqarnas: An Annual on the Visual Culture of the Islamic World*, 14 (1997), 103–17.

Kubicek, Robert, 'British Expansion, Empire, and Technological Change', in Andrew Porter (ed.), *The Oxford History of the British Empire*, vol. 3: *The Nineteenth Century* (Oxford University Press, 1999), pp. 247–69.

'The Proliferation and Diffusion of Steamship Technology and the Beginnings of "New Imperialism"', in D. Killingray, M. Lincoln and N. Rigby (eds.), *Maritime Empires: British Imperial Maritime Trade in the Nineteenth Century* (Woodbridge: The Boydell Press, 2004), pp. 100–10.

Kuhnke, LaVerne, *Lives at Risk: Public Health in Nineteenth-Century Egypt* (Berkeley: University of California Press, 1990).

Laak, Dirk van, *Imperiale Infrastruktur: Deutsche Planungen für eine Erschließung Afrikas 1880 bis 1960* (Paderborn.: Ferdinand Schöningh, 2004).

'Infra-Strukturgeschichte', *Geschichte und Gesellschaft* 27/3 (2001), 367–93.

Lackany, Radames, *Quelques célèbres Allemands en Egypte* (Alexandrie, 1971).

Lajard de Puyjalon, Jacques, *L'influence des Saint-Simoniens sur la réalisation de l'isthme de Suez et des chemins de fer* (Paris: L. Chauny et L. Quinsac, 1926).

Lambert, David and Lester, Alan (eds.), *Colonial Lives across the British Empire: Imperial Careering in the Long Nineteenth Century* (Cambridge University Press, 2006).

Lambert, David, Martins, Luciana and Ogborn, M., 'Currents, Visions and Voyages: Historical Geographies of the Sea', *Journal of Historical Geography* 32/3 (2006), 479–93.

Landau, Jacob M., *The Politics of Pan-Islam: Ideology and Organization* (Oxford: Clarendon Press, 1990).

Lane, Tony, 'The Political Imperatives of Bureaucracy and Empire: The Case of the Coloured Alien Seamen Order, 1925', *Immigrants & Minorities* 13/2–3 (1994), 104–29.

Lawless, Dick, 'The Role of Seamen's Agents in the Migration for Employment of Arab Seafarers in the Early Twentieth Century', *Immigrants & Minorities* 13/2–3 (1994), 34–58.

Leigh Star, Susan, 'The Ethnography of Infrastructure', *American Behavioral Scientist* 43/3 (1999), 377–91.

Lerner, Daniel, *The Passing of Traditional Society: Modernizing the Middle East* (New York: The Free Press, 1958).

van der Linden, Marcel, *Workers of the World: Essays Towards a Global Labor History* (Leiden/Boston: Brill, 2008).

Low, Michael Christopher, 'Empire and the Hajj: Pilgrims, Plagues and Pan-Islam under British Surveillance, 1865–1908', *International Journal of Middle Eastern Studies* 40 (2008), 269–290.

Lucassen, Leo, 'Eternal Vagrants? State Formation, Migration, and Travelling Groups in Western Europe, 1350–1914', in Jan Lucassen and Leo Lucassen (eds.), *Migration, Migration History: Old Paradigms and New Perspectives* (Bern: Peter Lang, 1999), pp. 225–51.

Ludden, David, 'Presidential Address: Maps in the Mind and the Mobility of Asia', *Journal of Asian Studies* 62/1 (2003), 1057–78.

Macfie, A. L., *The Eastern Question 1774–1923* (revised edition, London/New York: Longman, 1996 [1989]).

Mackenzie, John M., 'Empires of Travel: British Guide Books and Cultural Imperialism in the Nineteenth and Twentieth Centuries', in John K. Walton, *Histories of Tourism: Representation, Identity and Conflict* (Clevedon: Channel View Publications, 2005), pp. 19–38.

'Points of Entry: Victoria Terminus, Bombay', *History Today* 39/1 (1989), 60–1.

MacMillan, Margaret, *Women of the Raj* (London: Thames & Hudson, 1988).

Magee, Gary B. and Thompson, Andrew S., *Empire and Globalisation: Networks of People, Goods and Capital in the British World, c. 1850–1914* (Cambridge University Press, 2010).

Maier, Charles S., 'Consigning the Twentieth Century to History: Alternative Narratives for the Modern Era', *American Historical Review* 105/3 (2000), 807–31.

Markovits, Claude, *The Global World of Indian Merchants* (Cambridge University Press, 2000).

Markovits, Claude, Pouchepadass, Jacques and Subrahmanyam, Sanjay (eds.), *Society and Circulation: Mobile People and Itinerant Cultures in South Asia* (Delhi: Permanent Black, 2003).

Marks, Steven G., *Road to Power: The Trans-Siberian Railroad and the Colonization of Asian Russia, 1850–1917* (Ithaca NY: Cornell University Press, 1991).

Marlowe, John, *Perfidious Albion: The Origins of the Anglo-French Rivalry in the Levant* (London: Elek Books, 1971).

World Ditch: The Making of the Suez Canal (New York/Basingstoke: Macmillan, 1964).

Marsden, Ben and Smith, Crosbie, *Engineering Empires: A Cultural History of Technology in Nineteenth-Century Britain* (Basingstoke: Palgrave Macmillan, 2005).

Marshall, Ian, *Passage East* (Charlottesville: Howell Press, 1997).

Mayall, David, 'Egyptians and Vagabonds: Representations of the Gypsy in Early Modern Official and Rogue Literature', *Immigrants and Minorities* 16/3 (1997).

Salonica, City of Ghosts: Christians, Muslims and Jews 1430–1950 (London: HarperCollins, 2004).

McClelland, Keith and Rose, Sonya O., 'Citizenship and Empire, 1867–1928', in Catherine Hall and Sonya O. Rose, *At Home with the Empire: Metropolitan Culture and the Imperial World* (Cambridge University Press, 2006), pp. 275–97.

McKeown, Adam, 'Global Migration, 1846–1940', *Journal of World History* 15/2 (2004), 155–89.

Melancholy Order: Asian Migration and the Globalization of Borders (New York: Columbia University Press, 2008).

Metcalf, Thomas R., *Ideologies of the Raj* (Cambridge University Press, 1994).

Imperial Connections: India in the Indian Ocean Arena, 1860–1920 (Berkeley: University of California Press, 2007).

An Imperial Vision: Indian Architecture and Britain's Raj (Berkeley: University of California Press, 1989).

Miers, Suzanne, *Britain and the Ending of the Slave Trade* (London: Longman, 1975).

Miller, Michael B., 'Pilgrims' Progress: The Business of the Hajj', *Past & Present* 191 (2006), 189–228.

Missal, Alexander, *Seaway to the Future: Social Vision and the Construction of the Panama Canal* (Madison: University of Wisconsin Press, 2008).

Mitchell, Timothy, *Colonizing Egypt* (Berkeley: University of California Press, 1991 [1988]).

Moatti, Claudia and Kaiser, Wolfgang (eds.), *Gens de passage en Méditerranée de l'Antiquité à l'époque moderne: Procédures de contrôle et d'identification* (Paris: Maisonneuve & Larose, 2007).

Moch, Leslie Pages, 'Dividing Time: An Analytical Framework for Migration History Periodization', in Jan Lucassen and Leo Lucassen (eds.), *Migration, Migration History, History: Old Paradigms and New Perspectives* (Bern: Peter Lang, 1997), pp. 41–56.

Modelski, Sylvia, *Port Said Revisited* (Washington DC: Faros, 2000).

Moghira, Mohammed Anouar, *L'isthme de Suez: Passage millénaire (604–2000)* (Paris: L'Harmattan, 2002).

Mongia, Radhika Viyas, 'Race, Nationality, Mobility: A History of the Passport', in Antoinette Burton (ed.), *After the Imperial Turn: Thinking with and through the Nation* (Durham: Duke University Press, 2003), pp. 196–211.

Montel, Nathalie, *Le chantier du canal de Suez (1859–1869): Une histoire des pratiques techniques* (Paris: Editions In Forma, 1998).

Moore, Gene M., 'Newspaper Accounts of the "Jeddah" Affair', *The Canadian* 25/1 (2000) 104–39.

Moranian, Suzanne E., 'The Armenian Genocide and American Missionary Relief Efforts', in Jay Winter (ed.), *America and the Armenian Genocide of 1915* (Cambridge University Press, 2003), pp. 185–213.

Muhammad Ali, Abbas Ibrahim, *The British, the Slave Trade and Slavery in the Sudan 1820–1881* (Khartoum University Press, 1972).

Mundy, Martha and Musallam, Basim (eds.), *The Transformation of Nomadic Society in the Arab East* (Cambridge University Press, 2000).

Murray, Cara, *Imperial Ways: The Victorians, the Suez Canal and Narrative* (unpublished PhD dissertation, City University New York, 2005).

Nicholson, James, 'The Hejaz Railway', *Asian Affairs* 37/3 (2004), 320–447.

Nickel, Douglas R., *Francis Frith in Egypt and Palestine: A Victorian Photographer Abroad* (Princeton University Press, 2004).

Nickles, David Paull, *Under the Wire: How the Telegraph Changed Diplomacy* (Cambridge MA/London: Harvard University Press, 2003).

Northrup, David, *Indentured Labour in the Age of Imperialism* (Cambridge University Press, 1995).

Obieta, Joseph A., *The International Status of the Suez Canal* (The Hague: Martinus Nijhoff, 1960).

Omissi, David (ed.), *Indian Voices of the Great War: Soldiers' Letters, 1914–1918* (Basingstoke: Macmillan, 1999).

Orsi, Richard J., *Sunset Limited: The Southern Pacific Railroad and the Development of the American West 1850–1930* (Berkeley: University of California Press, 2005).

Osterhammel, Jürgen, 'Aufstieg und Fall der neuzeitlichen Sklaverei. Oder: Was ist ein weltgeschichtliches Problem?' in Osterhammel, *Geschichtswissenschaft jenseits des Nationalstaats: Studien zu Beziehungsgeschichte und Zivilisationsvergleich* (Göttingen: Vandenhoeck & Ruprecht, 2001) pp. 342–61.

Die Entzauberung Asiens: Europa und die asiatischen Reiche im 18. Jahrhundert (Munich: C. H.Beck, 1998).

'Globalizations', in Jerry H. Bentley (ed.), *The Oxford Handbook of World History* (Oxford University Press, 2011), pp. 89–104.

'"The Great Work of Uplifting Mankind": Zivilisierungsmission und Moderne', in Boris Barth and Jürgen Osterhammel (eds.), *Zivilisierungsmissionen: Imperiale Weltverbesserung seit dem 18. Jahrhundert* (Konstanz: UVK Verlagsgesellschaft, 2005).

'Raumerfassung und Universalgeschichte im 20. Jahrhundert', in Gangolf Hübinger, Jürgen Osterhammel and Erich Pelzer (eds.), *Universalgeschichte und Nationalgeschichten* (Freiburg im Breisgau: Rombach, 1994), pp. 51–72.

Sklaverei und die Zivilisation des Westens (Munich: Carl von Siemens Stiftung, 2009).

Die Verwandlung der Welt: Eine Geschichte des 19. Jahrhunderts (Munich: C. H. Beck, 2009).

Osterhammel, Jürgen and Petersson, Niels P., *Geschichte der Globalisierung: Dimensionen, Prozesse, Epochen* (Munich: C.H. Beck, 2003).

Otis, Laura, *Membranes: Metaphors of Invasion in Nineteenth-Century Literature, Science, and Politics* (Baltimore: Johns Hopkins University Press, 1999).

Owen, Roger, *Lord Cromer: Victorian Imperialist, Edwardian Proconsul* (Oxford University Press, 2004).

The Middle East in the World Economy 1800–1914 (London: I. B. Tauris & Co, 1981).

Power and the Politics in the Making of the Modern Middle East (London/New York: Routledge, 2004 [1992]).

Özcan, Azmi, *Pan-Islamism: Indian Muslims, the Ottomans and Britain (1877–1924)* (Leiden/Boston: Brill, 1997).

Palmowski, Jan, 'Travels with Baedeker: The Guidebook and the Middle Classes in Victorian and Edwardian England', in Rudy Koshar (ed.), *Histories of Leisure* (Oxford/New York: Berg, 2002), pp. 105–30.

Panzac, Daniel, *Quarantaines et Lazarets: L'Europe et la Peste d'Orient (XVIIe-XXe siècles)* (Aix-en-Provence: Édisud, 1986).

Parfond (Commandant), *Pilotes de Suez* (Paris: Editions France-Empire, 1957).

Parker, Matthew, *Panama Fever: The Epic Story of One of the Greatest Human Achievements of All Time – The Building of the Panama Canal* (New York: Doubleday, 2007).

Parsons, Nicholas T., *Worth the Detour: A History of the Guidebook* (Stroud: Sutton Publishers, 2007).

Patterson, Steven, 'Postcards from the Raj', *Patterns of Prejudice* 40/2 (2006), 142–58.

Le Pautremat, Pascal, *La politique musulmane de la France au XXe siècle: De l'Hexagone aux terres d'Islam. Espoirs, réussites, échecs* (Paris: Maisonneuve et Larose, 2003).

Pearson, Michael, *The Indian Ocean* (London/New York: Routledge, 2003).

Pemble, John, *The Mediterranean Passion: Victorians and Edwardians in the South* (Oxford: Clarendon Press, 1987).

Perez, Nissan N., *Focus East: Early Photography in the Near East (1839–1885)* (New York: Harry N. Abrams, 1988).

Perkins, K. J., *Port Sudan: The Evolution of a Colonial City* (Boulder: Westview Press, 1993).

Pesek, 'Von Europa nach Afrika: Deutsche Passagiere auf der Dampfer passage in die Kolonie Deutsch-Ostafrika', *Werkstatt Geschichte* 52 (2009), 71–90.

Peters, Tom F., *Building the Nineteenth Century* (Cambridge MA/London: MIT Press, 1996).

Picon, Antoine, *Les saint-simoniens: Raison, imaginaire et utopie* (Paris: Belin, 2002).

Pietsch, Tamson, 'A British Sea: Making Sense of Global Space in the Late Nineteenth Century', *Journal of Global History* 5 (3), 423–46

Piquet, Caroline, *La Compagnie du canal de Suez: Une concession française en Égypte (1888–1956)* (Paris: Presses de l'Université Paris-Sorbonne, 2008).

Histoire du canal de Suez (Paris: Perrin, 2009).

'The Suez Company's Concession in Egypt, 1854–1956: Modern Infrastructure and Local Economic Development', *Enterprise and Society* 5/1 (2004), 107–27.

Pouchepadass, Jacques, 'Itinerant Kings and Touring Officials: Circulation as a Modality of Power in India, 1700–1947', in Claude Markovits, Jacques Pouchepadass and Sanjay Subrahmanyam (eds.), *Society and Circulation: Mobile People and Itinerant Cultures in South Asia* (Delhi: Permanent Black, 2003), pp. 240–74.

Prakash, Gyan, *Another Reason: Science and the Imagination of Modern India* (Princeton University Press, 1999).

Pratt, Mary Louise, *Imperial Eyes: Travel Writing and Transculturation* (London/ New York: Routledge, 1992).

Rabinowitz, Dan, 'Themes in the Economy of the Bedouin of South Sinai in the Nineteenth and Twentieth Centuries', *International Journal of Middle Eastern Studies* 17/2 (1985), 211–28.

Rafeq, Abdul-Karim, 'Damascus and the Pilgrim Caravan', in Leila Tarazi, Fawaz and Christopher A. Bayly (eds.), *Modernity and Culture: From the Mediterranean to the Indian Ocean* (New York: Columbia University Press, 2002) pp. 130–57.

Ramaḍān, ʿAbd al-ʿAẓīm Muḥammad Ibrāhīm, *al-Ḥaqīqa al-tārīkhīyya ḥawla qarār taʾmīm sharikat qanāt al-Suways* (Cairo: al-Hayʾa al-Miṣrīyya al-ʿĀmma li-l-Kitāb, 2000).

Raphael, Lutz, *Recht und Ordnung: Herrschaft durch Verwaltung im 19. Jahrhundert* (Frankfurt am Main: Fischer, 2000).

Raymond, André, 'A Divided Sea: The Cairo Coffee Trade in the Red Sea Area during the Seventeenth and Eighteenth Centuries', in Leila Tarazi Fawaz and C. A. Bayly (eds.), *Modernity and Culture: From the Mediterranean to the Indian Ocean* (New York: Columbia University Press, 2002), pp. 46–57.

Reinecke, Christiane, *Grenzen der Freizügigkeit: Migrationskontrollen in Großbritannien und Deutschland, 1880–1930* (Munich: Oldenbourg, 2010).

Revel, Jacques (ed.), *Jeux d'échelles: La microanalyse à l'expérience* (Paris: Gallimard Le Seuil, 1996).

Reymond, Paul, *Le Port de Port-Said* (Le Caire: Imprimerie du Scribe Egyptien, 1950).

Richards, Jeffrey and MacKenzie, John M., *The Railway Station: A Social History* (Oxford University Press, 1986).

Roche, Daniel, *Humeurs vagabondes: De la circulation des hommes et de l'utilité des voyages* (Paris: Fayard, 2003).

Rosenberg, Emily (ed.), *A World Connecting (1870–1945)* (Cambridge, MA/ London: Harvard University Press, 2012).

Rothschild, Victor, *'You have it, Madam': The Purchase, in 1875, of Suez Canal Shares by Disraeli and Baron Lionel de Rothschild* (London: W. & J. Mackay, 1980).

Ruiz, Mario M., 'Manly Spectacles and Imperial Soldiers in Wartime Egypt, 1914–19', *Middle Eastern Studies* 45/3 (2009), 351–71.

Said, Edward, *Orientalism* (New York: Vintage Books, 1979).

Sassen, Saskia, *Guests and Aliens* (New York: New Press, 1999).

Satia, Priya, 'The Defense of Inhumanity: Air Control and the British Idea of Arabia', *American Historical Review* 111 (2006), 16–51.

Satya, Laxman D., 'Colonial Sedentarisation and Subjugation: The Case of the Banjaras of Berar 1850–1900', *Journal of Peasant Studies* 24/4 (1997), 314–36.

Schivelbusch, Wolfgang, *Geschichte der Eisenbahnreise: Zur Industrialisierung von Raum und Zeit im 19. Jahrhundert* (Munich: Carl Hanser, 1977).

'Railroad Space and Railroad Time', *New German Critique* 14 (1978), 31–40.

Schlögel, Karl, *Im Raume lesen wir die Zeit: Über Zivilisationsgeschichte und Geopolitik* (Munich: Carl Hanser, 2003).

Schmidt, Jan, *Through the Legation Window 1876–1926: Four Essays on Dutch, Dutch-Indian and Ottoman History* (Istanbul: Nederlands Historisch-Archaeologisch Instituut te Istanbul, 1992).

Schneider, Ute, *Die Macht der Karten: Eine Geschichte der Kartographie vom Mittelalter bis heute* (Darmstadt: Primus Verlag, 2004).

Schölch, Alexander, *Ägypten den Ägyptern! Die politische und gesellschaftliche Krise der Jahre 1878–1882 in Ägypten* (Zurich/Freiburg: Atlantis, 1972).

Schonfield, H. J., *The Suez Canal in World Affairs* (London: Constellation Books, 1952).

Searight, Sarah, 'The Charting of the Red Sea', *History Today* 53/3 (2003), 40–46.

Sengoopta, Chandak, *Imprint of the Raj: How Fingerprinting Was Born in Colonial India* (Basingstoke: Macmillan, 2003).

Sengupta, Indra (ed.), *Memory, History, and Colonialism: Engaging with Pierre Nora in Colonial and Postcolonial Contexts*, German Historical Institute London Bulletin Supplement 1 (2009).

Sheriff, Abdul, *Dhow Culture of the Indian Ocean: Cosmopolitanism, Commerce and Islam* (New York: Columbia University Press, 2010).

Siegert, Bernhard, *Passagiere und Papiere: Schreibakte auf der Schwelle zwischen Spanien und Amerika (1530–1600)* (Munich/Zurich: Wilhelm Fink Verlag, 2006).

Simmons, James C., *Passionate Pilgrims: English Travelers to the World of the Desert Arabs* (New York: William Morrow and Company, 1987).

Simoën, Jean-Claude, *Le voyage en Egypte: Les grands voyageurs au XIXe siècle* (Paris: Lattès, 1989).

Simons, Oliver, 'Dichter am Kanal: Deutsche Ingenieure in Ägypten', in Alexander Honold and Oliver Simons (eds.), *Kolonialismus als Kultur: Literatur, Medien, Wissenschaft in der deutschen Gründerzeit des Fremden* (Tübingen/Basel: A. Francke Verlag, 2002), pp. 243–62.

'Heinrich von Stephan und die Idee der Weltpost – November 1869: Die Eröffnung des Suezkanals', in Alexander Honold and Klaus R. Scherpe (eds.), *Mit Deutschland um die Welt: Eine Kulturgeschichte des Fremden in der Kolonialzeit* (Stuttgart/Weimar: Verlag J. B. Metzler, 2004), pp. 26–35.

Singha, Radhika, 'Settle, Mobilize, Verify: Identification Practices in Colonial India', *Studies in History* 16/2 (2000), 151–98.

Slight, John P. 'British Imperial Rule and the Hajj, 1865–1939', in David Motadel (ed.), *Islam and Empire* (Oxford University Press, forthcoming).

Spillmann, Georges, 'Le percement de l'isthme de Suez', *Revue du Souvenir Napoléonien* 266 (1997), 6–10.

Steel, Frances, *Oceania Under Steam: Sea Transport and the Cultures of Colonialism, c.1870–1914* (Manchester University Press, 2011).

'Women, Men and the Southern Octopus: Shipboard Gender Relations in the Age of Steam, 1870–1910s', *International Journal of Maritime History* 20/2 (2008), 285–306.

Steensgard, Niels, *The Asian Trade Revolution of the Seventeenth Century: The East India Companies and the Decline of the Caravan Trade* (University of Chicago Press, 1973).

Stieg, Margret F., 'Indian Romances: Tracts for the Times', *Journal of Popular Culture* 18/4 (1985), 2–15.

Stoler, Ann Laura, *Carnal Knowledge and Imperial Power: Race and the Intimate in Colonial Rule* (Berkeley: University of California Press, 2002).

Swaminathan, Srividhya, *Debating the Slave Trade: Rhetoric of British National Identity, 1759–1815* (Farnham: Ashgate, 2009).

Tabili, Laura, 'The Construction of Racial Difference in Twentieth-Century Britain: The Special Restriction (Coloured Alien Seamen) Order, 1925', *Journal of British Studies* 33 (1994).

Tagliacozzo, Eric, *Secret Trades, Porous Borders: Smuggling and States along a Southeast Asian Frontier, 1865–1915* (New Haven/London: Yale University Press, 2005).

Tenner, Edward, 'Digging Across Panama', *Humanities* 32/1 (2011), 28–32.

Toledano, Ehud R., *The Ottoman Slave Trade and its Suppression: 1840–1890* (Princeton University Press, 1982).

Slavery and Abolition in the Ottoman Middle East (Seattle/London: University of Washington Press, 1998).

Torpey, John C., 'The Great War and the Birth of the Modern Passport System', in Jane Caplan and John Torpey (eds.), *Documenting Individual Identity: The Development of State Practices in the Modern World* (Princeton University Press, 2001), pp. 256–70.

The Invention of the Passport: Surveillance, Citizenships, and the State (Cambridge University Press, 2000).

Trautmann, Wolfgang, 'The Nomads of Algeria under French Rule: A Study of Social and Economic Change', *Journal of Historical Geography* 15/2 (1989), 126–38.

Troutt Powell, Eve M., *A Different Shade of Colonialism: Egypt, Great Britain and the Mastery of Sudan* (Berkeley: University of California Press, 2003).

'Will that Subaltern Ever Speak? Finding African Slaves in the Historiography of the Middle East', in Israel Gershoni, Amy Singer and Y. Hakan Erdem (eds.), *Middle East Historiographies: Narrating the Twentieth Century* (Seattle/London: University of Washington Press, 2006), pp. 242–61.

Tuchscherer, Michel, 'Trade and Port Cities in the Red Sea – Gulf of Aden Region in the Sixteenth and Seventeenth Century', in Leila Tarazi Fawaz and C. A. Bayly (eds.), *Modernity and Culture: From the Mediterranean to the Indian Ocean* (New York: Columbia University Press, 2002), pp. 28–45.

Tucker, Judith E., *Women in Nineteenth-Century Egypt* (Cambridge University Press, 1985).

Tuker, Francis, *The Yellow Scarf: The Story and the Life of Thuggee Sleeman or Major-General Sir William Henry Sleeman K. C. B. 1788–1856 of the Bengal Army and the Indian Political Service* (London: J. M. Dent & Sons, Ltd, 1961).

Ure, John, *In Search of Nomads: An English Obsession from Hester Stanhope to Bruce Chatwin* (London: Constable, 2003).

Urry, John, *Mobilities* (Cambridge: Polity Press, 2007).

Sociology beyond Societies: Mobilities for the Twenty-First Century (London/New York: Routledge, 2000).

The Tourist Gaze (London: Sage Publications 2002 [1990]).

Verbeek, Bertjan, *Decision-Making in Great Britain During the Suez Crisis: Small Groups and a Persistent Leader* (Aldershot: Ashgate, 2003).

Walters, William, 'Schiffahrtsindustrie und die gouvernementale Verwaltung des blinden Passagiers', *Comparativ* 18/1 (2008), 70–91.

Watts, Sheldon, 'From Rapid Change to Stasis: Official Responses to Cholera in British-Ruled India and Egypt 1860 to c. 1921', *Journal of World History* 12/2 (2001), 321–74.

Wenzlhuemer, Roland, *Connecting the Nineteenth-Century World: The Telegraph and Globalization* (Cambridge University Press, 2013).

(ed.), *Global Communication: Telecommunication and Global Flows of Information in the Late 19th and Early 20th Century*, special issue of *Historical Social Research* 35/1 (2010).

Withey, Lynne, *Grand Tours and Cook's Tours: A History of Leisure Travel, 1750 to 1915* (London: Aurum Press, 1997).

Woollacott, Angela, '"All this is the Empire, I told Myself": Australian Women's Voyages "Home" and the articulation of Colonial Whiteness', *American Historical Review* 102/4 (1997), 1003–29.

Yūnus, Maḥmūd, *Qanāt al-Suways: māḍīhā, ḥāḍirihā, mustaqbalhā* (Cairo: al-Haram, 2006).

Index

A Passage to India (Forster), 55
Abbas II, Khedive, 105, 200
Abdülmecid I, Sultan, 27
acceleration and deceleration, 6–7, 142, 318
  acceleration aided by 'desert mobilities',
  164–71
  acceleration and Western modernity, 2–3
  acceleration associated with the Suez
  Canal, 1–2
  camels versus steam, 164–6
  deceleration of 'desert mobilities',
  152–64
  and disease, 241–2
  restriction of dhow mobilities, 173
  tensions between mobilities, 1–2, 6–7
  theme in portrayals of the Canal
  journey, 38, 51
  and troops, 103–4
accidents in the Suez Canal, 110, 111,
  250
Aden, 50, 93, 247, 287, 316
  coaling station, 117, 122–3
  Gulf of, 195
  prostitution, 303
  repatriation of destitute travellers, 288–9
Alexandria, 46
  1882 riots and bombardment, 83–4
  Egyptianisation, 307
  lazaretto, 256
  medical checks, 267
  overland route, 21–3
Algeria
  Algerian pilgrims, 161, 204
  Army of Africa, 169
  and citizenship status, 234
  and fears of pan-Islam, 219
  French troops, 101
  regulation of pilgrim movements, 221–5,
  230–6
anti-imperial ideas, fear of spread, 213–14,
  216–20

anti-slavery movement, 28, 181
Armenian refugees, 308, 310–12
Aouat, Brahim, 217–18
Arnoux, Hippolyte, 64, 65, 148, 154, 155,
  166, 177
Aubert-Roche, Louis, 46
Australia, 56, 96
  Australian emigrants, 134
  Australian troops in the First World
  War, 308
  destitute and stowaways, 283, 291
  emigration to, 14
Austrian Lloyd, 24, 278
Azizie Company, 182

Baedeker travel guides, 60, 91, 152,
  160, 277
baghla (sailing boat), 174
Baijnath, Lala, 46, 52
Baring, Evelyn, from 1892 Lord Cromer,
  92, 98, 105, 115, 160–1, 185, 198, 201,
  207, 246, 265
Barrows, John Henry, 105, 125, 150
Bartlett, W. H., 59
Bauer, Marie-Bernard, 41
Bedouin, 19
  abandonment of nomadic way of life,
  155–8
  acceleration aided by 'desert mobilities',
  164–71
  Bedouin attacks on pilgrim caravans,
  161–4, 224
  Bedouin camp at Canal opening, 40
  contrast with Canal mobility, 31
  dwindling opportunities, 155–8
  employment as local experts, 166–8
  mobility despised by European travellers,
  144–7
  resistance to European presence,
  158–64
  restrictions caused by the Canal, 153–5

CPSIA information can be obtained
at www.ICGtesting.com
Printed in the USA
LVOW04s2221130116

470490LV00012B/229/P